D0779261

Sherlock Bones 4

Miki & Sherdog & Takeru

Story: Yuma Ando   Art: Yuki Sato

CHARACTERS

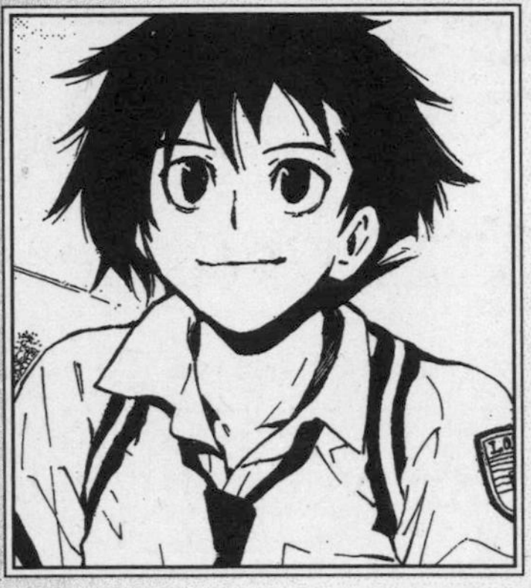

Takeru Wajima

A second-year at London Academy High School, he is an ordinary student who loves dogs. He is Sherdog's owner and the one person who can understand him. He and Sherdog must team up to solve all kinds of difficult cases. He has a crush on his childhood friend Miki.

Sherdog
(Sherlock Holmes)

The mixed-breed puppy that Takeru adopted. His true identity is that of the world-famous detective, Sherlock Holmes. When he has the Wajima family's heirloom pipe in his mouth, he can speak to Takeru. He solves crimes with Takeru, learning about the modern world in the process.

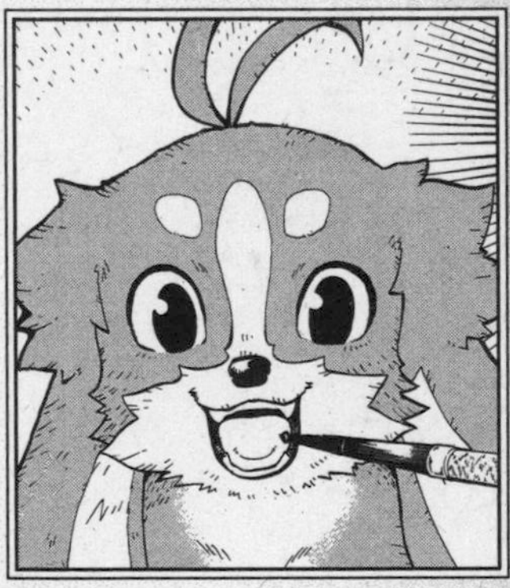

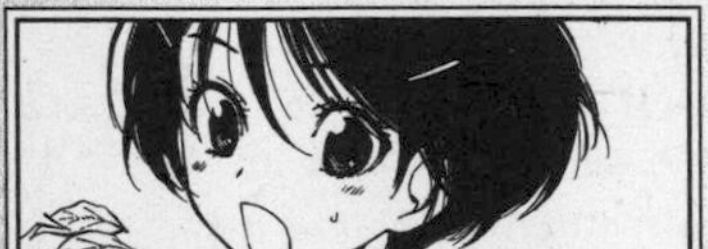

Miki Arisaka

A second-year at London Academy High School. Takeru's friend since childhood, and a member of the school newspaper staff.

Members of the Wajima Family

Airin Wajima

Takeru's sister, an inspector in the Violent Crimes Division. Sherdog calls her Irene.

Kōsuke Wajima

Takeru's father. A sergeant in the police force.

Satoko Wajima

Takeru's mother. She really hates it when Sherdog sits in her favorite rocking chair.

Akane Nanami

A second-year at London Academy High School, and friend of Takeru and Miki. President of the volunteer club.

THE STORY SO FAR

The puppy Sherdog— reincarnation of Sherlock Holmes—and the ordinary high school student Takeru Wajima team up to solve tough cases!! It's ASB election time at London Academy, and presidential candidate Akane is in danger of losing the election when her mud-slinging opponent distributes an obscene photo of her.

STORY

Volume.4

CONTENTS

Coffee Time 2 : Typographical Testimony (Conclusion)

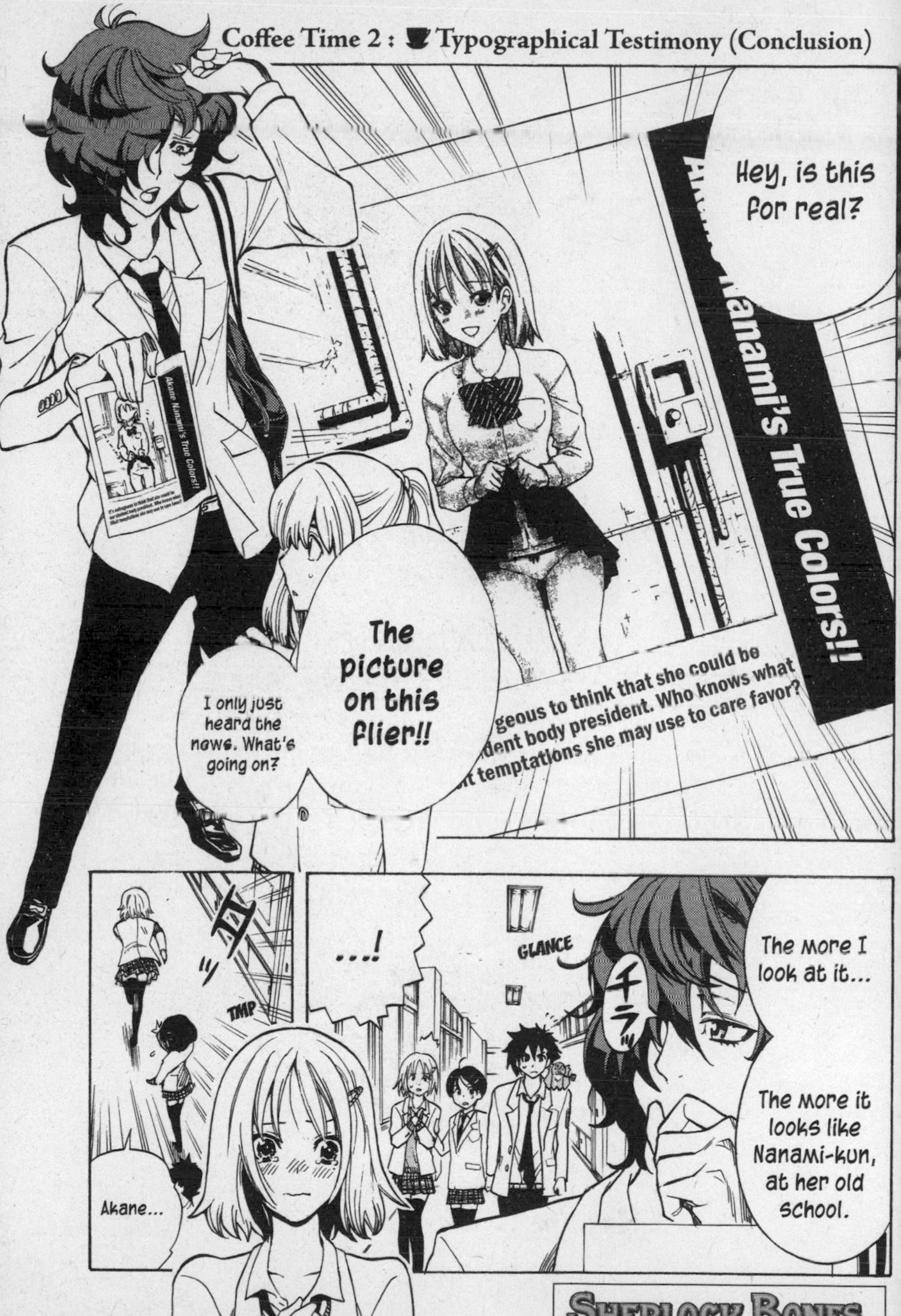
Hey, is this for real?
Akane Nanami's True Colors!!
geous to think that she could be
dent body president. Who knows what
temptations she may use to care favor?
The picture on this flier!!
I only just heard the news. What's going on?
The more I look at it...
The more it looks like Nanami-kun, at her old school.
GLANCE
チラッ
...!
TMP
Akane...
SHERLOCK BONES

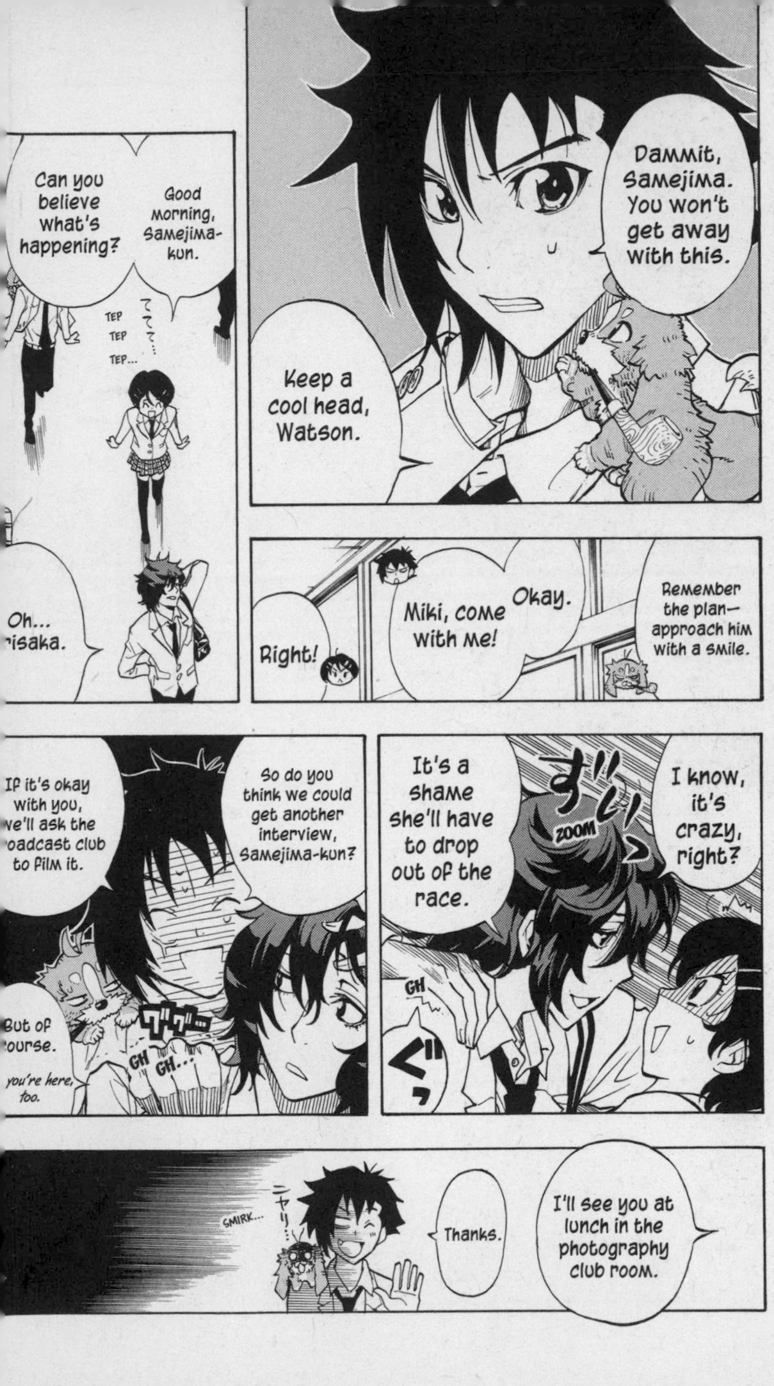
Dammit, Samejima. You won't get away with this.
Keep a cool head, Watson.
Remember the plan— approach him with a smile.
Okay.
Miki, come with me!
Right!
Good morning, Samejima-kun.
Can you believe what's happening?
TEP TEP TEP...
Oh... risaka.
I know, it's crazy, right?
ZOOM
It's a shame she'll have to drop out of the race.
GH
So do you think we could get another interview, Samejima-kun?
If it's okay with you, ve'll ask the oadcast club to film it.
GH GH...
But of ourse.
you're here, too.
I'll see you at lunch in the photography club room.
Thanks.
SMIRK...

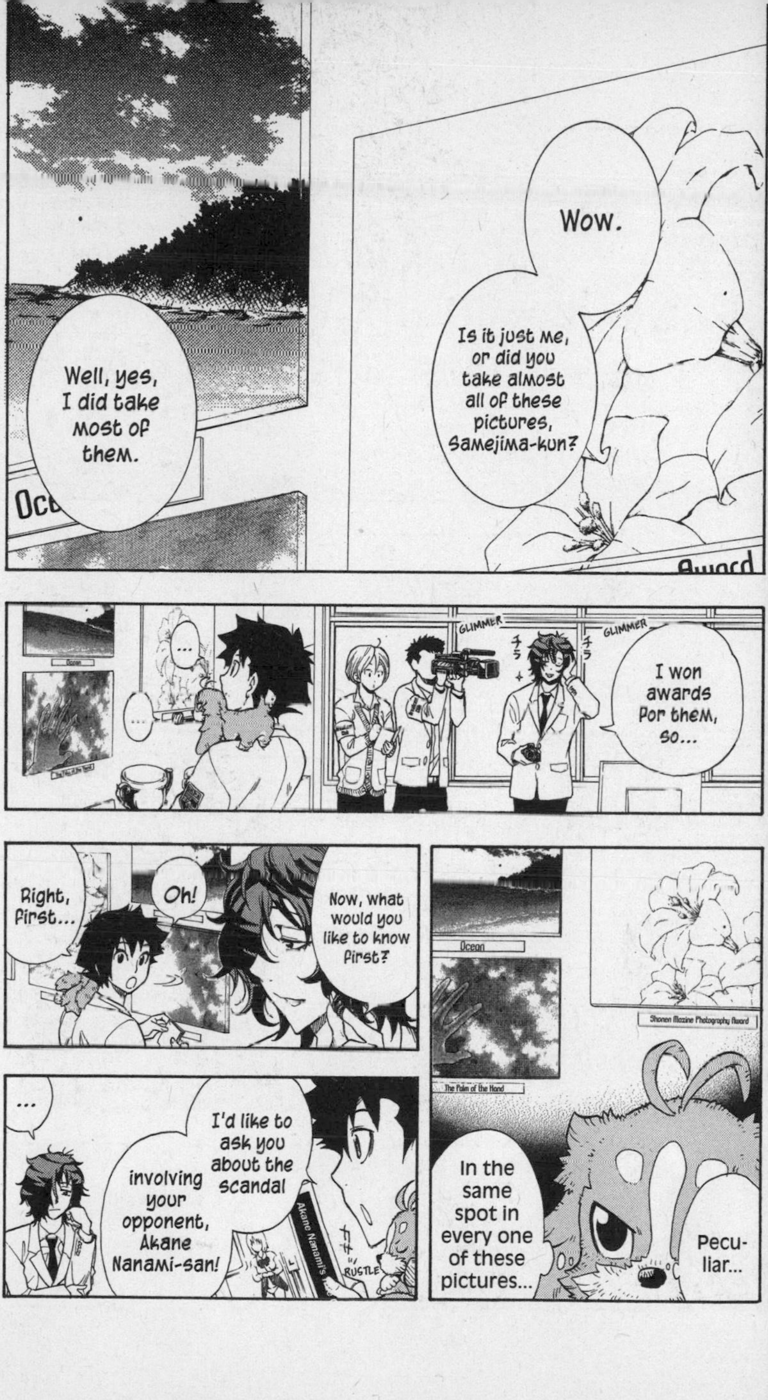
Wow.
Is it just me, or did you take almost all of these pictures, Samejima-kun?
Award
Well, yes, I did take most of them.
GLIMMER
I won awards for them, so...
GLIMMER
...
...
Shonen Mazine Photography Award
Ocean
The Palm of the Hand
In the same spot in every one of these pictures...
Peculiar...
Now, what would you like to know first?
Oh!
Right, first...
I'd like to ask you about the scandal
involving your opponent, Akane Nanami-san!
Akane Nanami's
RUSTLE
...

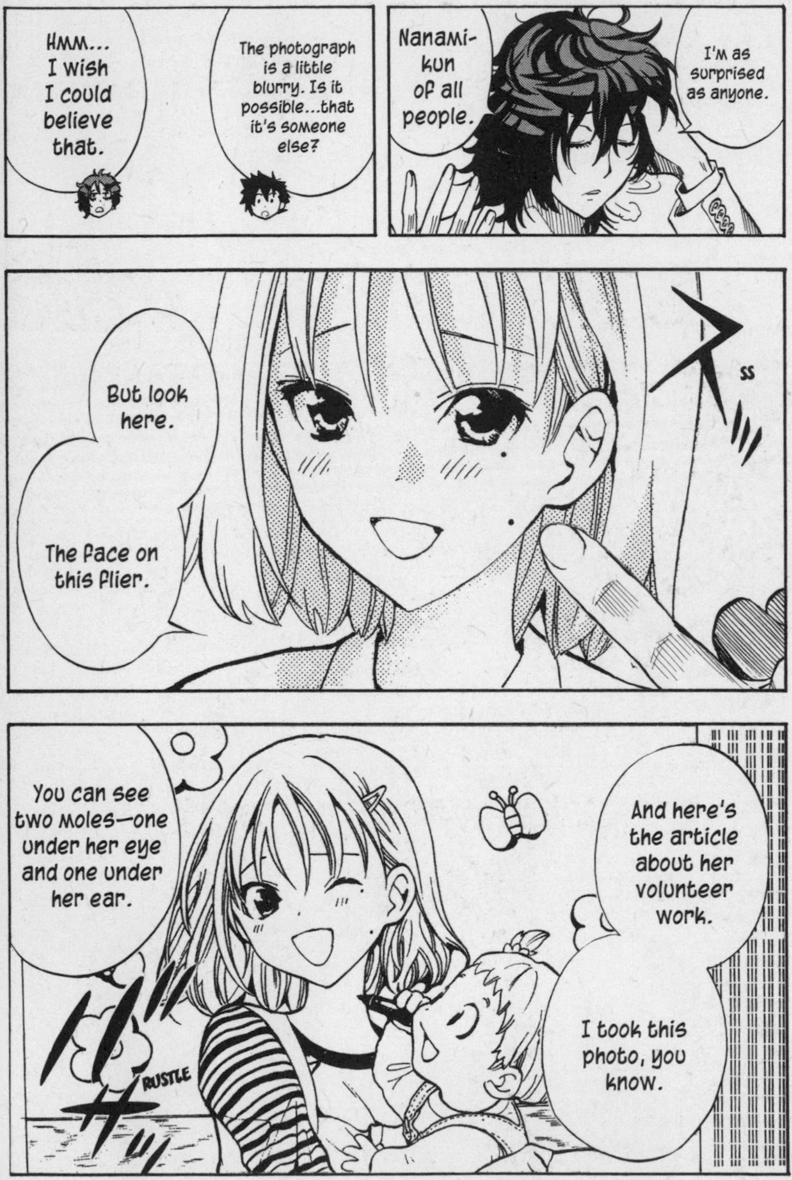
I'm as surprised as anyone.
Nanami-kun of all people.
The photograph is a little blurry. Is it possible...that it's someone else?
Hmm... I wish I could believe that.
SS
But look here.
The face on this flier.
And here's the article about her volunteer work.
I took this photo, you know.
You can see two moles—one under her eye and one under her ear.
RUSTLE

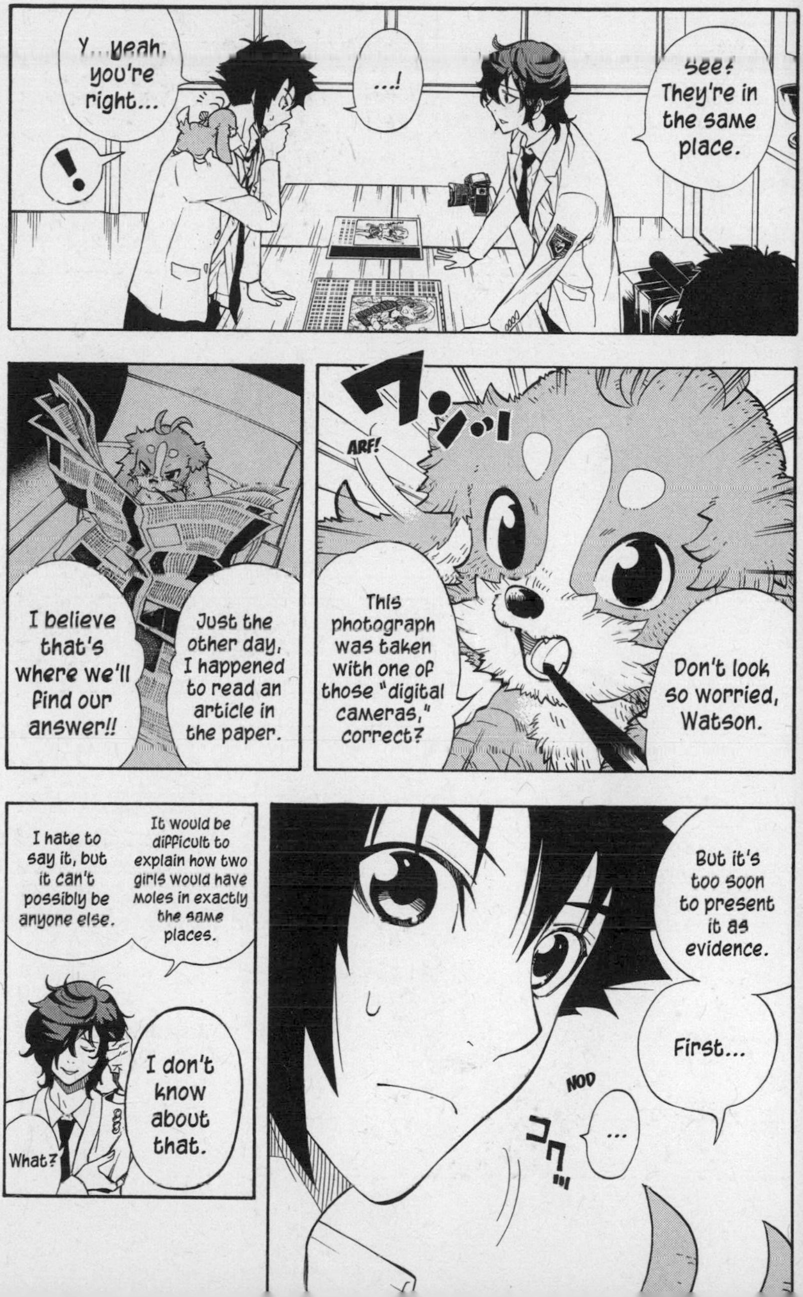
See? They're in the same place.
...!
Y... yeah, you're right...
!
ARF!
Don't look so worried, Watson.
This photograph was taken with one of those "digital cameras," correct?
Just the other day, I happened to read an article in the paper.
I believe that's where we'll find our answer!!
But it's too soon to present it as evidence.
First...
NOD
...
It would be difficult to explain how two girls would have moles in exactly the same places.
I hate to say it, but it can't possibly be anyone else.
I don't know about that.
What?

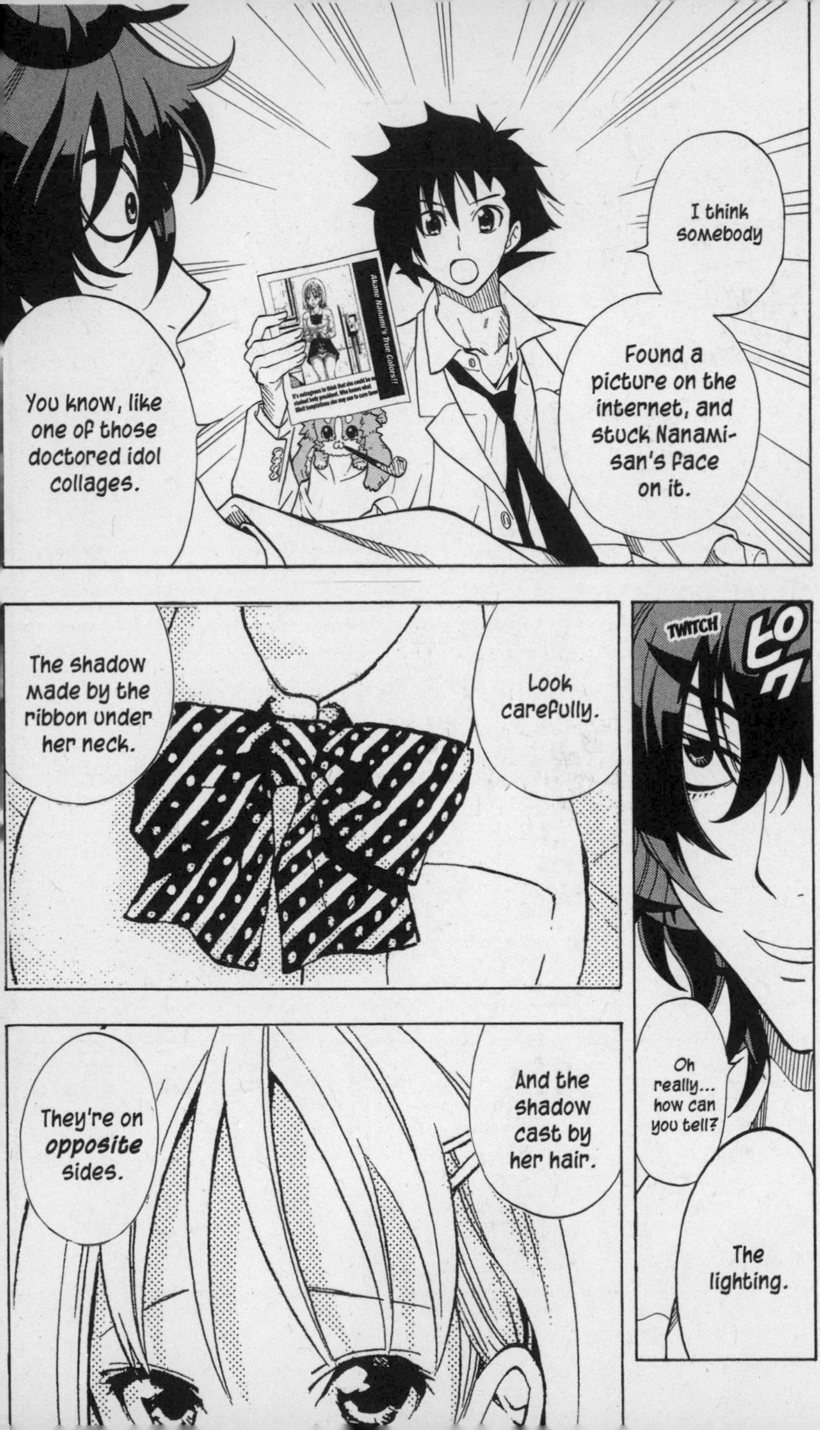
I think somebody
Found a picture on the internet, and stuck Nanami-san's face on it.
Akane Nanami's True Colors!!
You know, like one of those doctored idol collages.
TWITCH
ピク
Oh really... how can you tell?
The lighting.
Look carefully.
The shadow made by the ribbon under her neck.
And the shadow cast by her hair.
They're on *opposite* sides.

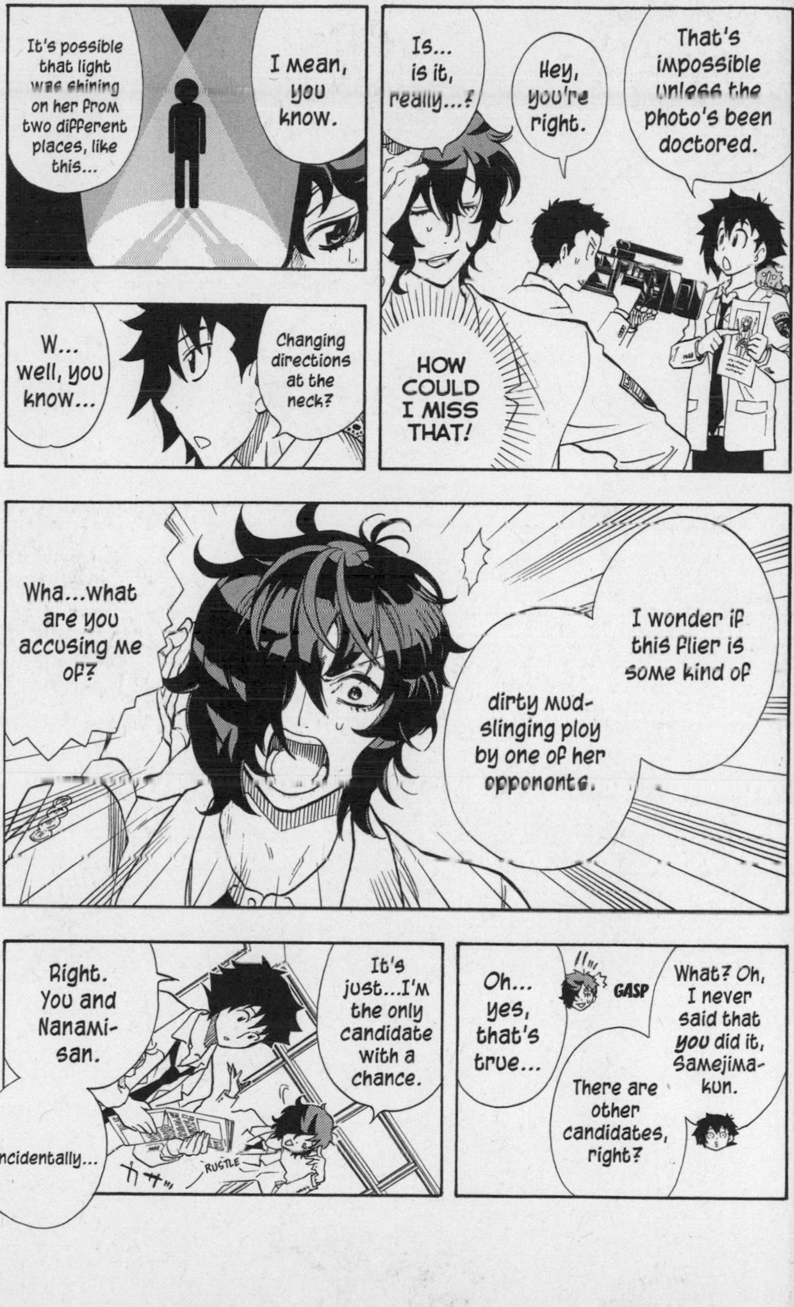
That's impossible unless the photo's been doctored.
Hey, you're right.
Is... is it, really...?
HOW COULD I MISS THAT!
I mean, you know.
It's possible that light was shining on her from two different places, like this...
Changing directions at the neck?
W... well, you know...
I wonder if this flier is some kind of dirty mud-slinging ploy by one of her opponents.
Wha...what are you accusing me of?
What? Oh, I never said that *you* did it, Samejima-kun.
GASP
There are other candidates, right?
Oh... yes, that's true...
It's just...I'm the only candidate with a chance.
Right. You and Nanami-san.
RUSTLE
Incidentally...

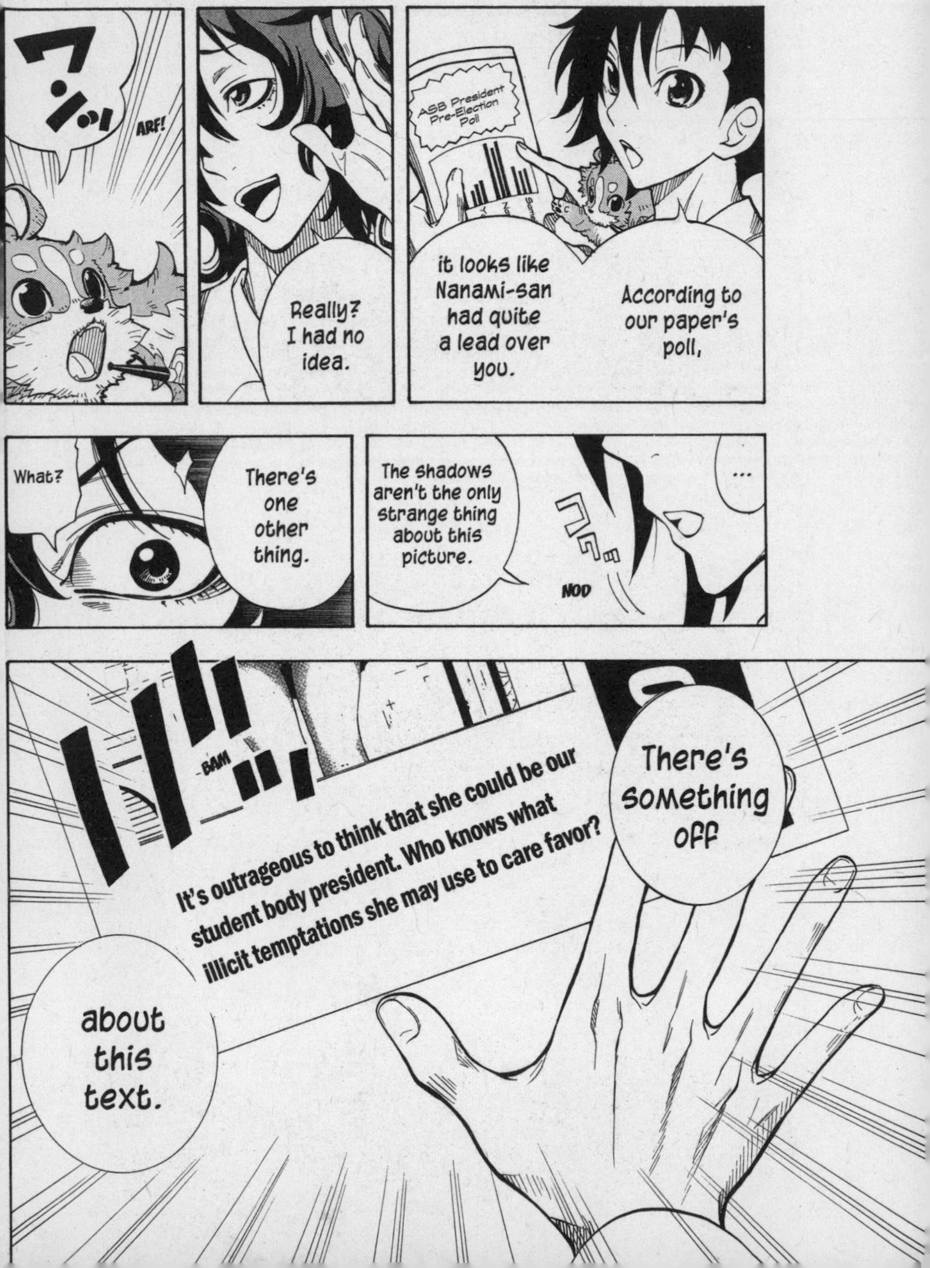
ASB President Pre-Election Poll
According to our paper's poll,
it looks like Nanami-san had quite a lead over you.
Really? I had no idea.
ARF!
...
NOD
The shadows aren't the only strange thing about this picture.
There's one other thing.
What?
There's something off
BAM
It's outrageous to think that she could be our student body president. Who knows what illicit temptations she may use to care favor?
about this text.

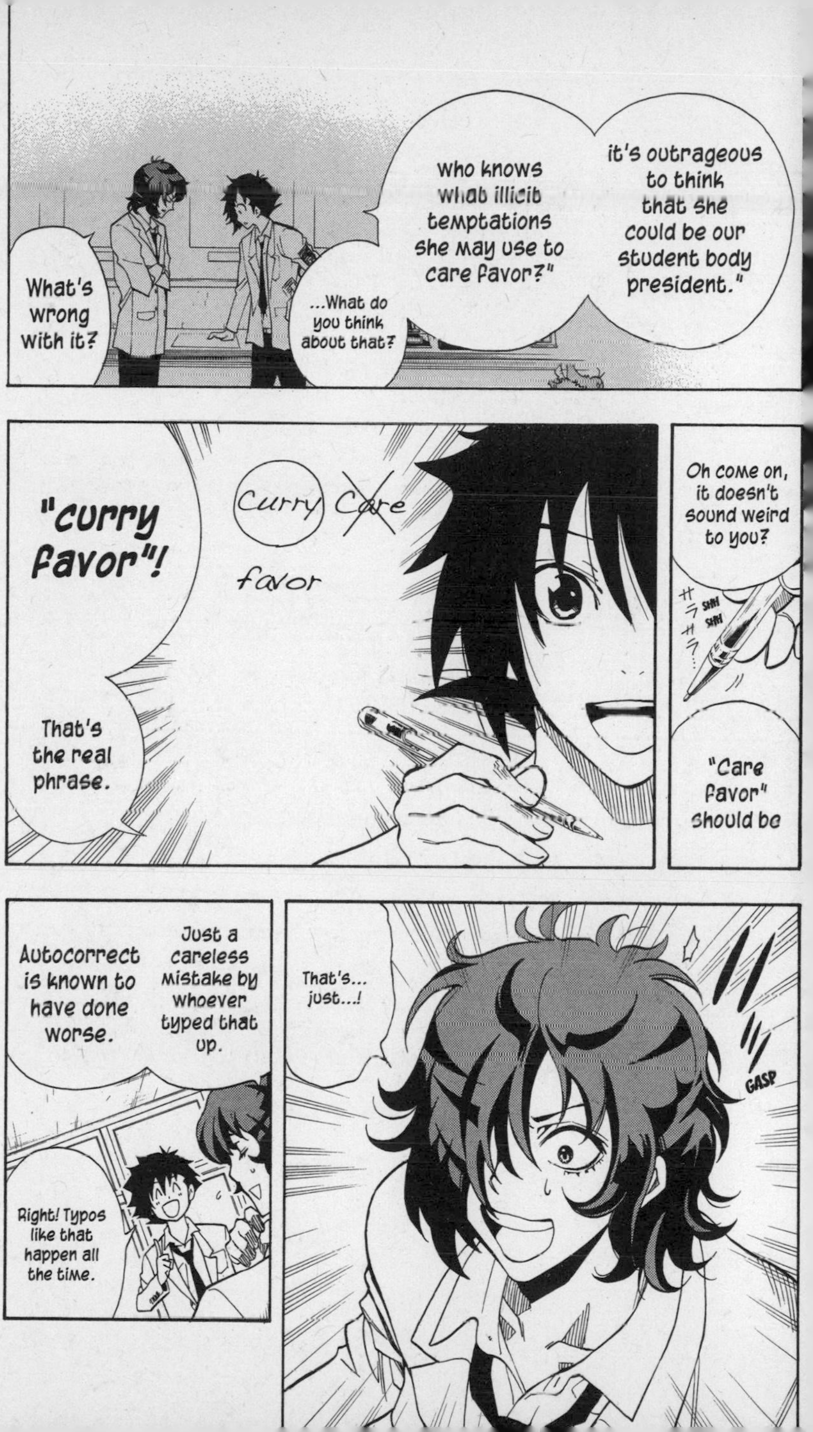
it's outrageous to think that she could be our student body president."
who knows what illicit temptations she may use to care favor?"
...What do you think about that?
What's wrong with it?
Oh come on, it doesn't sound weird to you?
サラサラ
SHH SHH
"Care favor" should be
Curry Care
favor
"curry favor"!
That's the real phrase.
That's... just...!
GASP
Just a careless mistake by whoever typed that up.
Autocorrect is known to have done worse.
Right! Typos like that happen all the time.

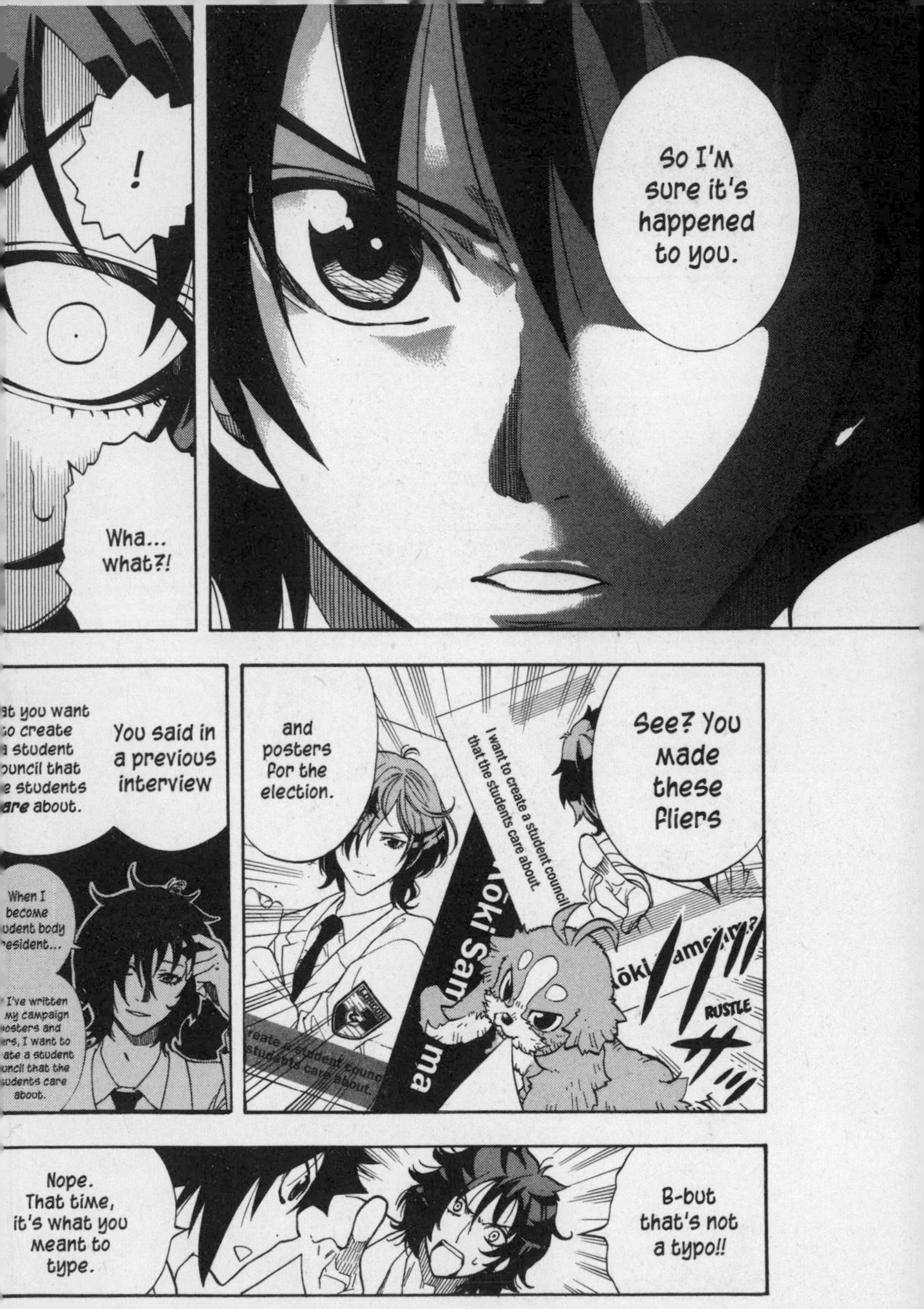
So I'm sure it's happened to you.
!
Wha... what?!
See? You made these fliers
and posters for the election.
I want to create a student council that the students care about.
RUSTLE
You said in a previous interview
at you want to create a student council that the students care about.
When I become udent body resident...
I've written my campaign posters and ers, I want to ate a student uncil that the udents care about.
B-but that's not a typo!!
Nope. That time, it's what you meant to type.

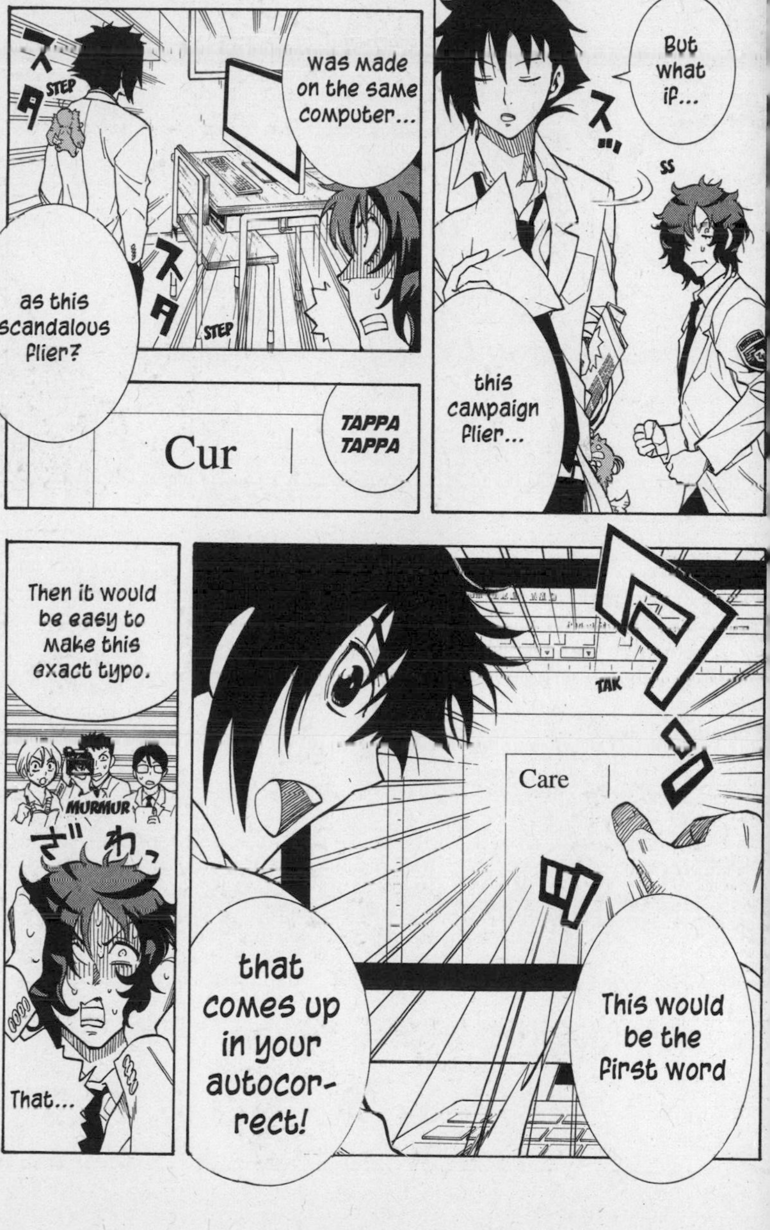
But what if...
SS
this campaign flier...
was made on the same computer...
STEP
STEP
as this scandalous flier?
TAPPA TAPPA
Cur
This would be the first word
that comes up in your autocorrect!
TAK
Care
Then it would be easy to make this exact typo.
MURMUR
ざわっ
That...

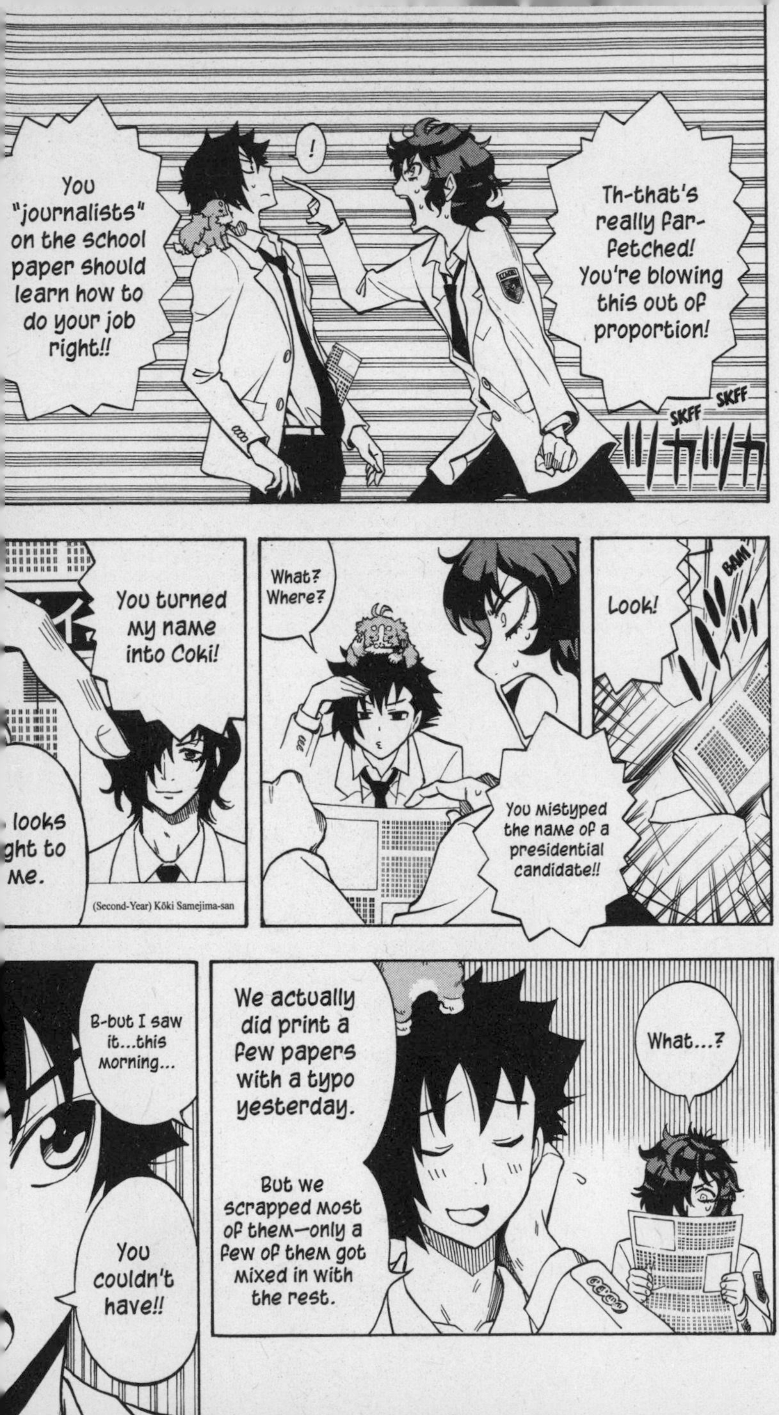
Th-that's really far-fetched! You're blowing this out of proportion!
!
You "journalists" on the school paper should learn how to do your job right!!
SKFF
SKFF
Look!
BAM
You mistyped the name of a presidential candidate!!
What? Where?
You turned my name into Coki!
looks
ght to
me.
(Second-Year) Kōki Samejima-san
What...?
We actually did print a few papers with a typo yesterday.
But we scrapped most of them—only a few of them got mixed in with the rest.
B-but I saw it...this morning...
You couldn't have!!

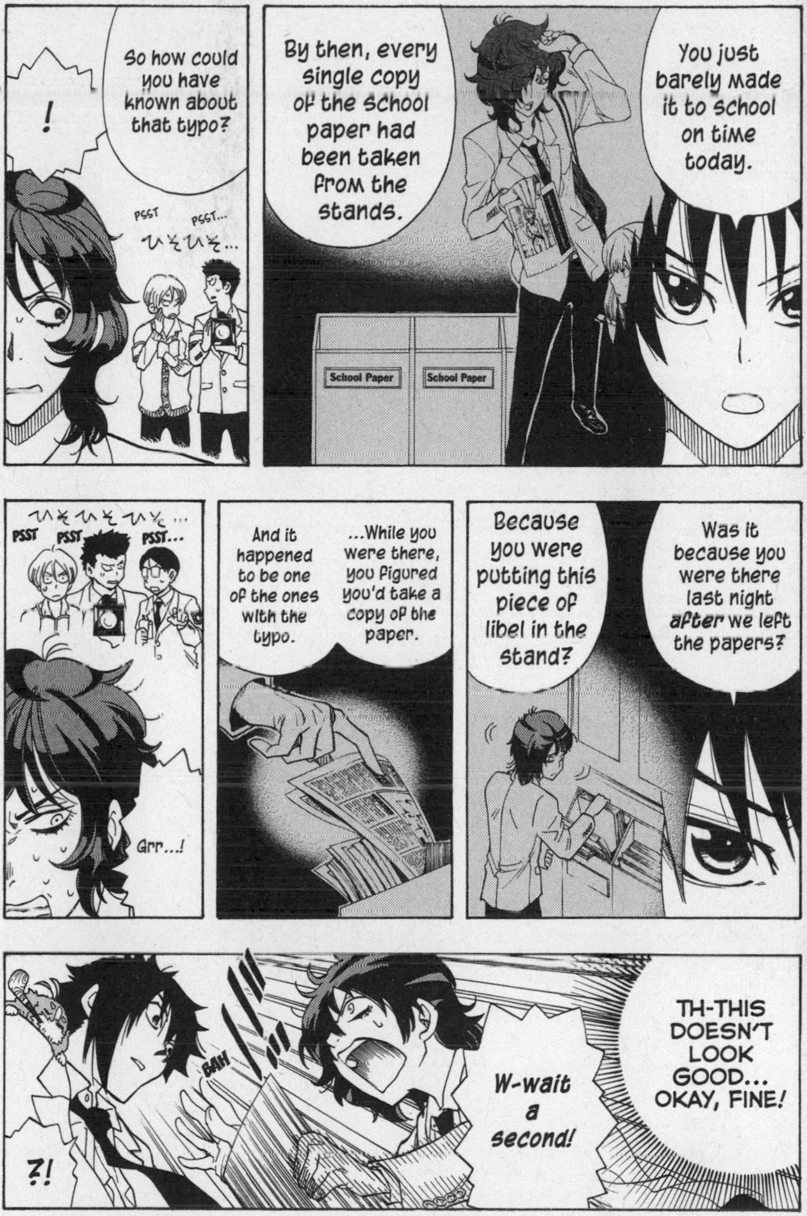
You just barely made it to school on time today.
By then, every single copy of the school paper had been taken from the stands.
School Paper
School Paper
So how could you have known about that typo?
!
PSST
PSST...
ひそひそ...
Was it because you were there last night *after* we left the papers?
Because you were putting this piece of libel in the stand?
...While you were there, you figured you'd take a copy of the paper.
And it happened to be one of the ones with the typo.
ひそひそひそ...
PSST
PSST
PSST...
Grr...!
TH-THIS DOESN'T LOOK GOOD... OKAY, FINE!
W-wait a second!
BAH
?!

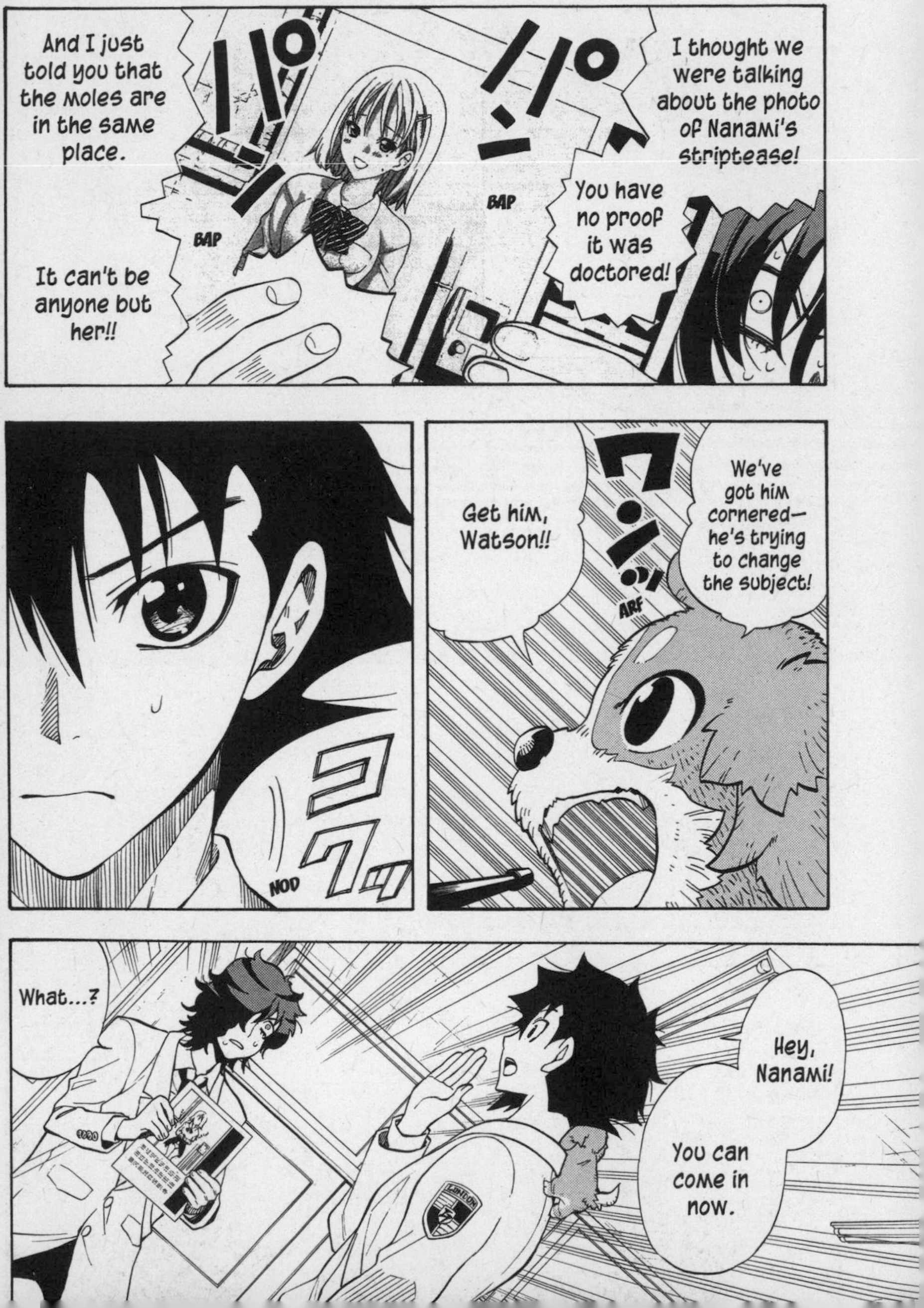
I thought we were talking about the photo of Nanami's striptease!
BAP
You have no proof it was doctored!
And I just told you that the moles are in the same place.
BAP
It can't be anyone but her!!
We've got him cornered—he's trying to change the subject!
ARF
Get him, Watson!!
NOD
Hey, Nanami!
You can come in now.
What...?

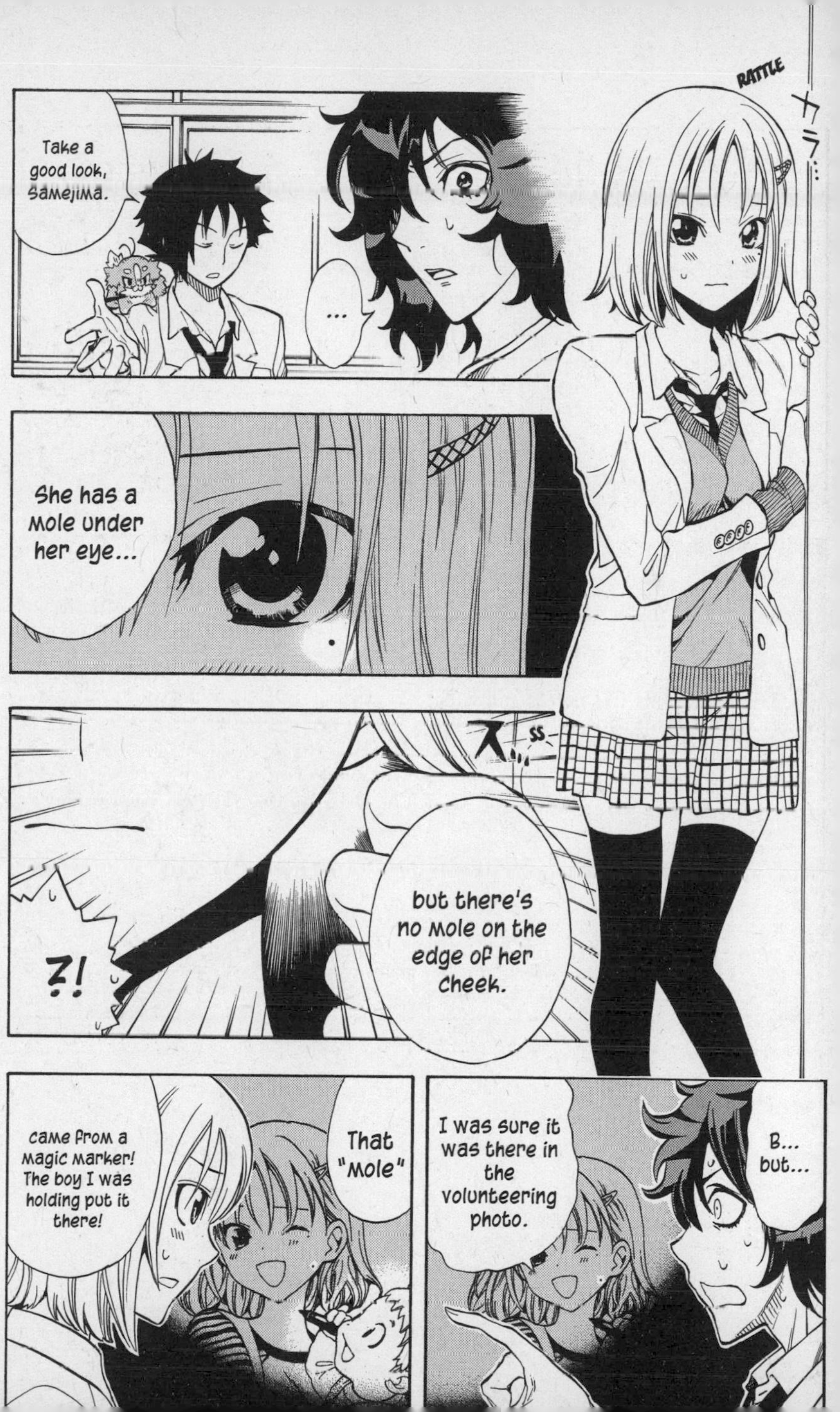
RATTLE
カラ…
…
Take a good look, Samejima.
She has a mole under her eye…
SS…
?!
but there's no mole on the edge of her cheek.
B… but…
I was sure it was there in the volunteering photo.
That "Mole"
came from a magic marker! The boy I was holding put it there!

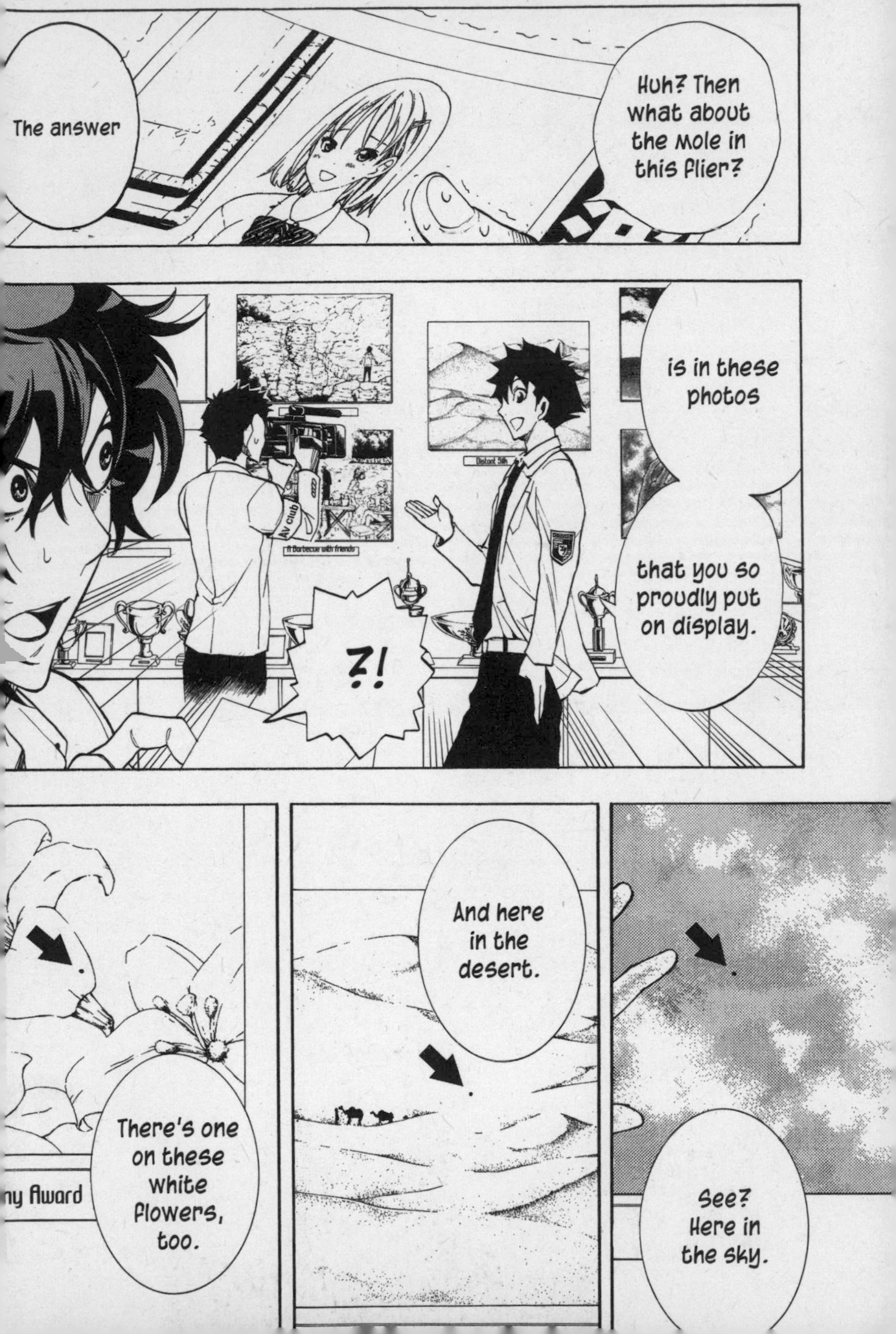
Huh? Then what about the mole in this flier?
The answer
is in these photos
that you so proudly put on display.
?!
See? Here in the sky.
And here in the desert.
There's one on these white flowers, too.
ny Award

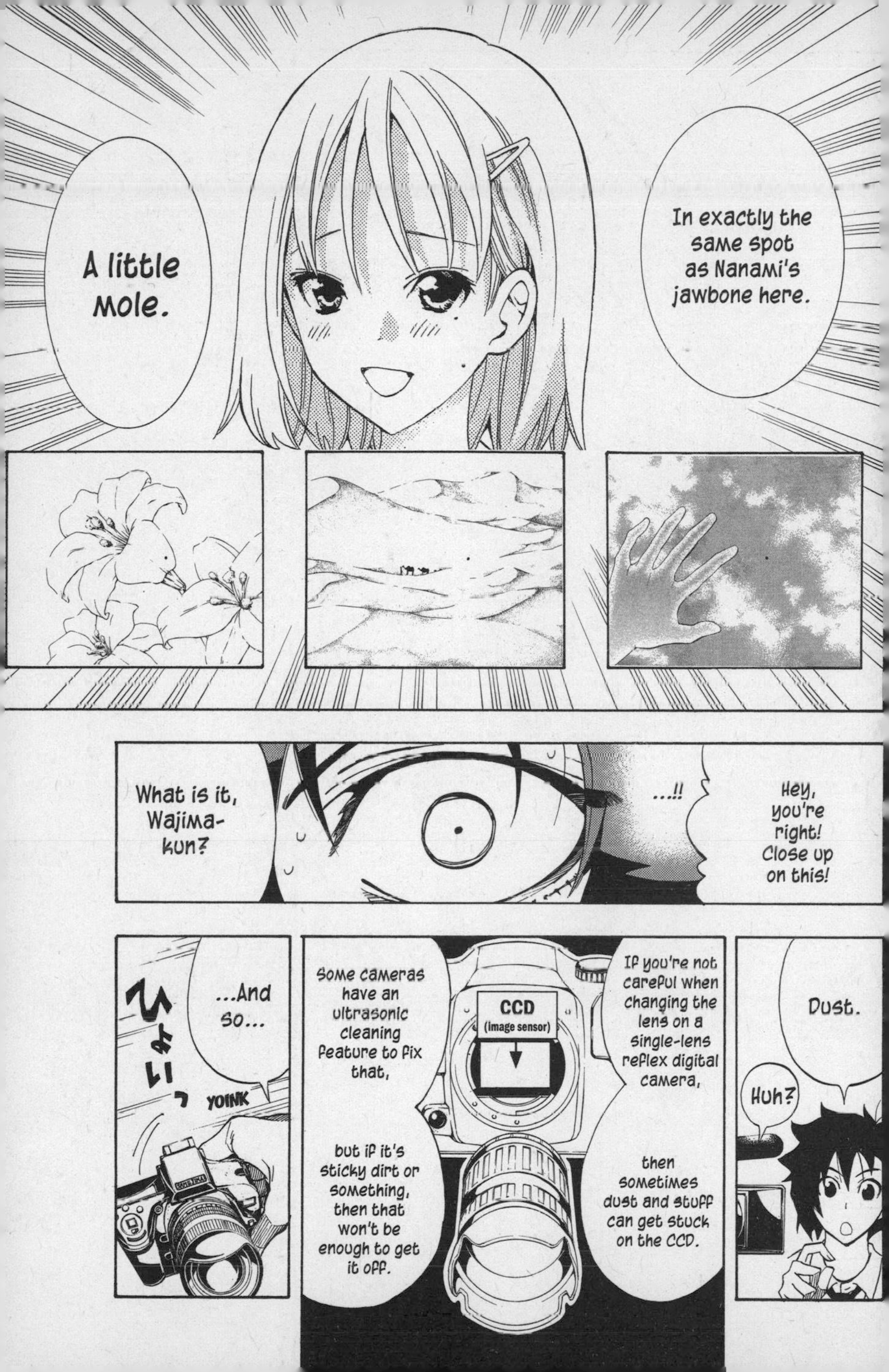
In exactly the same spot as Nanami's jawbone here.
A little mole.
Hey, you're right! Close up on this!
...!!
What is it, Wajima-kun?
Dust.
Huh?
If you're not careful when changing the lens on a single-lens reflex digital camera,
then sometimes dust and stuff can get stuck on the CCD.
CCD (image sensor)
Some cameras have an ultrasonic cleaning feature to fix that,
but if it's sticky dirt or something, then that won't be enough to get it off.
...And so...
ひょいっ
YOINK

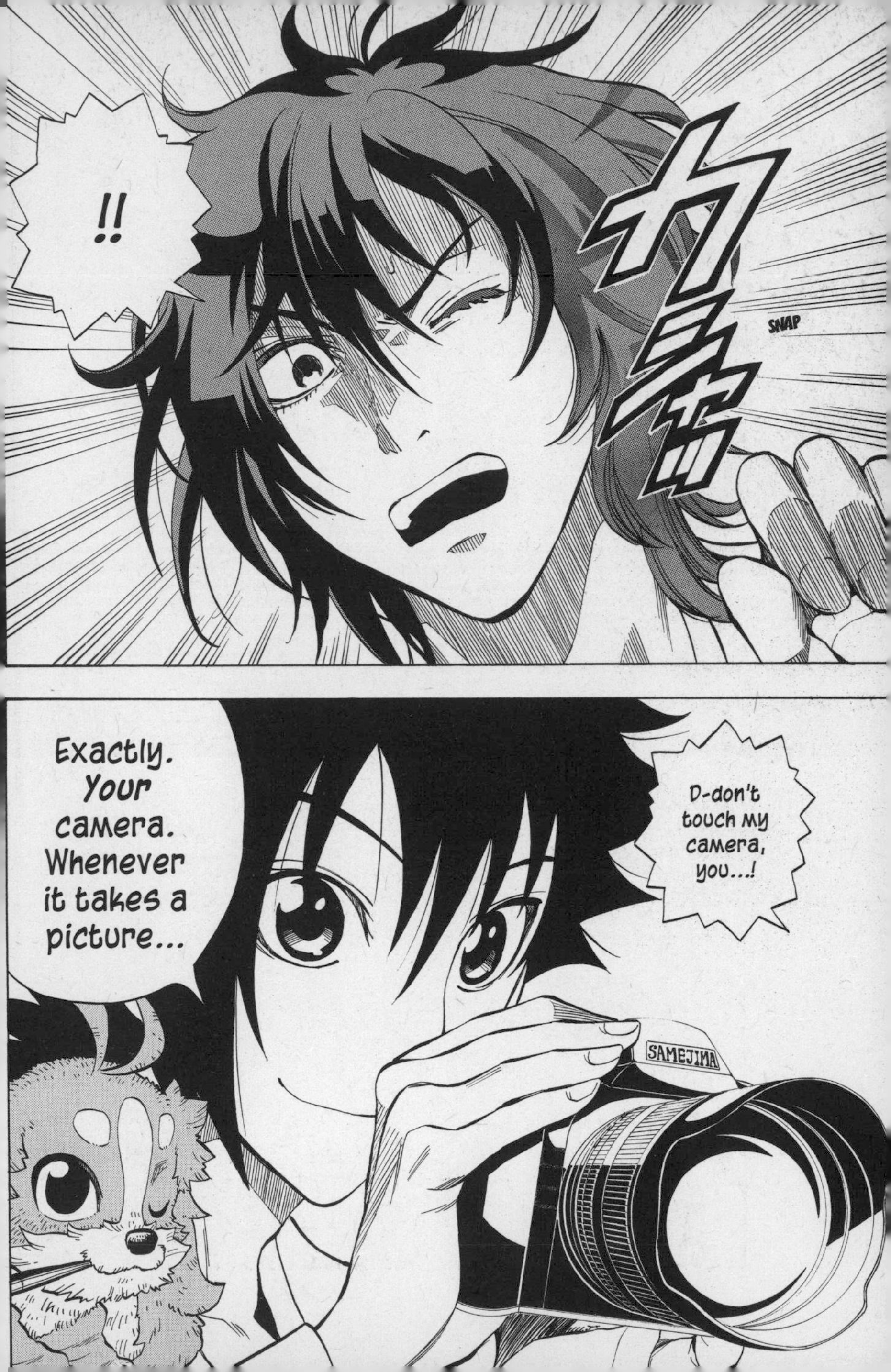
SNAP
!!
D-don't touch my camera, you...!
Exactly. Your camera. Whenever it takes a picture...
SAMEJIMA

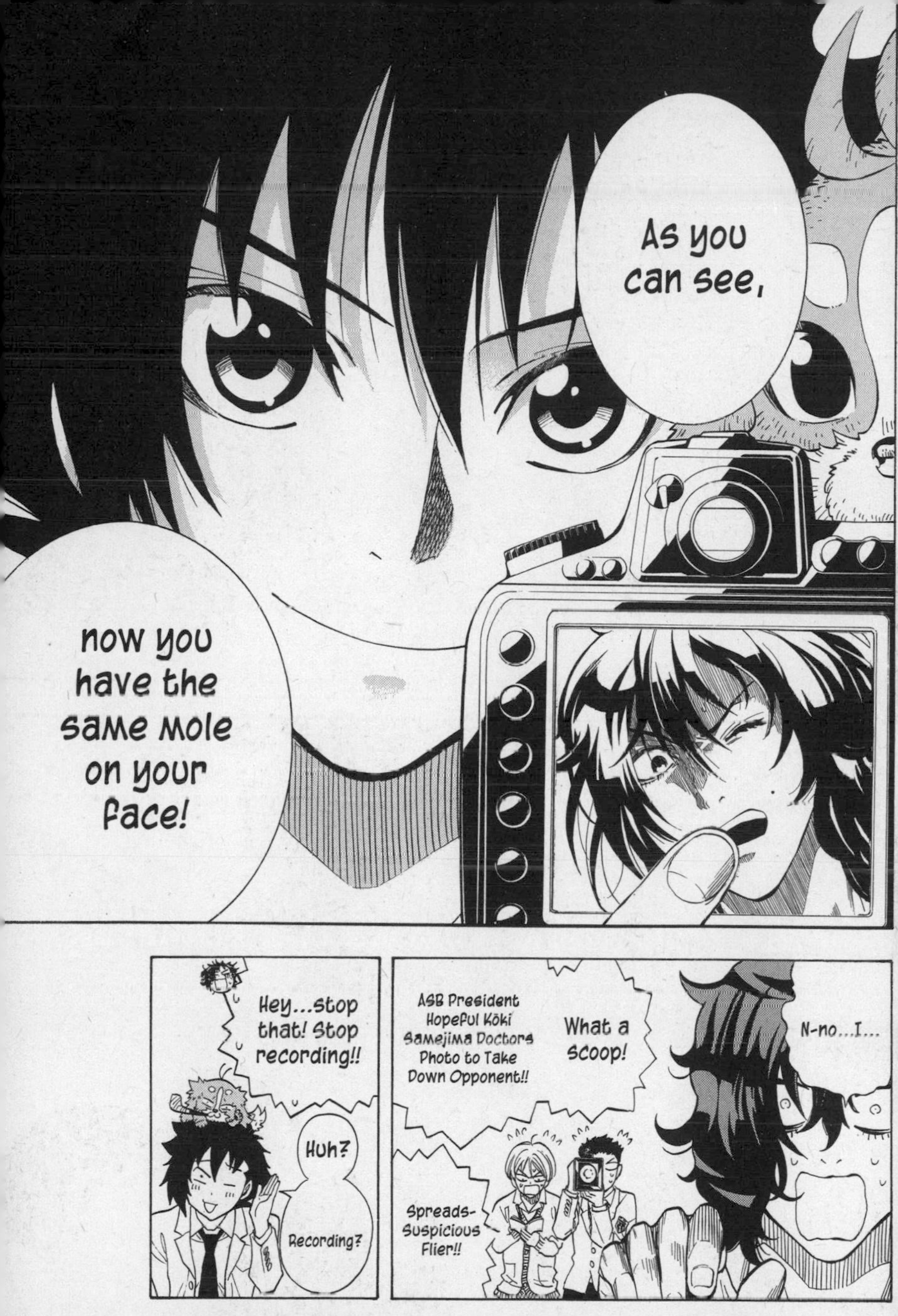
As you can see,
now you have the same mole on your face!
N-no...I...
What a scoop!
ASB President Hopeful Kōki Samejima Doctors Photo to Take Down Opponent!!
Spreads-Suspicious Flier!!
Hey...stop that! Stop recording!!
Huh?
Recording?

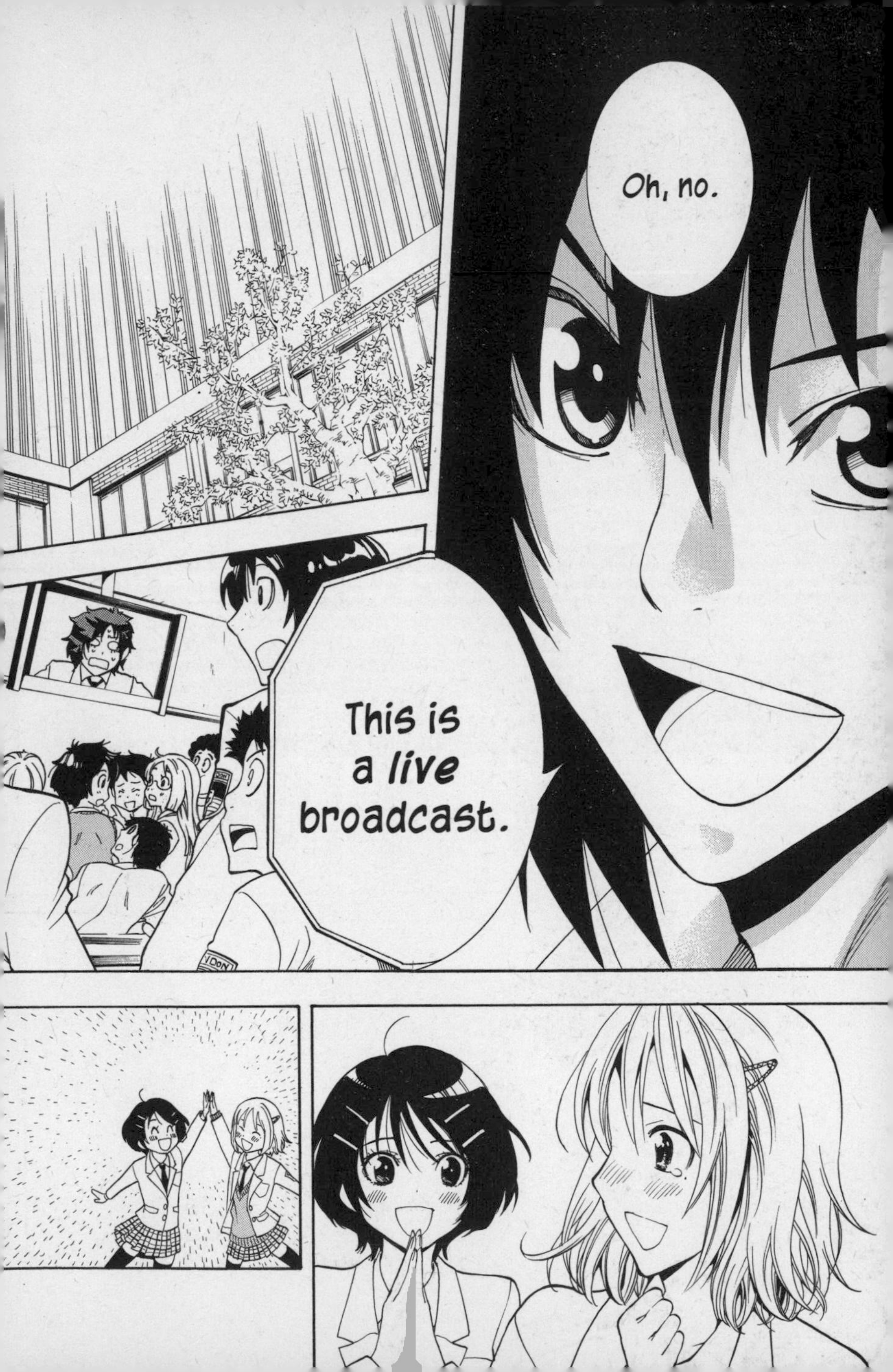
Oh, no.
This is a *live* broadcast.

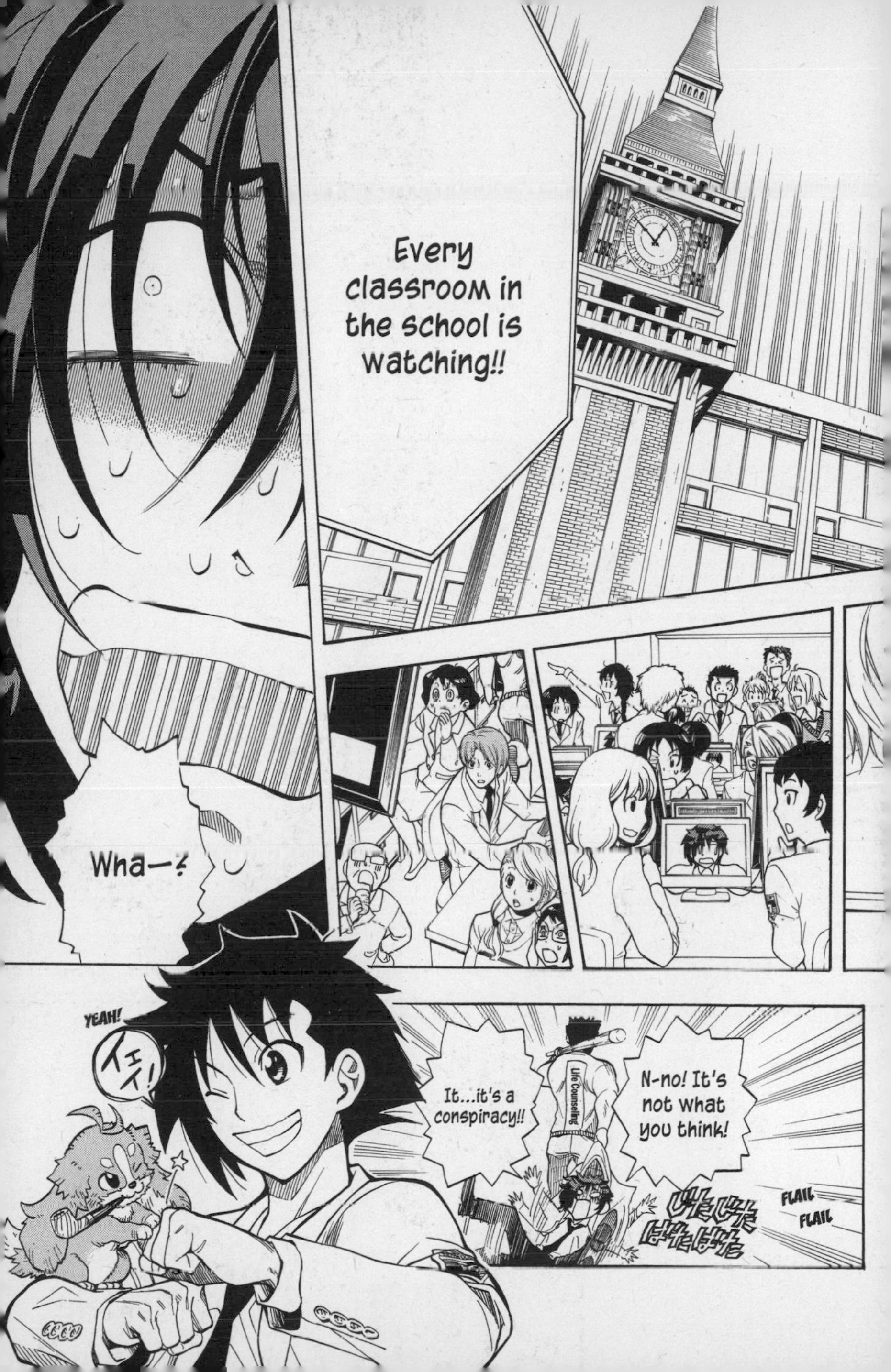
Every classroom in the school is watching!!
Wha—?
N-no! It's not what you think!
FLAIL
FLAIL
Life Counseling
It...it's a conspiracy!!
YEAH!
イエイ!

Defending to the
Death

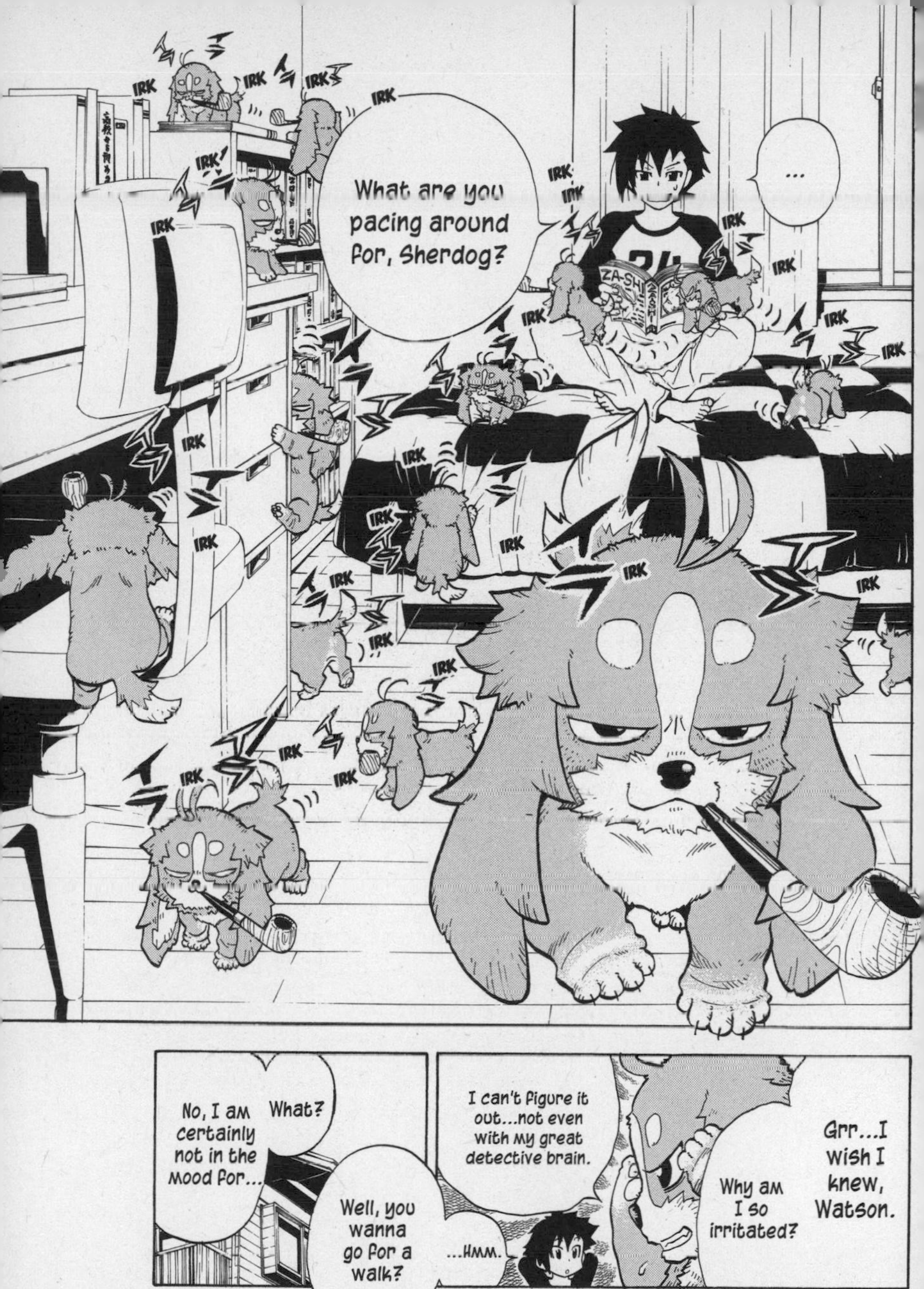
...
IRK
IRK
IRK
IRK
IRK
IRK
What are you pacing around for, Sherdog?
IRK
IRK
IRK
IRK
IRK
IRK
IRK
IRK
IRK
IRK
IRK
IRK
IRK
IRK
IRK
IRK
IRK
IRK
IRK
Grr...I wish I knew, Watson.
Why am I so irritated?
I can't figure it out...not even with my great detective brain.
...Hmm.
Well, you wanna go for a walk?
What?
No, I am certainly not in the mood for...

Sherlock Bones

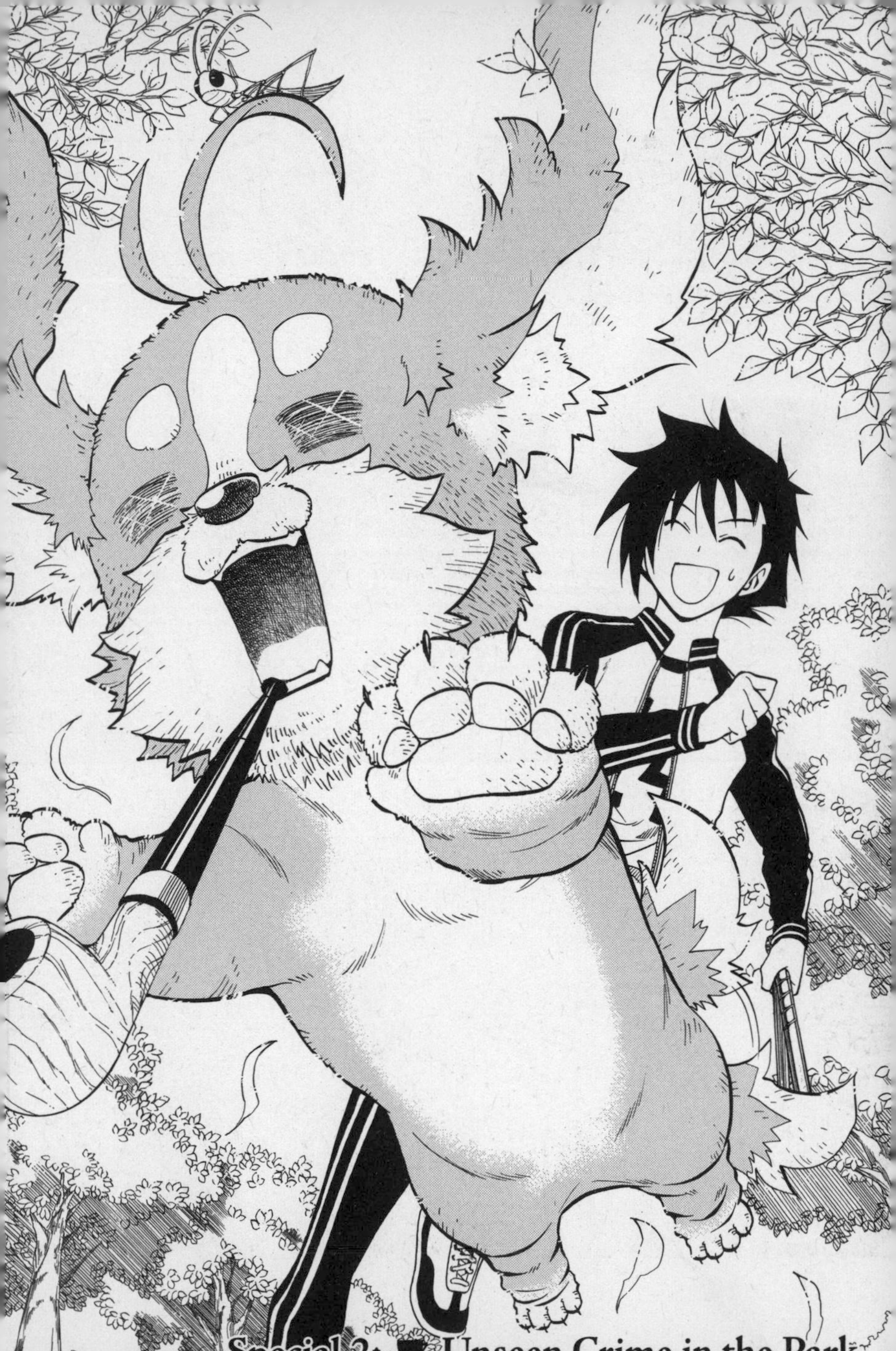

Special 2: Unseen Crime in the Park

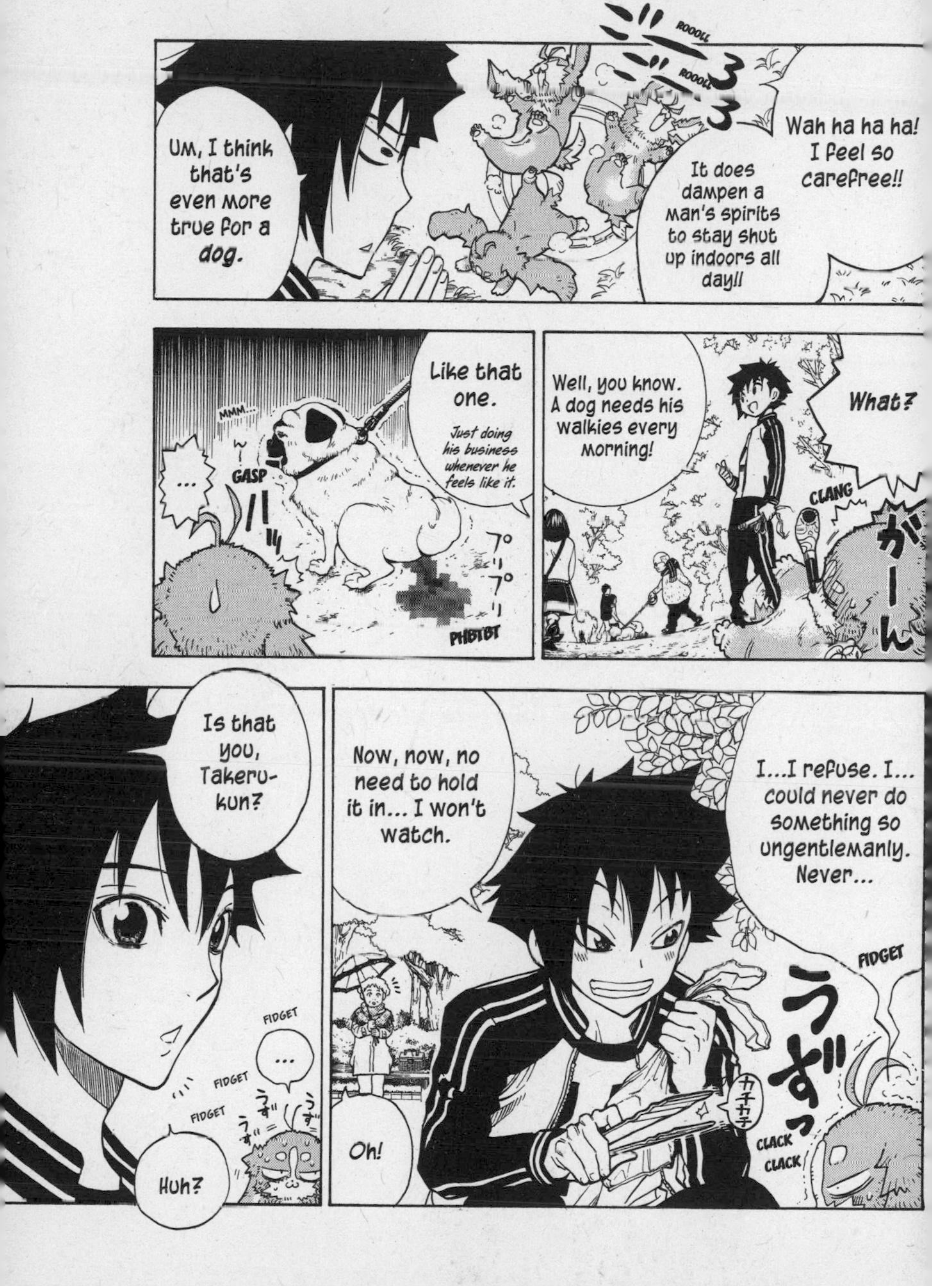
ROOOLL
ROOOLL
Wah ha ha ha! I feel so carefree!!
It does dampen a man's spirits to stay shut up indoors all day!!
Um, I think that's even more true for a dog.
What?
CLANG
Well, you know. A dog needs his walkies every morning!
Like that one.
Just doing his business whenever he feels like it.
MMM...
GASP
...
PHBTBT
I...I refuse. I... could never do something so ungentlemanly. Never...
FIDGET
CLACK
CLACK
Now, now, no need to hold it in... I won't watch.
Oh!
Is that you, Takeru-kun?
FIDGET
FIDGET
FIDGET
...
Huh?

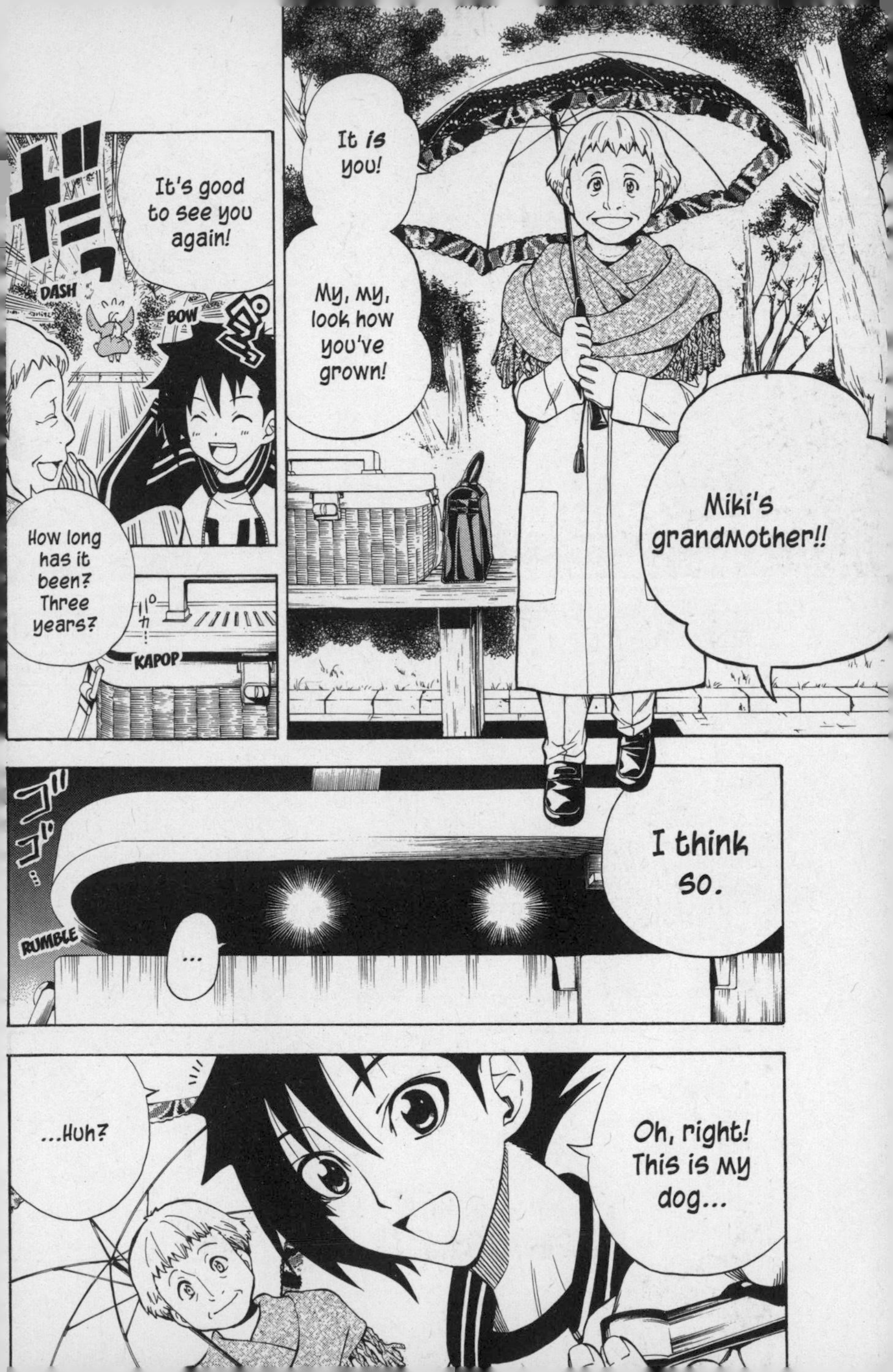
It is you!
My, my, look how you've grown!
Miki's grandmother!!
It's good to see you again!
DASH
BOW
How long has it been? Three years?
KAPOP
I think so.
...
RUMBLE
Oh, right! This is my dog...
...Huh?

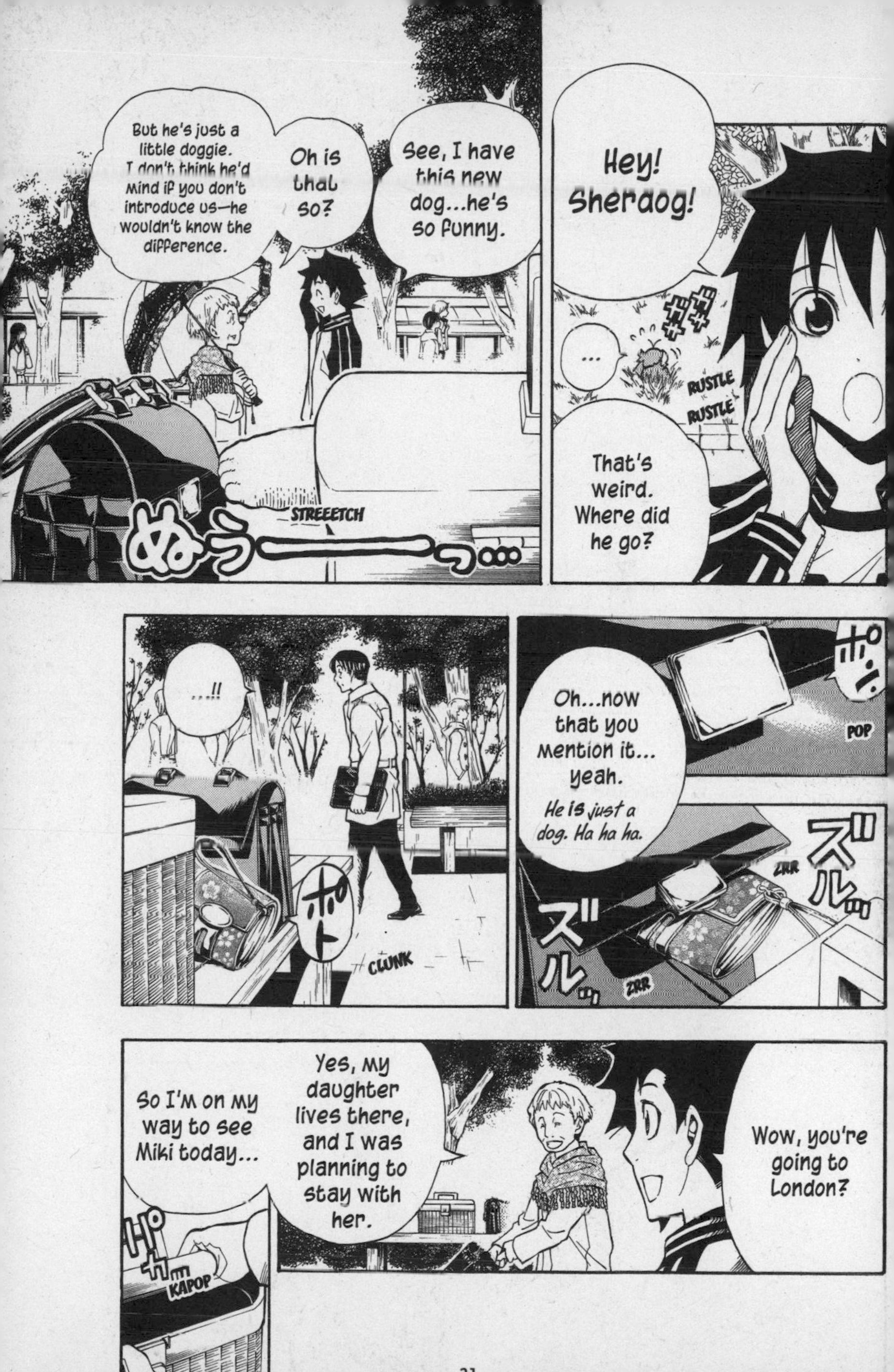

Hey! Sheradog!
...
RUSTLE
RUSTLE
That's weird. Where did he go?
See, I have this new dog...he's so funny.
Oh is that so?
But he's just a little doggie. I don't think he'd mind if you don't introduce us—he wouldn't know the difference.
STREEETCH
ぬうーーっ…
ポン
POP
Oh...now that you mention it... yeah.
He is just a dog. Ha ha ha.
ズルッ
ZRR
ズルッ
ZRR
...!!
ポト
CLUNK
Wow, you're going to London?
Yes, my daughter lives there, and I was planning to stay with her.
So I'm on my way to see Miki today...
パカ
KAPOP

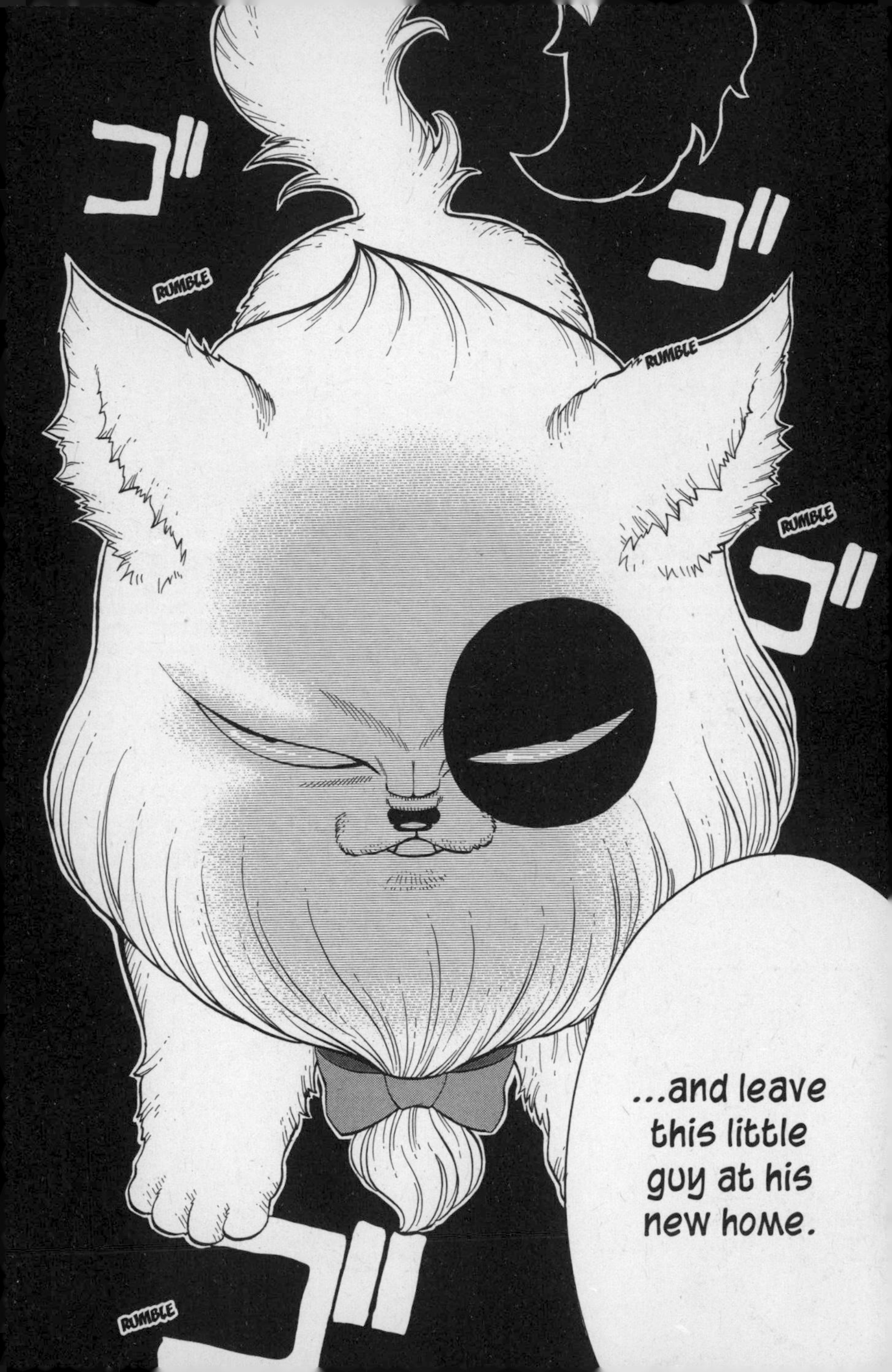
ゴ
RUMBLE
ゴ
RUMBLE
RUMBLE
ゴ
...and leave this little guy at his new home.
ゴ
RUMBLE

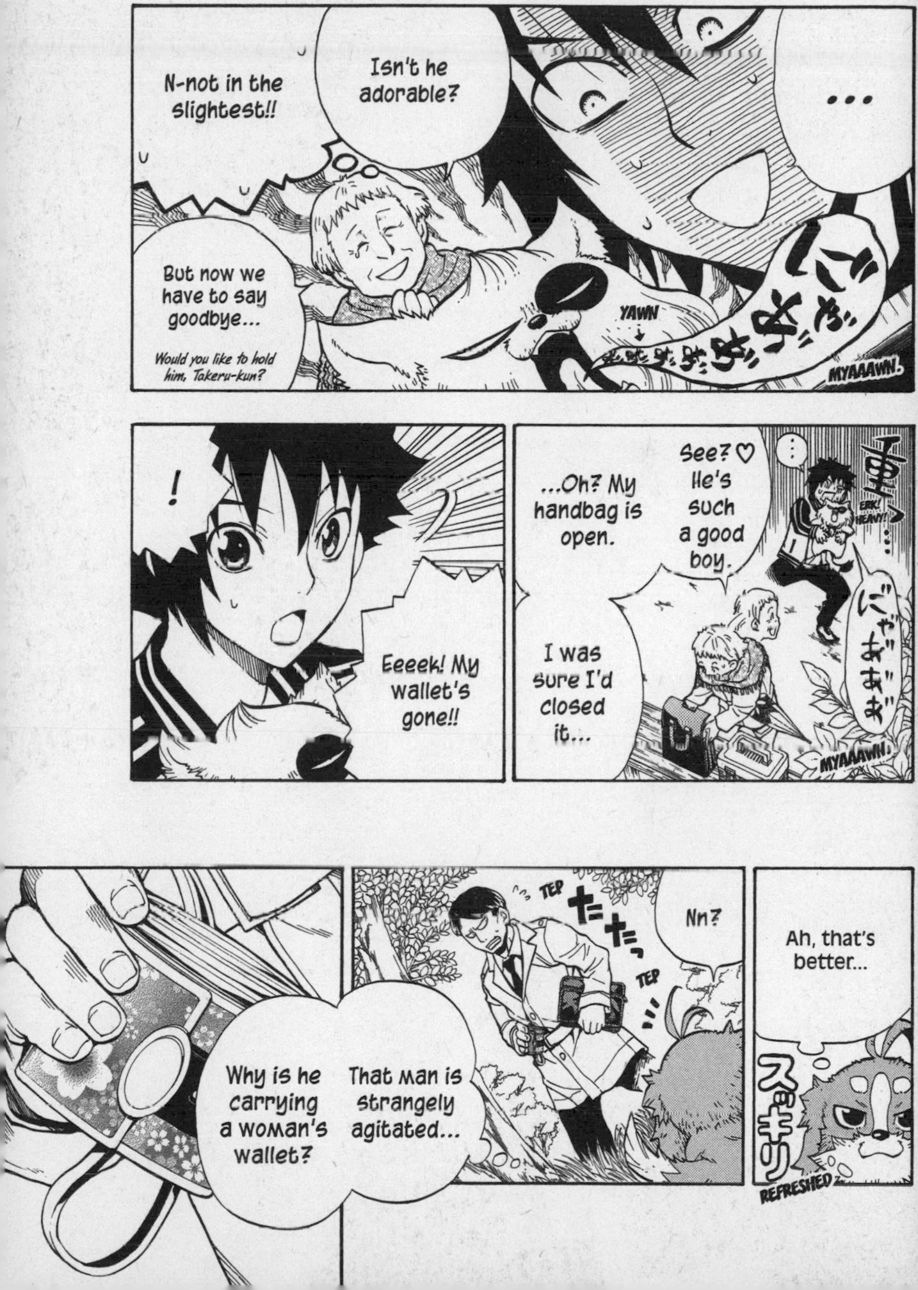
...
MYAAAWN.
Isn't he adorable?
N-not in the slightest!!
YAWN
But now we have to say goodbye...
Would you like to hold him, Takeru-kun?
...
重
ERK! HEAVY!
See? ♡ He's such a good boy.
...Oh? My handbag is open.
MYAAAWN.
I was sure I'd closed it...
!
Eeeek! My wallet's gone!!
Ah, that's better...
スッキリ
REFRESHED
TEP
たたっ
TEP
Nn?
That man is strangely agitated...
Why is he carrying a woman's wallet?

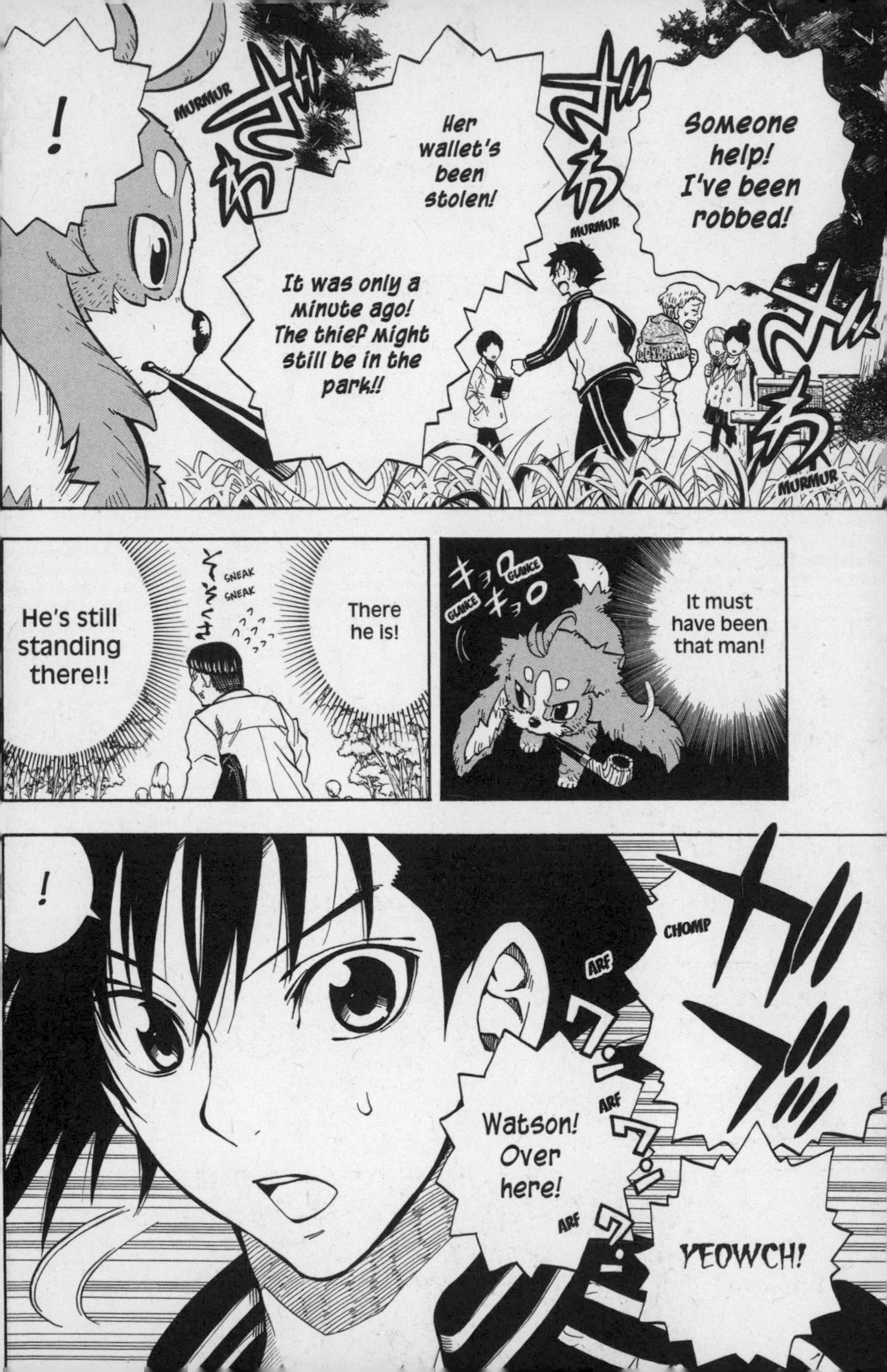
Someone help! I've been robbed!
MURMUR
MURMUR
Her wallet's been stolen!
MURMUR
It was only a minute ago! The thief might still be in the park!!
!
GLANCE
GLANCE
It must have been that man!
There he is!
SNEAK
SNEAK
He's still standing there!!
CHOMP
ARF
YEOWCH!
ARF
Watson! Over here!
ARF
!

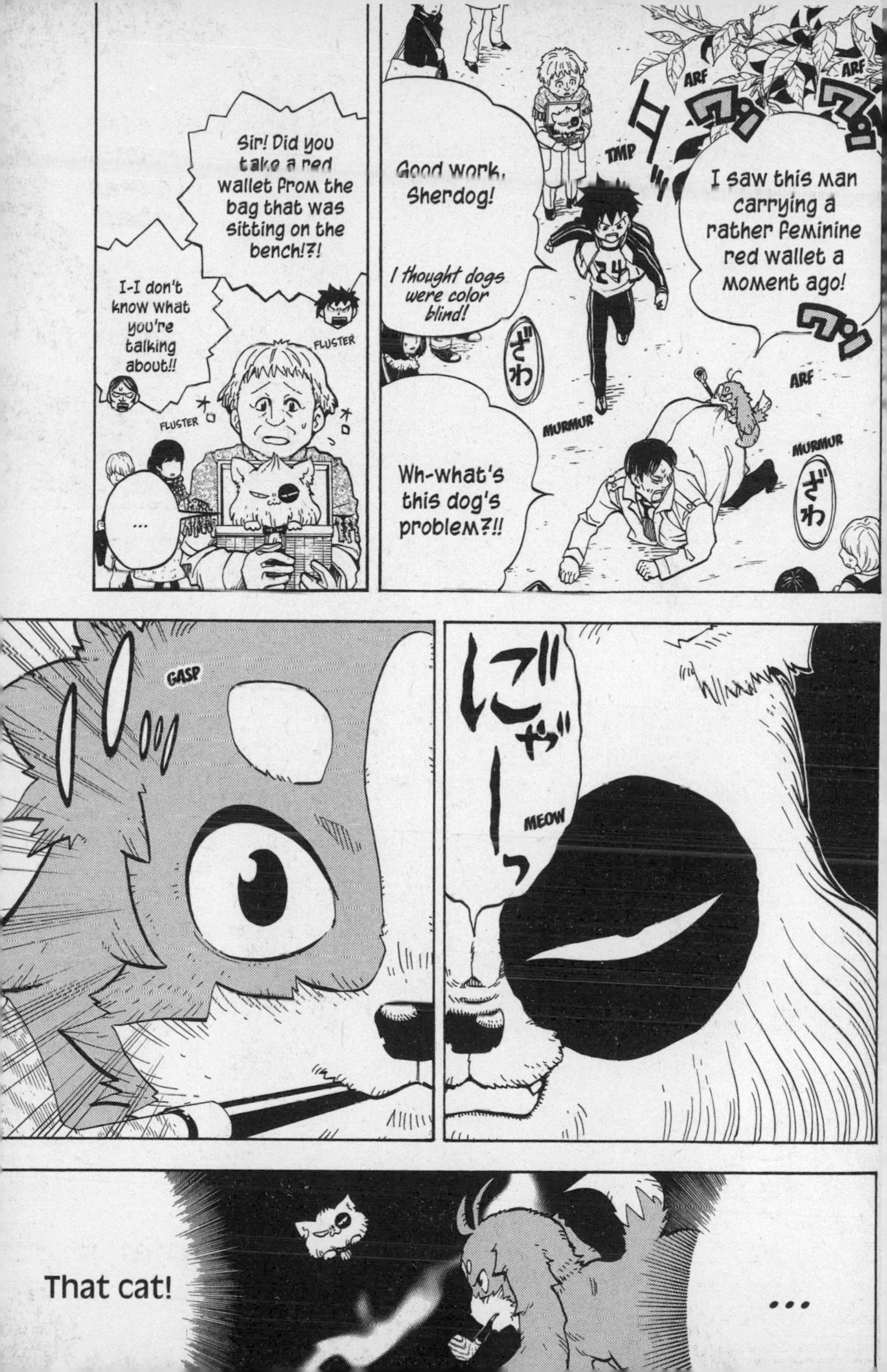
ARF
ARF
I saw this man carrying a rather feminine red wallet a moment ago!
TMP
Good work, Sherdog!
I thought dogs were color blind!
ARF
ざわ
MURMUR
MURMUR
ざわ
Wh-what's this dog's problem?!!
Sir! Did you take a red wallet from the bag that was sitting on the bench!?!
FLUSTER
I-I don't know what you're talking about!!
FLUSTER
...
MEOW
GASP
...
That cat!

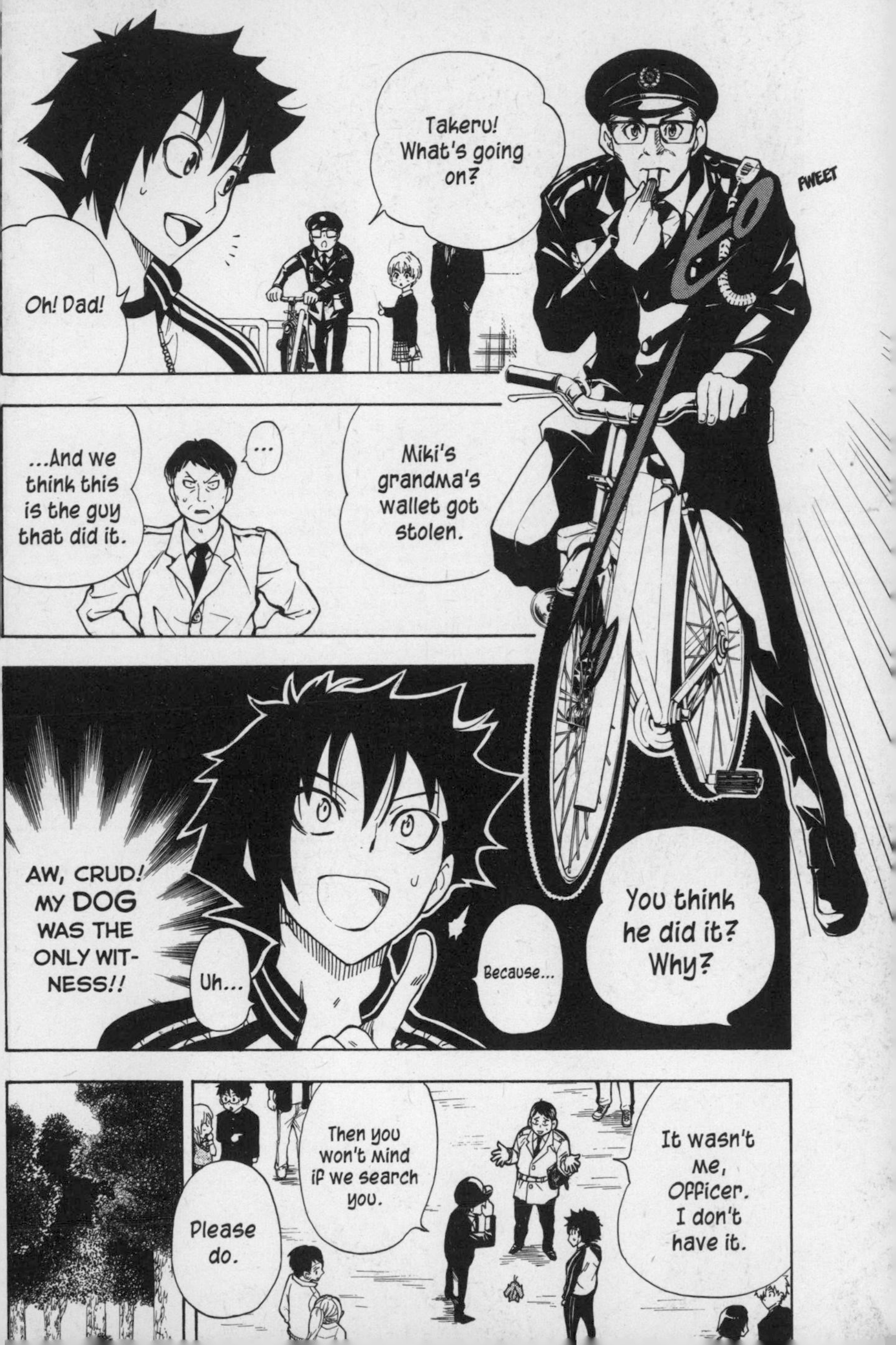
FWEET
Takeru! What's going on?
Oh! Dad!
Miki's grandma's wallet got stolen.
...
...And we think this is the guy that did it.
You think he did it? Why?
Because...
Uh...
AW, CRUD! MY DOG WAS THE ONLY WIT-NESS!!
It wasn't me, Officer. I don't have it.
Then you won't mind if we search you.
Please do.

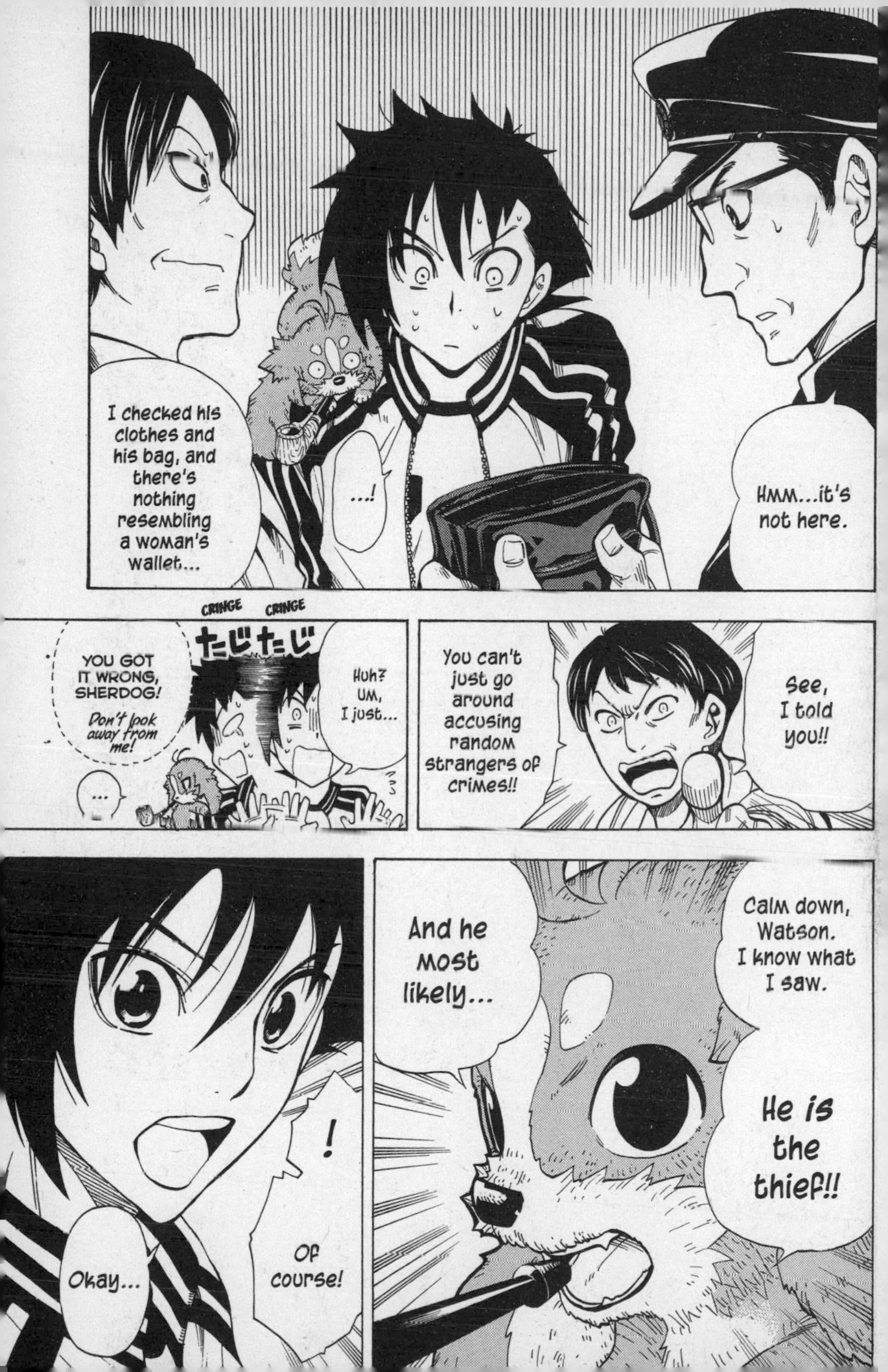
HMM...it's not here.
...!
I checked his clothes and his bag, and there's nothing resembling a woman's wallet...
See, I told you!!
You can't just go around accusing random strangers of crimes!!
Huh? UM, I just...
CRINGE CRINGE
たじたじ
YOU GOT IT WRONG, SHERDOG!
Don't look away from me!
...
Calm down, Watson. I know what I saw.
And he most likely...
He is the thief!!
!
Of course!
Okay...

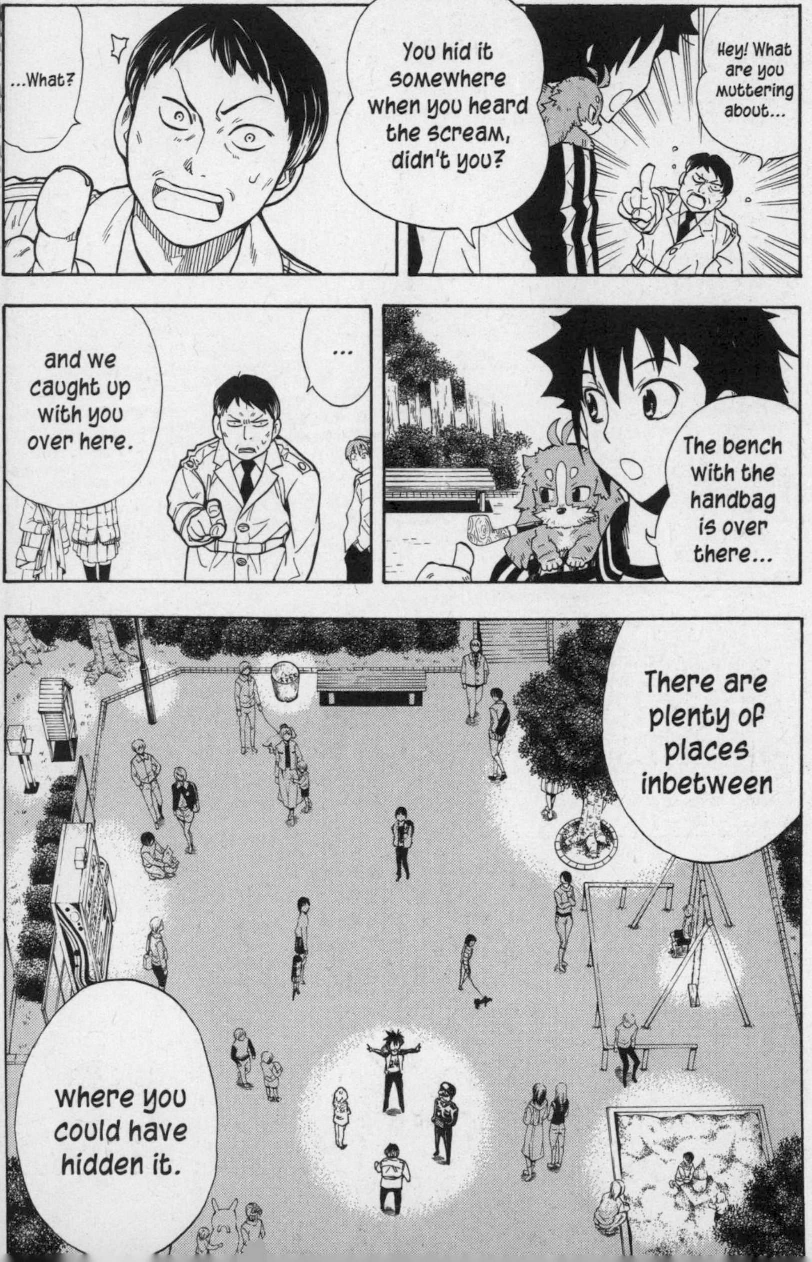
Hey! What are you muttering about...
You hid it somewhere when you heard the scream, didn't you?
...What?
The bench with the handbag is over there...
...
and we caught up with you over here.
There are plenty of places inbetween
where you could have hidden it.

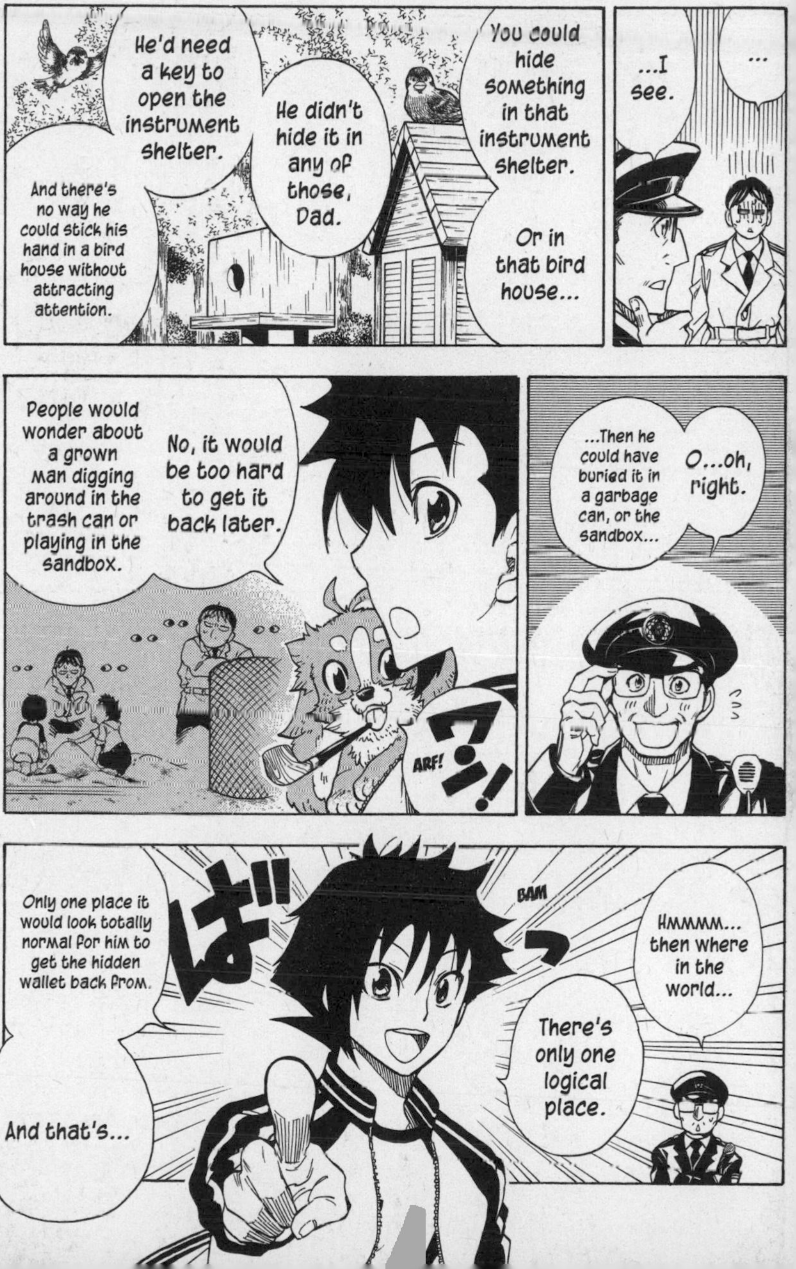
...
...I see.
You could hide something in that instrument shelter.
Or in that bird house...
He didn't hide it in any of those, Dad.
He'd need a key to open the instrument shelter.
And there's no way he could stick his hand in a bird house without attracting attention.
O...oh, right.
...Then he could have buried it in a garbage can, or the sandbox...
No, it would be too hard to get it back later.
People would wonder about a grown man digging around in the trash can or playing in the sandbox.
ワン!
ARF!
HMMMM... then where in the world...
There's only one logical place.
ばっ
BAM
Only one place it would look totally normal for him to get the hidden wallet back from.
And that's...

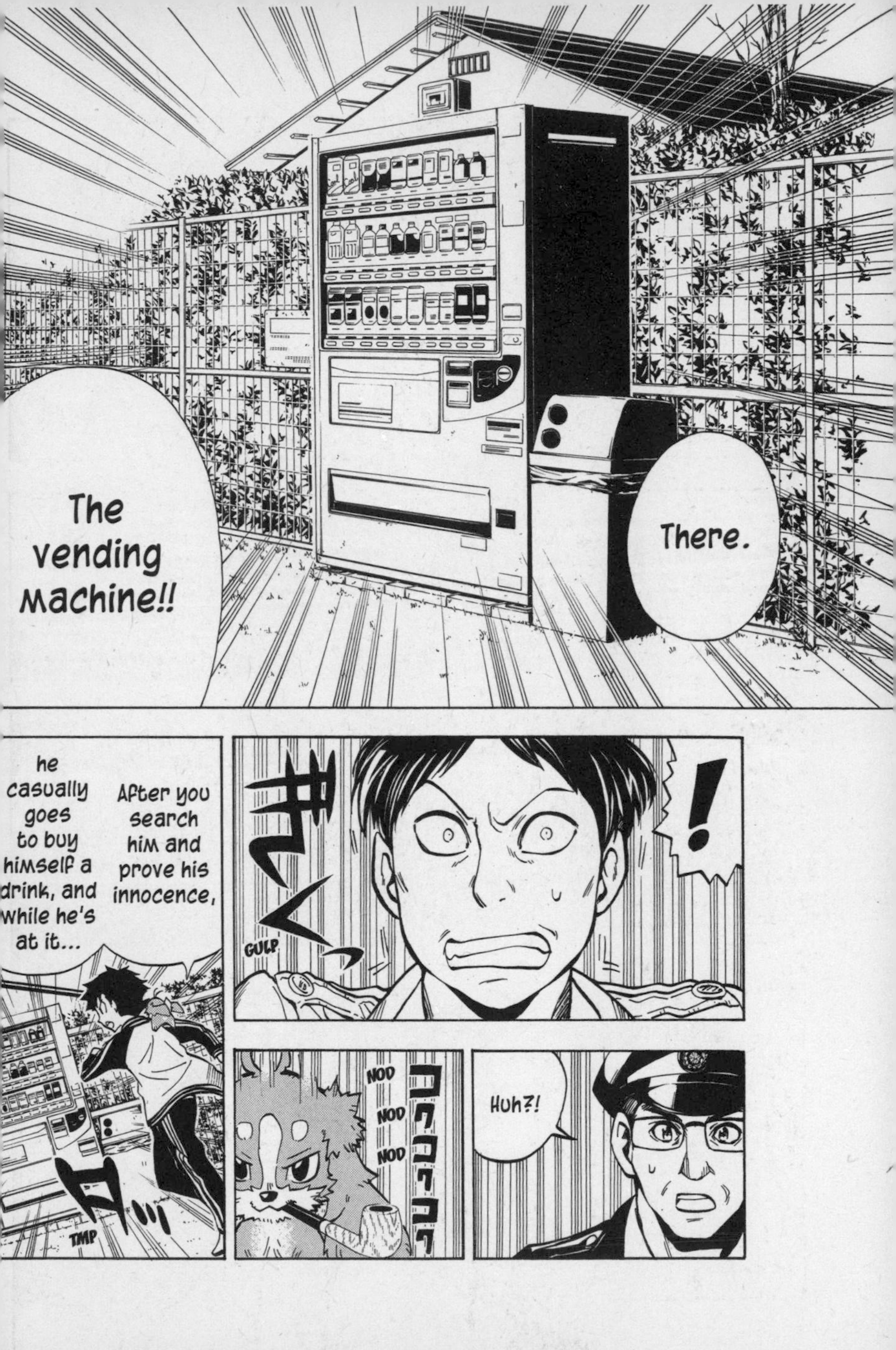
There.
The vending machine!!
!
GULP
Huh?!
NOD NOD NOD
After you search him and prove his innocence,
he casually goes to buy himself a drink, and while he's at it...
TMP

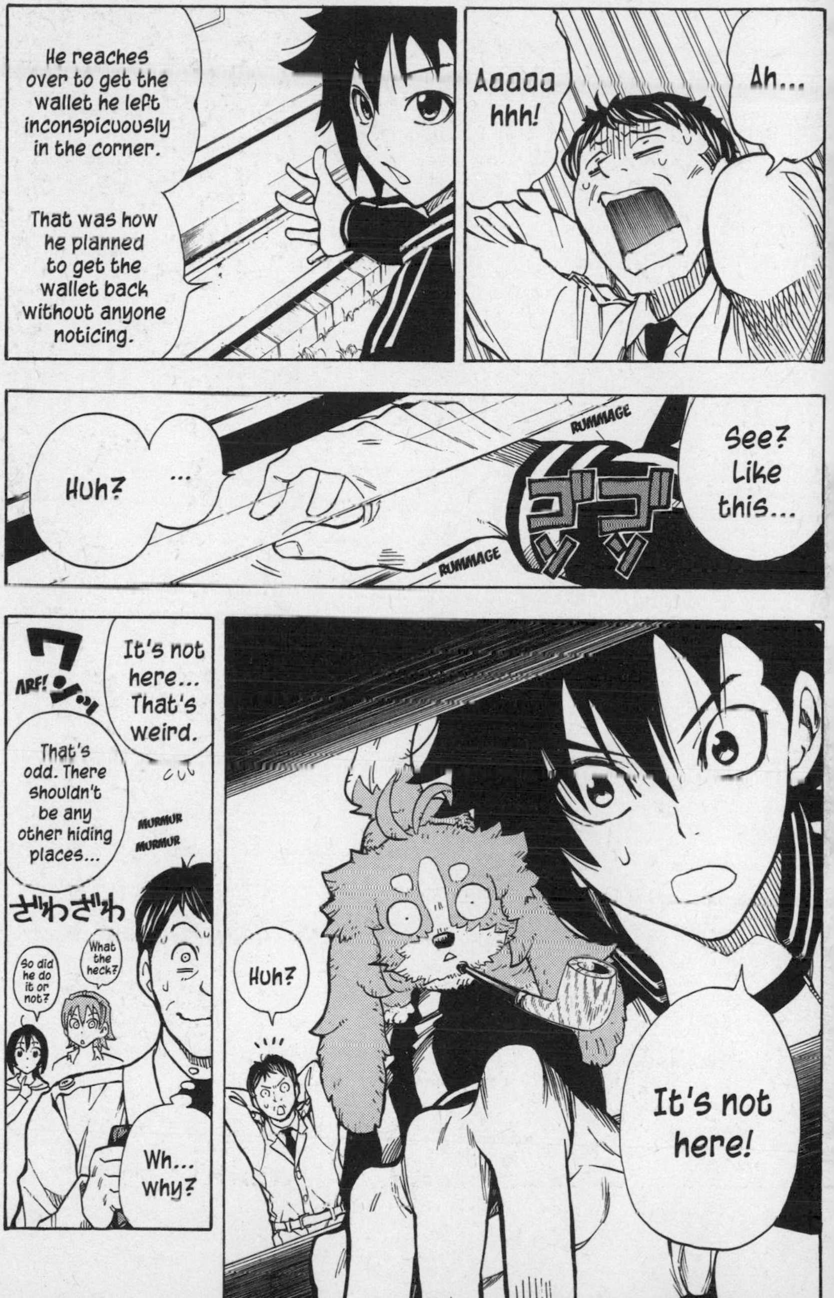
Ah...
Aaaaa hhh!
He reaches over to get the wallet he left inconspicuously in the corner.
That was how he planned to get the wallet back without anyone noticing.
See? Like this...
RUMMAGE
ゴソゴソ
RUMMAGE
...
Huh?
It's not here!
Huh?
It's not here... That's weird.
ワンッ
ARF!
That's odd. There shouldn't be any other hiding places...
MURMUR
MURMUR
ざわざわ
What the heck?
So did he do it or not?
Wh... why?

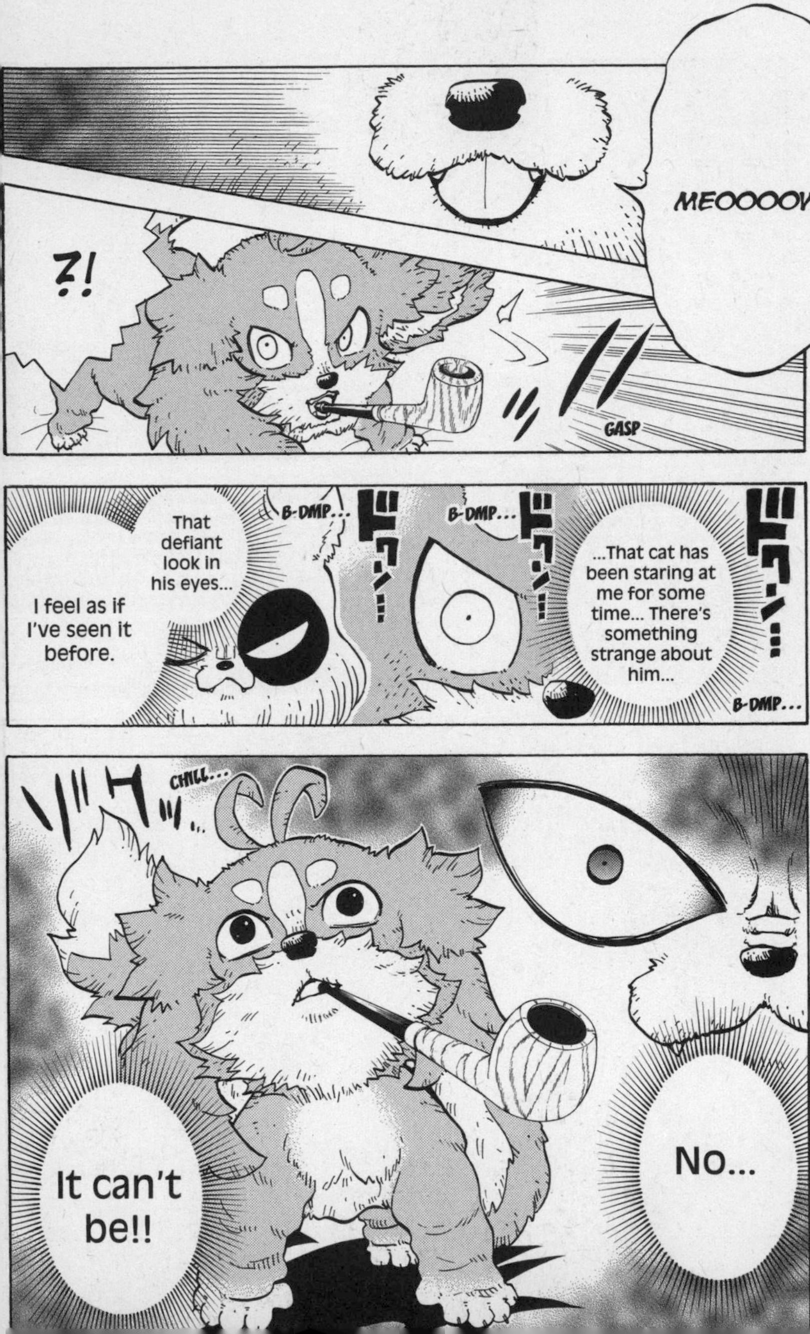
MEOOOOW.
?!
GASP
...That cat has been staring at me for some time... There's something strange about him...
B-DMP...
B-DMP...
B-DMP...
That defiant look in his eyes...
I feel as if I've seen it before.
CHILL...
No...
It can't be!!

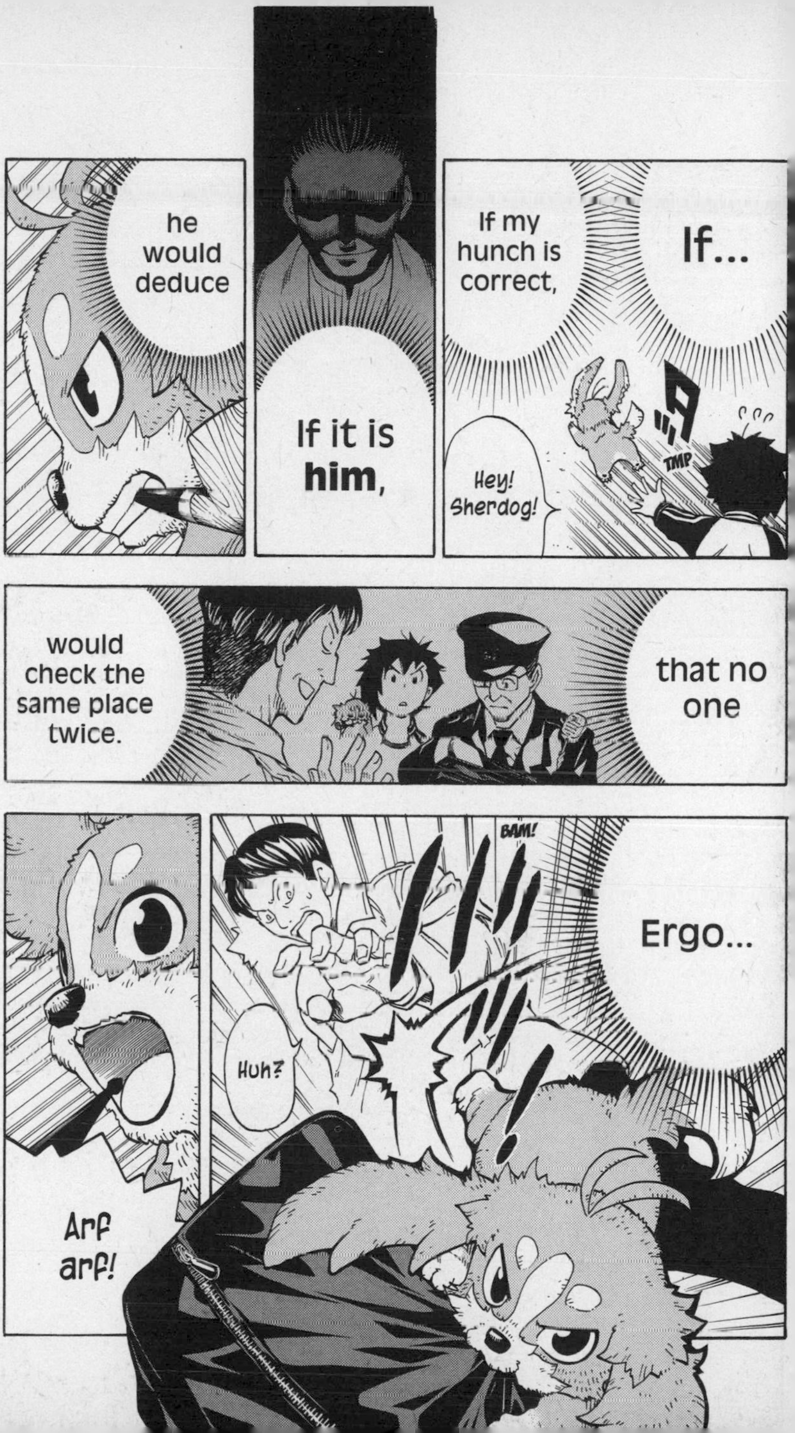
If...
If my hunch is correct,
Hey! Sherdog!
TMP
If it is **him**,
he would deduce
that no one
would check the same place twice.
Ergo...
BAM!
Huh?
Arf arf!

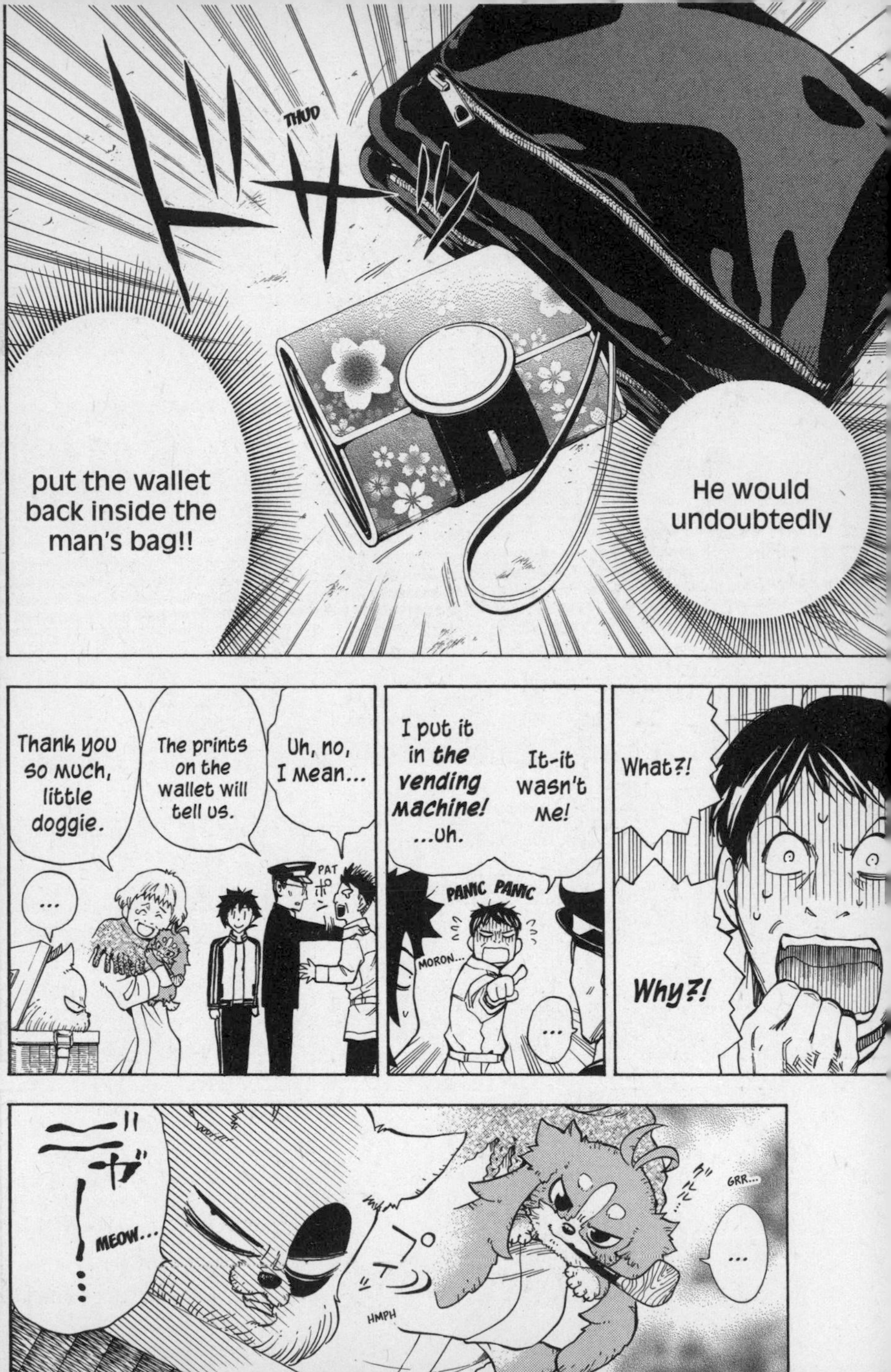

THUD
He would undoubtedly
put the wallet back inside the man's bag!!
What?!
Why?!
It-it wasn't me!
I put it in the vending machine! ...uh.
PANIC PANIC
MORON...
...
Uh, no, I mean...
PAT
The prints on the wallet will tell us.
Thank you so much, little doggie.
...
GRR...
...
HMPH
MEOW...

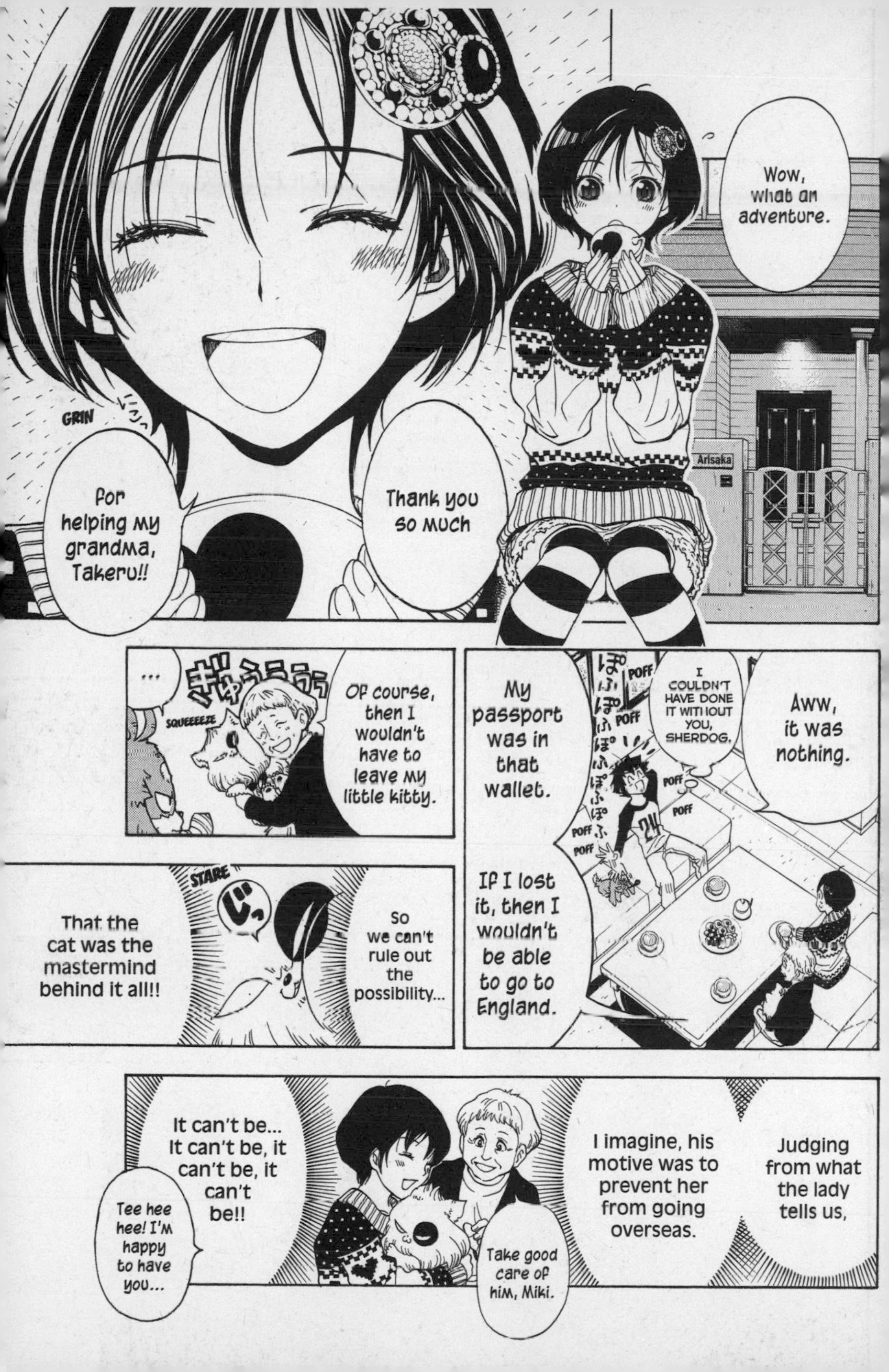
Wow, what an adventure.
Thank you so much
for helping my grandma, Takeru!!
GRIN
Aww, it was nothing.
I COULDN'T HAVE DONE IT WITHOUT YOU, SHERDOG.
POFF
POFF
POFF
POFF
POFF
POFF
My passport was in that wallet.
If I lost it, then I wouldn't be able to go to England.
Of course, then I wouldn't have to leave my little kitty.
SQUEEEEZE
...
So we can't rule out the possibility...
That the cat was the mastermind behind it all!!
STARE
Judging from what the lady tells us,
I imagine, his motive was to prevent her from going overseas.
Take good care of him, Miki.
It can't be... It can't be, it can't be, it can't be!!
Tee hee hee! I'm happy to have you...

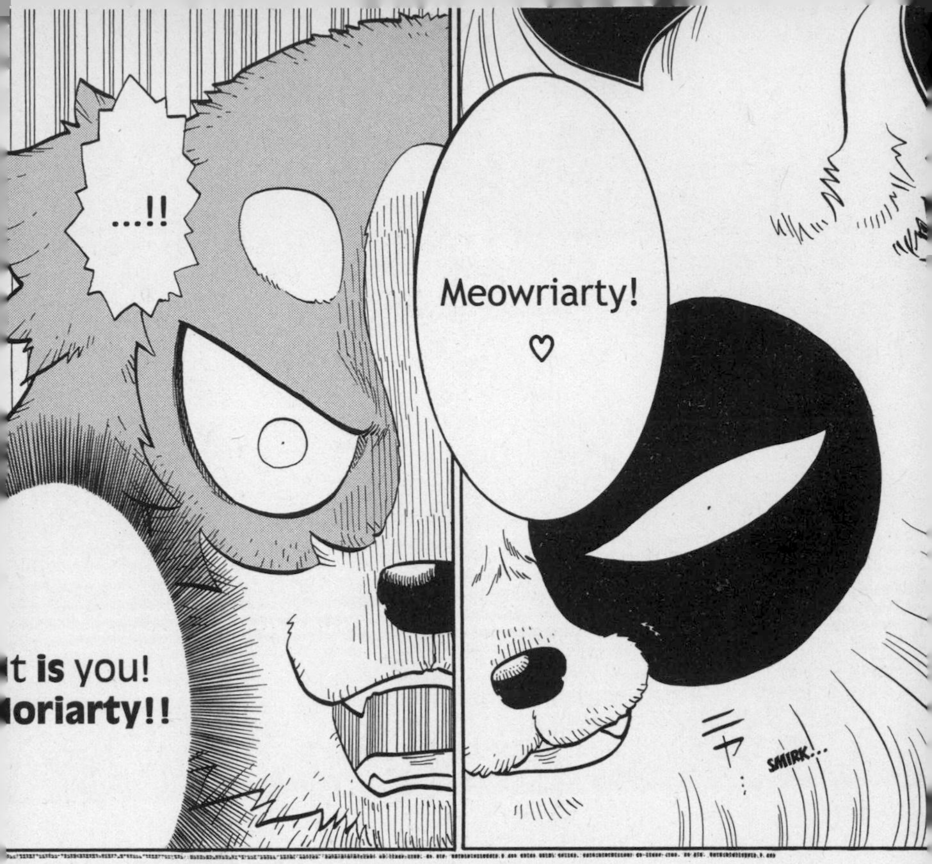
Meowriarty! ♡
ニヤ…
SMIRK…
...!!
t is you!
oriarty!!

Holmes Trivia
~James Moriarty~

The criminal mastermind said to be Holmes's greatest rival.

To the general public, he is a retired math professor, but in the underworld he is the head of a massive criminal organization.

He never dirties his own hands, but accomplishes crime by controlling others.

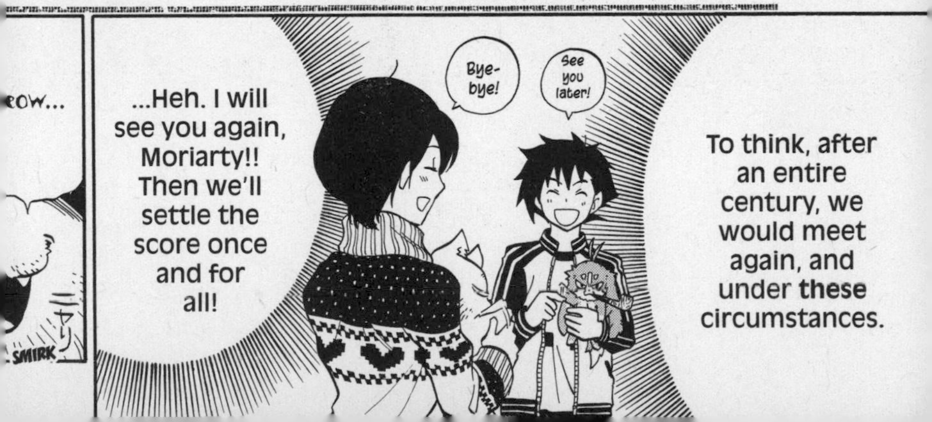
To think, after an entire century, we would meet again, and under these circumstances.
See you later!
Bye-bye!
...Heh. I will see you again, Moriarty!! Then we'll settle the score once and for all!
eow...
ニヤリ
SMIRK

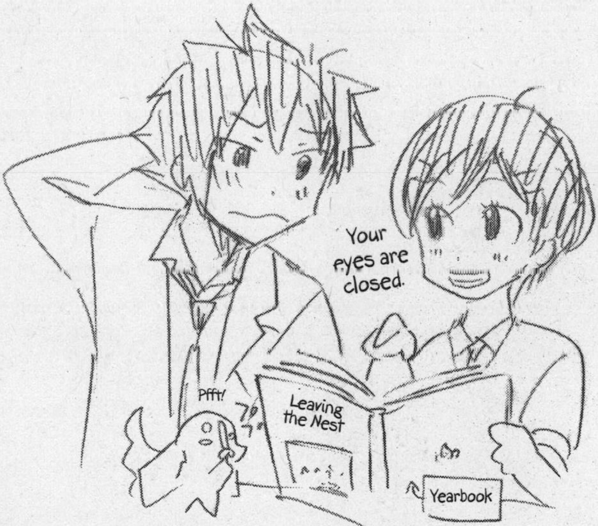
Your eyes are closed.
Leaving the Nest
Yearbook
Pfft!

SHERLOCK BONES

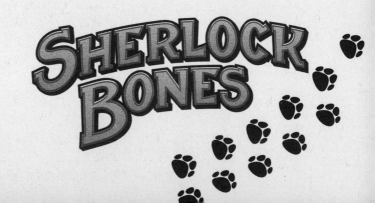

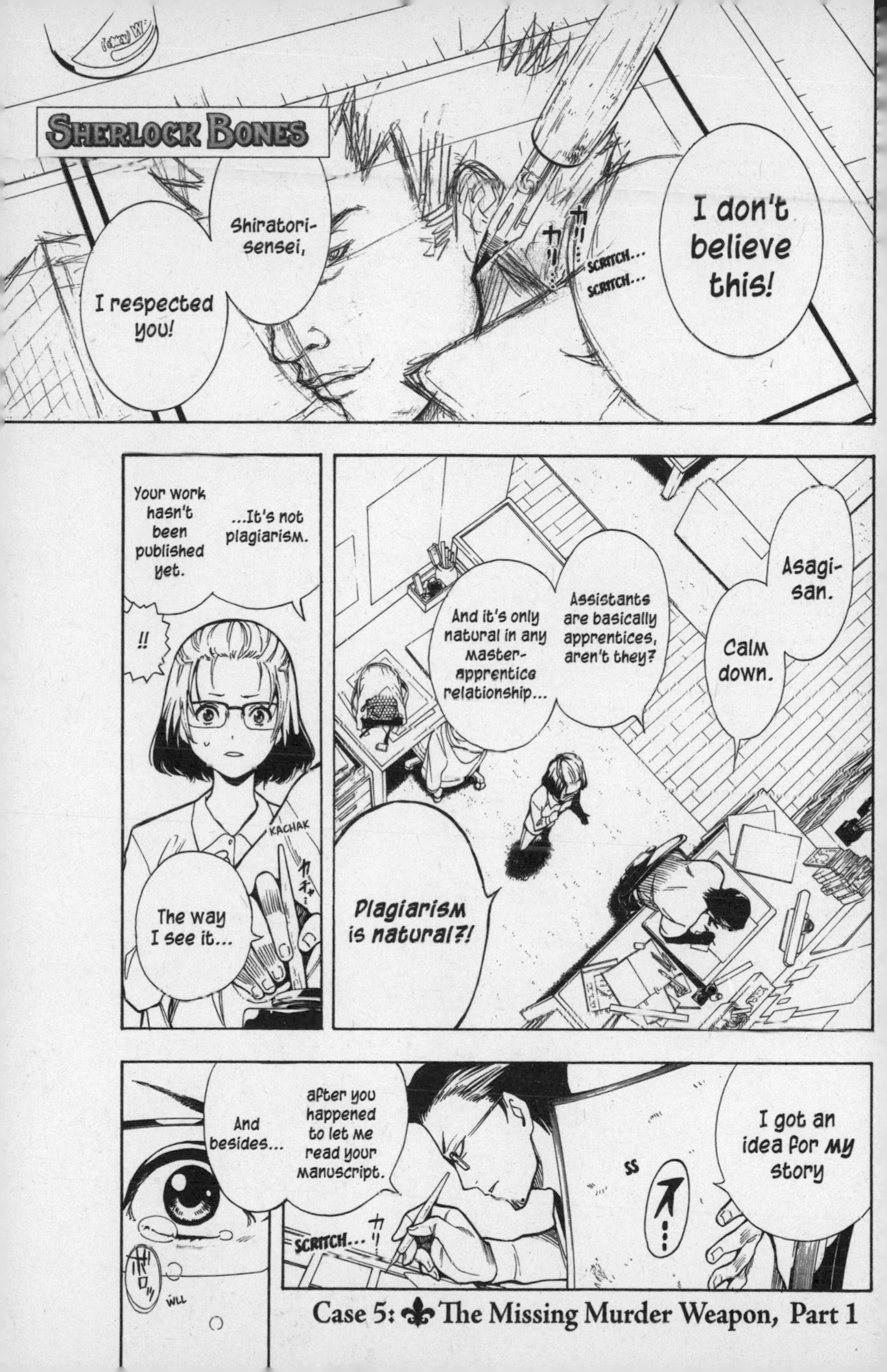
SHERLOCK BONES
I don't believe this!
SCRITCH...
SCRITCH...
Shiratori-sensei,
I respected you!
Asagi-san.
Calm down.
Assistants are basically apprentices, aren't they?
And it's only natural in any master-apprentice relationship...
Plagiarism is natural?!
...It's not plagiarism.
Your work hasn't been published yet.
!!
KACHAK
The way I see it...
I got an idea for my story
...!
SS
after you happened to let me read your manuscript.
And besides...
SCRITCH...
WLL

Case 5: ⚜ The Missing Murder Weapon, Part 1

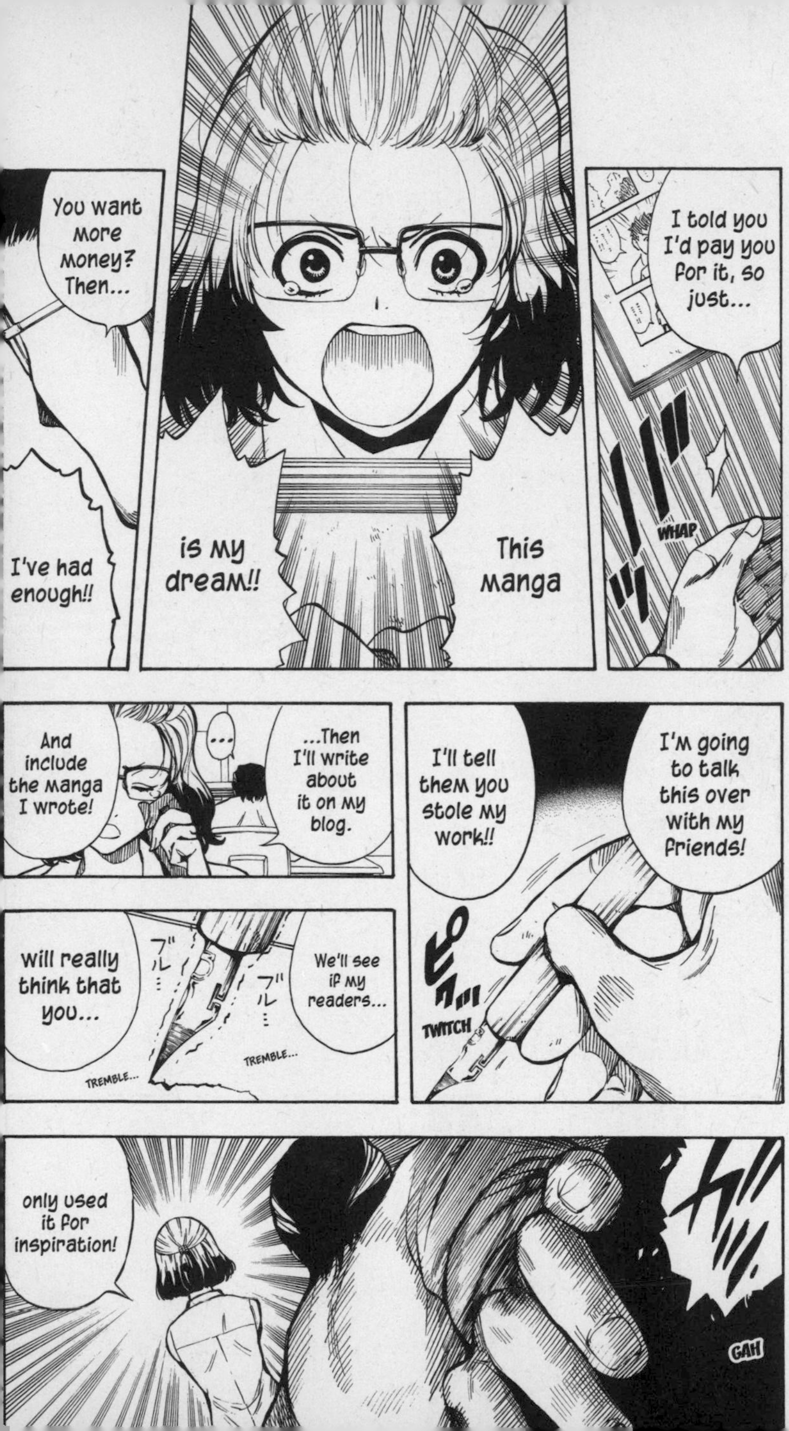
I told you I'd pay you for it, so just...
WHAP
This manga
is my dream!!
You want more money? Then...
I've had enough!!
I'm going to talk this over with my friends!
I'll tell them you stole my work!!
ピクッ
TWITCH
...Then I'll write about it on my blog.
And include the manga I wrote!
We'll see if my readers...
ブル...
TREMBLE...
ブル...
will really think that you...
TREMBLE...
only used it for inspiration!
GAH

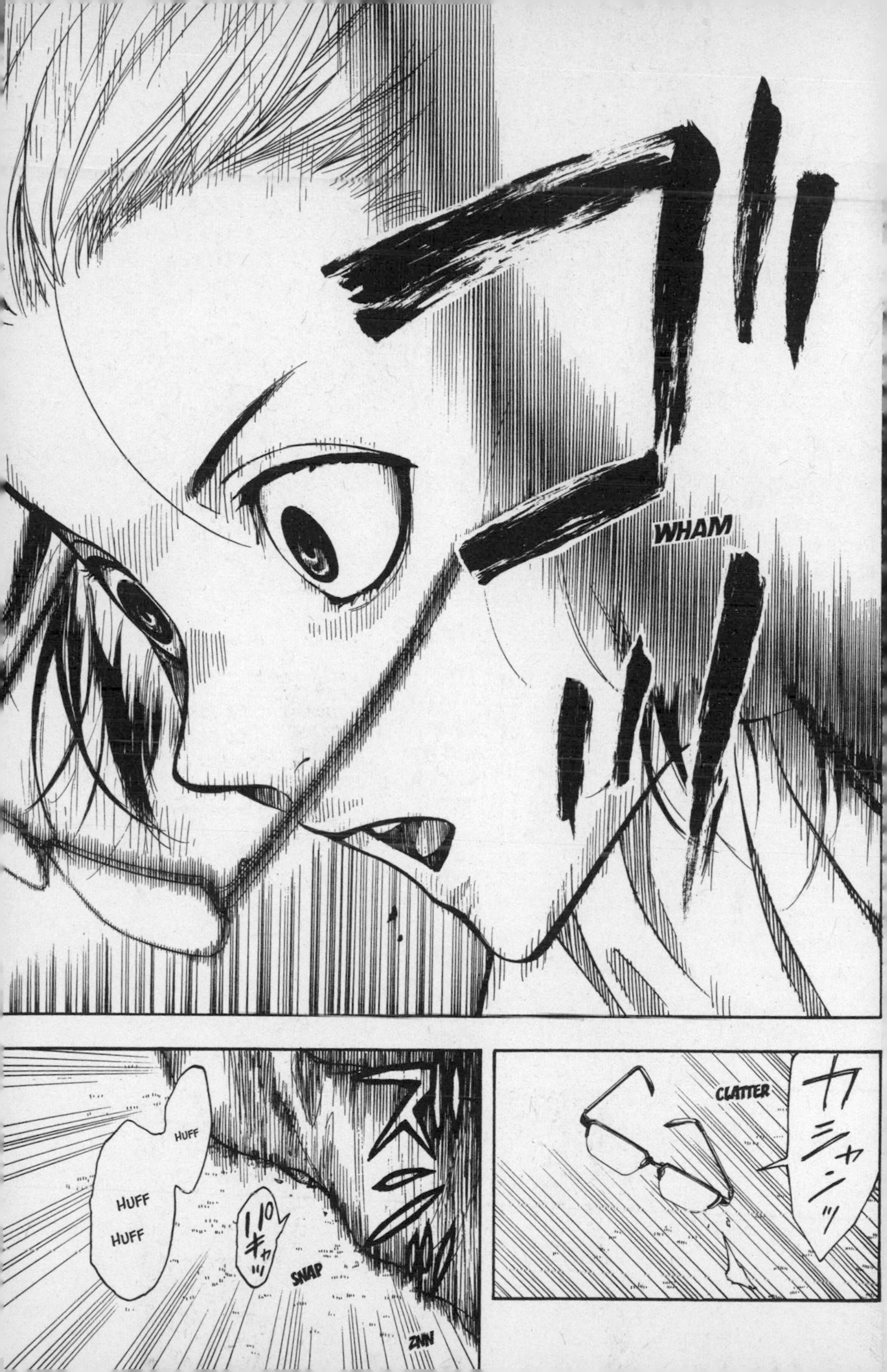
WHAM
CLATTER
カシャンッ
HUFF
HUFF
HUFF
SNAP
ZNN

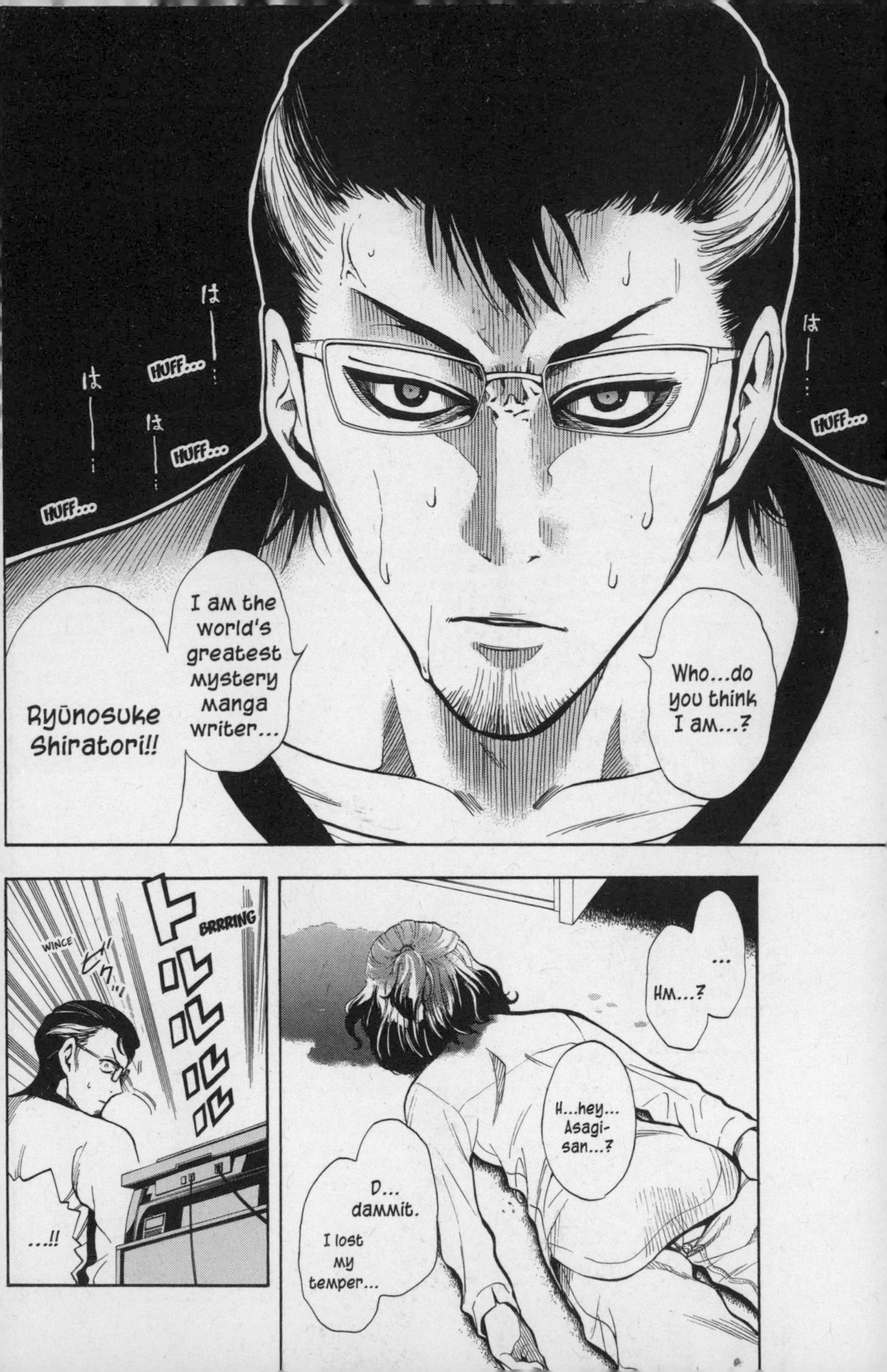
は―…
HUFF...
は―…
HUFF...
は―…
HUFF...
HUFF...
Who...do you think I am...?
I am the world's greatest mystery manga writer...
Ryūnosuke Shiratori!!
...
HM...?
H...hey... Asagi-san...?
D... dammit.
I lost my temper...
BRRRING
WINCE
...!!

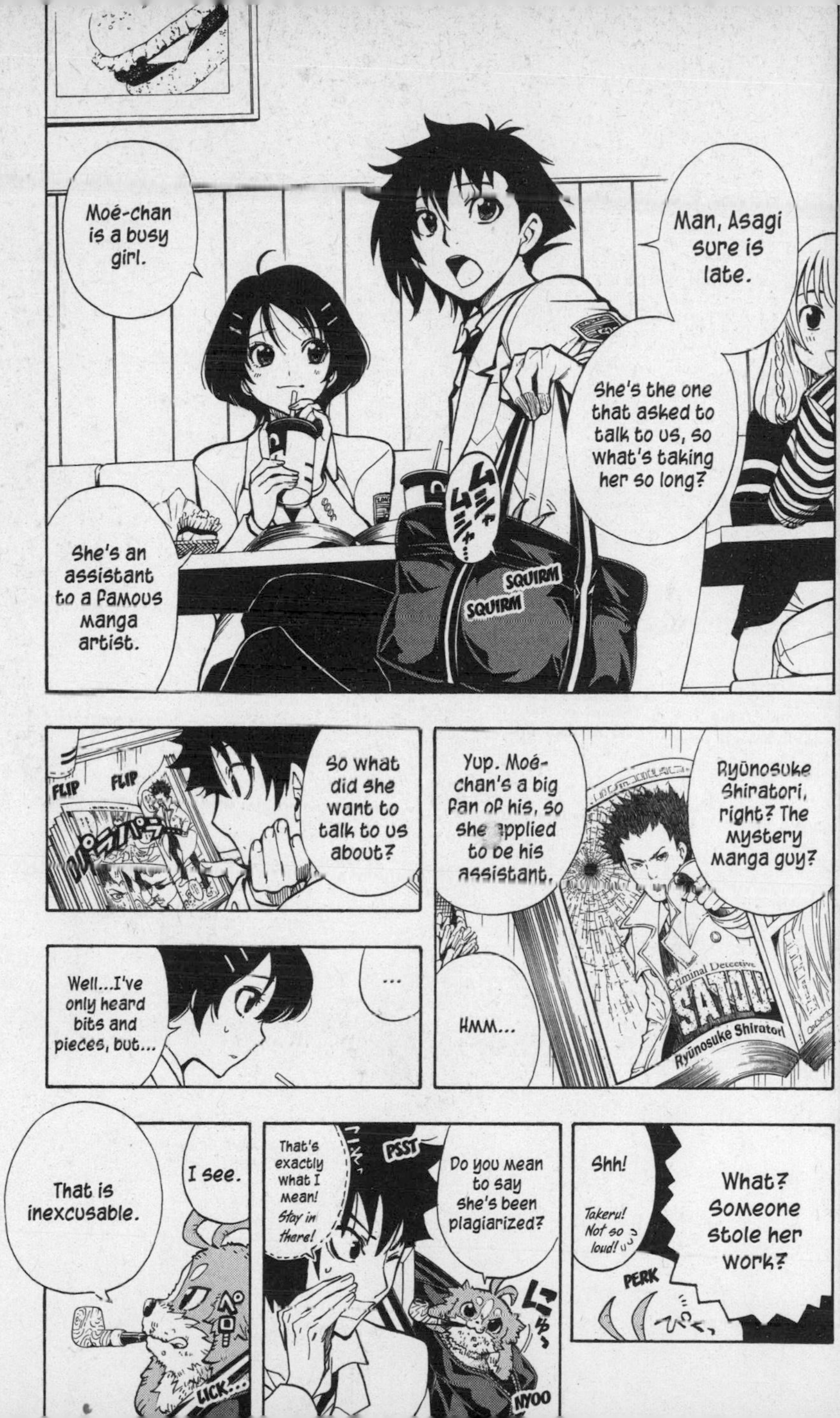
Man, Asagi sure is late.
She's the one that asked to talk to us, so what's taking her so long?
Moé-chan is a busy girl.
She's an assistant to a famous manga artist.
SQUIRM
SQUIRM
Ryūnosuke Shiratori, right? The mystery manga guy?
Yup. Moé-chan's a big fan of his, so she applied to be his assistant.
Criminal Detective SATOU
Ryūnosuke Shiratori
HMM...
FLIP
FLIP
So what did she want to talk to us about?
...
Well...I've only heard bits and pieces, but...
What? Someone stole her work?
Shh!
Takeru! Not so loud!
PERK
Do you mean to say she's been plagiarized?
PSST
That's exactly what I mean! Stay in there!
NYOO
I see.
That is inexcusable.
LICK...

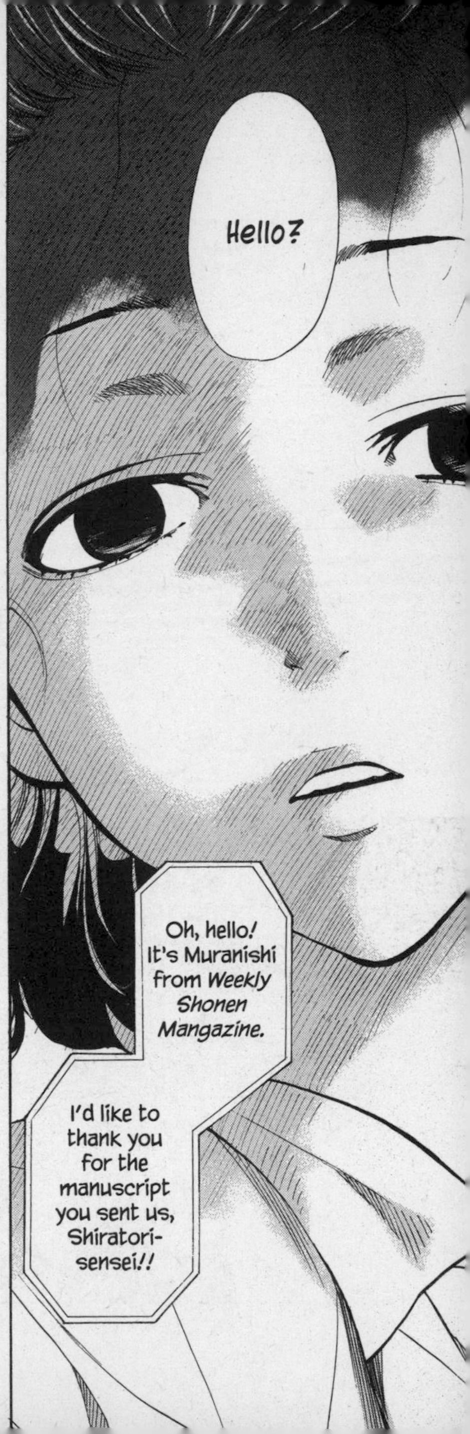
Hello?
Oh, hello! It's Muranishi from *Weekly Shonen Mangazine.*
I'd like to thank you for the manuscript you sent us, Shiratori-sensei!!

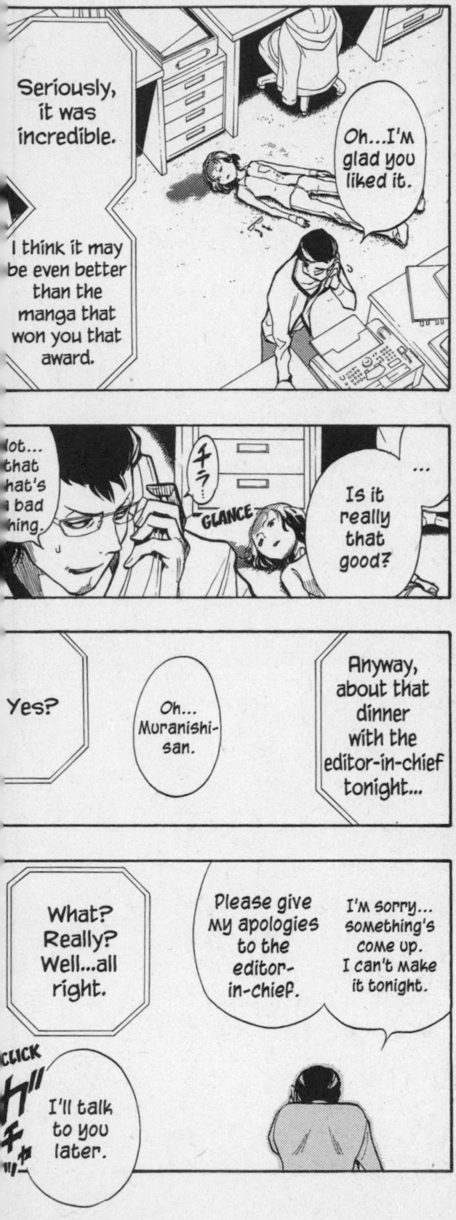
Seriously, it was incredible.
Oh...I'm glad you liked it.
I think it may be even better than the manga that won you that award.
...
Is it really that good?
チラ…
GLANCE
ot... that hat's a bad hing.
Anyway, about that dinner with the editor-in-chief tonight...
Oh... Muranishi-san.
Yes?
I'm sorry... something's come up. I can't make it tonight.
Please give my apologies to the editor-in-chief.
What? Really? Well...all right.
CLICK
ガチャ
I'll talk to you later.

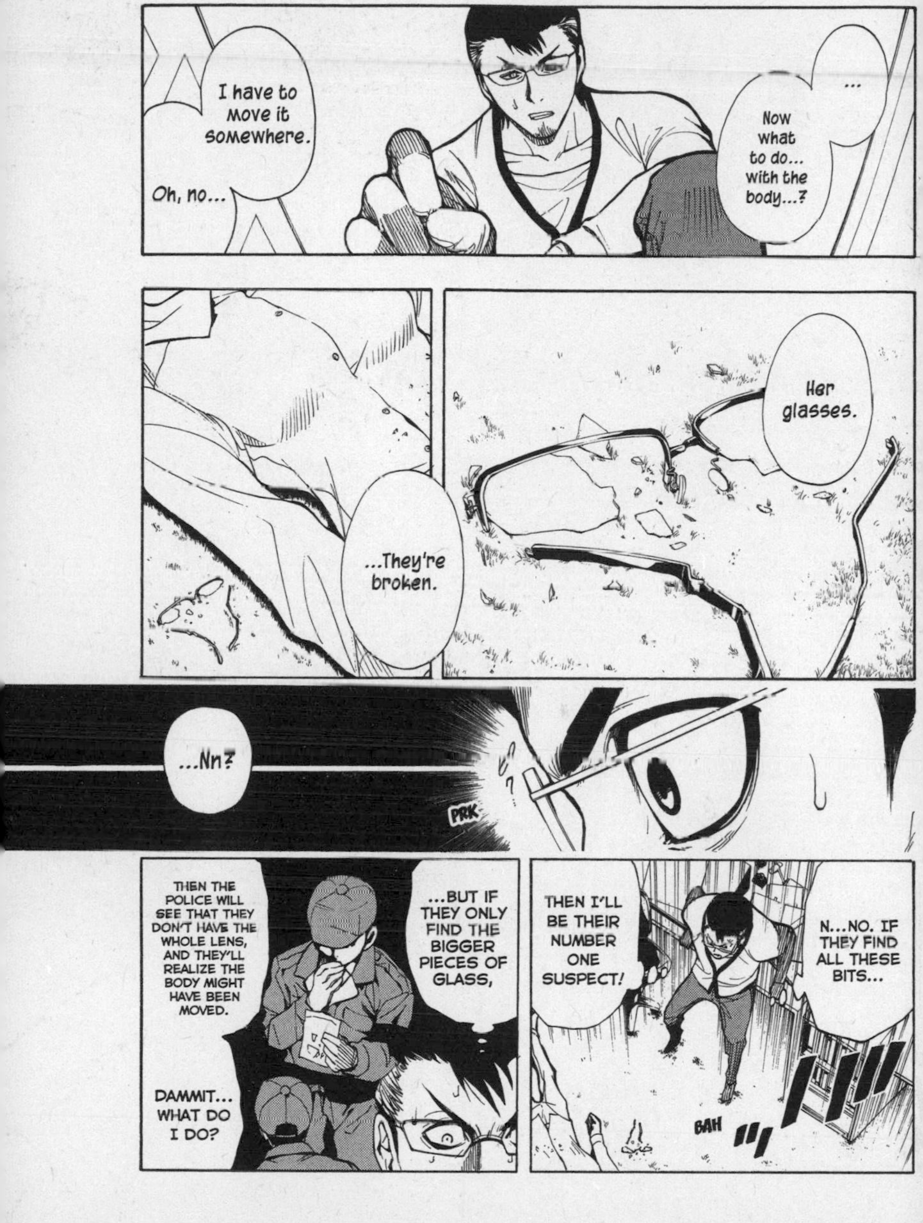
...
Now what to do... with the body...?
I have to move it somewhere.
Oh, no...
Her glasses.
...They're broken.
PRK
...Nn?
N...NO. IF THEY FIND ALL THESE BITS...
THEN I'LL BE THEIR NUMBER ONE SUSPECT!
BAH
...BUT IF THEY ONLY FIND THE BIGGER PIECES OF GLASS,
THEN THE POLICE WILL SEE THAT THEY DON'T HAVE THE WHOLE LENS, AND THEY'LL REALIZE THE BODY MIGHT HAVE BEEN MOVED.
DAMMIT... WHAT DO I DO?

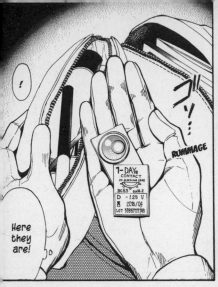

!

RUMMAGE

1-DAY
CONTACT
UV BLOCKING CARE

BC 8.5 DIA14.2
D -1.25 V
B 2015/01
LOT 3395727148

Here
they
are!

!

WAIT.
IF I'M NOT
MISTAKEN...

She
sometimes
wore
contact
lenses.

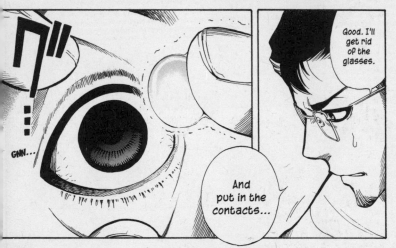

Good. I'll
get rid
of the
glasses.

GNN...

And
put in the
contacts...

SPLITCH

Blegh.

Urp.

56

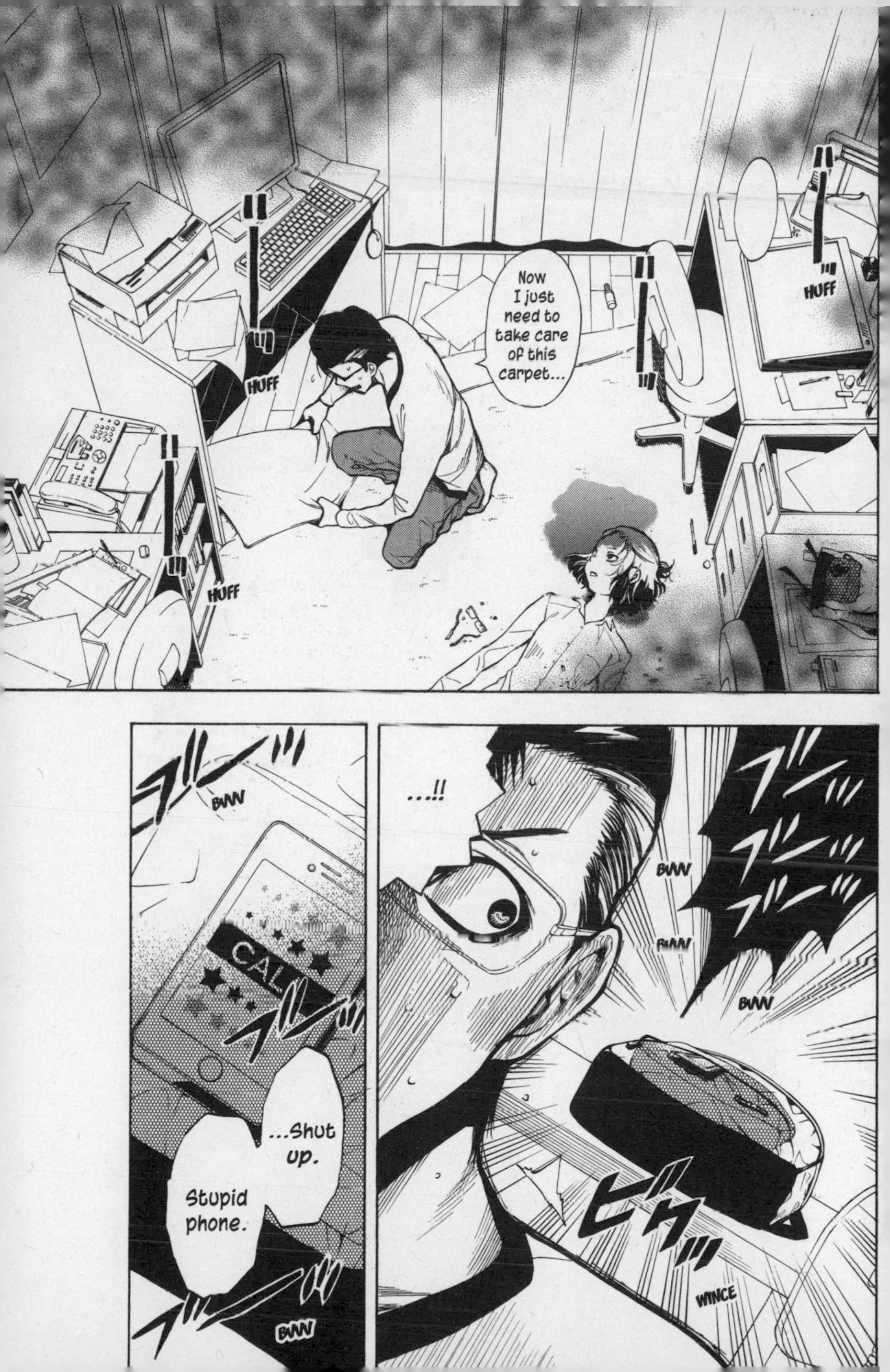
HUFF
Now I just need to take care of this carpet...
HUFF
HUFF
...!!
BWW
BWW
BWW
WINCE
BWW
...Shut up.
Stupid phone.
BWW

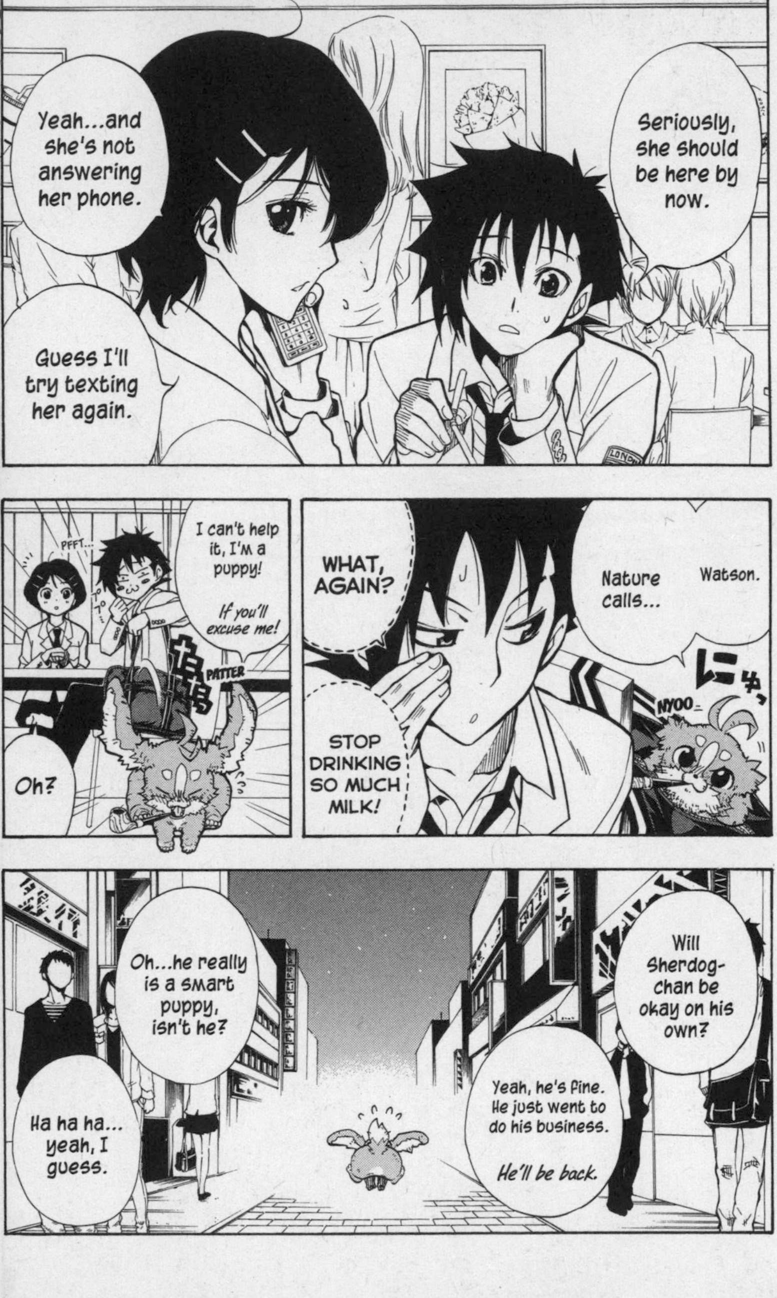
Seriously, she should be here by now.
Yeah...and she's not answering her phone.
Guess I'll try texting her again.
Watson.
Nature calls...
NYOO
WHAT, AGAIN?
STOP DRINKING SO MUCH MILK!
I can't help it, I'm a puppy!
If you'll excuse me!
PFFT...
PATTER
Oh?
Will Sherdog-chan be okay on his own?
Yeah, he's fine. He just went to do his business.
He'll be back.
Oh...he really is a smart puppy, isn't he?
Ha ha ha... yeah, I guess.

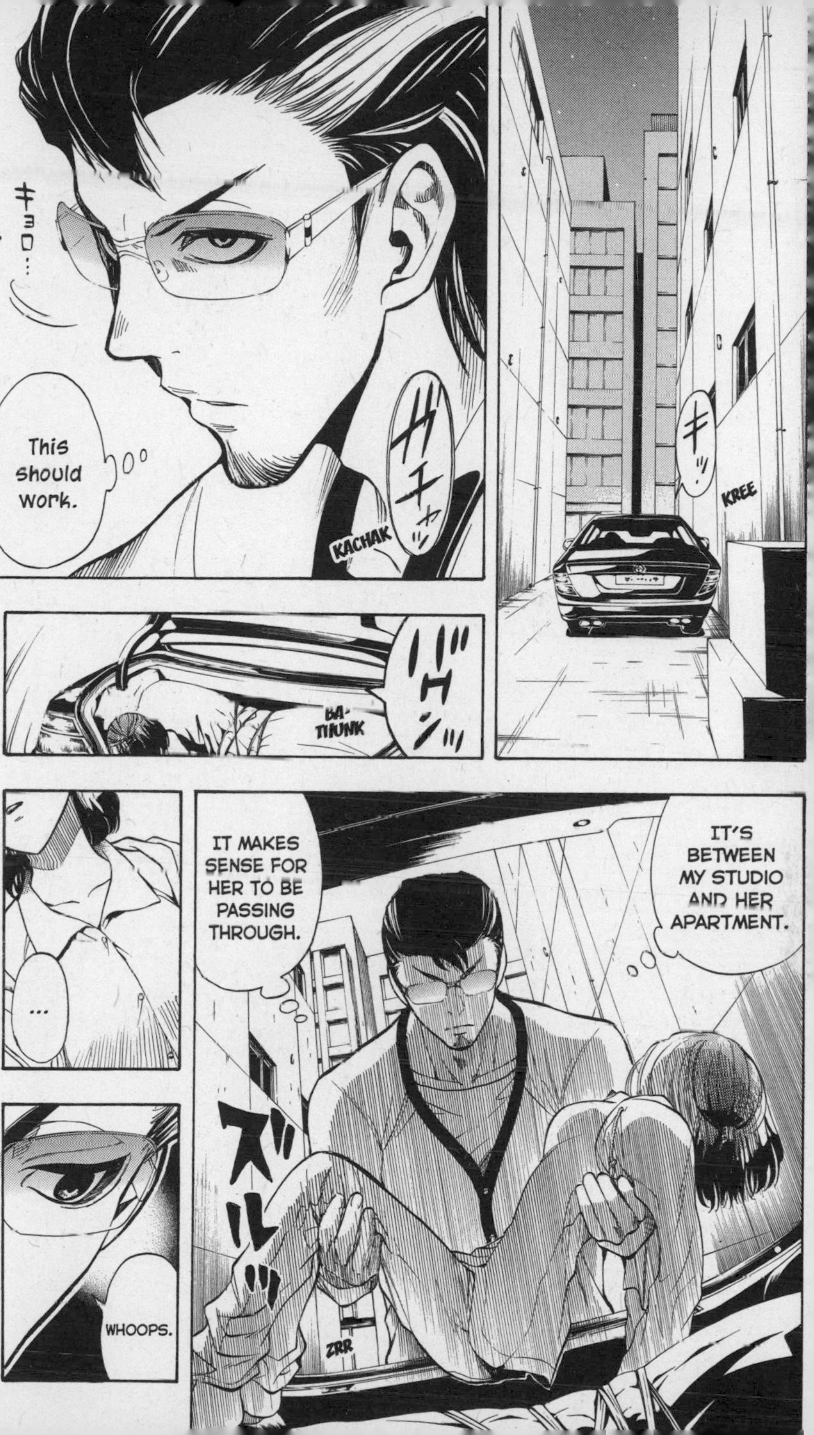
キッ
KREE
キョロ…
GLANCE
This should work.
ガチャッ
KACHAK
BA-THUNK
IT'S BETWEEN MY STUDIO AND HER APARTMENT.
IT MAKES SENSE FOR HER TO BE PASSING THROUGH.
ズルッ
ZRR
...
WHOOPS.

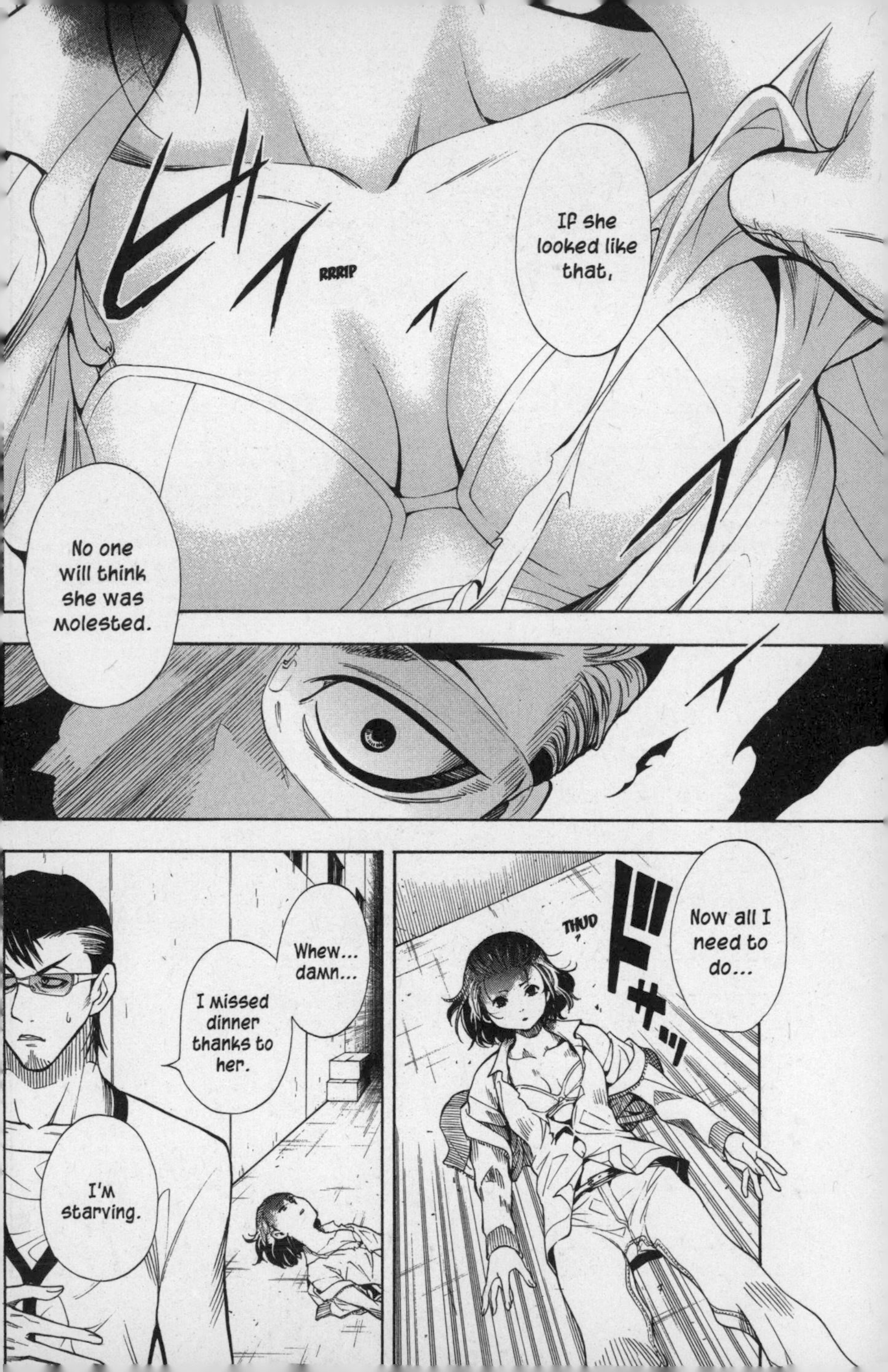
If she looked like that,
RRRIP
No one will think she was molested.
Now all I need to do...
THUD
ドサッ
Whew... damn...
I missed dinner thanks to her.
I'm starving.

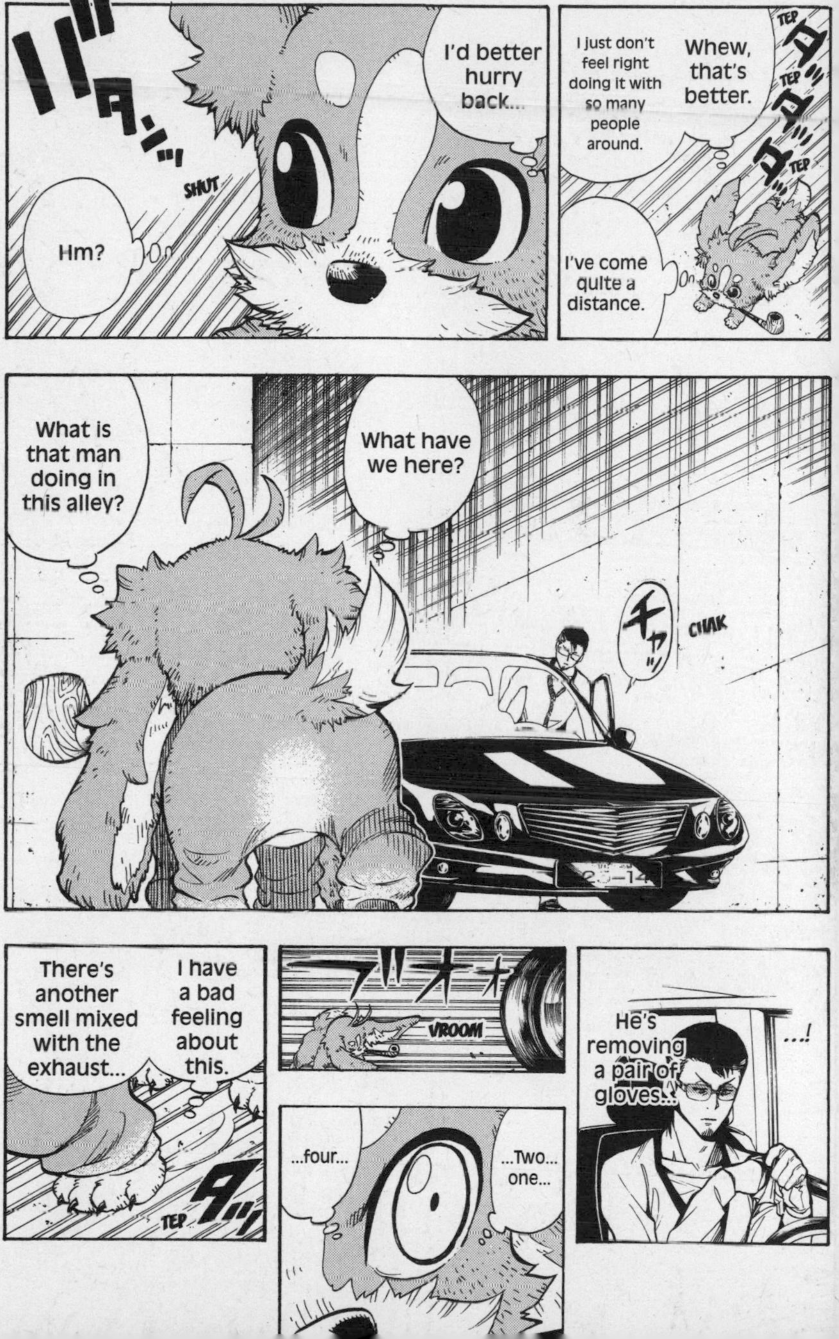
Whew, that's better.
I just don't feel right doing it with so many people around.
TEP
TEP
TEP
I've come quite a distance.
I'd better hurry back...
SHUT
Hm?
What have we here?
What is that man doing in this alley?
CHAK
He's removing a pair of gloves...
...!
VROOM
...Two... one...
...four...
I have a bad feeling about this.
There's another smell mixed with the exhaust...
TEP

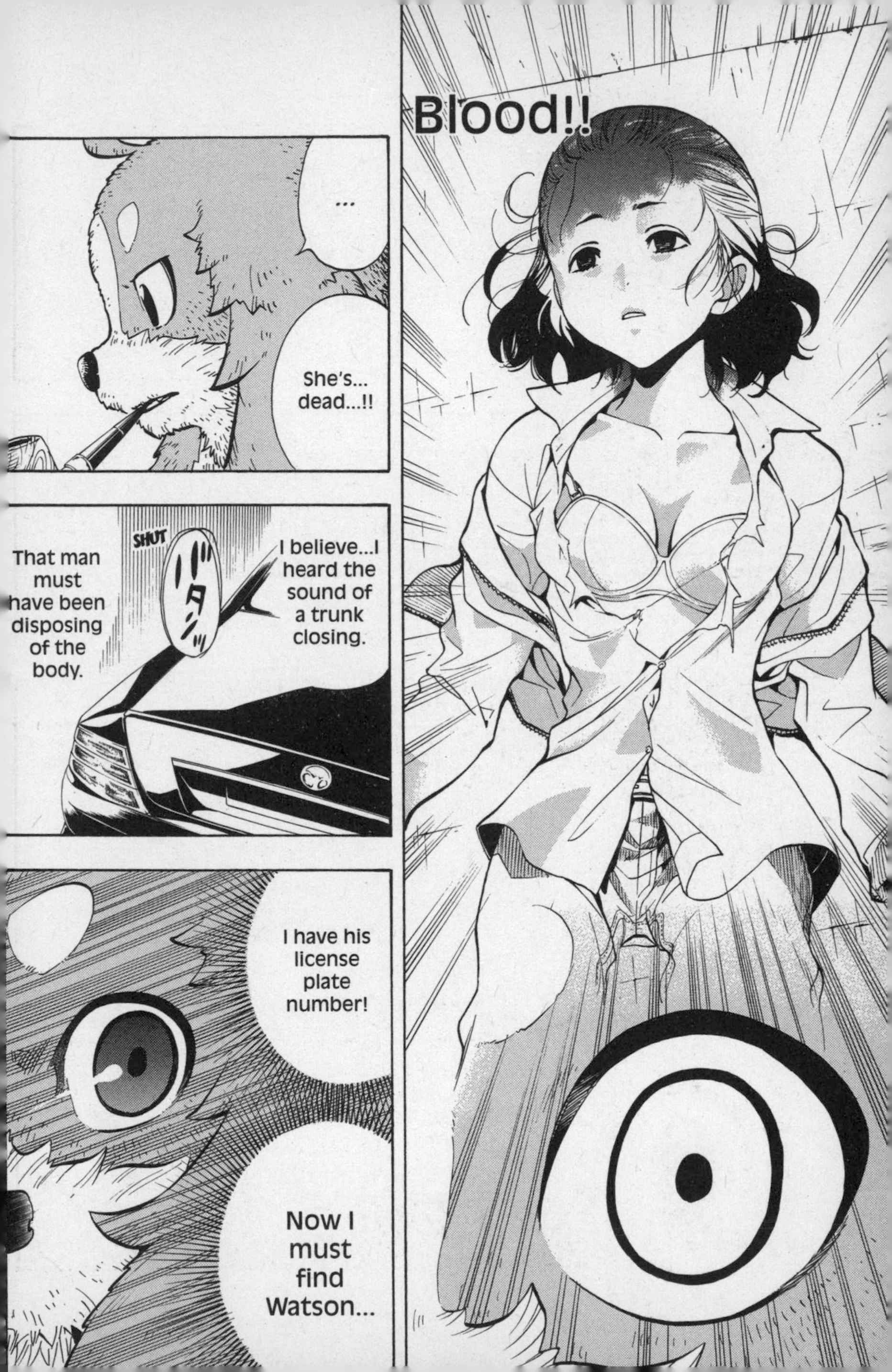
Blood!!
...
She's... dead...!!
I believe...I heard the sound of a trunk closing.
SHUT
バタン
That man must have been disposing of the body.
I have his license plate number!
Now I must find Watson...

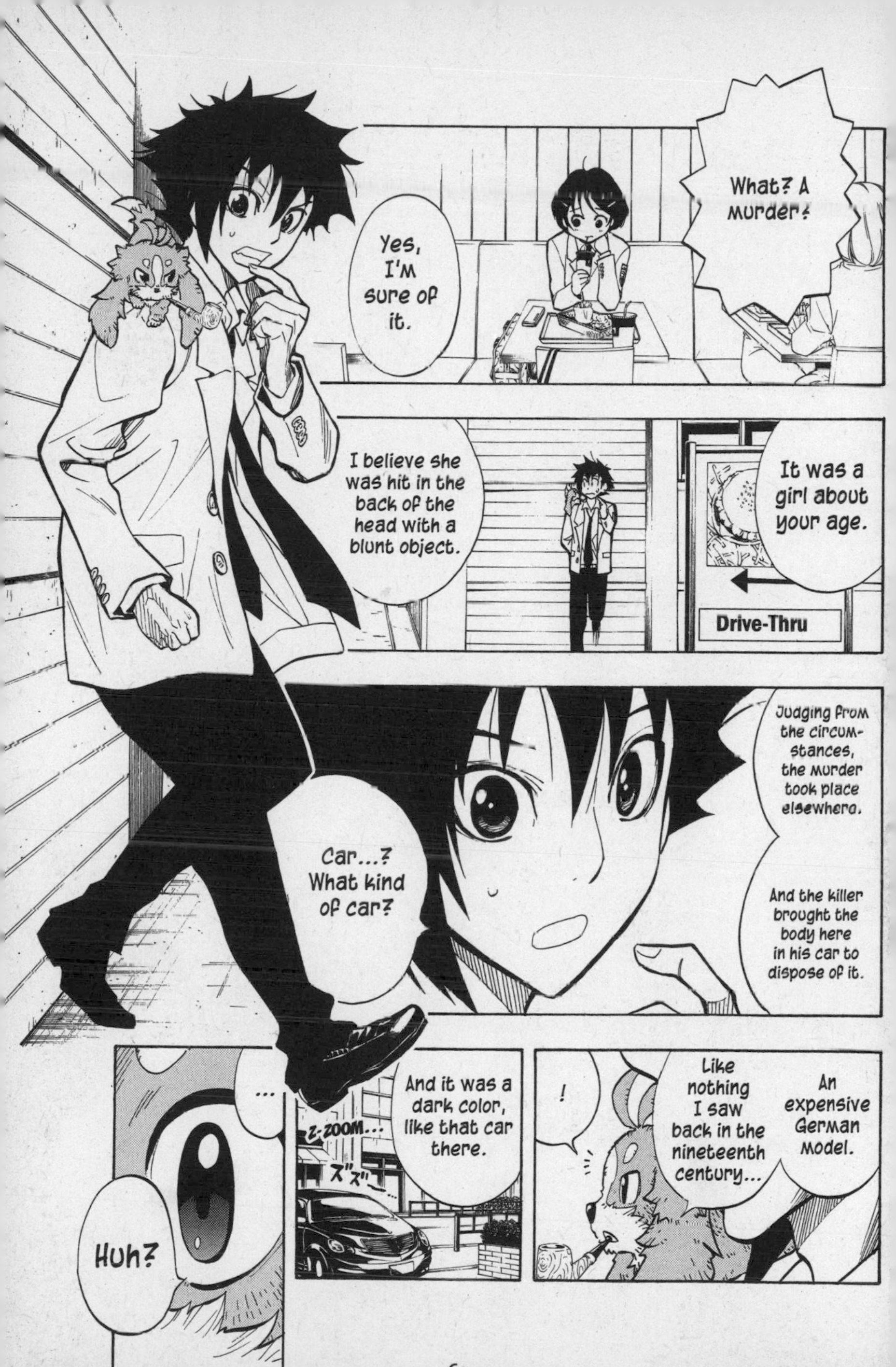
What? A murder?
Yes, I'm sure of it.
It was a girl about your age.
Drive-Thru
I believe she was hit in the back of the head with a blunt object.
Judging from the circumstances, the murder took place elsewhere.
And the killer brought the body here in his car to dispose of it.
Car...? What kind of car?
An expensive German model.
Like nothing I saw back in the nineteenth century...
!
And it was a dark color, like that car there.
Z-ZOOM...
ズズー...
...
Huh?

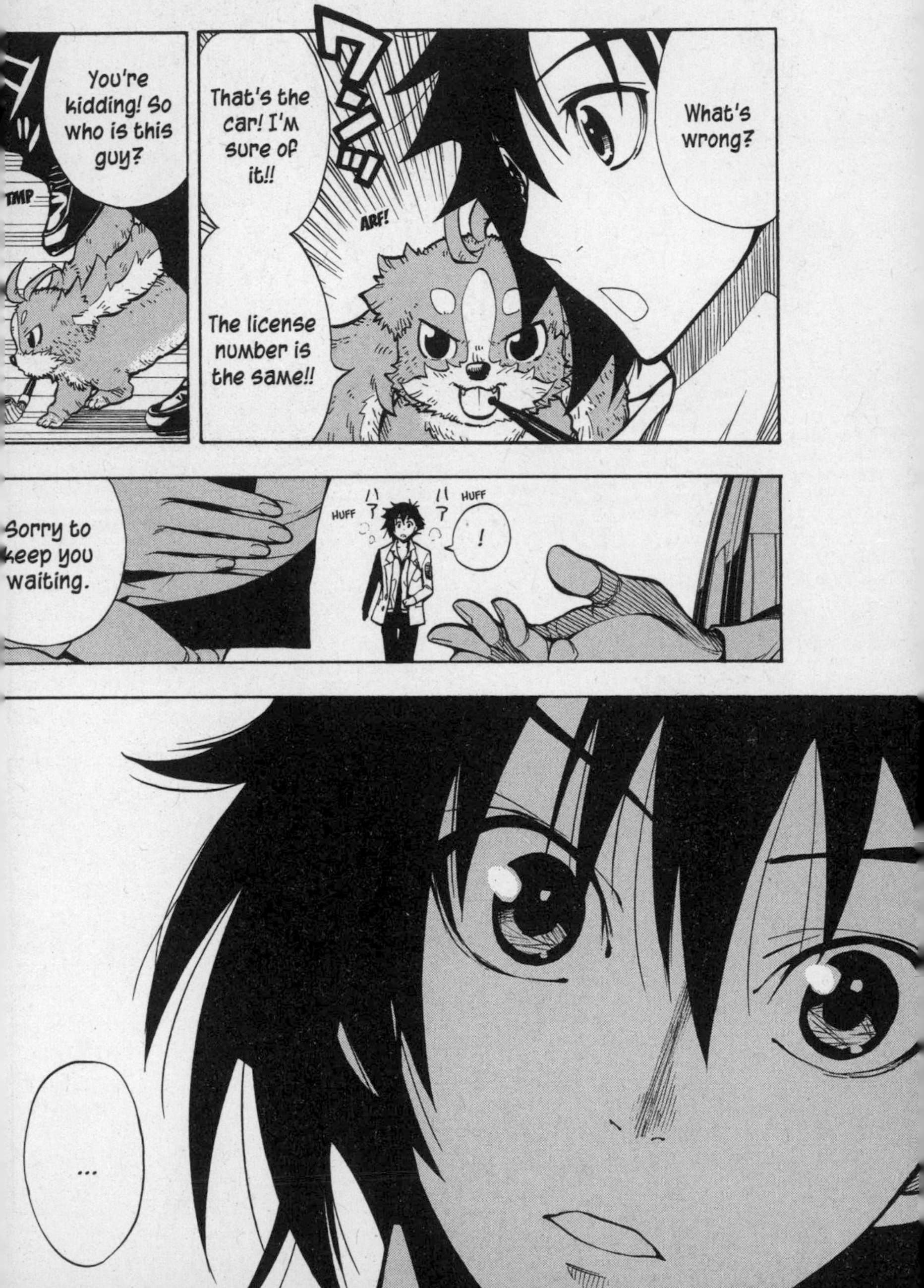
What's wrong?
That's the car! I'M sure of it!!
ARF!
The license number is the same!!
You're kidding! So who is this guy?
TMP
HUFF
ハァ
!
ハァ
HUFF
Sorry to keep you waiting.
...

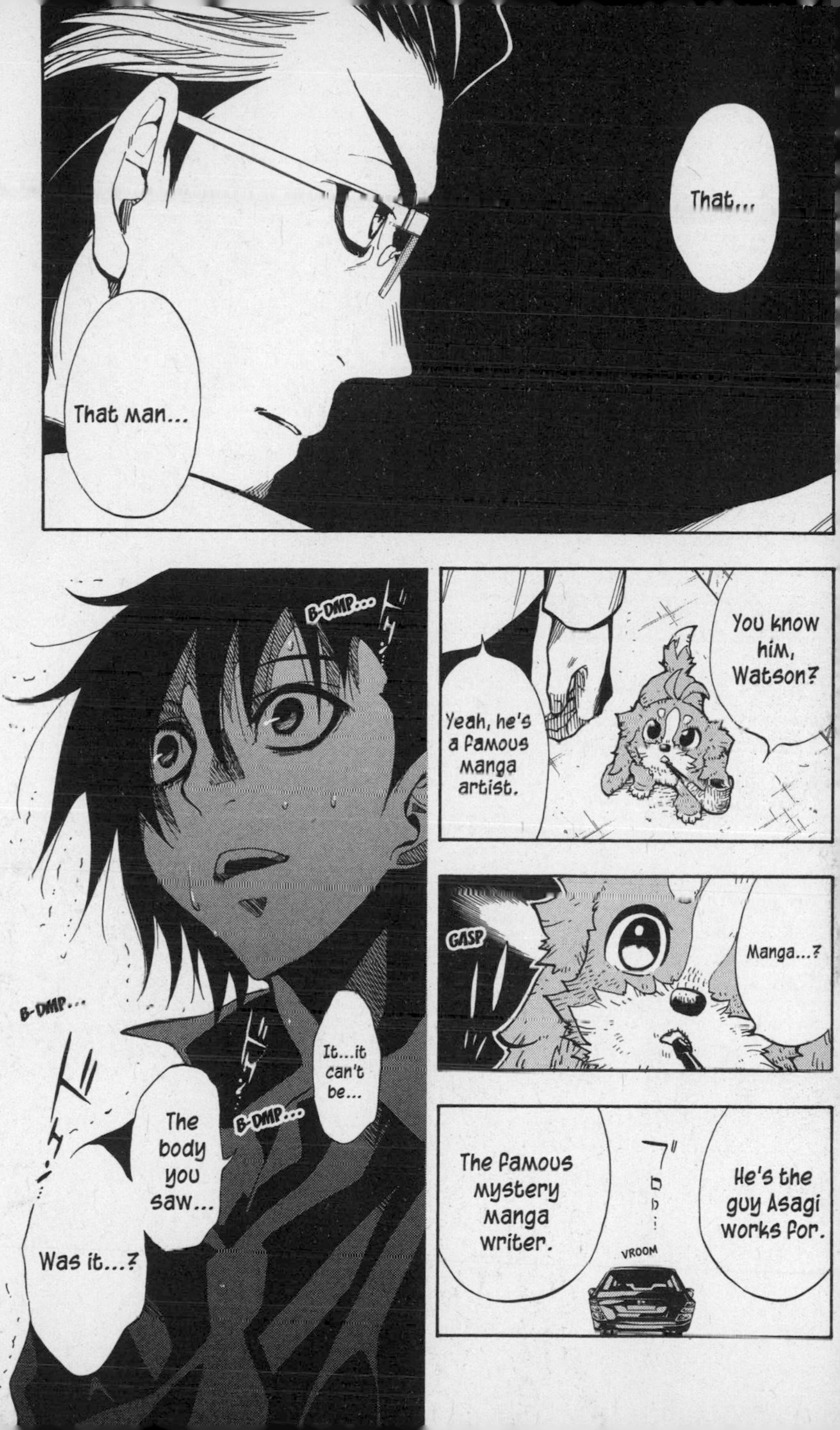
That...
That man...
You know him, Watson?
Yeah, he's a famous manga artist.
Manga...?
GASP
He's the guy Asagi works for.
The famous mystery manga writer.
VROOM
B-DMP...
It...it can't be...
B-DMP...
B-DMP...
The body you saw...
Was it...?

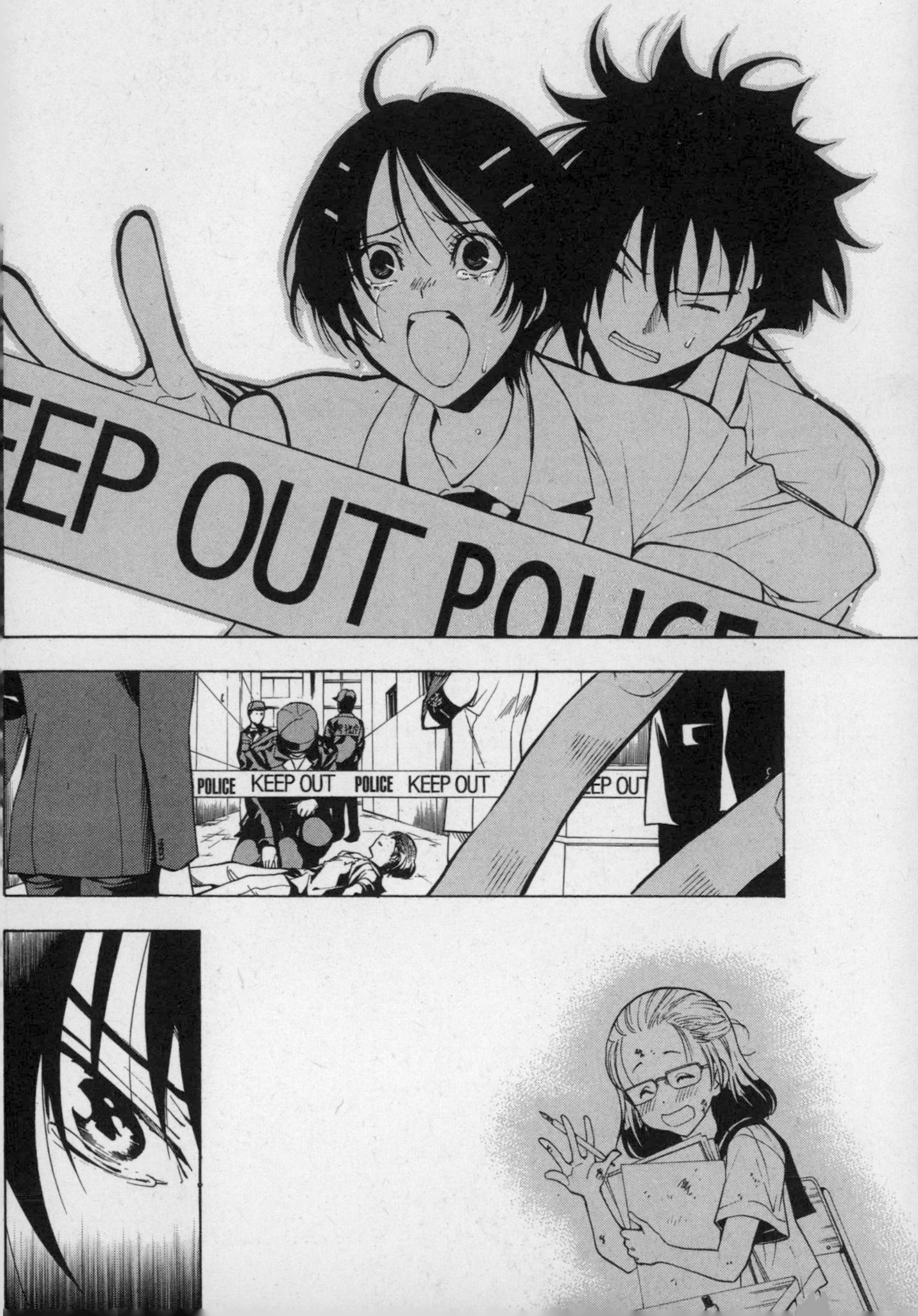
POLICE KEEP OUT POLICE KEEP OUT

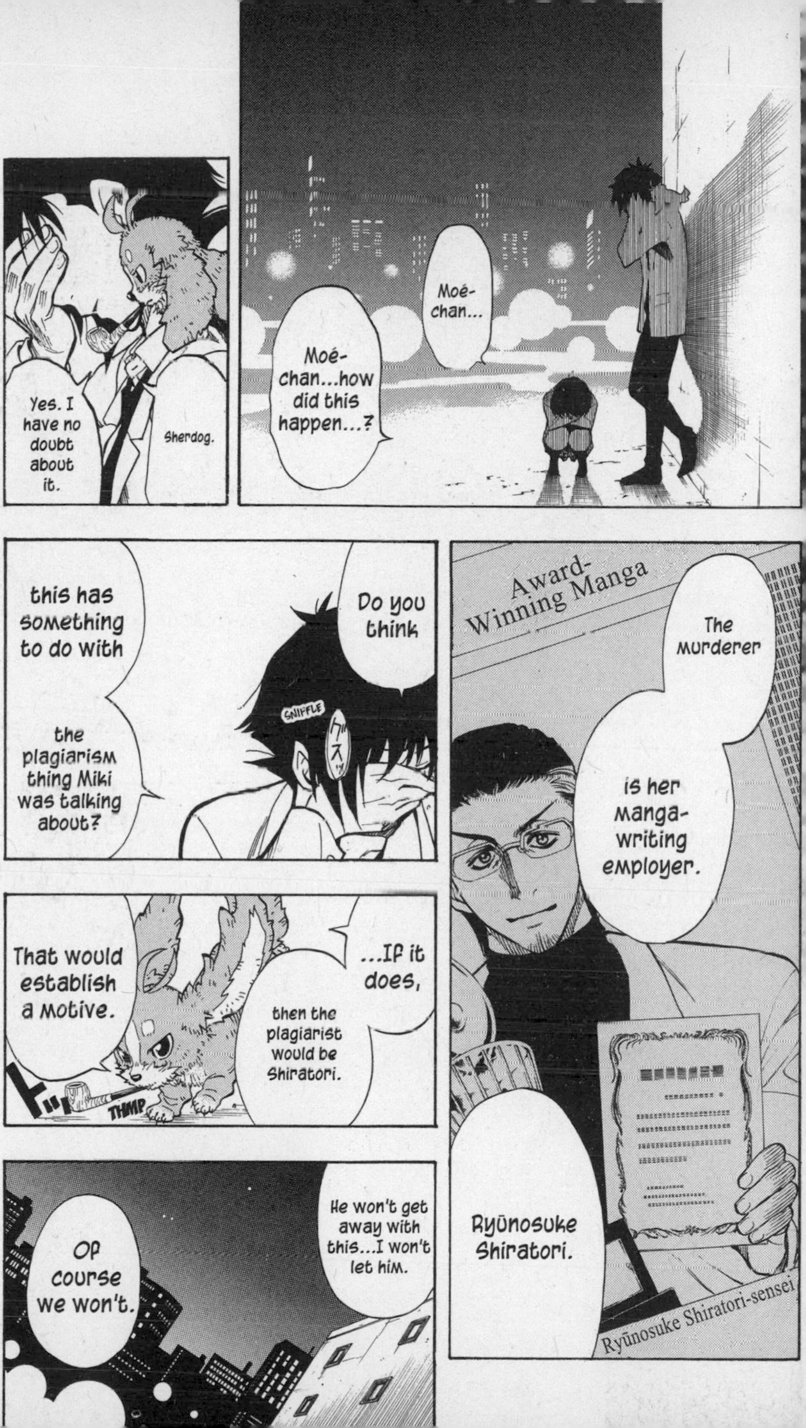
Moé-chan...
Moé-chan...how did this happen...?
Sherdog.
Yes. I have no doubt about it.
Award-Winning Manga
The murderer
is her manga-writing employer.
Ryūnosuke Shiratori.
Ryūnosuke Shiratori-sensei
Do you think
SNIFFLE
this has something to do with
the plagiarism thing Miki was talking about?
...If it does,
then the plagiarist would be Shiratori.
That would establish a motive.
THMP
He won't get away with this...I won't let him.
Of course we won't.

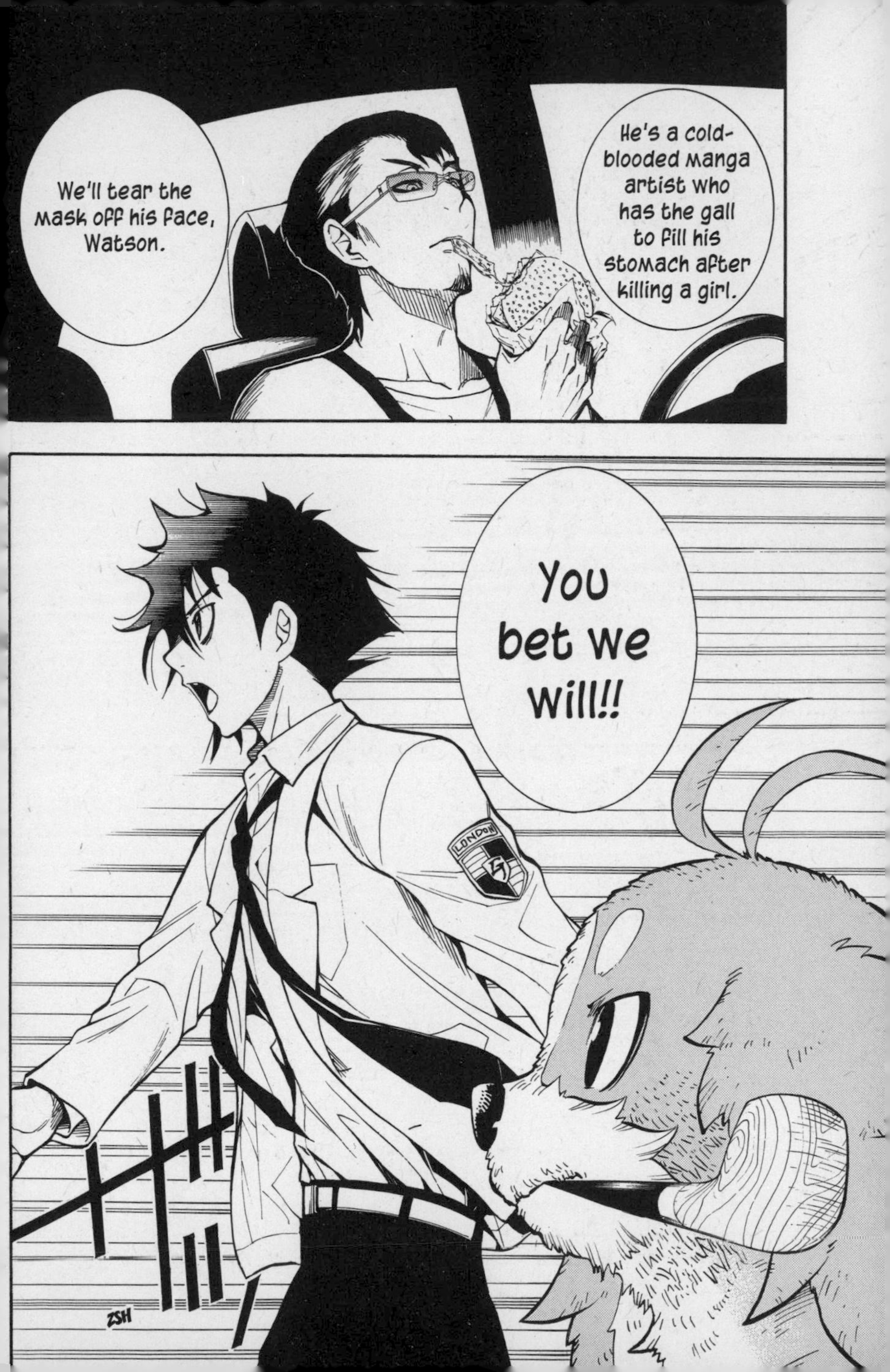
He's a cold-blooded manga artist who has the gall to fill his stomach after killing a girl.
We'll tear the mask off his face, Watson.
You bet we will!!
LONDON
ZSH

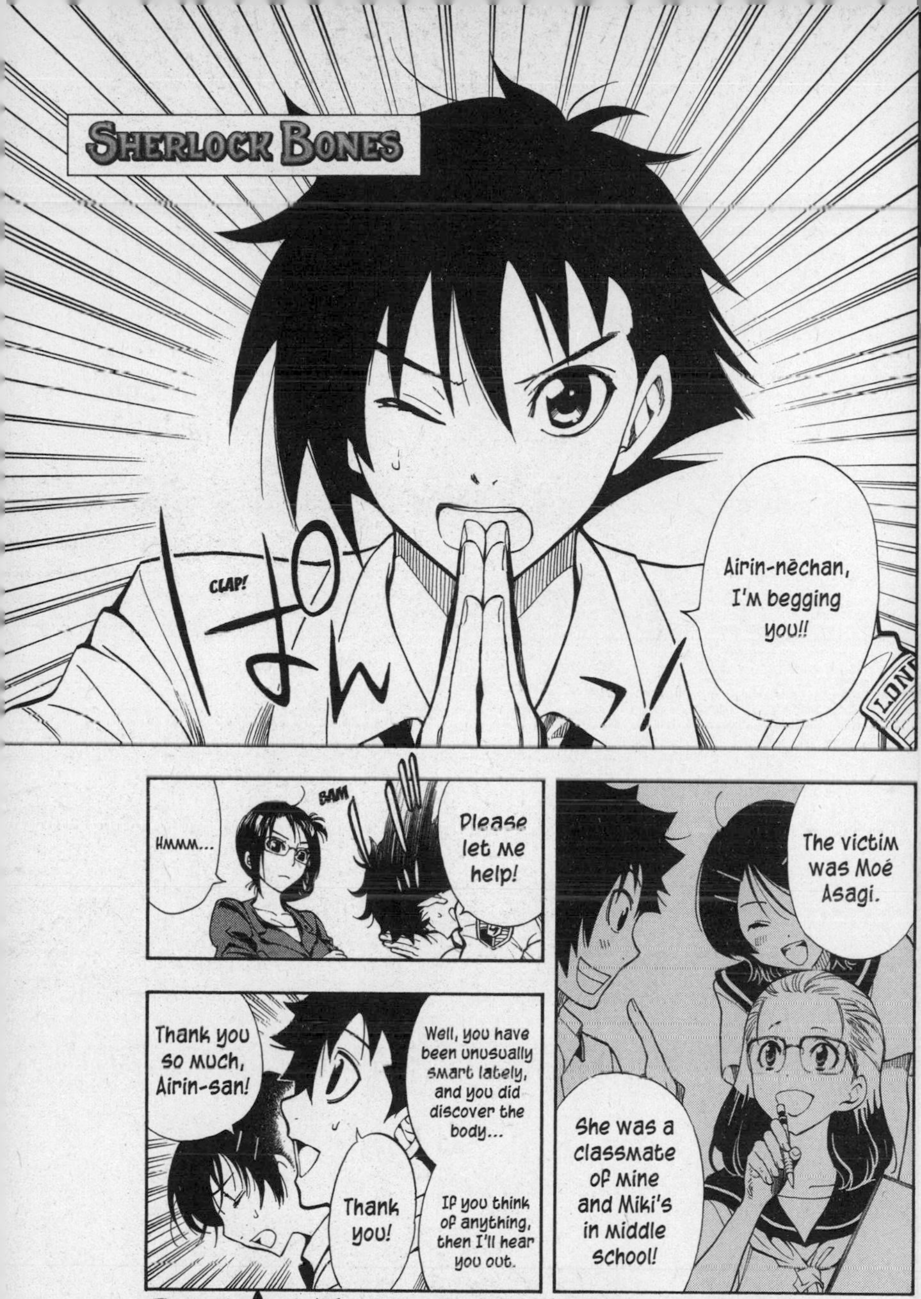
SHERLOCK BONES
Airin-nēchan, I'm begging you!!
ぱんッ!
CLAP!
The victim was Moé Asagi.
She was a classmate of mine and Miki's in middle school!
Please let me help!
BAM
Hmmm...
Well, you have been unusually smart lately, and you did discover the body...
If you think of anything, then I'll hear you out.
Thank you!
Thank you so much, Airin-san!

Case 5: ⚜ A The Missing Murder Weapon, Part 2

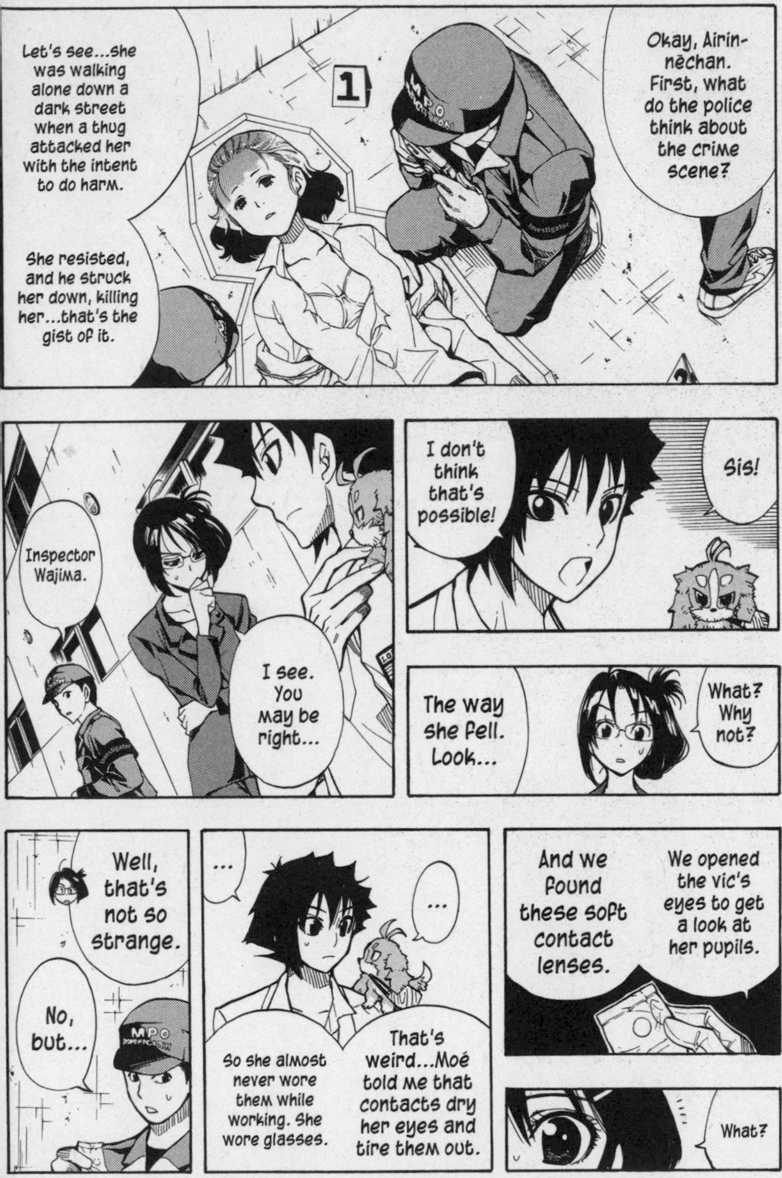
Okay, Airin-nēchan. First, what do the police think about the crime scene?
Let's see...she was walking alone down a dark street when a thug attacked her with the intent to do harm.
She resisted, and he struck her down, killing her...that's the gist of it.
Sis!
I don't think that's possible!
What? Why not?
The way she fell. Look...
I see. You may be right...
Inspector Wajima.
We opened the vic's eyes to get a look at her pupils.
And we found these soft contact lenses.
What?
...
...
That's weird...Moé told me that contacts dry her eyes and tire them out.
So she almost never wore them while working. She wore glasses.
Well, that's not so strange.
No, but...

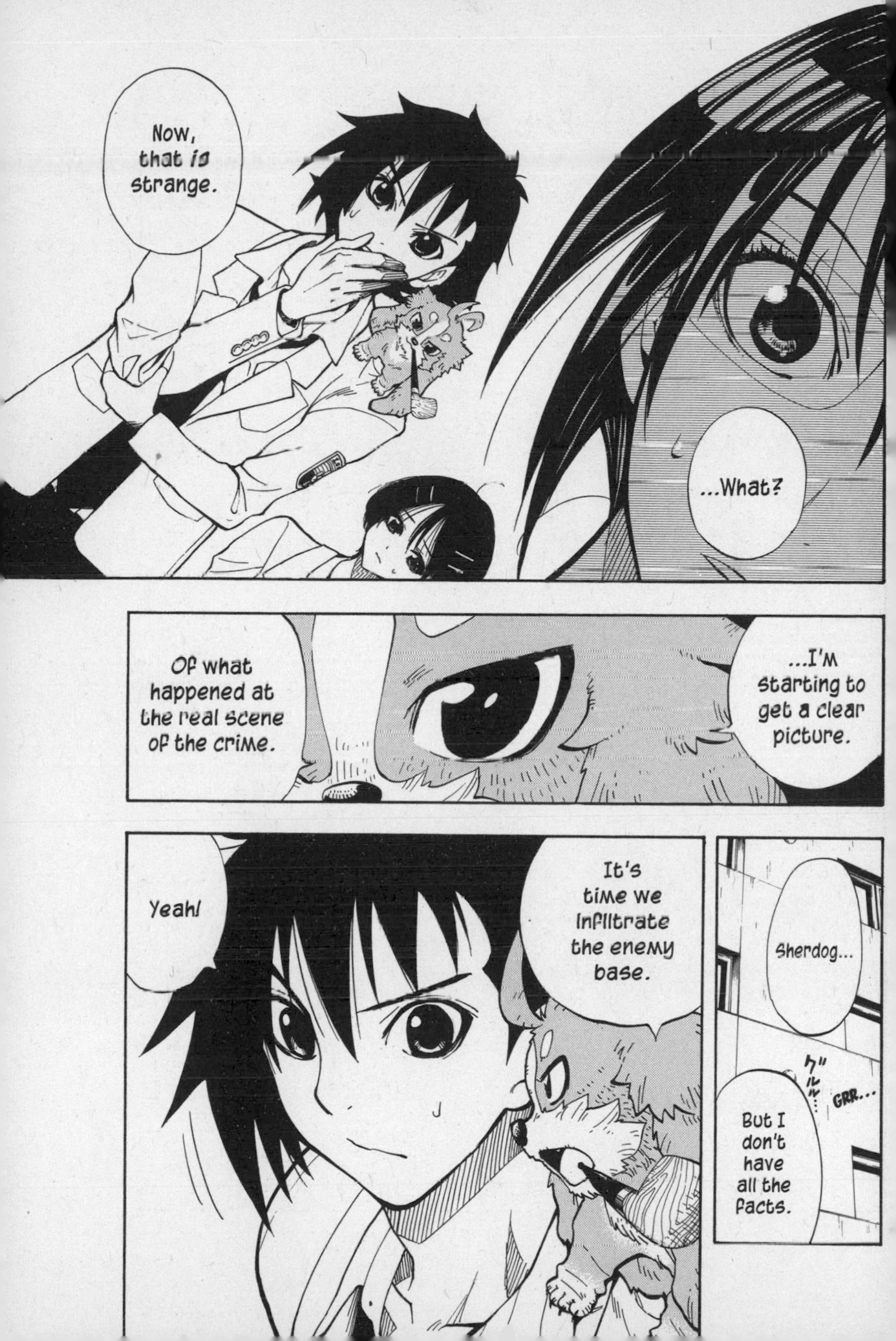
Now, that *is* strange.
...What?
...I'm starting to get a clear picture.
Of what happened at the real scene of the crime.
Sherdog...
GRR...
But I don't have all the facts.
It's time we infiltrate the enemy base.
Yeah!

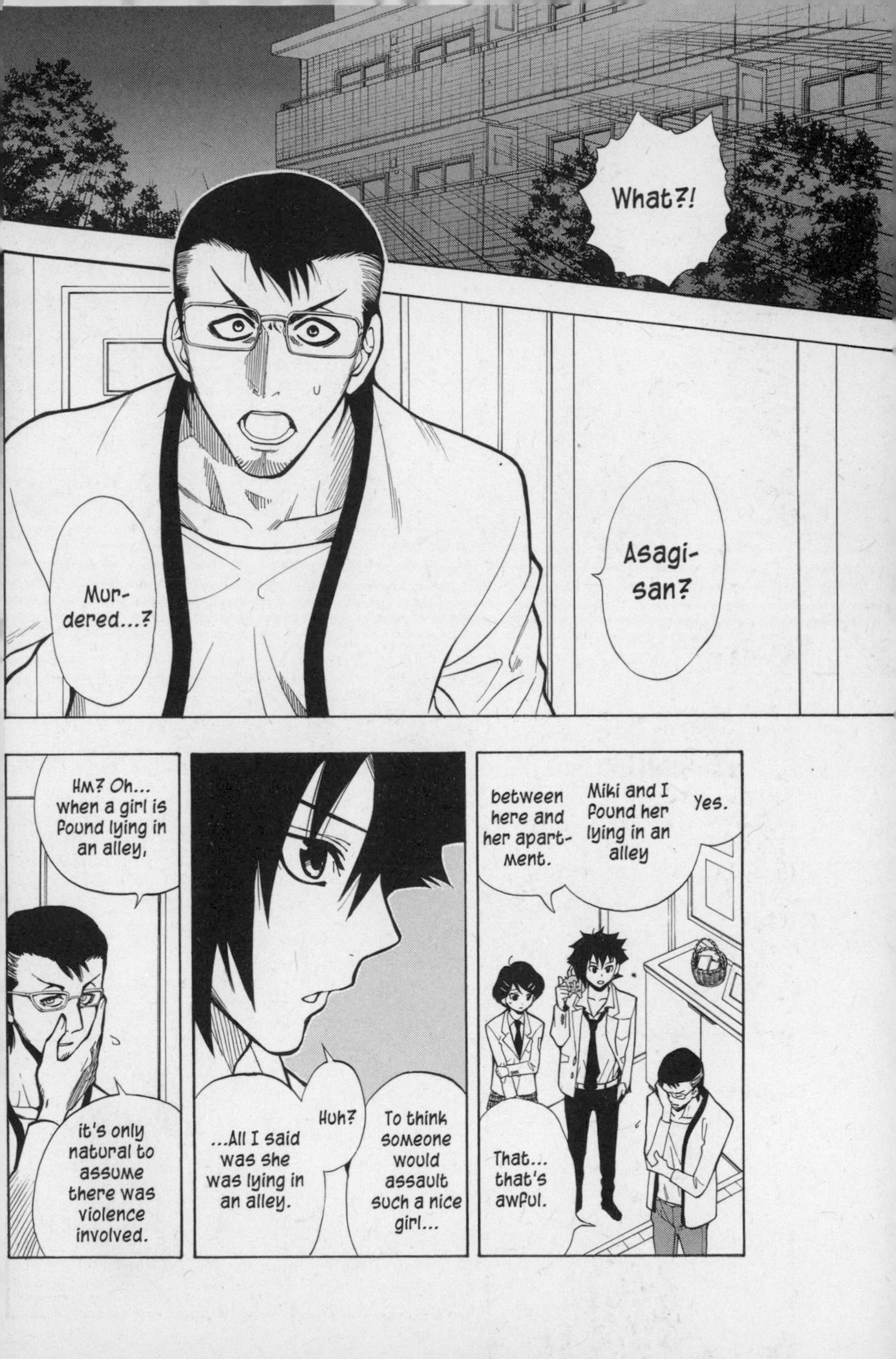
What?!
Asagi-san?
Mur-dered...?
Yes.
Miki and I found her lying in an alley
between here and her apart-ment.
That... that's awful.
To think someone would assault such a nice girl...
Huh?
...All I said was she was lying in an alley.
Hm? Oh... when a girl is found lying in an alley,
it's only natural to assume there was violence involved.

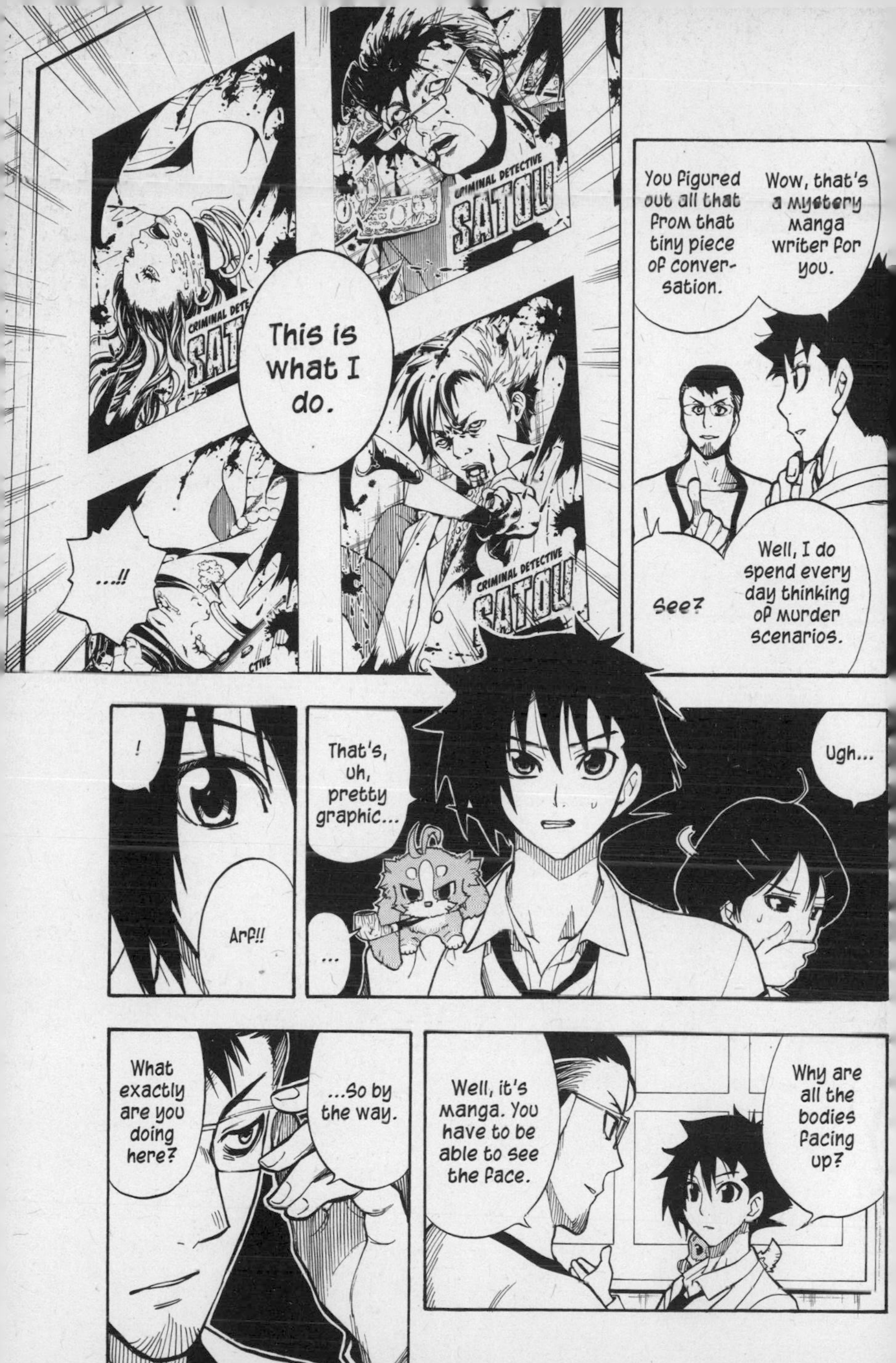

Wow, that's a mystery manga writer for you.
You figured out all that from that tiny piece of conversation.
Well, I do spend every day thinking of murder scenarios.
See?
CRIMINAL DETECTIVE SATOU
This is what I do.
...!!
Ugh...
That's, uh, pretty graphic...
...
!
Arf!!
Why are all the bodies facing up?
Well, it's manga. You have to be able to see the face.
...So by the way.
What exactly are you doing here?

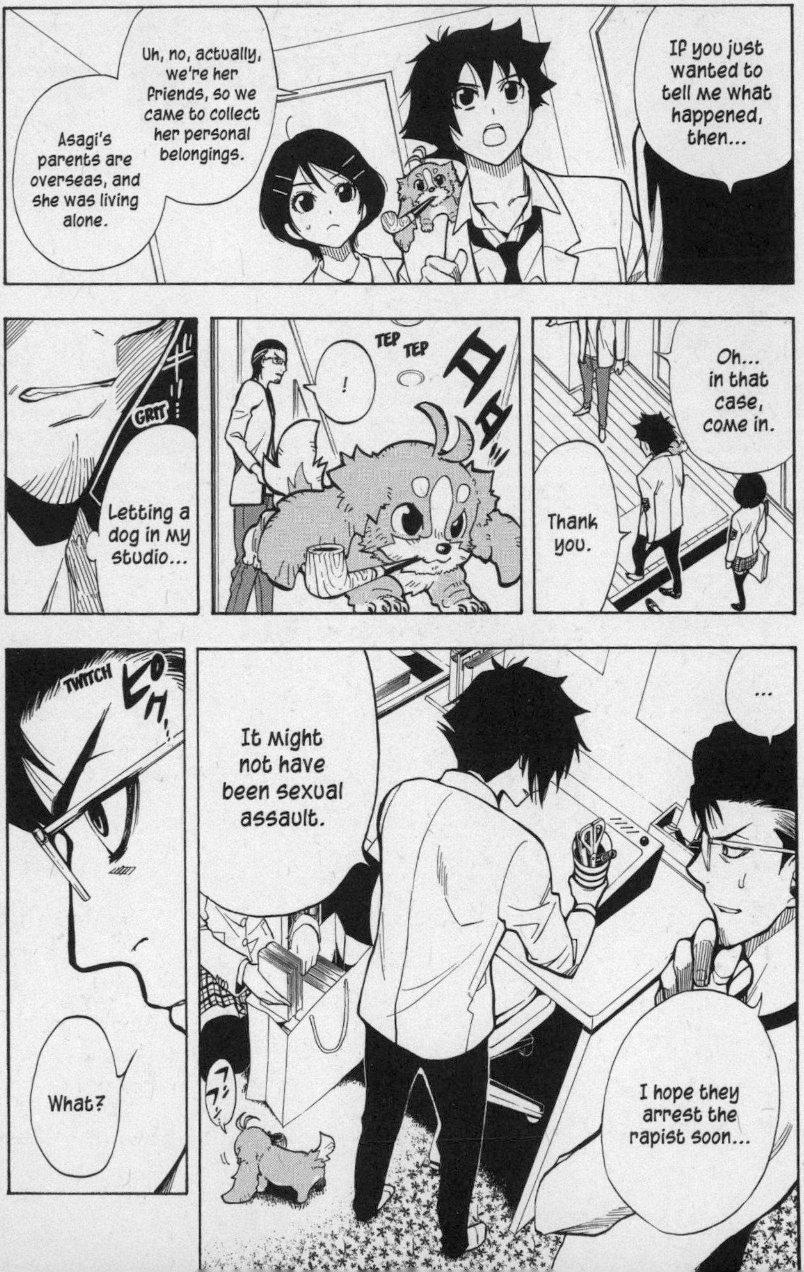
If you just wanted to tell me what happened, then...
Uh, no, actually, we're her friends, so we came to collect her personal belongings.
Asagi's parents are overseas, and she was living alone.
Oh... in that case, come in.
Thank you.
!
TEP TEP
GRIT
Letting a dog in my studio...
I hope they arrest the rapist soon...
...
It might not have been sexual assault.
TWITCH
What?

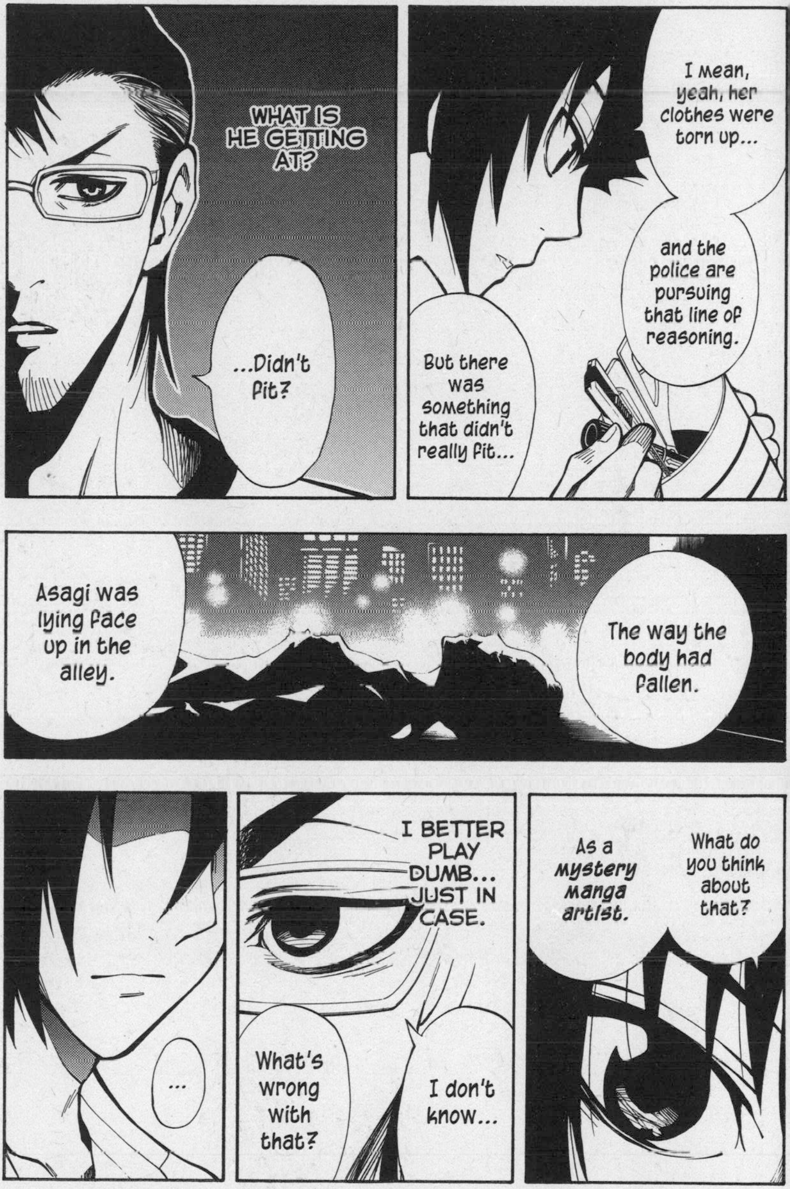
I mean, yeah, her clothes were torn up...
and the police are pursuing that line of reasoning.
But there was something that didn't really fit...
WHAT IS HE GETTING AT?
...Didn't fit?
The way the body had fallen.
Asagi was lying face up in the alley.
What do you think about that?
As a *mystery manga artist*.
I BETTER PLAY DUMB... JUST IN CASE.
I don't know...
What's wrong with that?
...

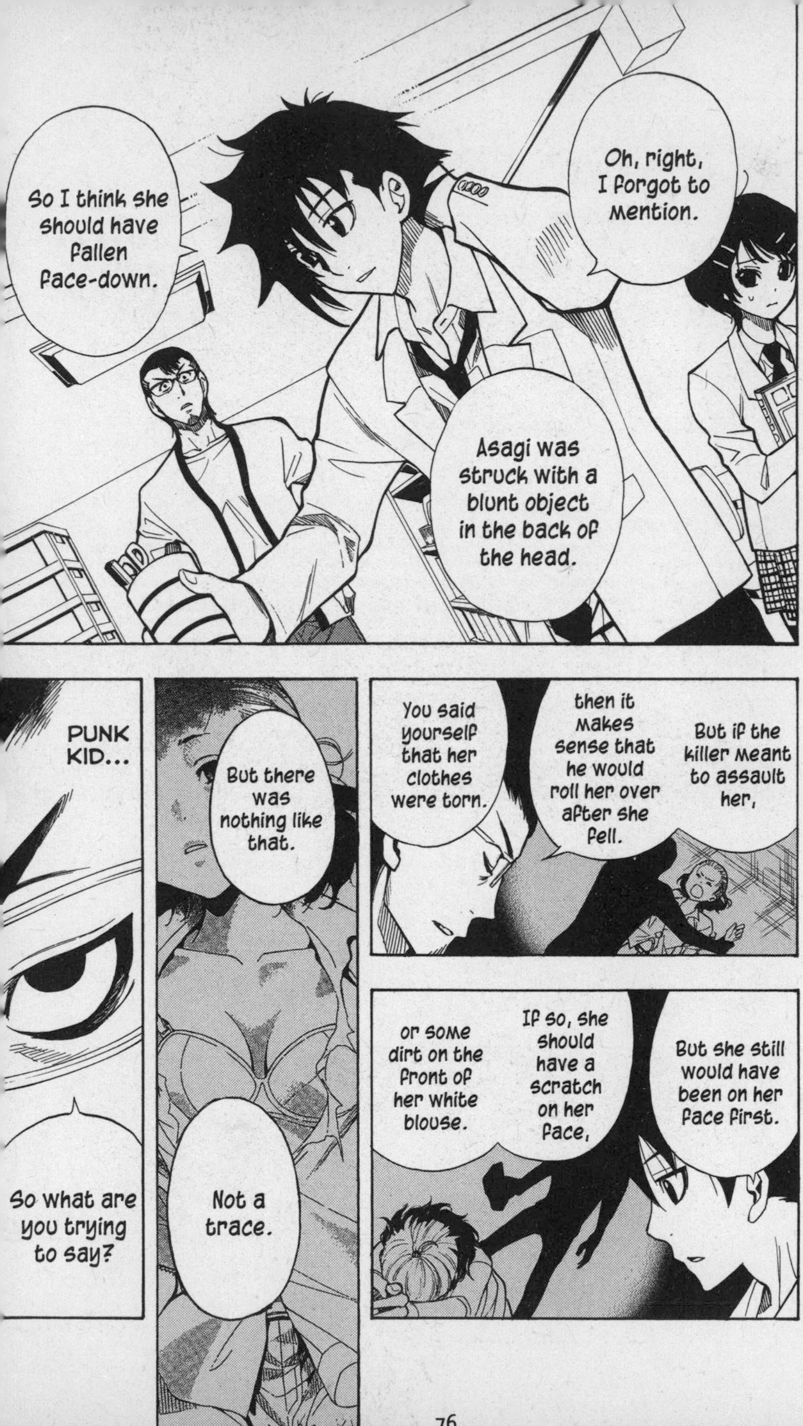
Oh, right, I forgot to mention.
Asagi was struck with a blunt object in the back of the head.
So I think she should have fallen face-down.
But if the killer meant to assault her,
then it makes sense that he would roll her over after she fell.
You said yourself that her clothes were torn.
But she still would have been on her face first.
If so, she should have a scratch on her face,
or some dirt on the front of her white blouse.
But there was nothing like that.
Not a trace.
PUNK KID...
So what are you trying to say?

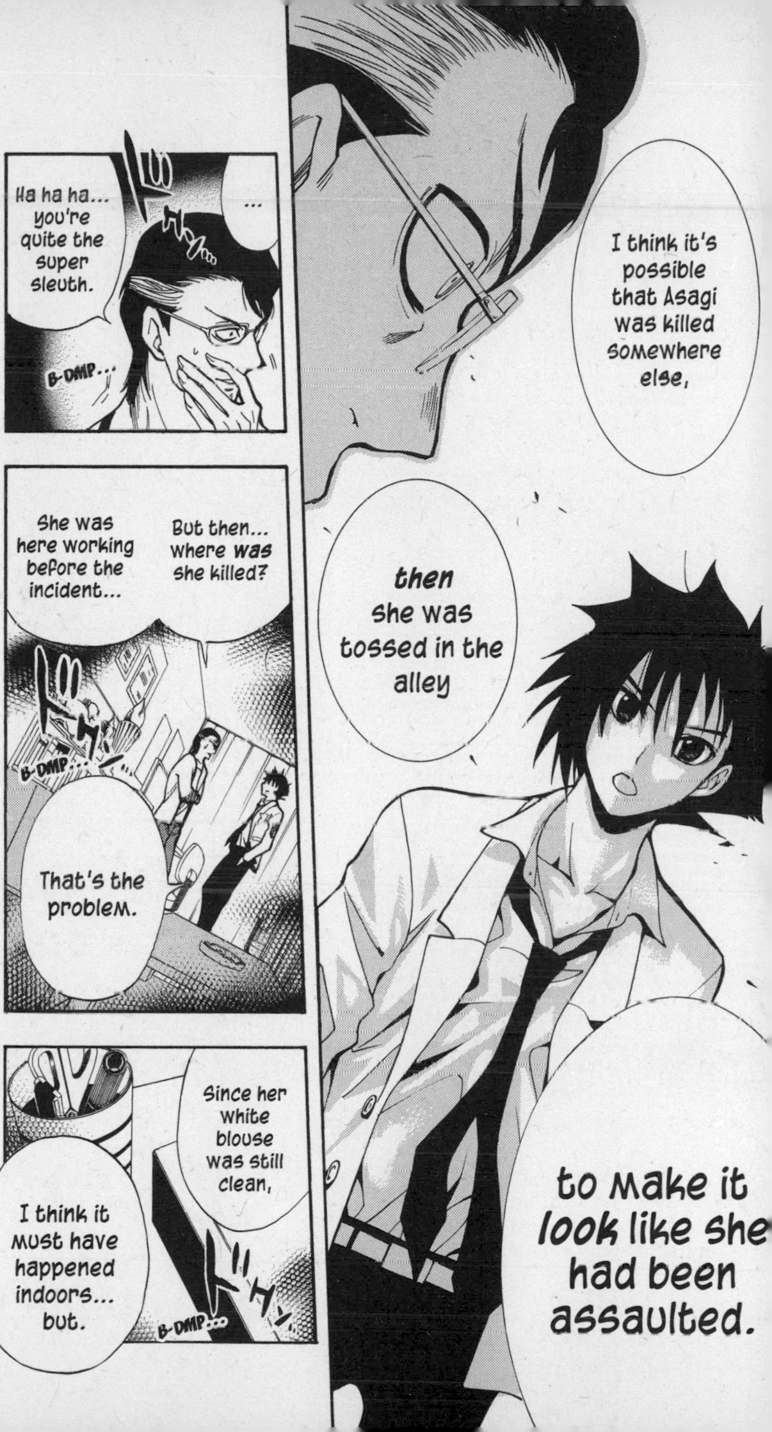
I think it's possible that Asagi was killed somewhere else,
then she was tossed in the alley
to make it look like she had been assaulted.
...
Ha ha ha... you're quite the super sleuth.
B-DMP...
But then... where was she killed?
She was here working before the incident...
B-DMP...
That's the problem.
Since her white blouse was still clean,
I think it must have happened indoors... but.
B-DMP...

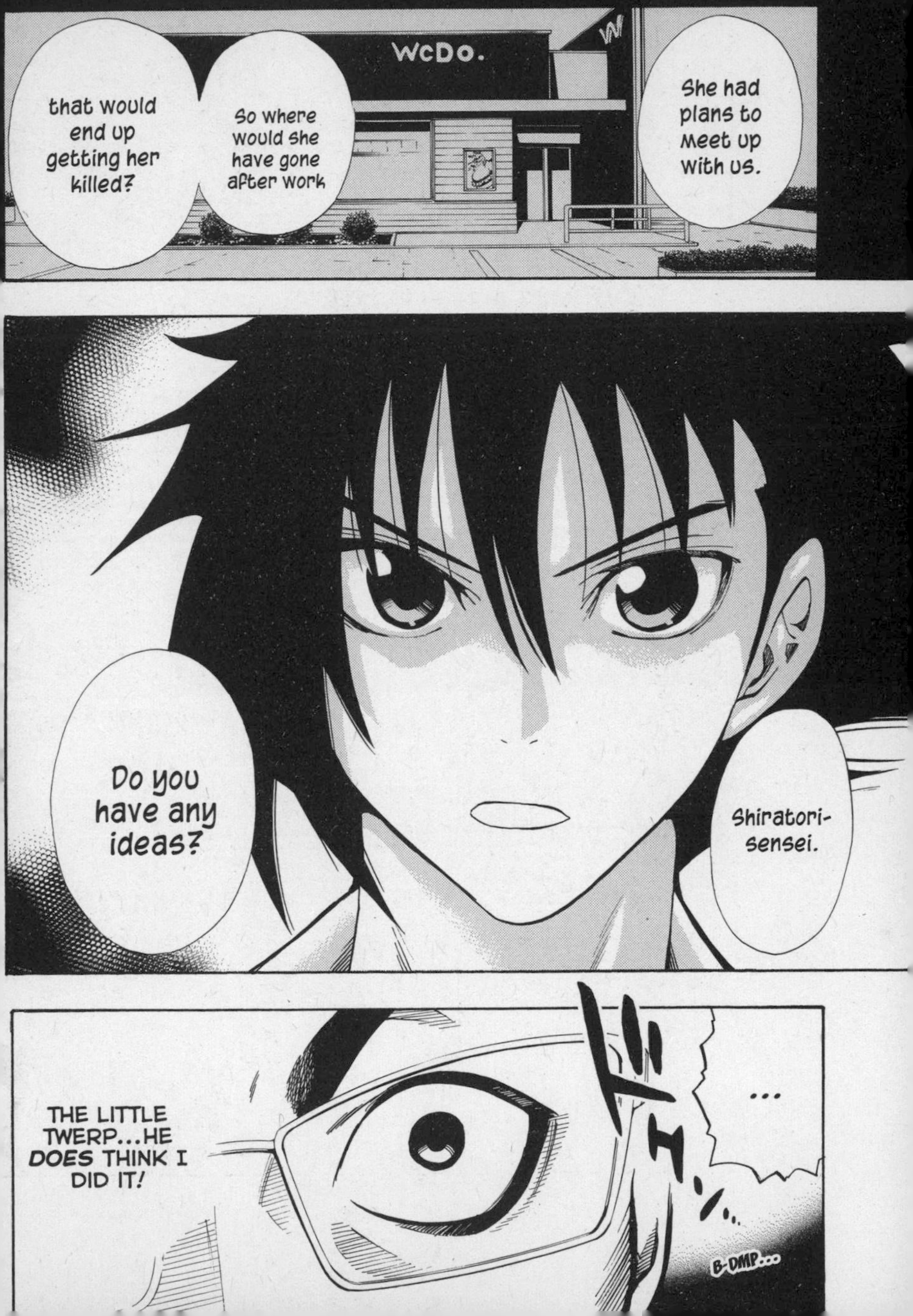
WcDo.
She had plans to meet up with us.
So where would she have gone after work
that would end up getting her killed?
Shiratori-sensei.
Do you have any ideas?
...
THE LITTLE TWERP...HE *DOES* THINK I DID IT!
B-DMP...

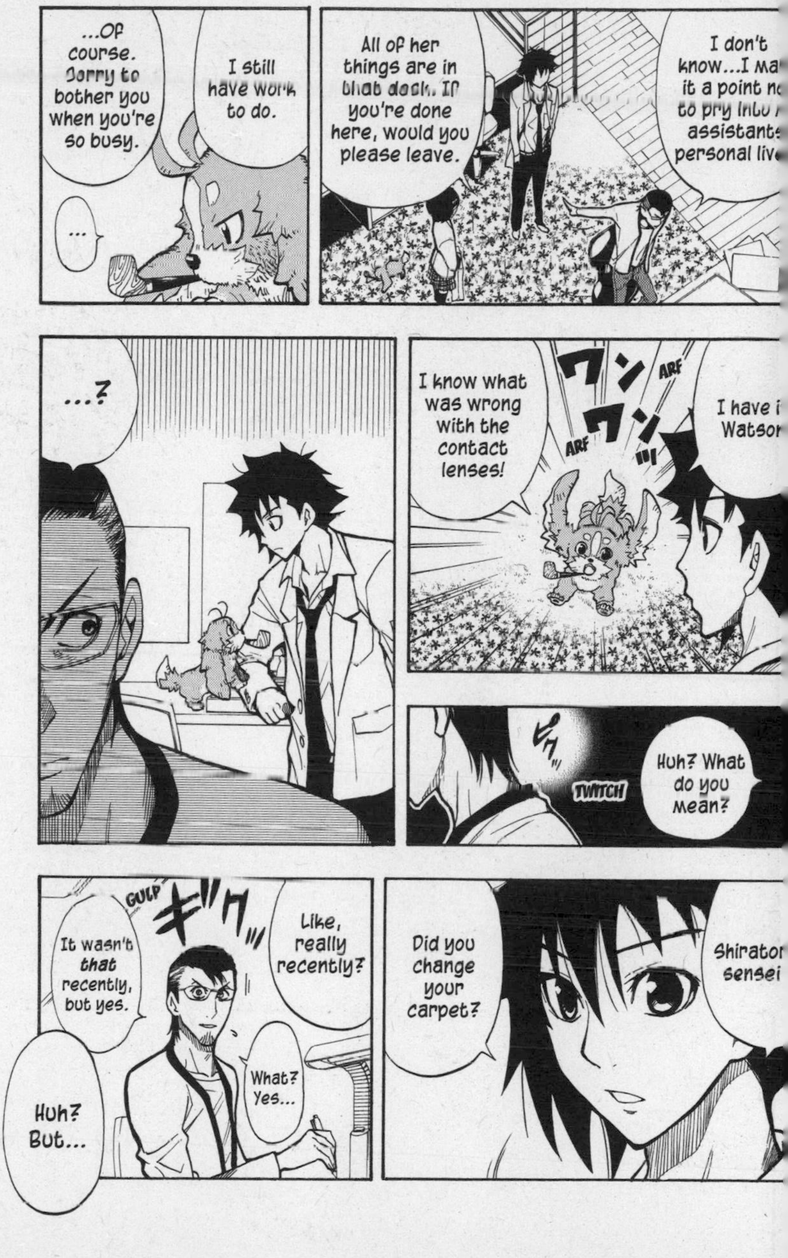
I don't know...I ma it a point n to pry into assistant personal liv
All of her things are in that desk. If you're done here, would you please leave.
I still have work to do.
...Of course. Sorry to bother you when you're so busy.
...
I have i Watson
ARF
ARF
I know what was wrong with the contact lenses!
TWITCH
Huh? What do you mean?
...?
Shirator sensei
Did you change your carpet?
Like, really recently?
GULP
What? Yes...
It wasn't *that* recently, but yes.
Huh? But...

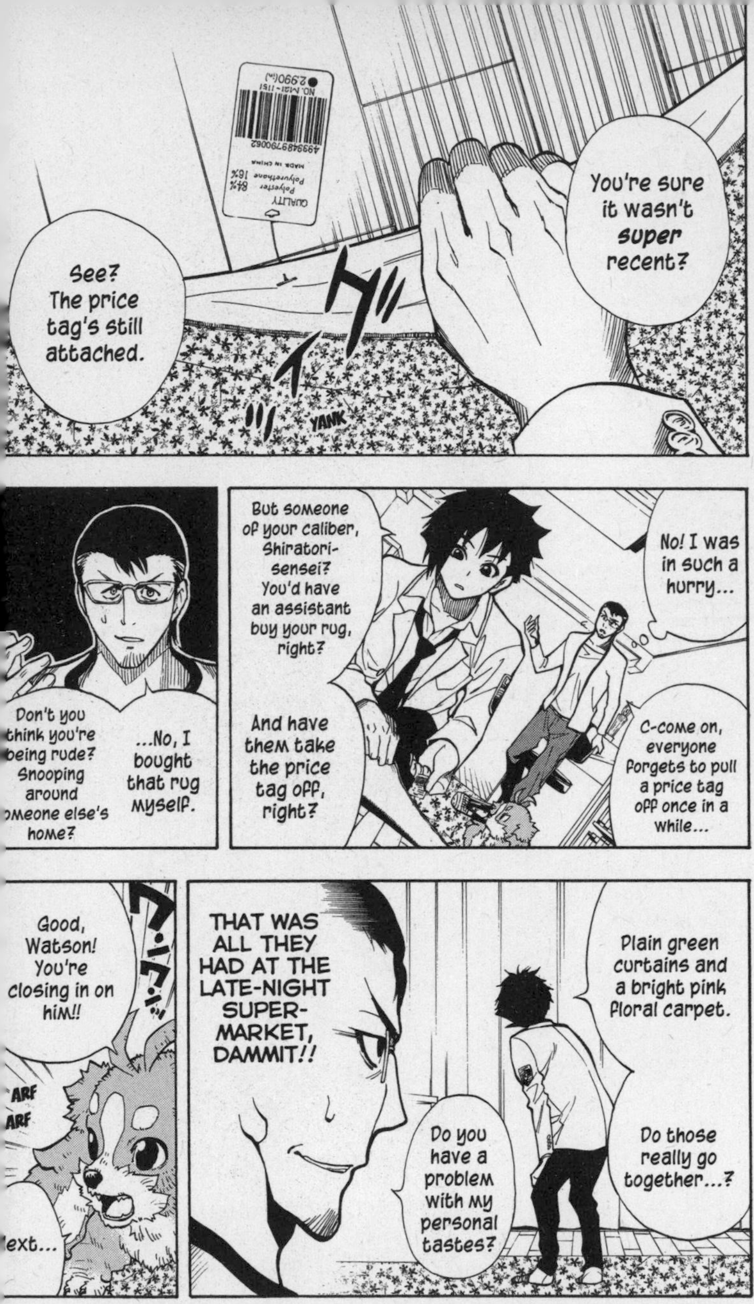
You're sure it wasn't super recent?
See? The price tag's still attached.
YANK
No! I was in such a hurry...
But someone of your caliber, Shiratori-sensei? You'd have an assistant buy your rug, right?
C-come on, everyone forgets to pull a price tag off once in a while...
And have them take the price tag off, right?
...No, I bought that rug myself.
Don't you think you're eing rude? Snooping around omeone else's home?
Plain green curtains and a bright pink floral carpet.
Do those really go together...?
THAT WAS ALL THEY HAD AT THE LATE-NIGHT SUPER-MARKET, DAMMIT!!
Do you have a problem with my personal tastes?
Good, Watson! You're closing in on him!!
ARF ARF
ext...

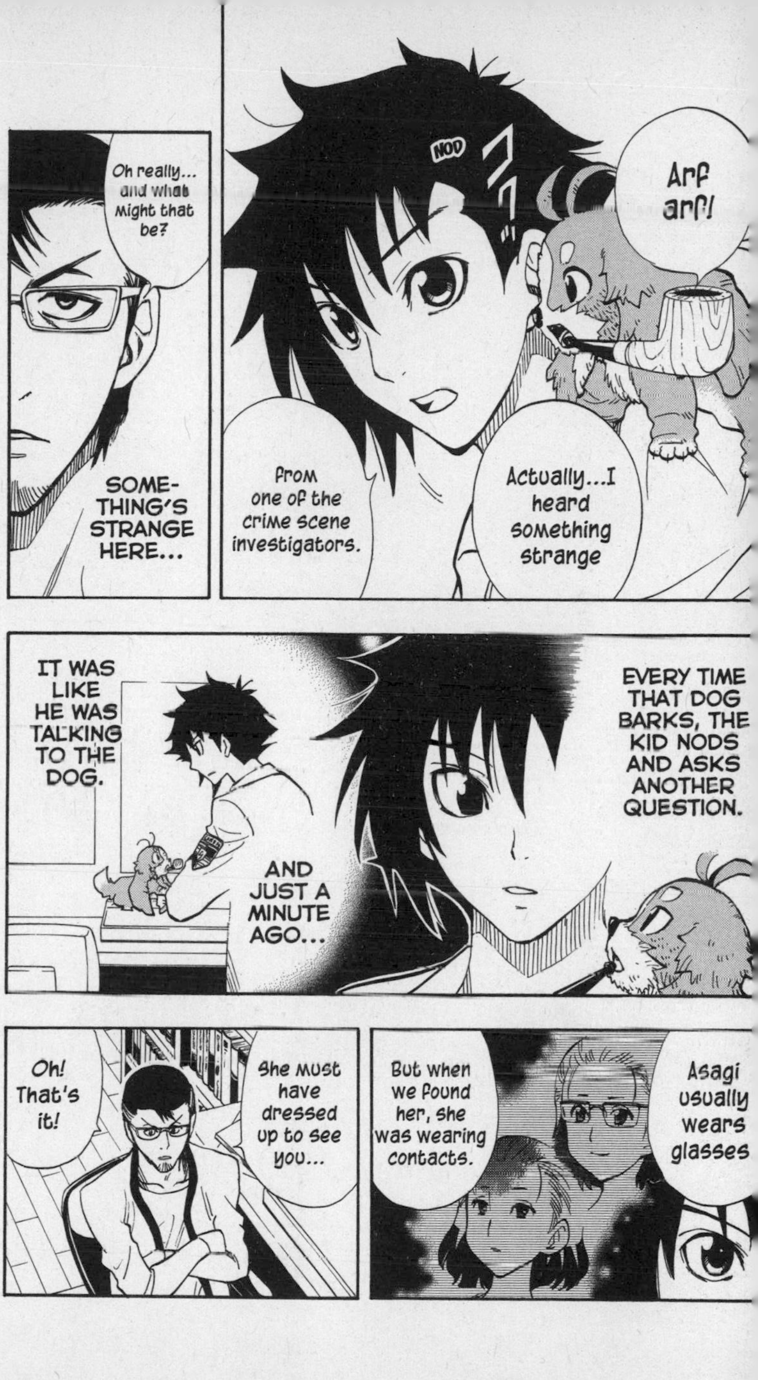
NOD
Arf arf!
Actually...I heard something strange
from one of the crime scene investigators.
Oh really... and what might that be?
SOME-THING'S STRANGE HERE...
EVERY TIME THAT DOG BARKS, THE KID NODS AND ASKS ANOTHER QUESTION.
AND JUST A MINUTE AGO...
IT WAS LIKE HE WAS TALKING TO THE DOG.
Asagi usually wears glasses
But when we found her, she was wearing contacts.
She must have dressed up to see you...
Oh! That's it!

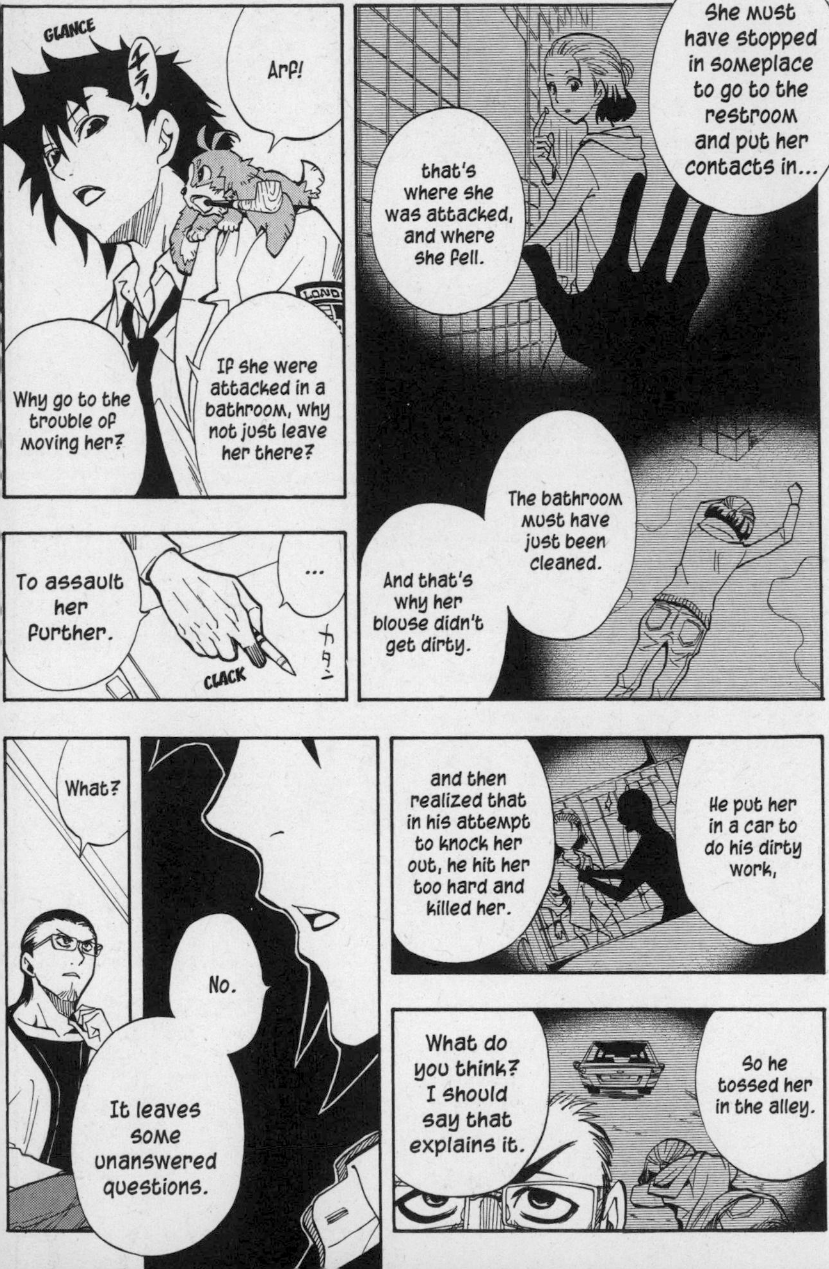
She must have stopped in someplace to go to the restroom and put her contacts in...
that's where she was attacked, and where she fell.
The bathroom must have just been cleaned.
And that's why her blouse didn't get dirty.
GLANCE
Arf!
If she were attacked in a bathroom, why not just leave her there?
Why go to the trouble of moving her?
...
CLACK
To assault her further.
He put her in a car to do his dirty work,
and then realized that in his attempt to knock her out, he hit her too hard and killed her.
So he tossed her in the alley.
What do you think? I should say that explains it.
No.
It leaves some unanswered questions.
What?

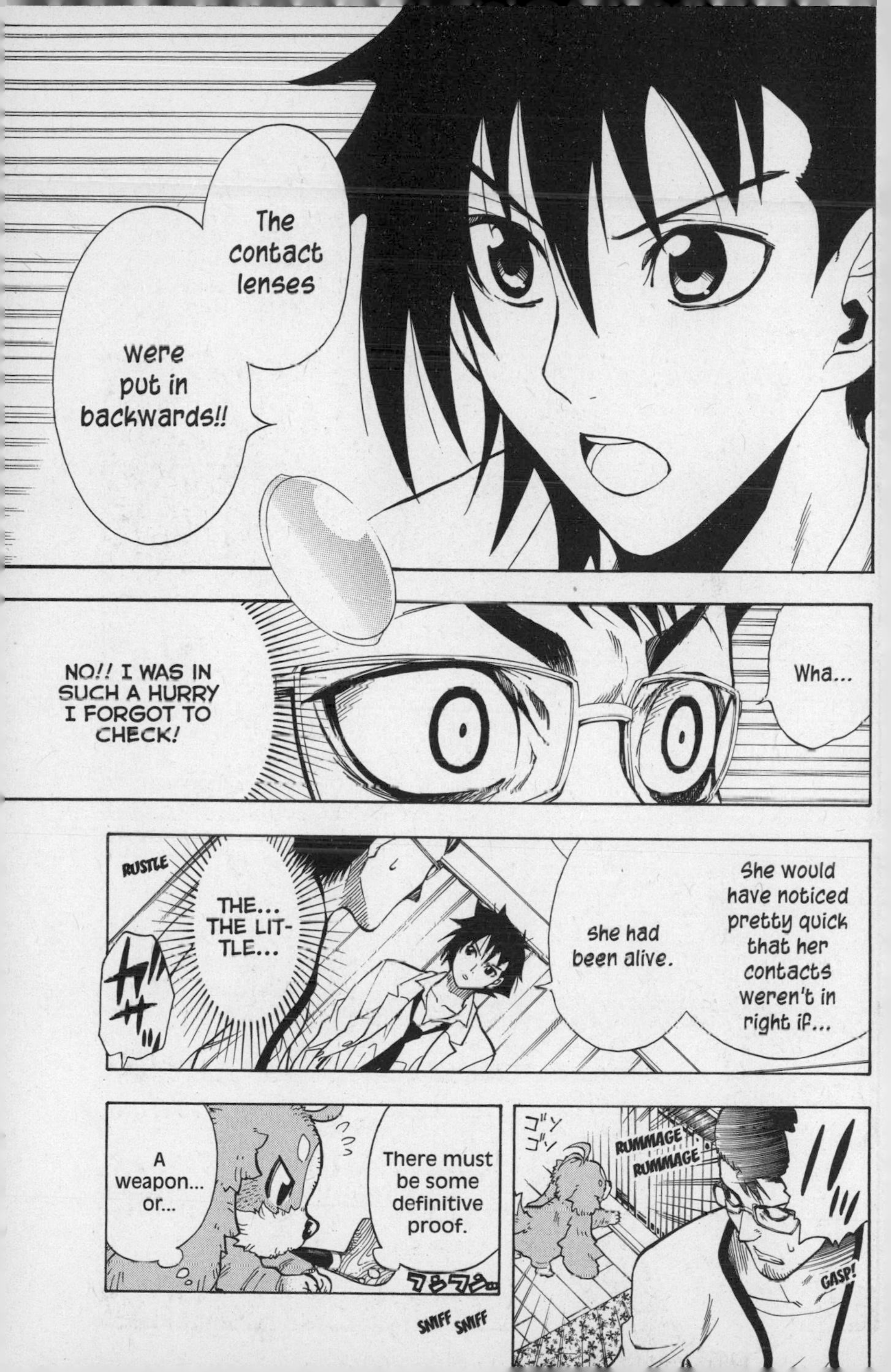
The contact lenses
were put in backwards!!
Wha...
NO!! I WAS IN SUCH A HURRY I FORGOT TO CHECK!
She would have noticed pretty quick that her contacts weren't in right if...
she had been alive.
THE... THE LIT-TLE...
RUSTLE
RUMMAGE
RUMMAGE
GASP!
There must be some definitive proof.
A weapon... or...
SNIFF SNIFF

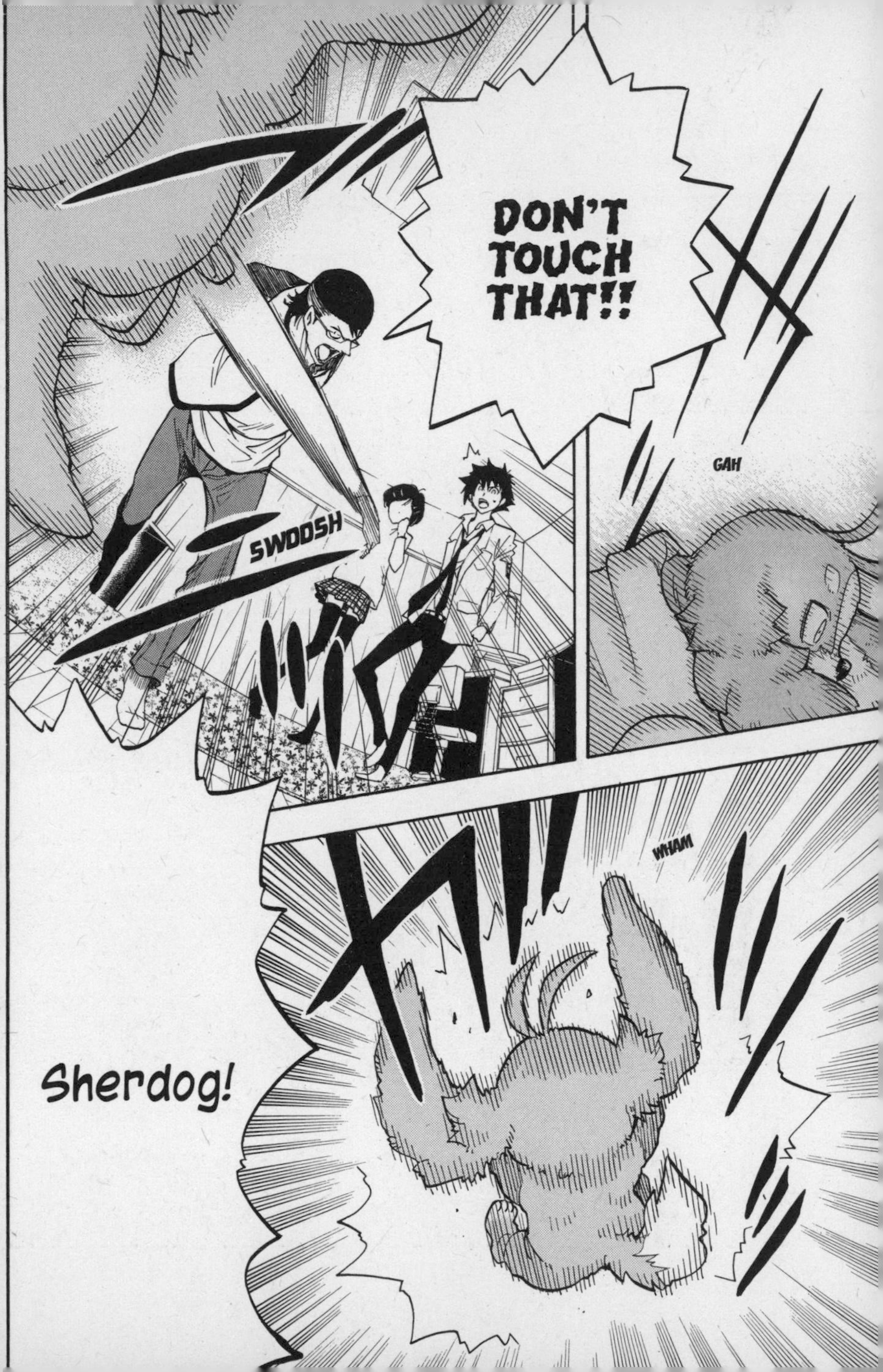
DON'T TOUCH THAT!!
SWOOSH
GAH
WHAM
Sherdog!

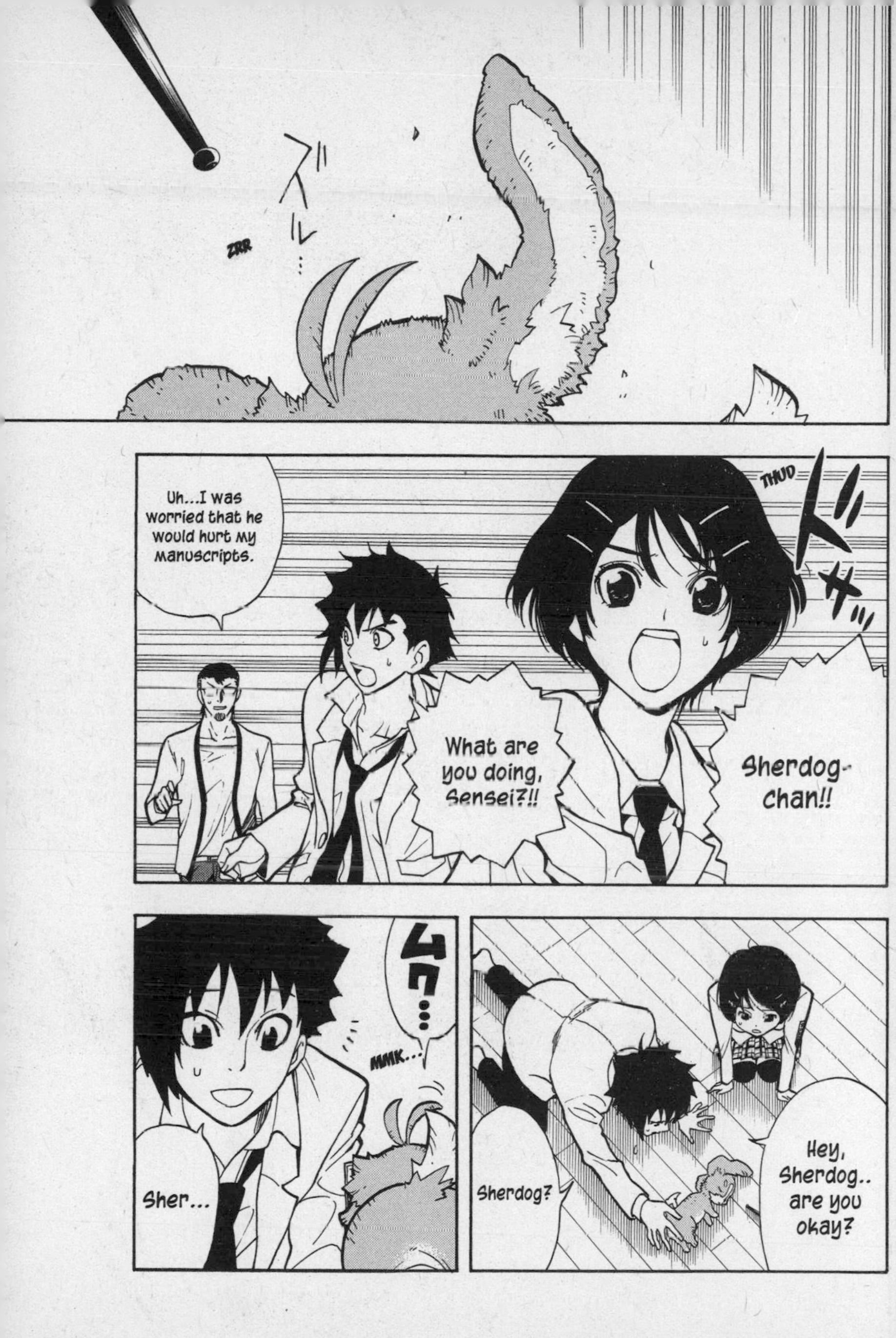
ズル…
ZRR
THUD
ドサッ
Sherdog-chan!!
What are you doing, Sensei?!!
Uh...I was worried that he would hurt my manuscripts.
Hey, Sherdog.. are you okay?
Sherdog?
ムク…
MMK...
Sher...

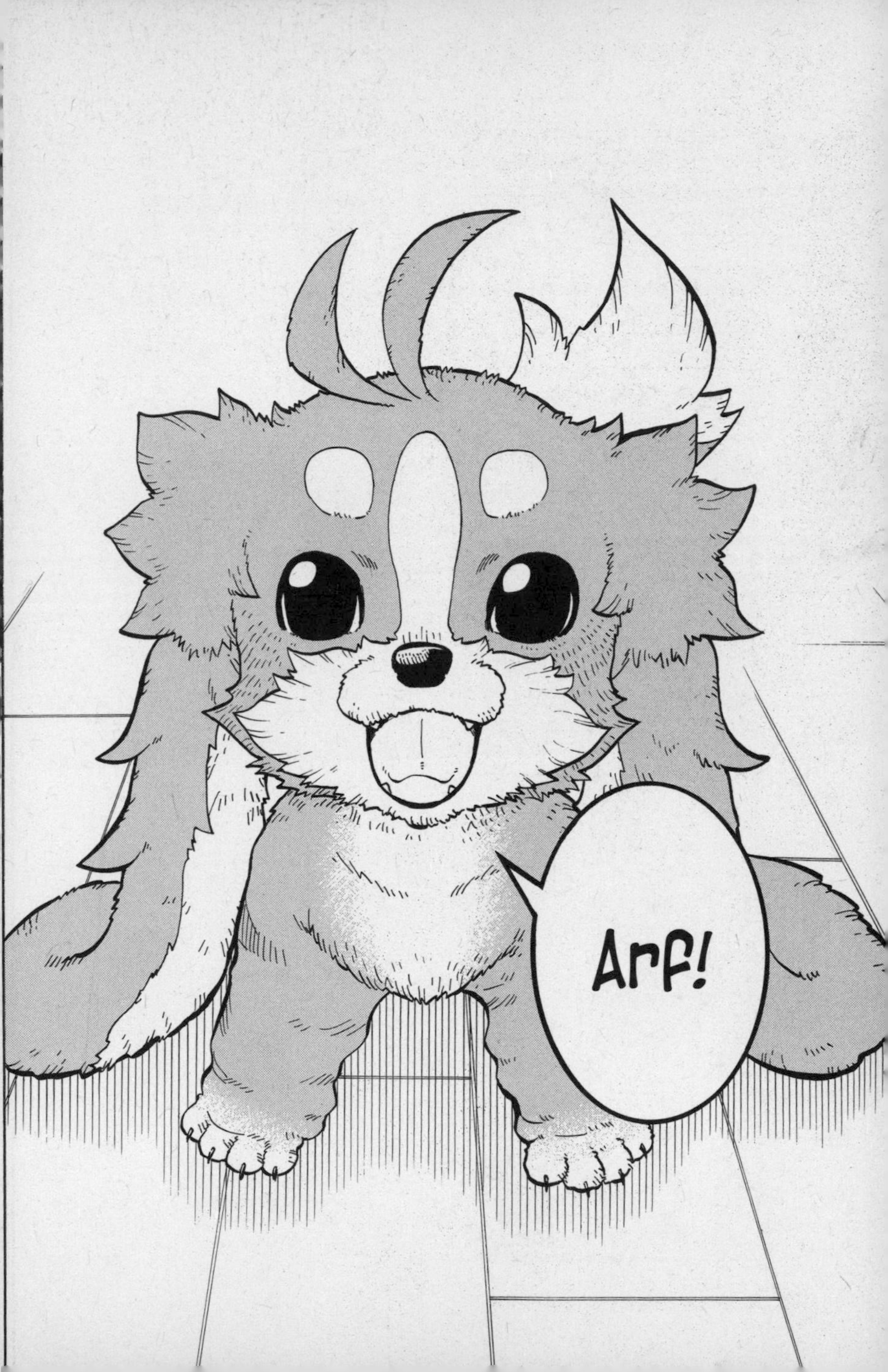
Arf!

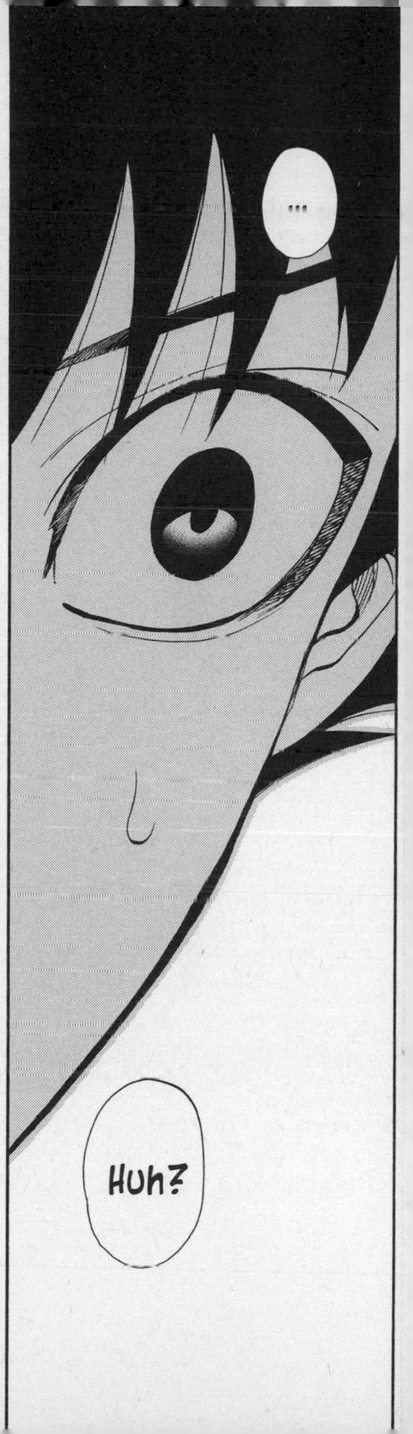
...
Huh?
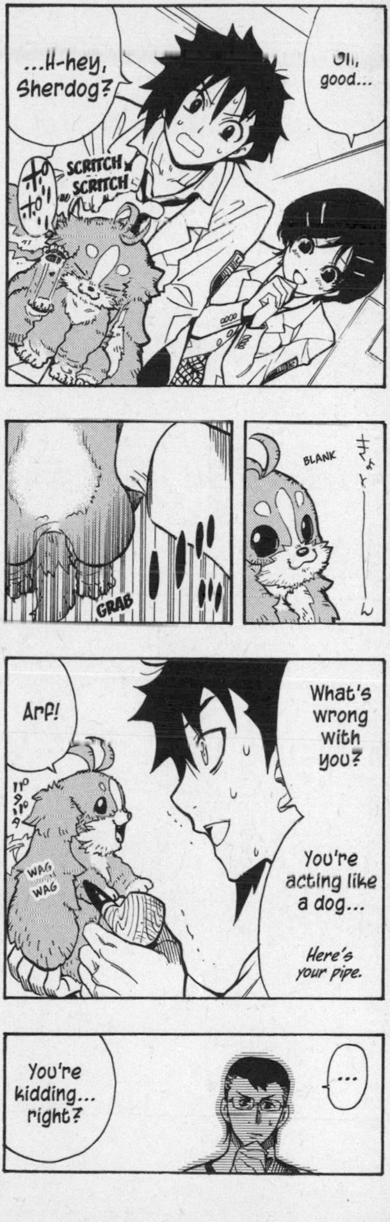
Oh, good...
...H-hey, Sherdog?
SCRITCH SCRITCH
BLANK
GRAB
What's wrong with you?
You're acting like a dog...
Here's your pipe.
Arf!
WAG WAG
...
You're kidding... right?

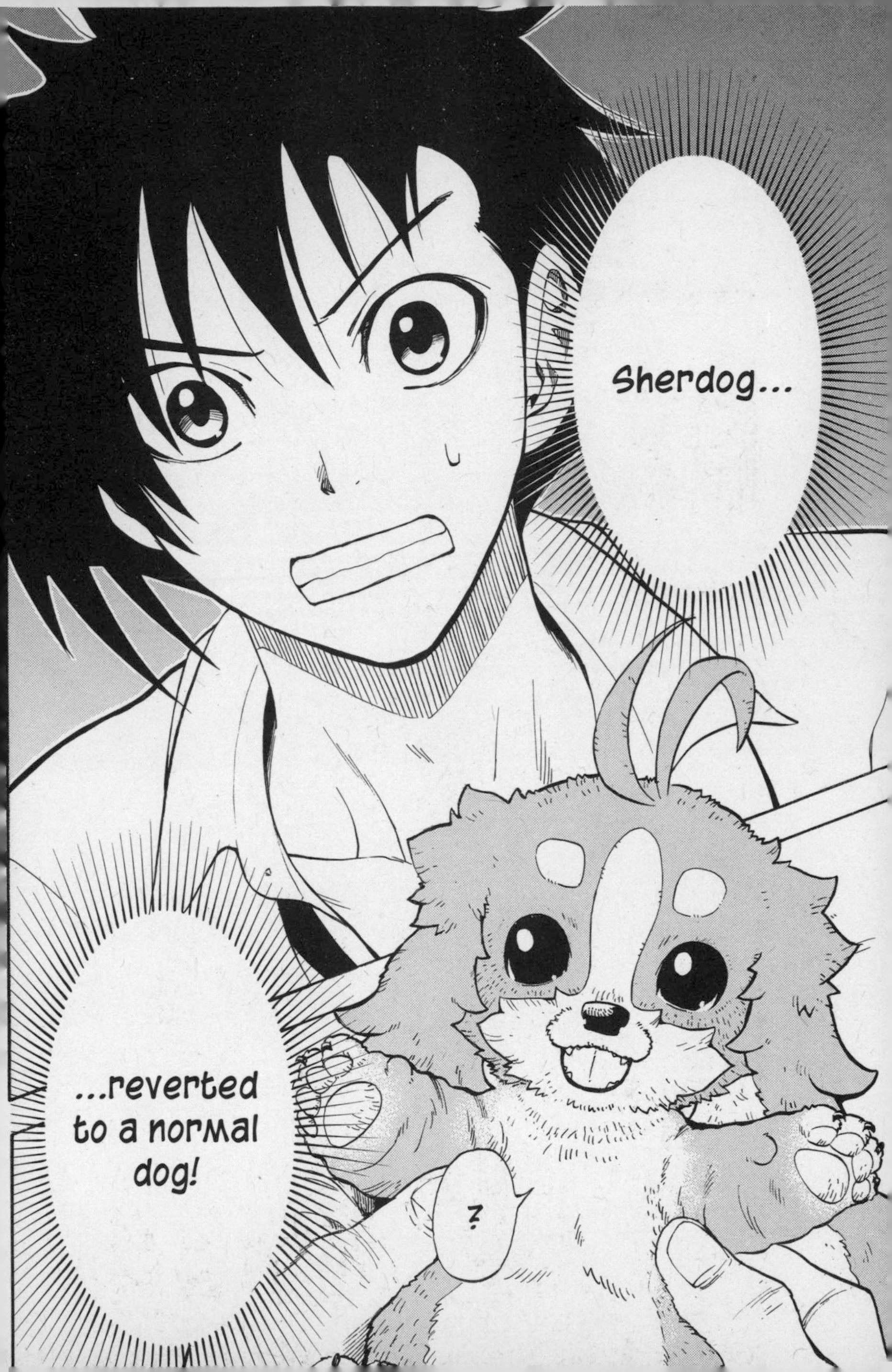
Sherdog...
...reverted to a normal dog!
?

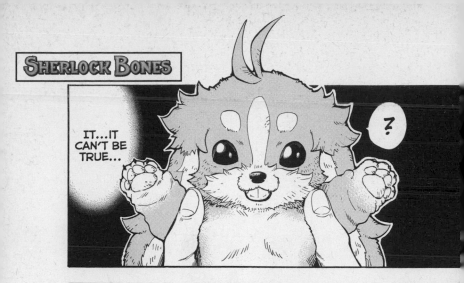

SHERLOCK BONES

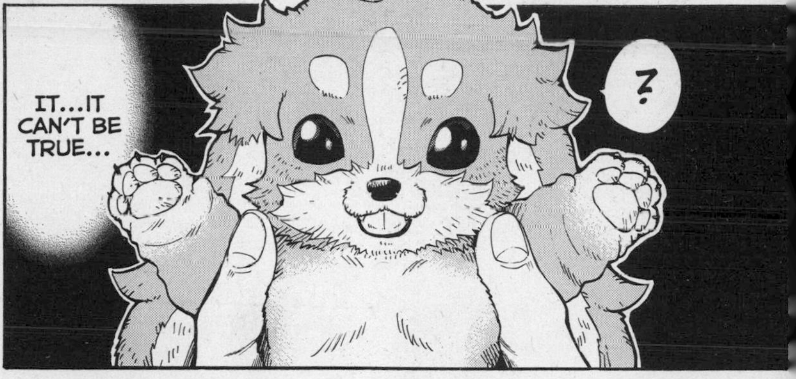
?
IT...IT CAN'T BE TRUE...

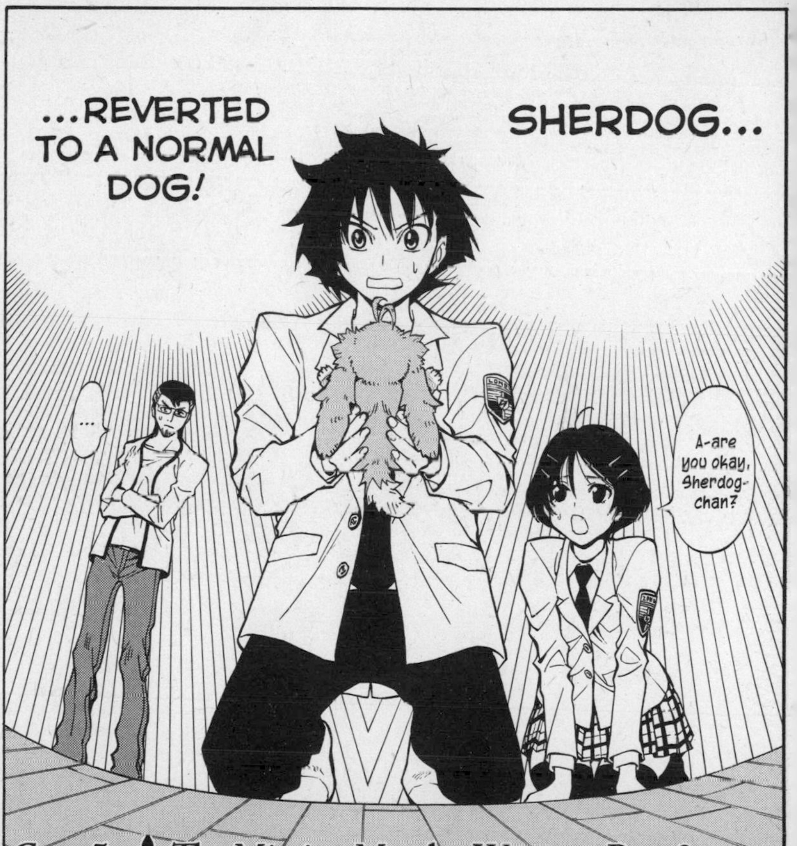
SHERDOG...
...REVERTED TO A NORMAL DOG!
A-are you okay, Sherdog-chan?
...

Case 5: ⚜ The Missing Murder Weapon, Part 3

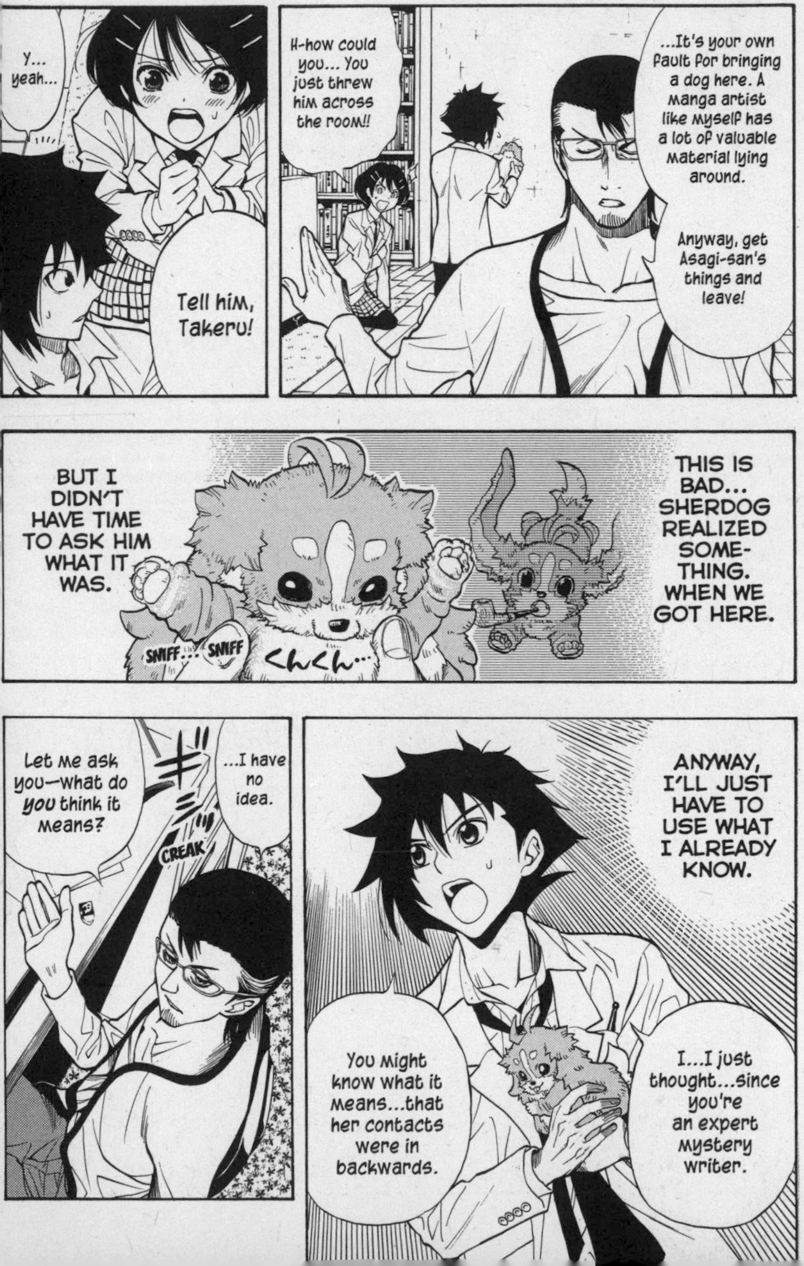
...It's your own fault for bringing a dog here. A manga artist like myself has a lot of valuable material lying around.
Anyway, get Asagi-san's things and leave!
H-how could you... You just threw him across the room!!
Tell him, Takeru!
Y... yeah...
THIS IS BAD... SHERDOG REALIZED SOMETHING. WHEN WE GOT HERE.
BUT I DIDN'T HAVE TIME TO ASK HIM WHAT IT WAS.
くんくん…
SNIFF... SNIFF
ANYWAY, I'LL JUST HAVE TO USE WHAT I ALREADY KNOW.
I...I just thought...since you're an expert mystery writer.
You might know what it means...that her contacts were in backwards.
...I have no idea.
CREAK
Let me ask you—what do you think it means?

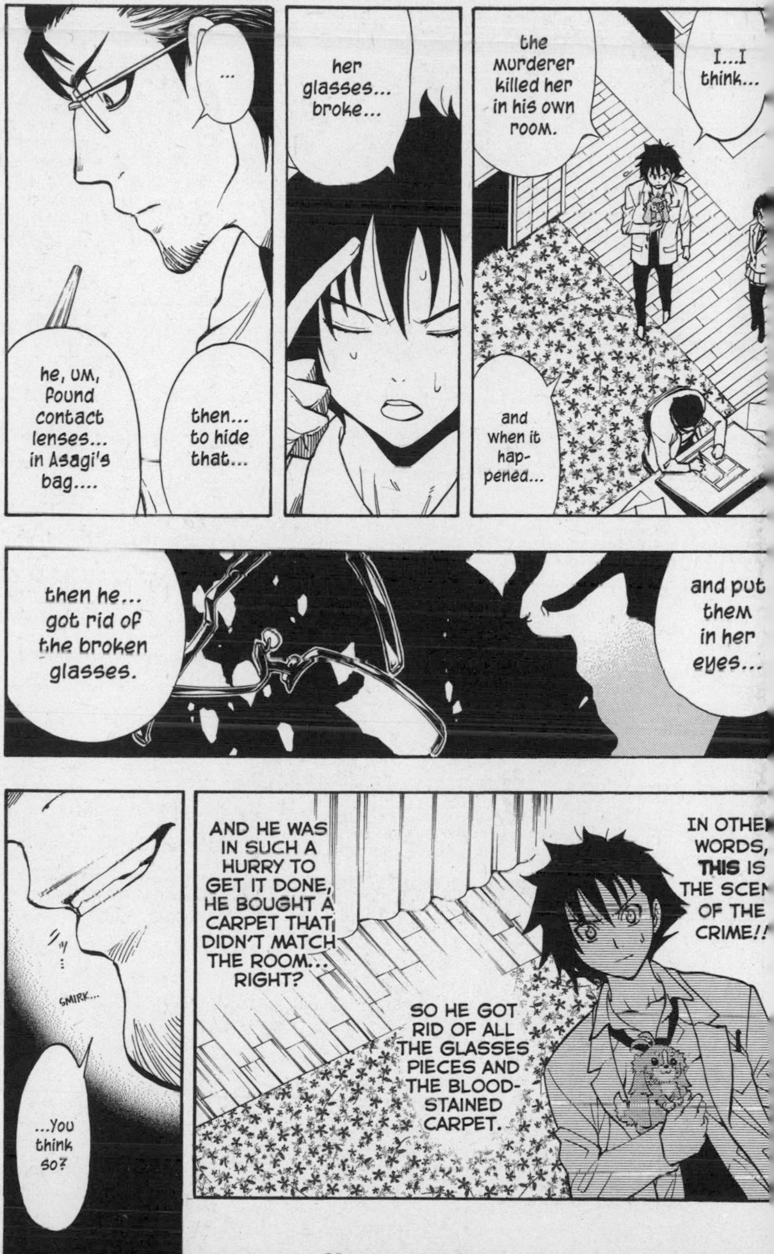
I...I think...
the murderer killed her in his own room.
and when it hap-pened...
her glasses... broke...
...
then... to hide that...
he, um, found contact lenses... in Asagi's bag....
and put them in her eyes...
then he... got rid of the broken glasses.
IN OTHE WORDS, THIS IS THE SCEN OF THE CRIME!!
AND HE WAS IN SUCH A HURRY TO GET IT DONE, HE BOUGHT A CARPET THAT DIDN'T MATCH THE ROOM... RIGHT?
SO HE GOT RID OF ALL THE GLASSES PIECES AND THE BLOOD-STAINED CARPET.
SMIRK...
...You think so?

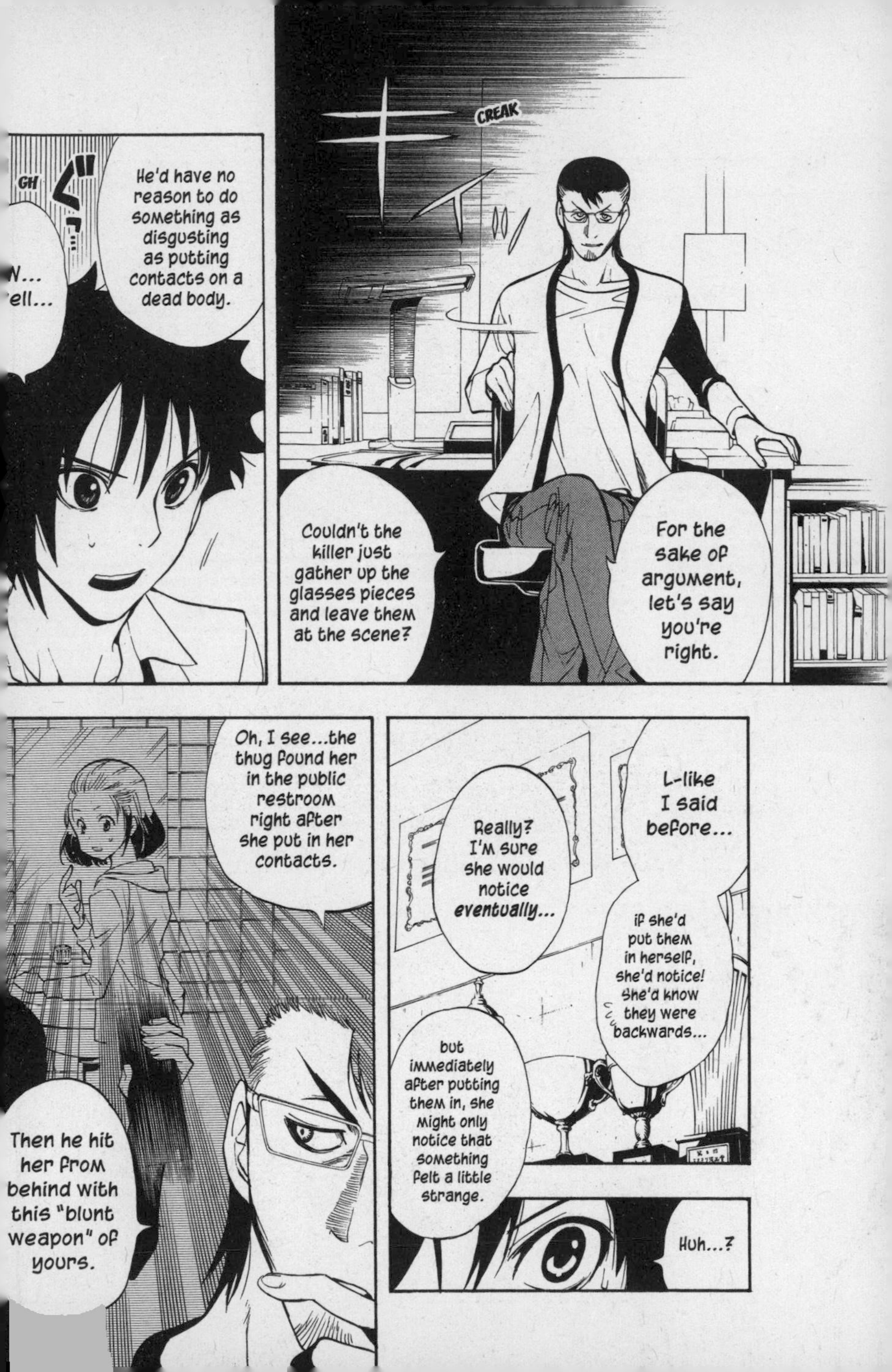
CREAK
For the sake of argument, let's say you're right.
Couldn't the killer just gather up the glasses pieces and leave them at the scene?
He'd have no reason to do something as disgusting as putting contacts on a dead body.
GH
W... ell...
L-like I said before...
Really? I'm sure she would notice eventually...
if she'd put them in herself, she'd notice! She'd know they were backwards...
but immediately after putting them in, she might only notice that something felt a little strange.
Huh...?
Oh, I see...the thug found her in the public restroom right after she put in her contacts.
Then he hit her from behind with this "blunt weapon" of yours.

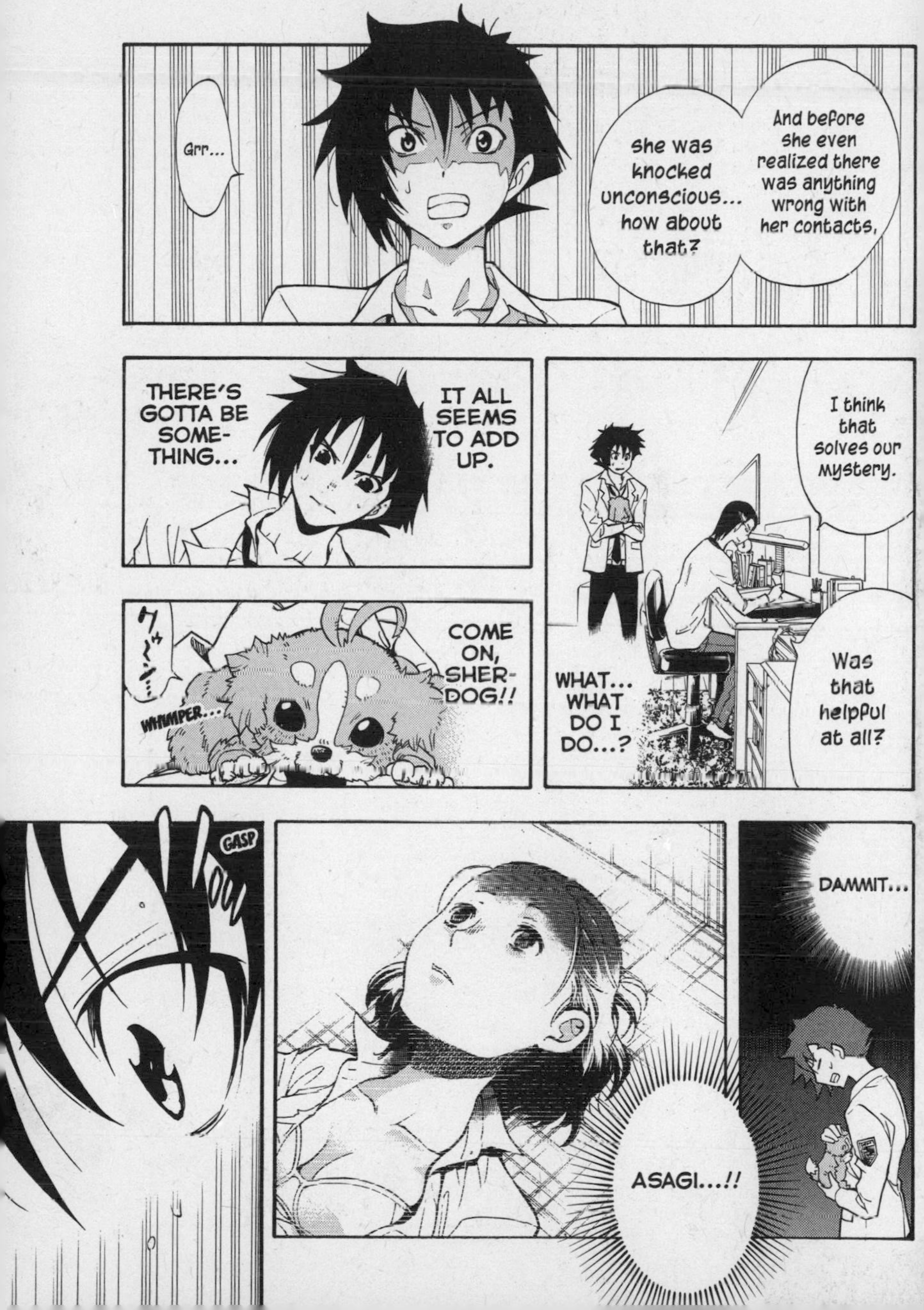
And before she even realized there was anything wrong with her contacts,
she was knocked unconscious... how about that?
Grr...
I think that solves our mystery.
Was that helpful at all?
WHAT... WHAT DO I DO...?
IT ALL SEEMS TO ADD UP.
THERE'S GOTTA BE SOMETHING...
COME ON, SHERDOG!!
クゥ～ン…
WHIMPER...
DAMMIT...
ASAGI...!!
GASP

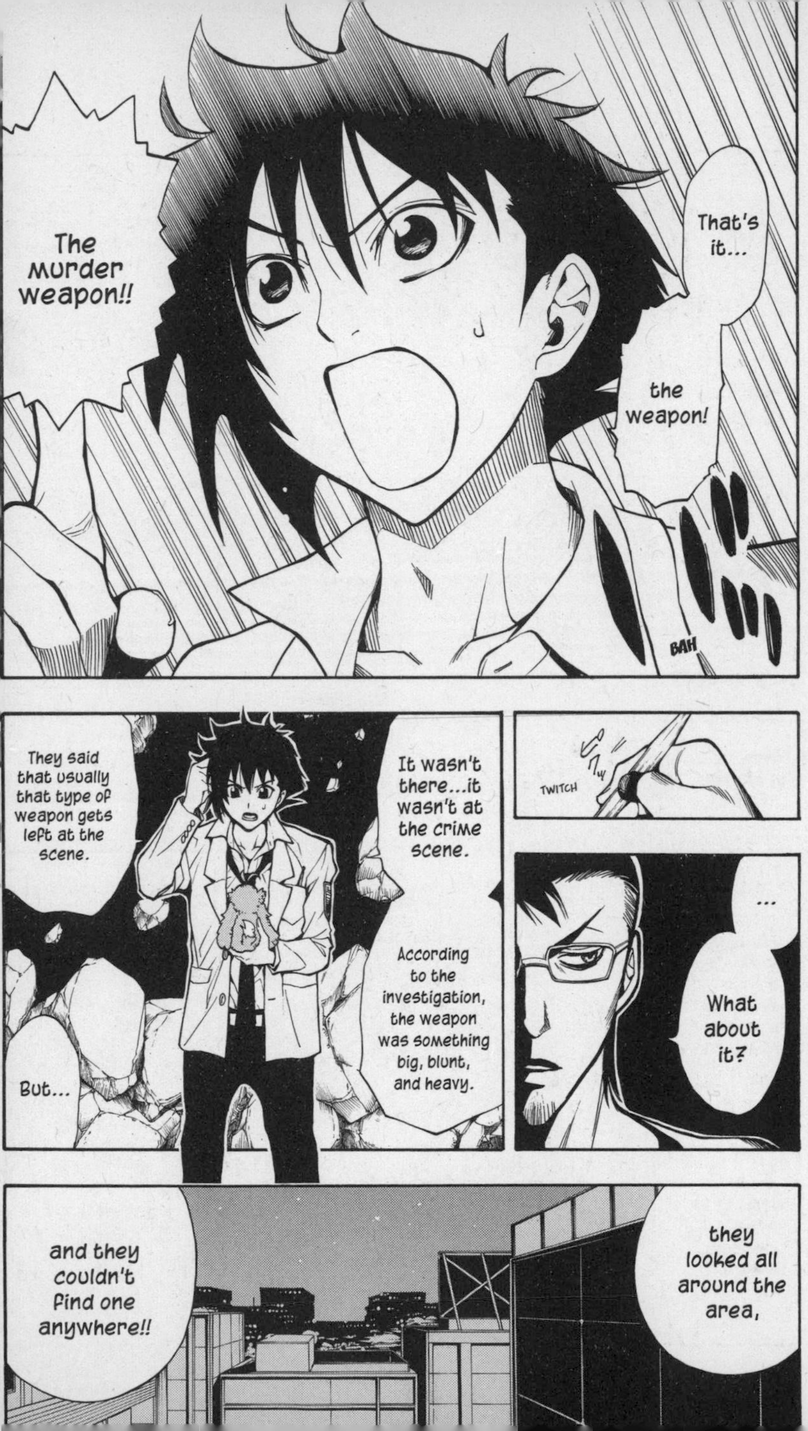

That's it...
the weapon!
The murder weapon!!
BAH
TWITCH
...
What about it?
It wasn't there...it wasn't at the crime scene.
According to the investigation, the weapon was something big, blunt, and heavy.
They said that usually that type of weapon gets left at the scene.
But...
they looked all around the area,
and they couldn't find one anywhere!!

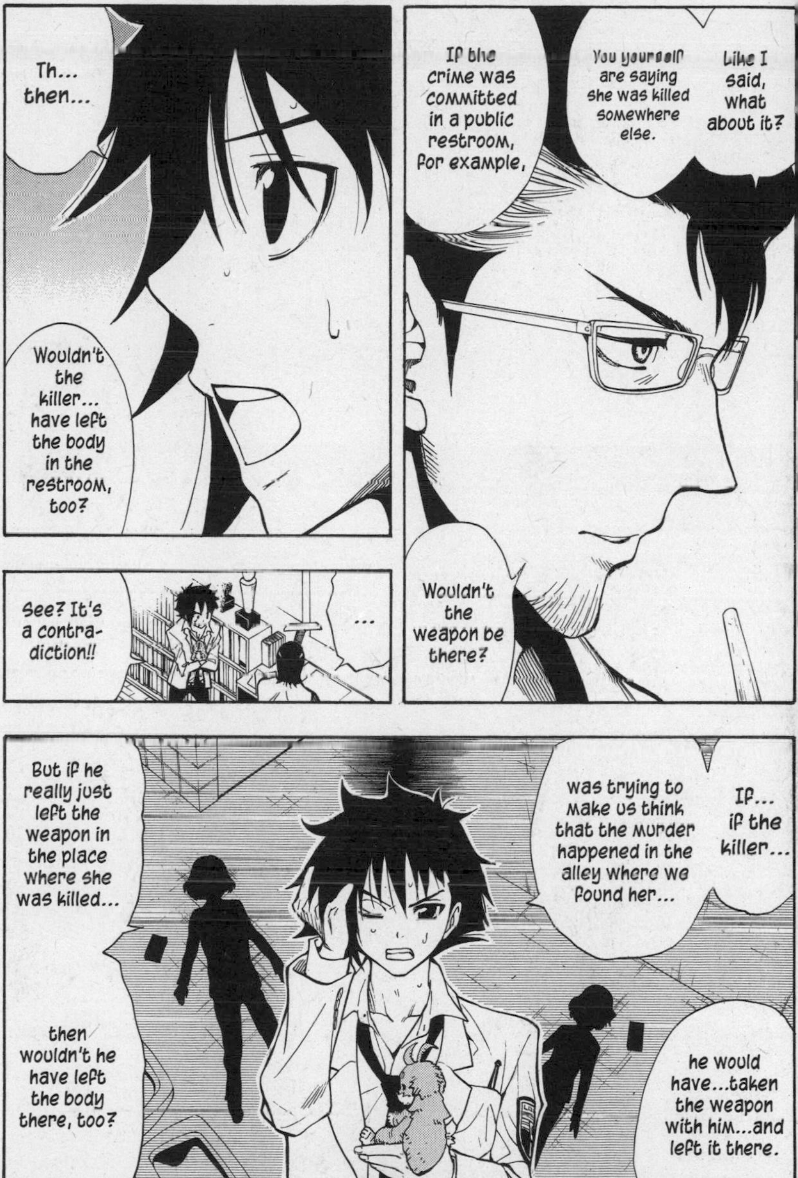
Like I said, what about it?
You yourself are saying she was killed somewhere else.
If the crime was committed in a public restroom, for example,
Wouldn't the weapon be there?
Th... then...
Wouldn't the killer... have left the body in the restroom, too?
...
See? It's a contradiction!!
If... if the killer...
was trying to make us think that the murder happened in the alley where we found her...
he would have...taken the weapon with him...and left it there.
But if he really just left the weapon in the place where she was killed...
then wouldn't he have left the body there, too?

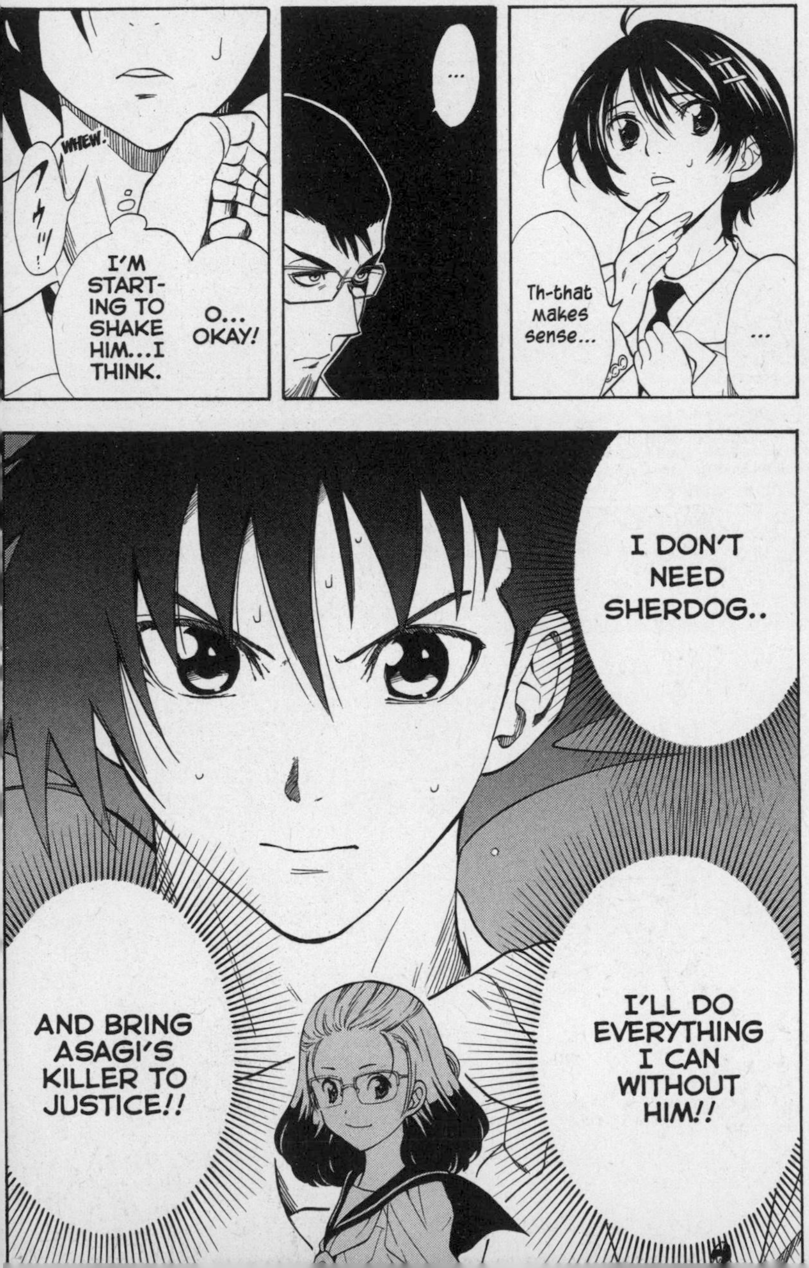
Th-that makes sense...
...
...
WHEW.
I'M STARTING TO SHAKE HIM...I THINK.
O... OKAY!
I DON'T NEED SHERDOG..
I'LL DO EVERYTHING I CAN WITHOUT HIM!!
AND BRING ASAGI'S KILLER TO JUSTICE!!

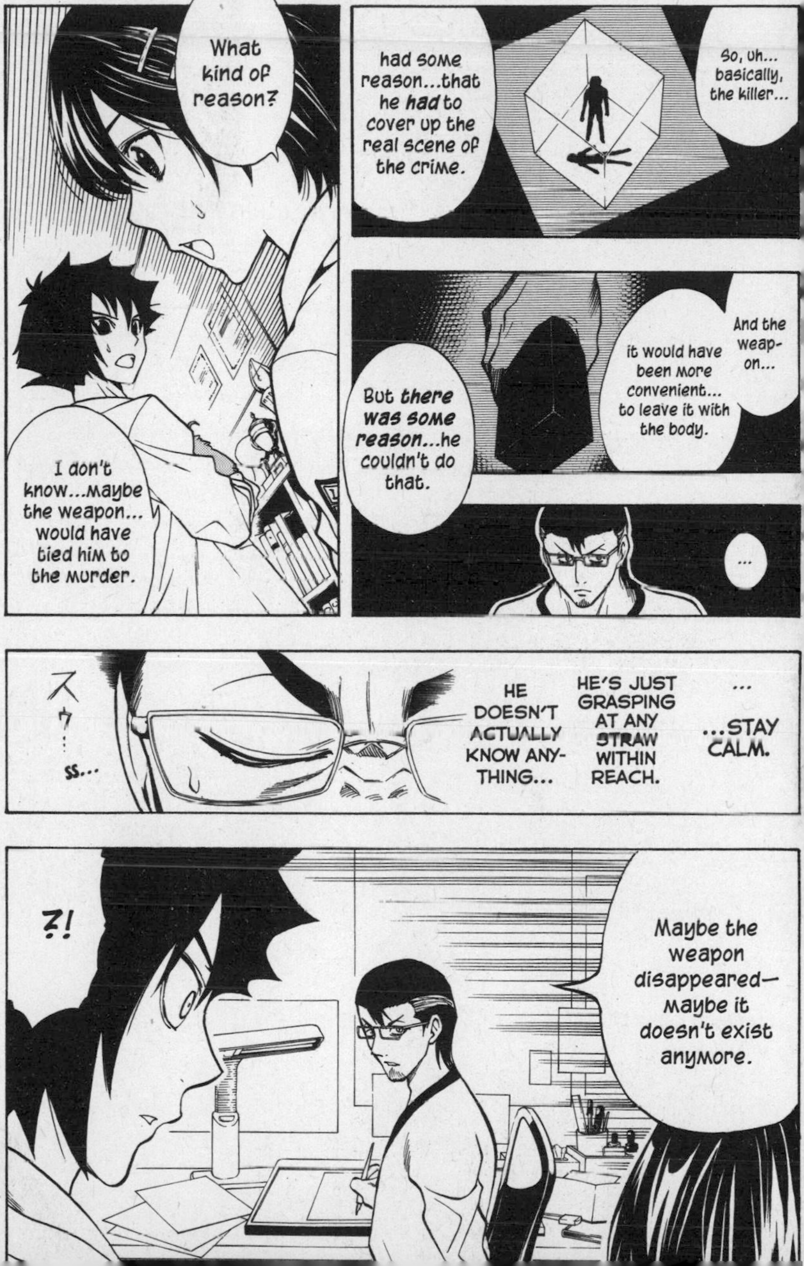
So, uh... basically, the killer...
had some reason...that he *had* to cover up the real scene of the crime.
And the weap-on...
it would have been more convenient... to leave it with the body.
But ***there was some reason...***he couldn't do that.
...
What kind of reason?
I don't know...maybe the weapon... would have tied him to the murder.
...
...STAY CALM.
HE'S JUST GRASPING AT ANY STRAW WITHIN REACH.
HE DOESN'T ACTUALLY KNOW ANY-THING...
スウ…
ss...
Maybe the weapon disappeared—maybe it doesn't exist anymore.
?!

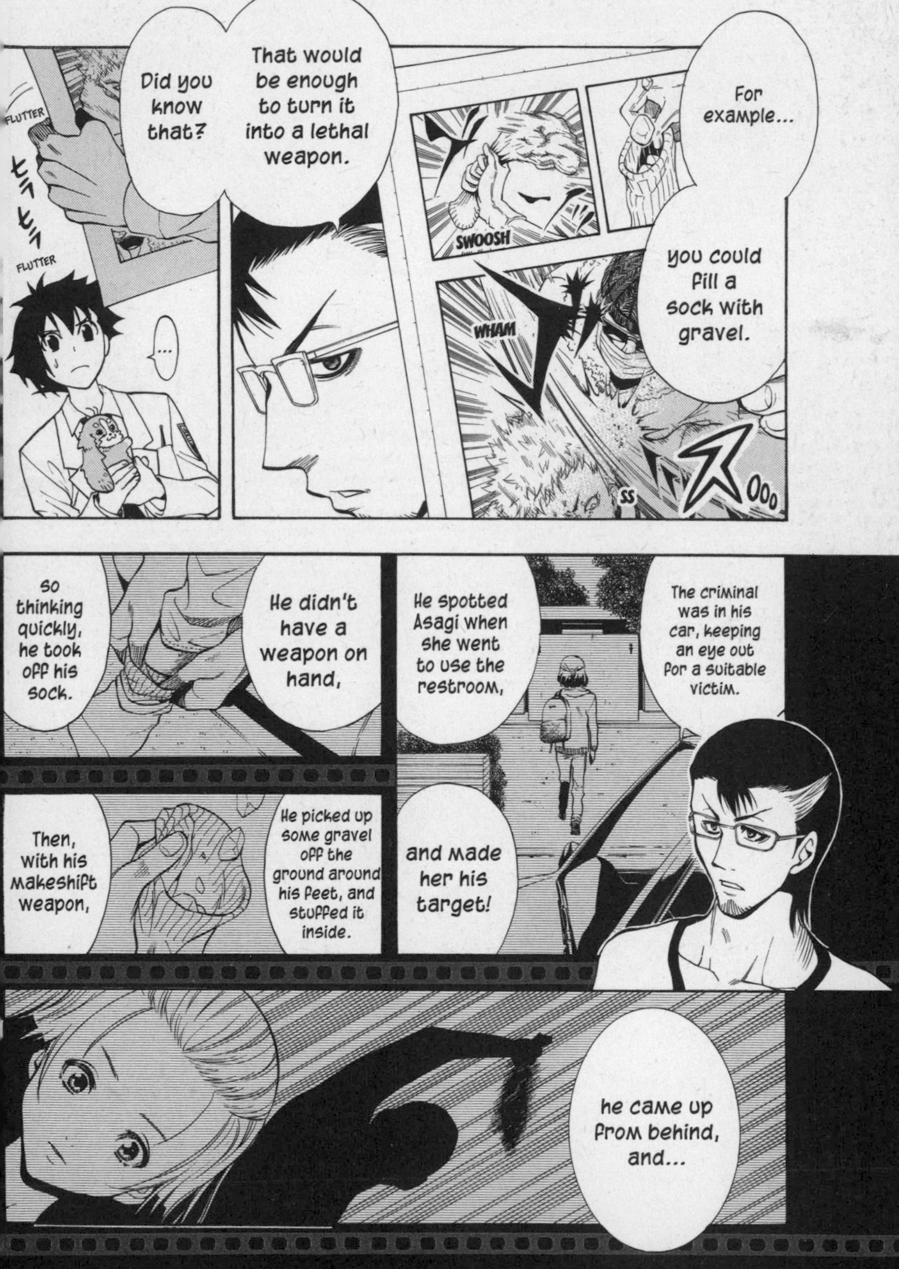
For example...
SWOOSH
WHAM
you could fill a sock with gravel.
SS
Ooo
That would be enough to turn it into a lethal weapon.
Did you know that?
FLUTTER
FLUTTER
...
The criminal was in his car, keeping an eye out for a suitable victim.
He spotted Asagi when she went to use the restroom,
and made her his target!
He didn't have a weapon on hand,
so thinking quickly, he took off his sock.
He picked up some gravel off the ground around his feet, and stuffed it inside.
Then, with his makeshift weapon,
he came up from behind, and...

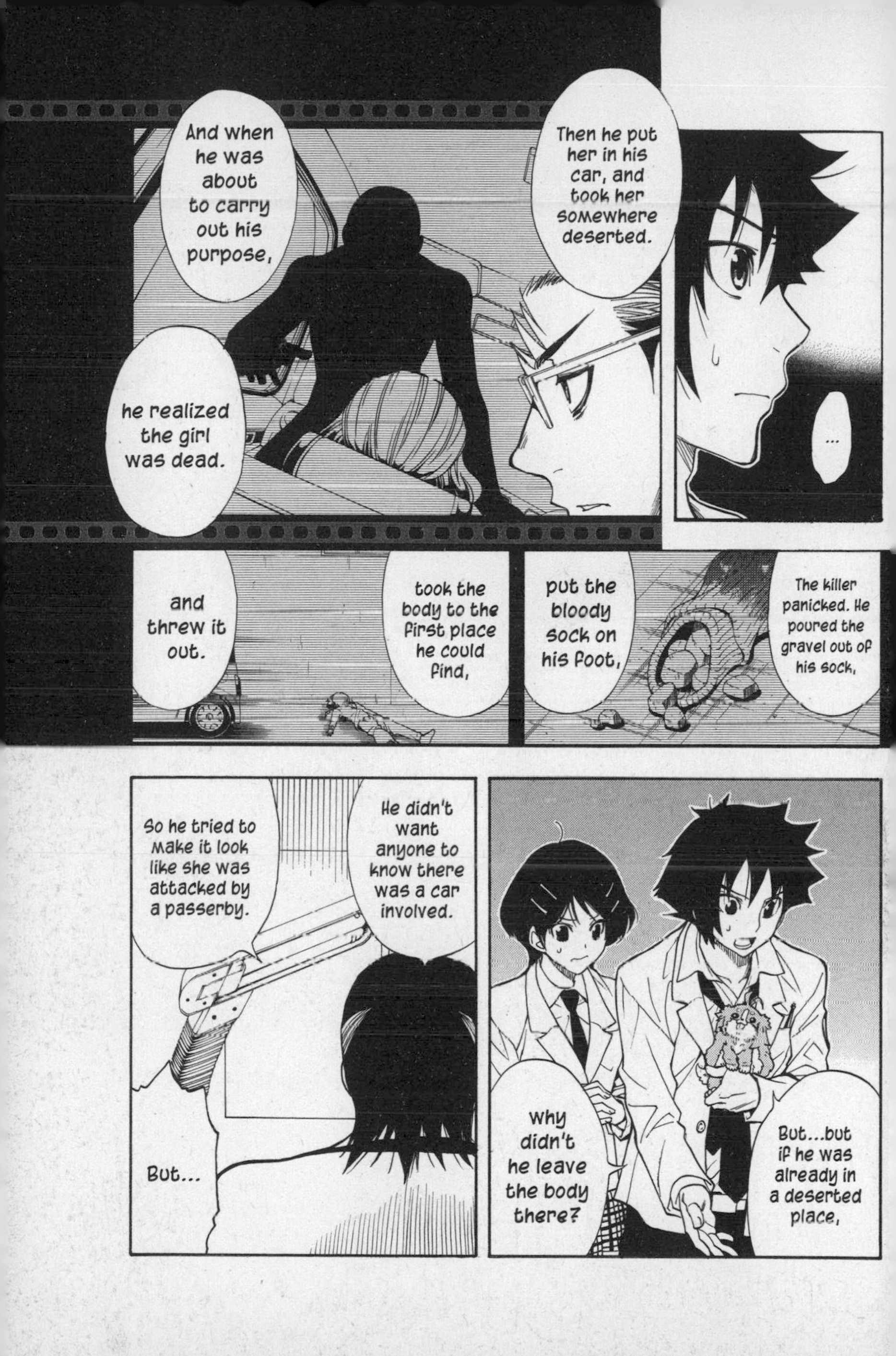
...
Then he put her in his car, and took her somewhere deserted.
And when he was about to carry out his purpose,
he realized the girl was dead.
The killer panicked. He poured the gravel out of his sock,
put the bloody sock on his foot,
took the body to the first place he could find,
and threw it out.
But...but if he was already in a deserted place,
Why didn't he leave the body there?
He didn't want anyone to know there was a car involved.
So he tried to make it look like she was attacked by a passerby.
But...

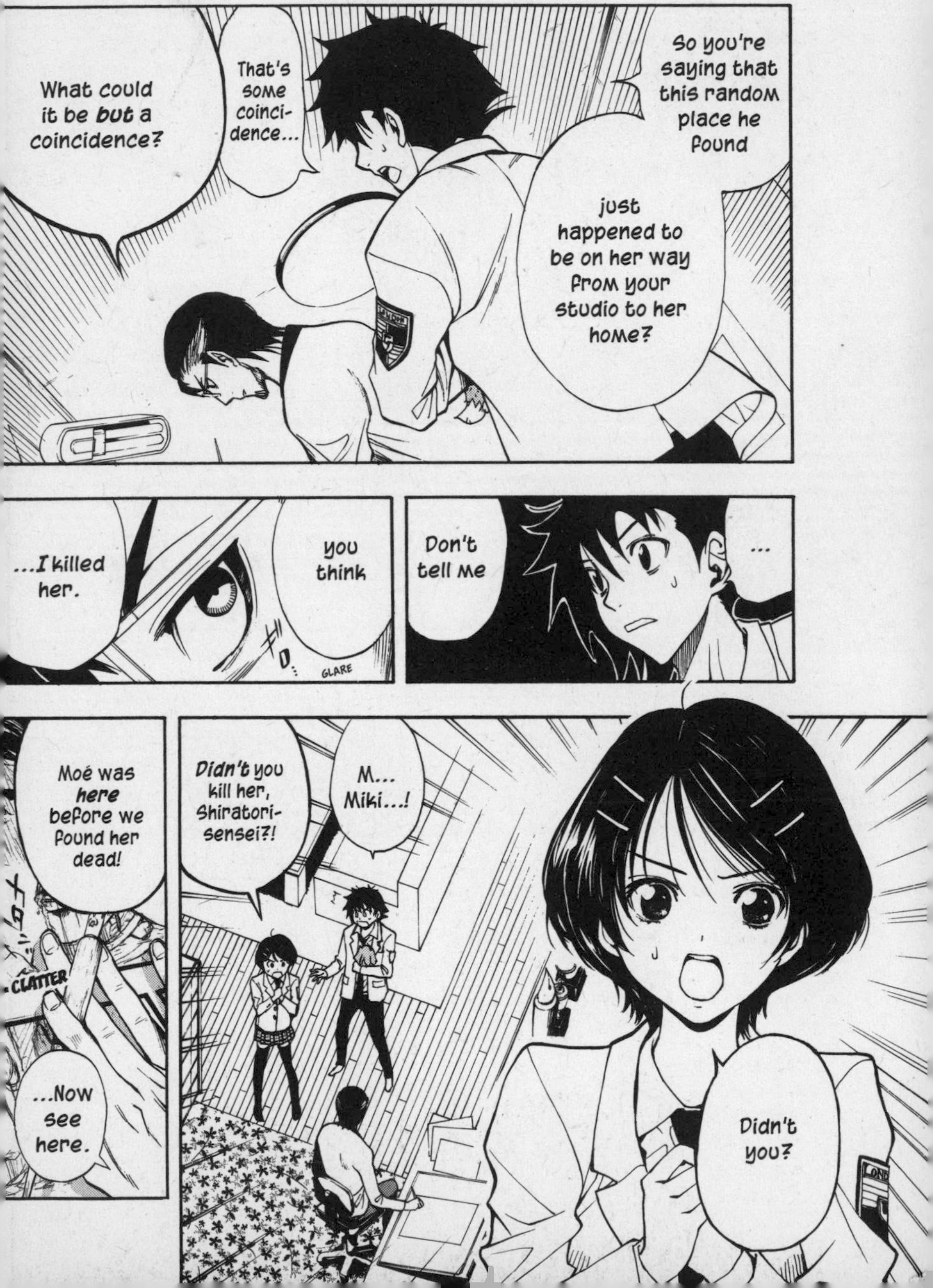
So you're saying that this random place he found
just happened to be on her way from your studio to her home?
That's some coincidence...
What could it be *but* a coincidence?
...
Don't tell me
you think
...I killed her.
GLARE
M... Miki...!
Didn't you kill her, Shiratori-sensei?!
Didn't you?
Moé was *here* before we found her dead!
CLATTER
...Now see here.

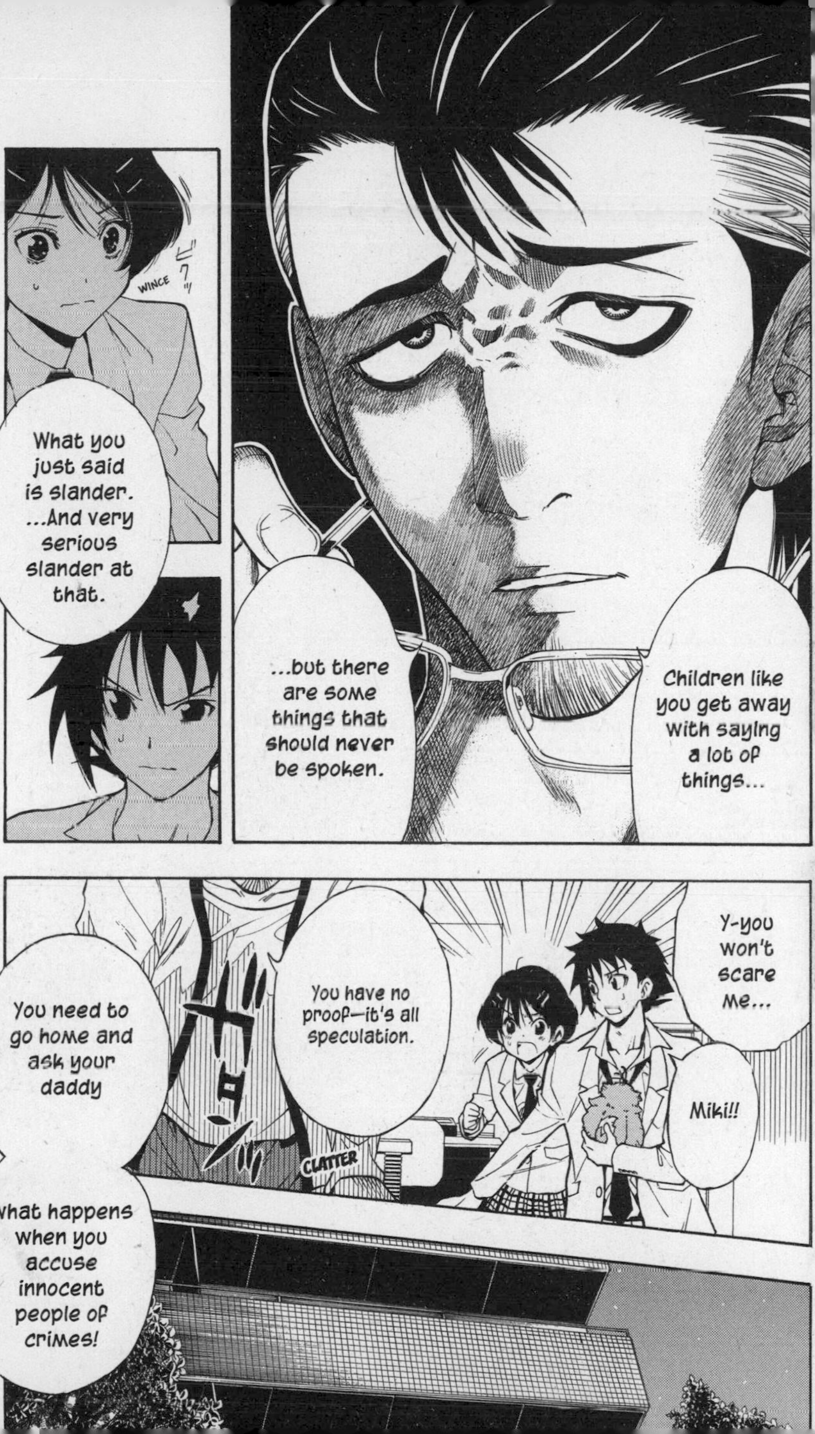
Children like you get away with saying a lot of things...
...but there are some things that should never be spoken.
WINCE
What you just said is slander. ...And very serious slander at that.
Y-you won't scare me...
Miki!!
You have no proof—it's all speculation.
CLATTER
You need to go home and ask your daddy
what happens when you accuse innocent people of crimes!

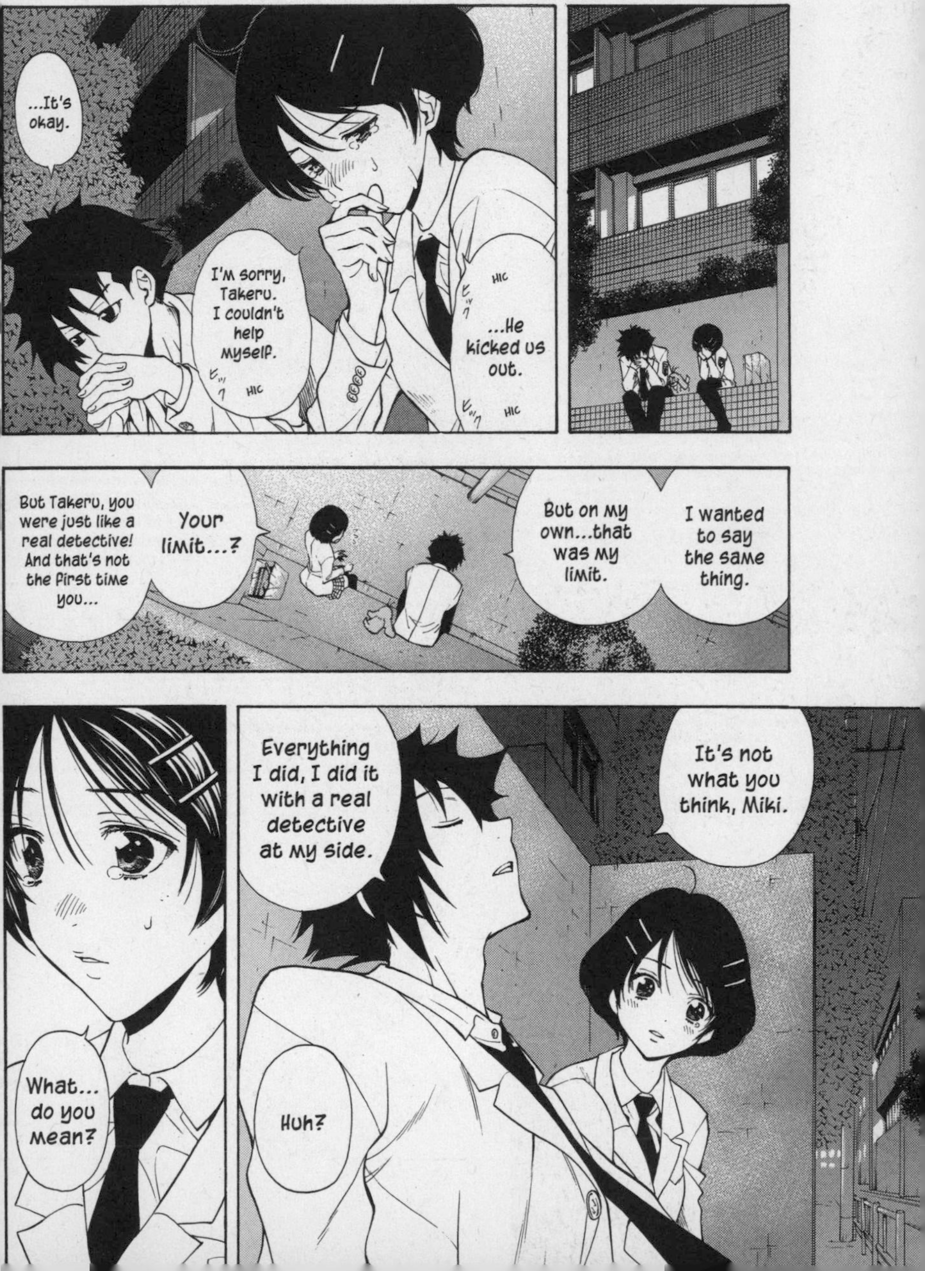

...He kicked us out.
HIC
HIC
I'm sorry, Takeru. I couldn't help myself.
HIC
...It's okay.
I wanted to say the same thing.
But on my own...that was my limit.
Your limit...?
But Takeru, you were just like a real detective! And that's not the first time you...
It's not what you think, Miki.
Everything I did, I did it with a real detective at my side.
Huh?
What... do you mean?

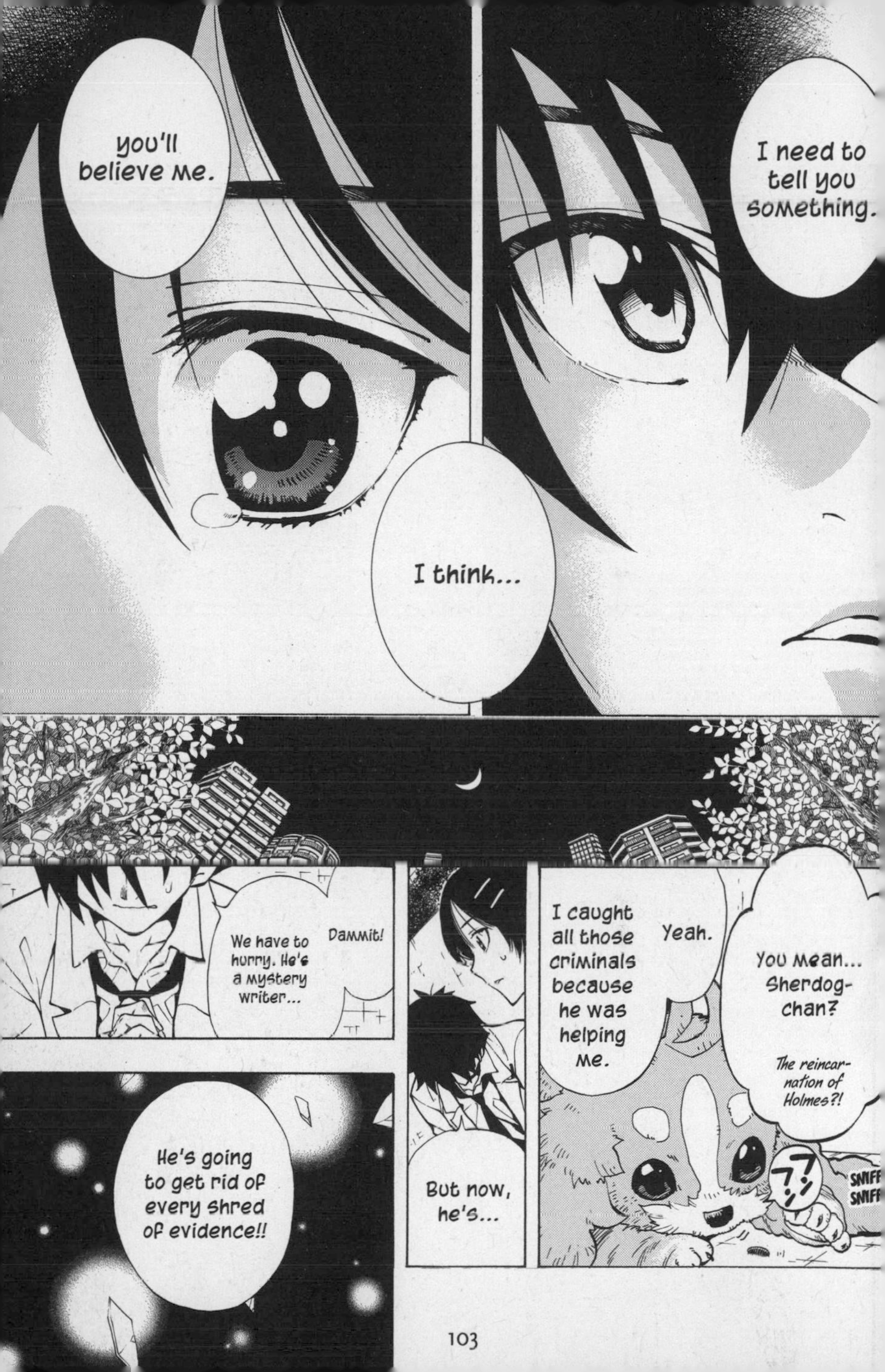
I need to tell you something.
I think...
you'll believe me.
You mean... Sherdog-chan?
The reincarnation of Holmes?!
SNIFF SNIFF
Yeah.
I caught all those criminals because he was helping me.
But now, he's...
Dammit!
We have to hurry. He's a mystery writer...
He's going to get rid of every shred of evidence!!

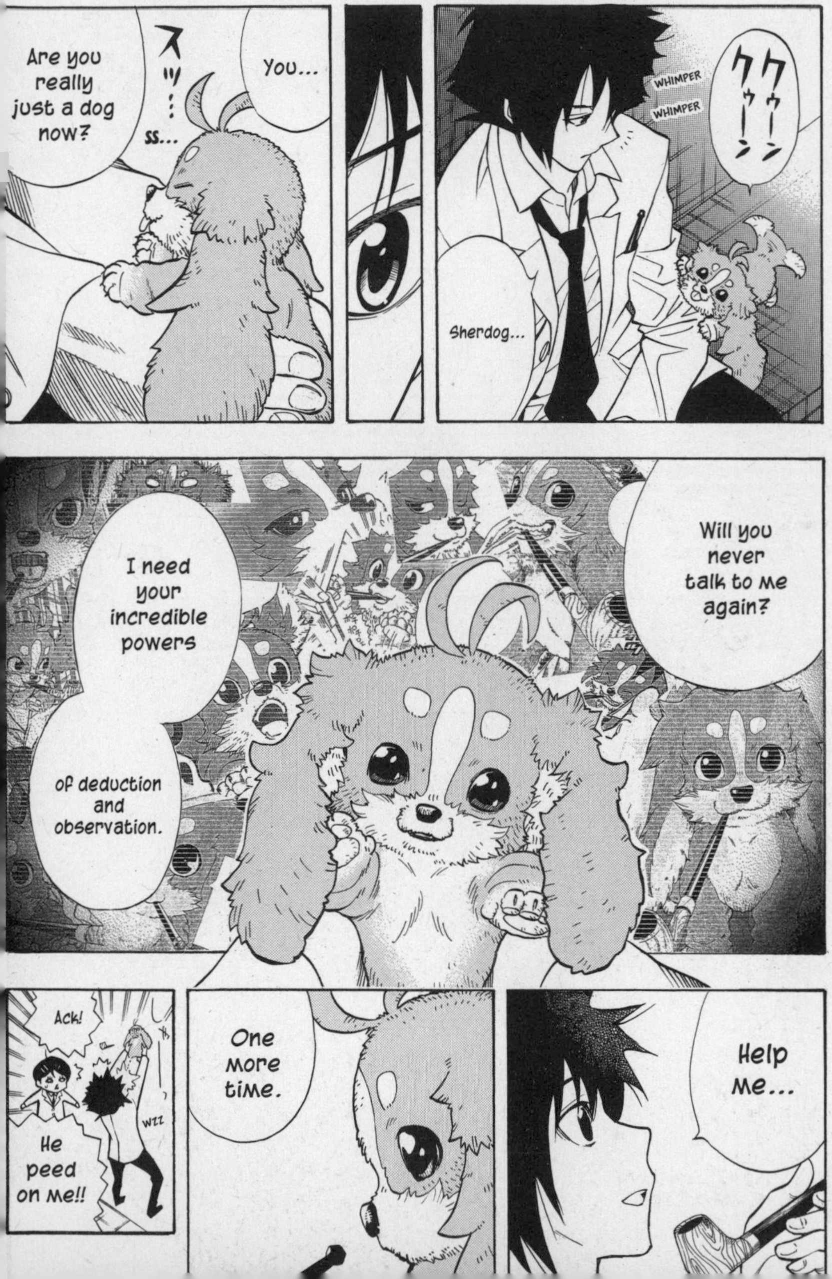
クゥーン クゥーン
WHIMPER
WHIMPER
Sherdog...
You...
スッ…
ss...
Are you really just a dog now?
Will you never talk to me again?
I need your incredible powers
of deduction and observation.
Help me...
One more time.
Ack!
WZZ
He peed on me!!

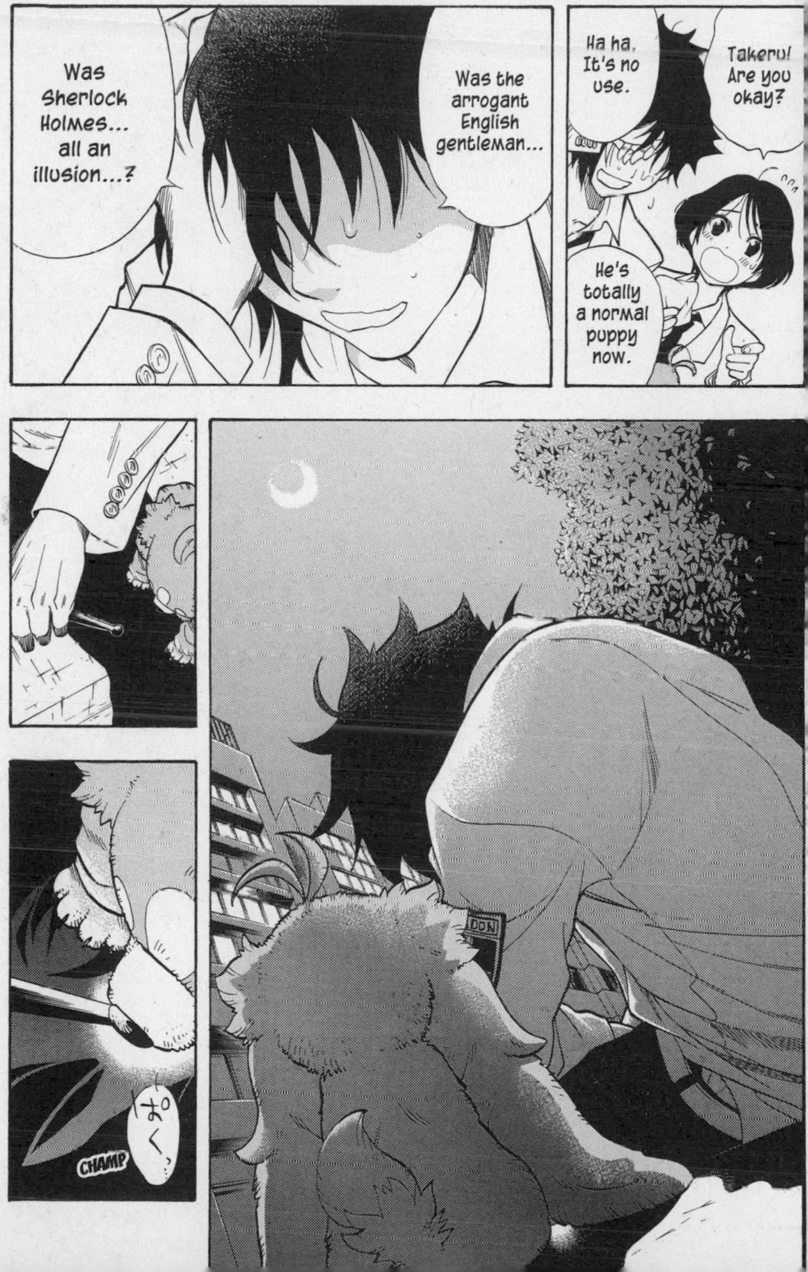
Takeru! Are you okay?
Ha ha. It's no use.
He's totally a normal puppy now.
Was the arrogant English gentleman...
Was Sherlock Holmes... all an illusion...?
ぱく
CHAMP

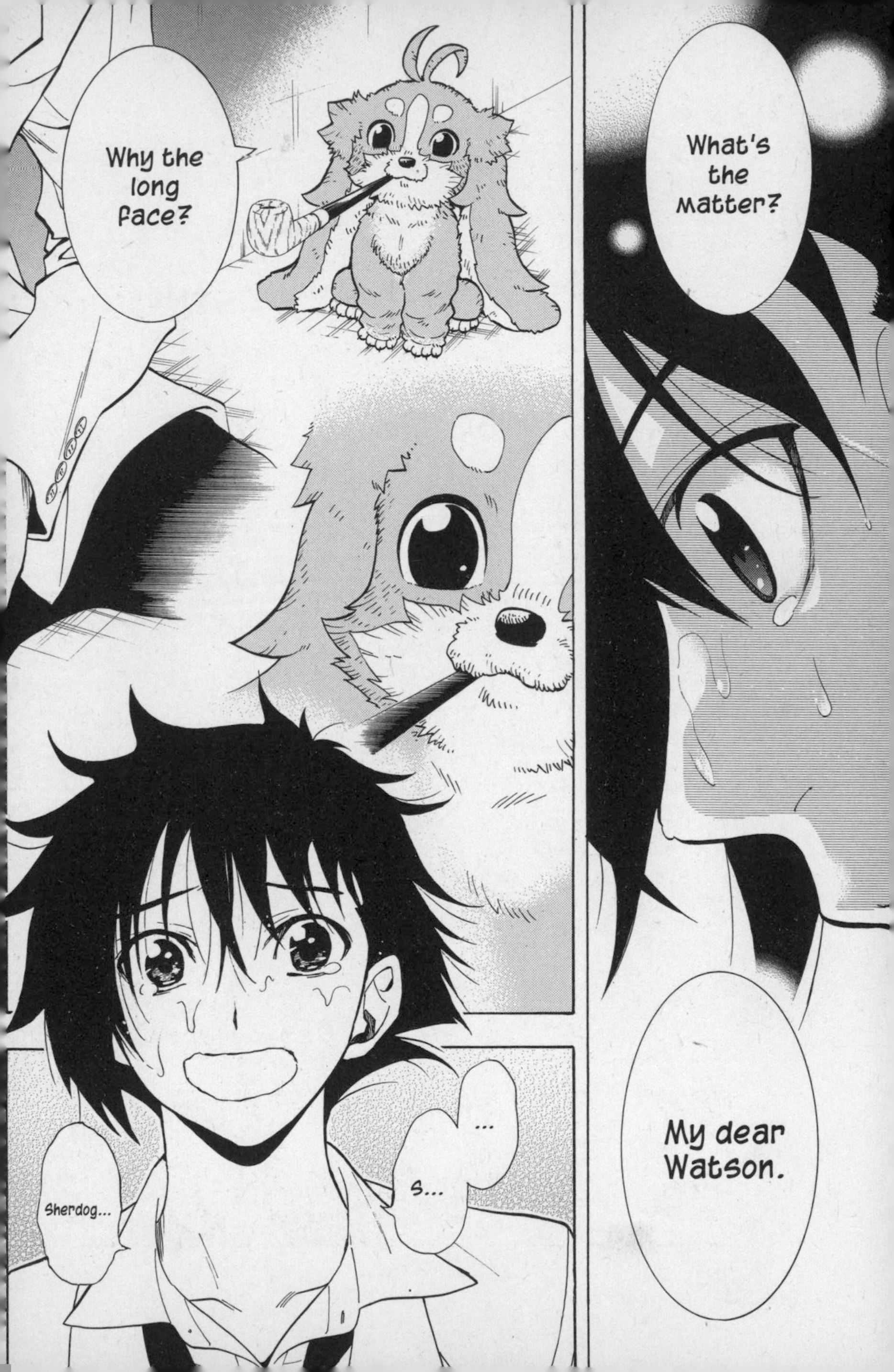
What's the matter?
Why the long face?
My dear Watson.
...
S...
Sherdog...

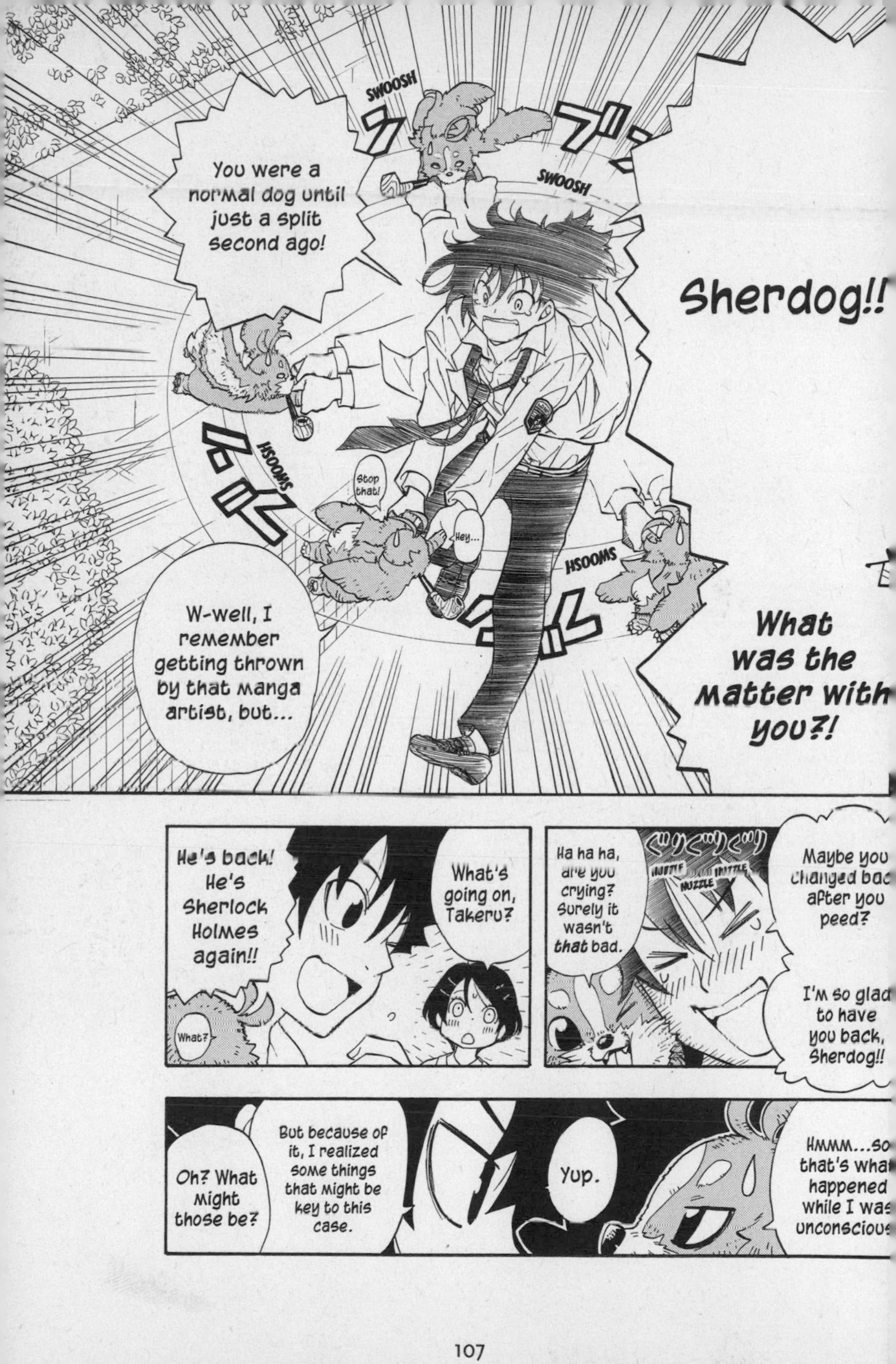

SWOOSH
SWOOSH
Sherdog!!
What was the matter with you?!
You were a normal dog until just a split second ago!
HSOOMS
HSOOMS
Stop that!
Hey...
W-well, I remember getting thrown by that manga artist, but...
Maybe you changed bac after you peed?
I'm so glad to have you back, Sherdog!!
NUZZLE
NUZZLE
NUZZLE
Ha ha ha, are you crying? Surely it wasn't *that* bad.
What's going on, Takeru?
He's back! He's Sherlock Holmes again!!
What?
HMMM...so that's wha happened while I was unconsciou
Yup.
But because of it, I realized some things that might be key to this case.
Oh? What might those be?

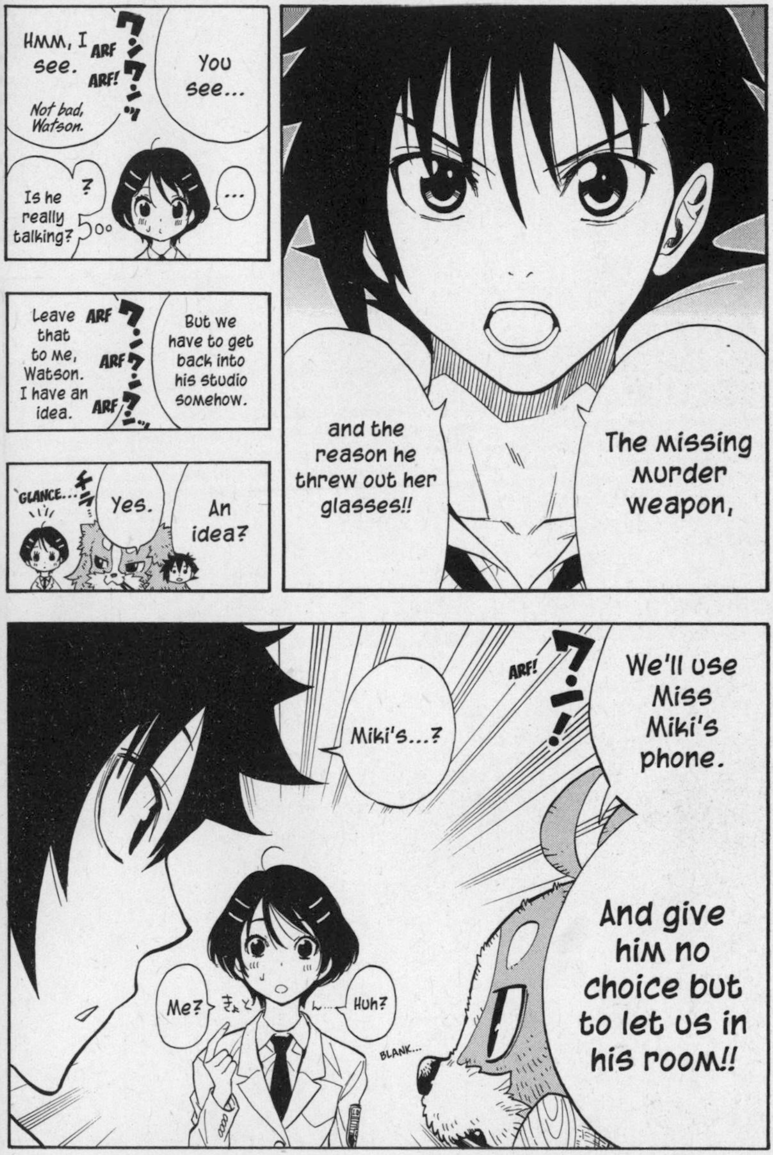
The missing murder weapon,
and the reason he threw out her glasses!!
You see...
ARF
ARF!
Hmm, I see.
Not bad, Watson.
...
?
Is he really talking?
But we have to get back into his studio somehow.
ARF
ARF
ARF
Leave that to me, Watson. I have an idea.
An idea?
Yes.
GLANCE...
We'll use Miss Miki's phone.
ARF!
Miki's...?
And give him no choice but to let us in his room!!
Huh?
BLANK...
Me?

Case 5: ⚜ The Missing Murder Weapon, Part 4

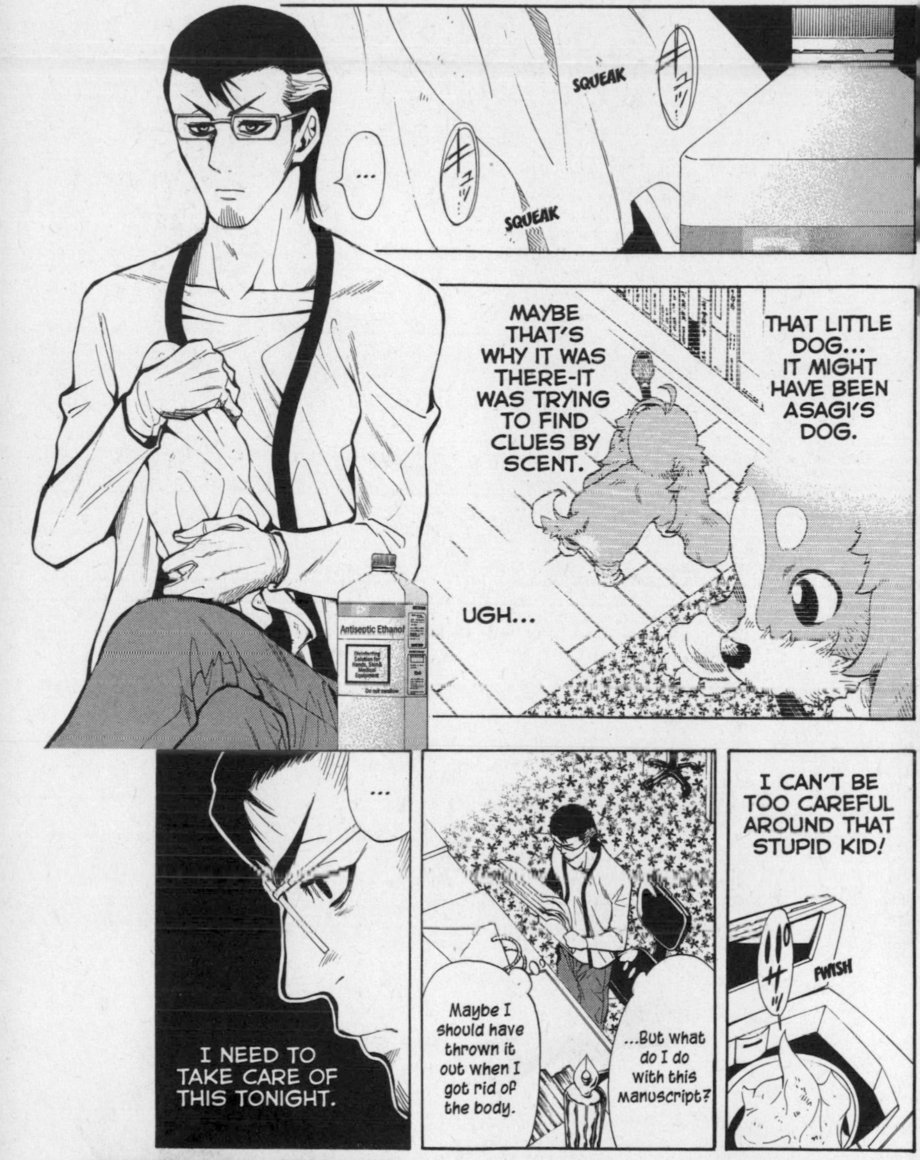
SQUEAK
...
SQUEAK
THAT LITTLE DOG... IT MIGHT HAVE BEEN ASAGI'S DOG.
MAYBE THAT'S WHY IT WAS THERE-IT WAS TRYING TO FIND CLUES BY SCENT.
UGH...
Antiseptic Ethanol
I CAN'T BE TOO CAREFUL AROUND THAT STUPID KID!
FWISH
...But what do I do with this manuscript?
Maybe I should have thrown it out when I got rid of the body.
...
I NEED TO TAKE CARE OF THIS TONIGHT.

SHERLOCK BONES

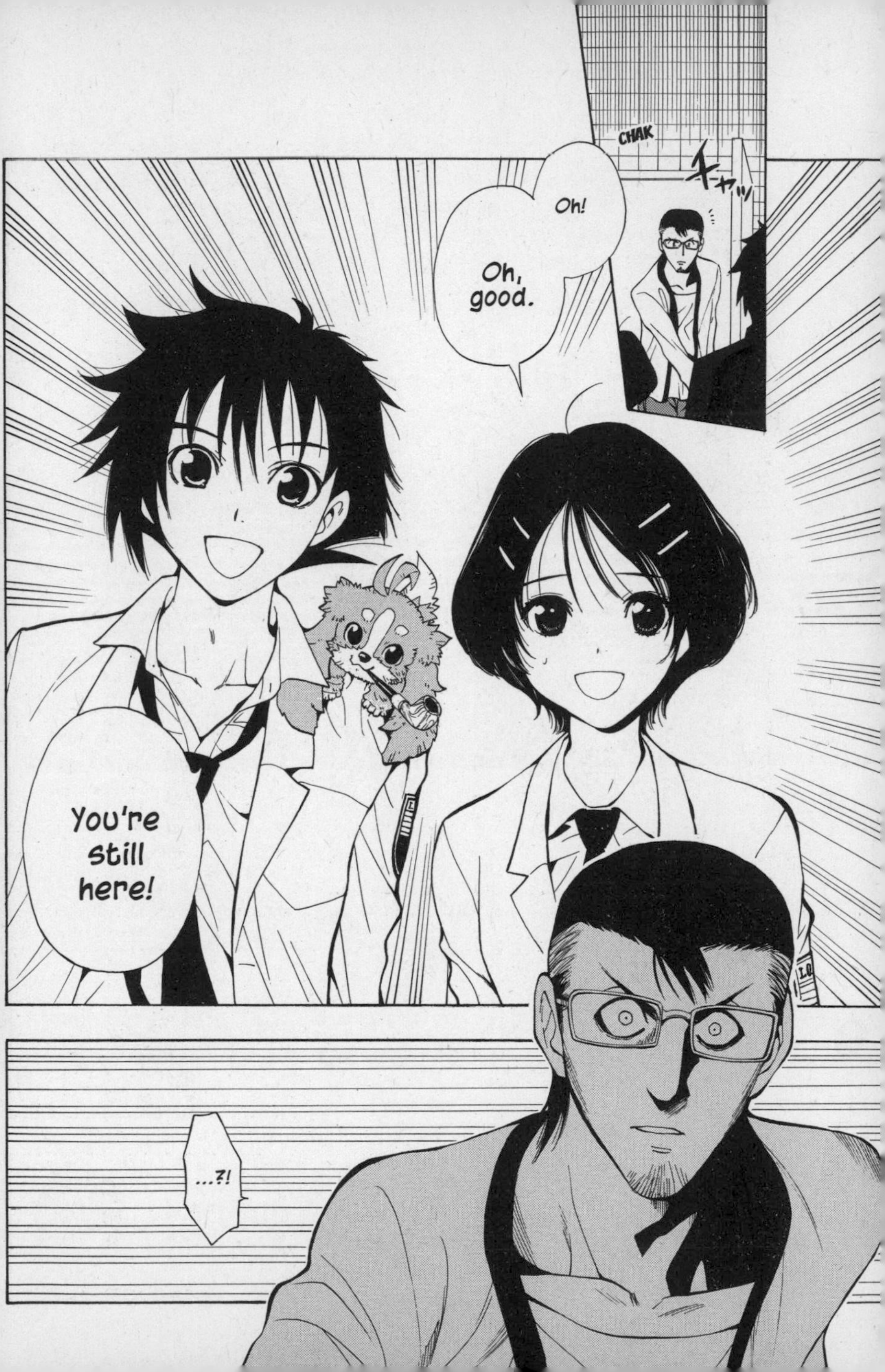
CHAK
Oh!
Oh, good.
You're still here!
...?!

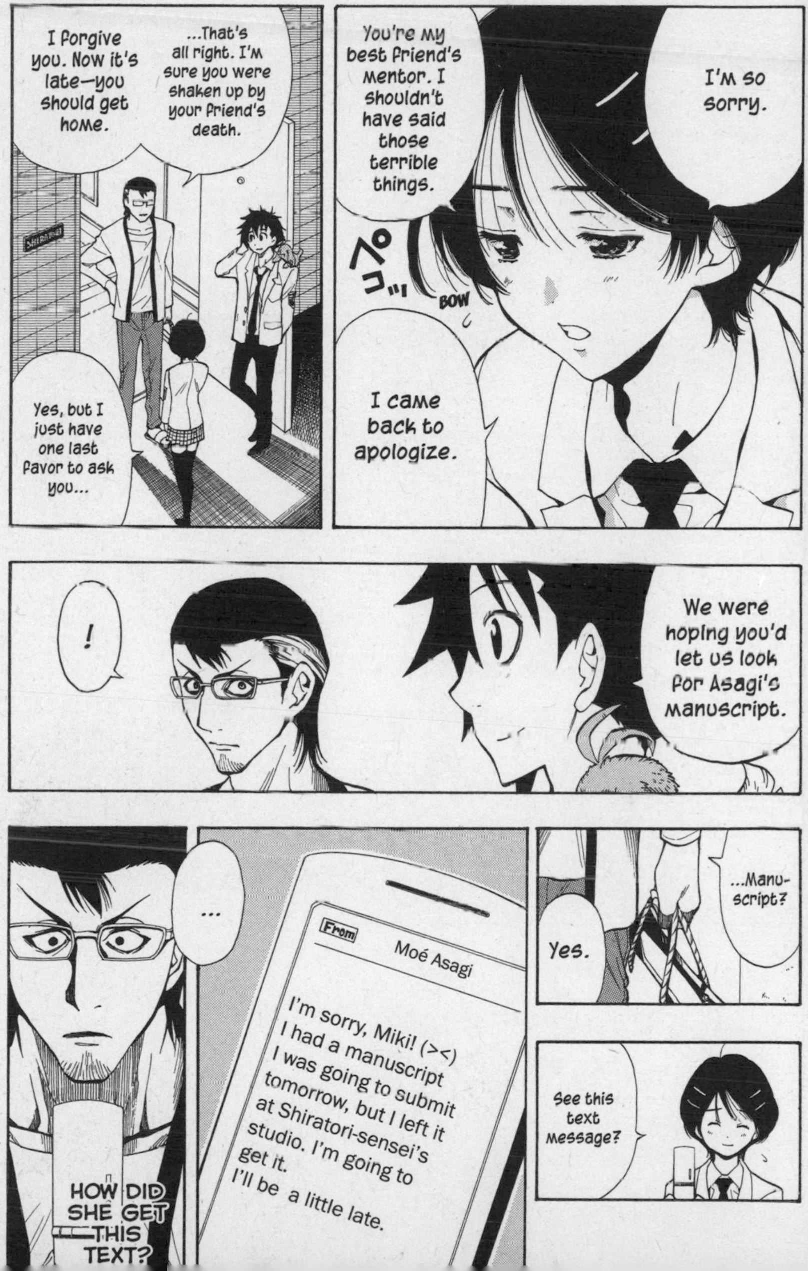
I'm so sorry.
You're my best friend's mentor. I shouldn't have said those terrible things.
ペコッ
BOW
I came back to apologize.
...That's all right. I'm sure you were shaken up by your friend's death.
I forgive you. Now it's late—you should get home.
Yes, but I just have one last favor to ask you...
We were hoping you'd let us look for Asagi's manuscript.
!
...Manu-script?
Yes.
See this text message?
From
Moé Asagi
I'm sorry, Miki! (><) I had a manuscript I was going to submit tomorrow, but I left it at Shiratori-sensei's studio. I'm going to get it. I'll be a little late.
...
HOW DID SHE GET THIS TEXT?

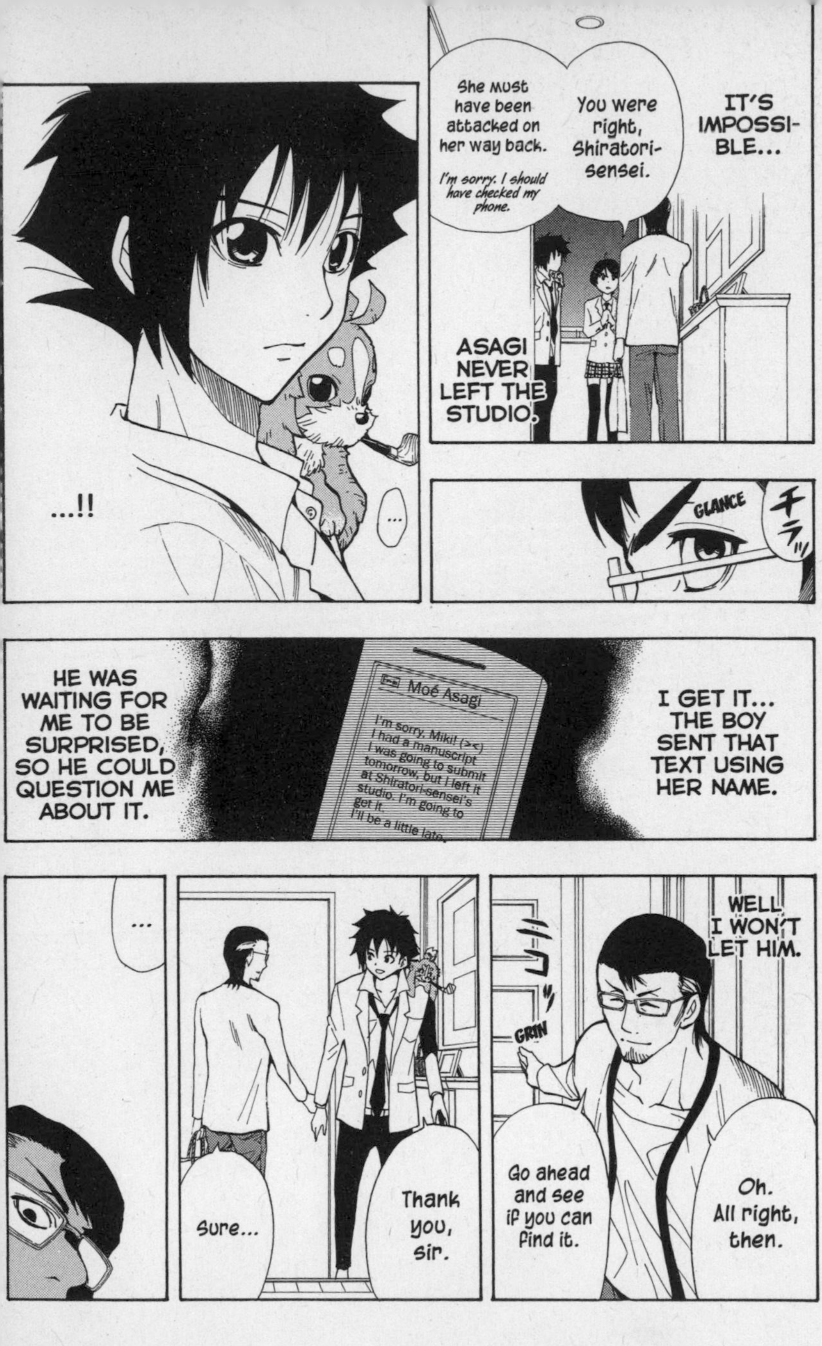
IT'S IMPOSSIBLE...
You were right, Shiratori-sensei.
She must have been attacked on her way back.
I'm sorry. I should have checked my phone.
ASAGI NEVER LEFT THE STUDIO.
チラッ
GLANCE
...
...!!
I GET IT... THE BOY SENT THAT TEXT USING HER NAME.
Moé Asagi
I'm sorry, Miki! (><) I had a manuscript I was going to submit tomorrow, but I left it at Shiratori-sensei's studio. I'm going to get it. I'll be a little late.
HE WAS WAITING FOR ME TO BE SURPRISED, SO HE COULD QUESTION ME ABOUT IT.
WELL I WON'T LET HIM.
ニコッ
GRIN
Oh. All right, then.
Go ahead and see if you can find it.
Thank you, sir.
Sure...
...

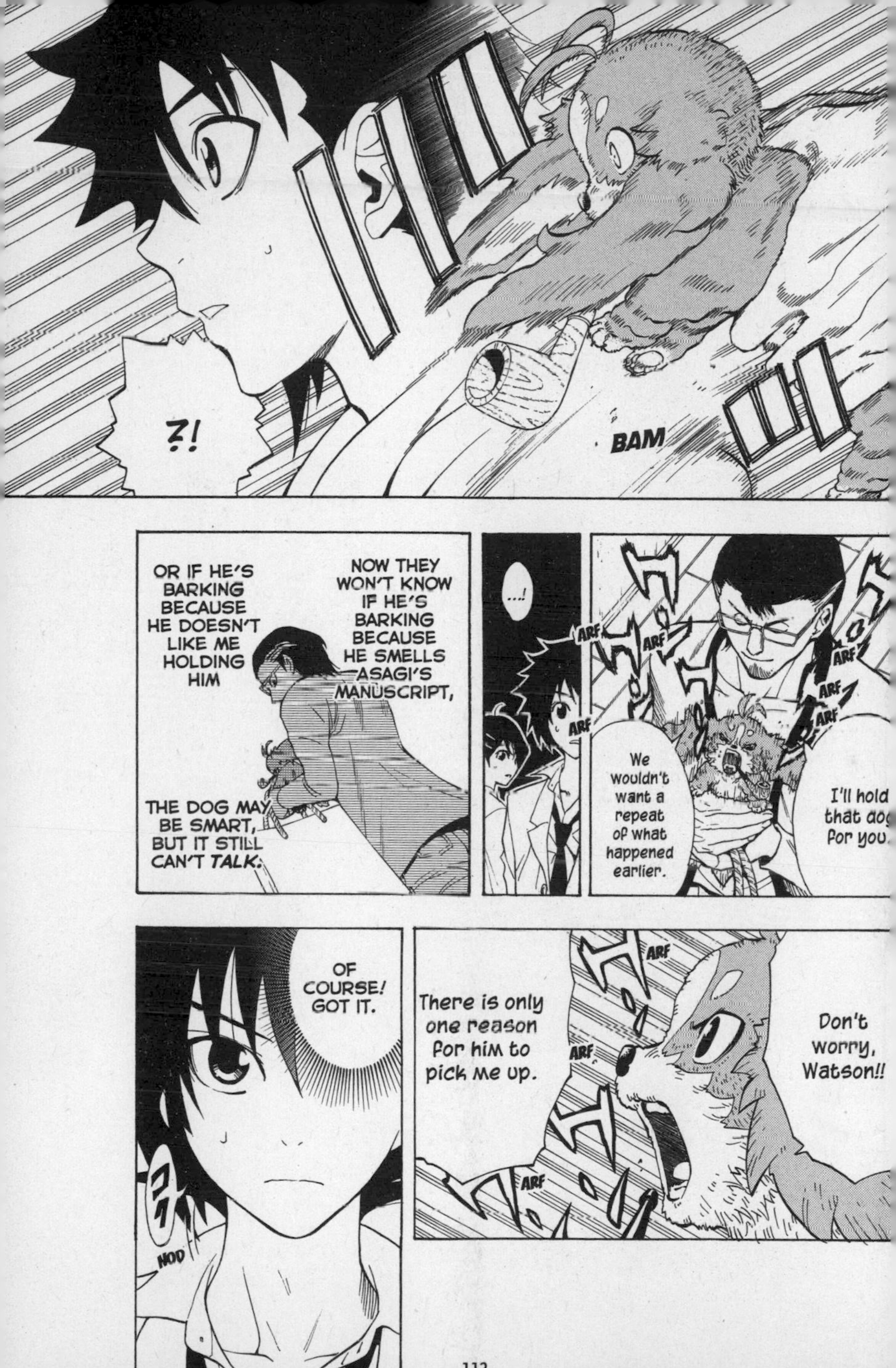
BAM
?!
I'll hold that do for you.
ARF
ARF
ARF
ARF
We wouldn't want a repeat of what happened earlier.
ARF
ARF
...!
NOW THEY WON'T KNOW IF HE'S BARKING BECAUSE HE SMELLS ASAGI'S MANUSCRIPT,
OR IF HE'S BARKING BECAUSE HE DOESN'T LIKE ME HOLDING HIM
THE DOG MAY BE SMART, BUT IT STILL CAN'T *TALK.*
Don't worry, Watson!!
ARF
There is only one reason for him to pick me up.
ARF
ARF
OF COURSE! GOT IT.
NOD

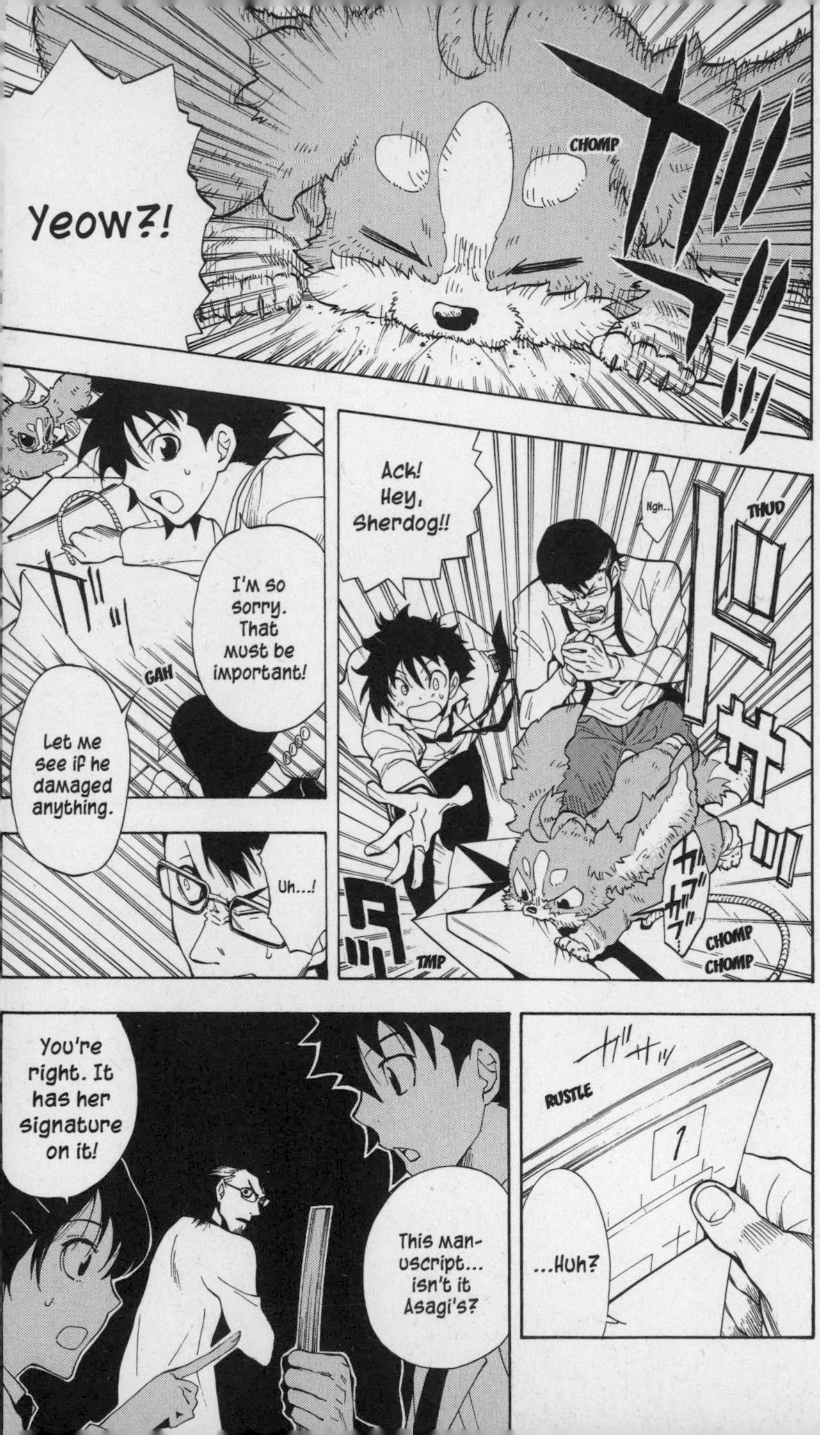
CHOMP
Yeow?!
THUD
Ngh..
Ack! Hey, Sherdog!!
CHOMP CHOMP
TMP
I'm so sorry. That must be important!
GAH
Let me see if he damaged anything.
Uh...!
RUSTLE
1
...Huh?
This man-uscript... isn't it Asagi's?
You're right. It has her signature on it!

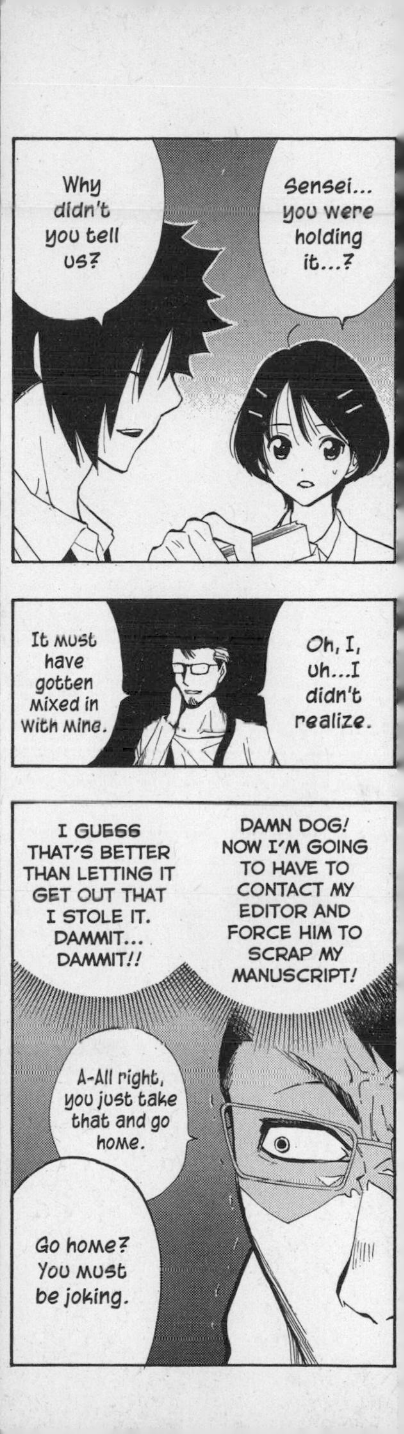
Sensei... you were holding it...?
Why didn't you tell us?
Oh, I, uh...I didn't realize.
It must have gotten mixed in with mine.
DAMN DOG! NOW I'M GOING TO HAVE TO CONTACT MY EDITOR AND FORCE HIM TO SCRAP MY MANUSCRIPT!
I GUESS THAT'S BETTER THAN LETTING IT GET OUT THAT I STOLE IT. DAMMIT... DAMMIT!!
A-All right, you just take that and go home.
Go home? You must be joking.
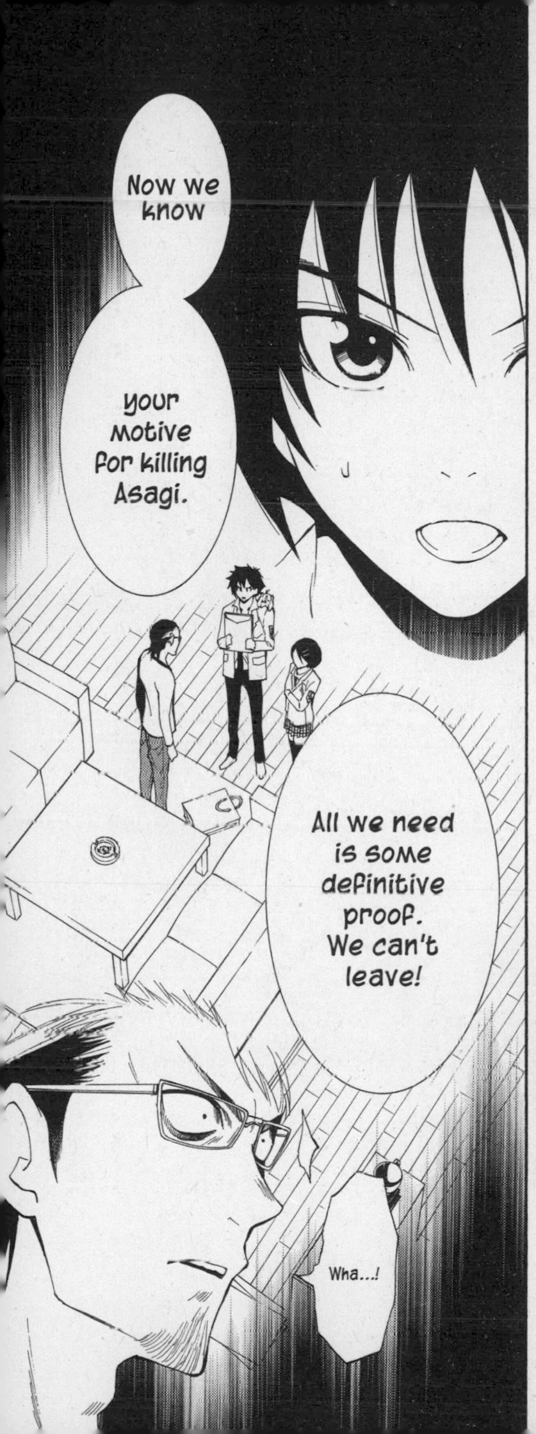
Now we know
your motive for killing Asagi.
All we need is some definitive proof. We can't leave!
Wha...!

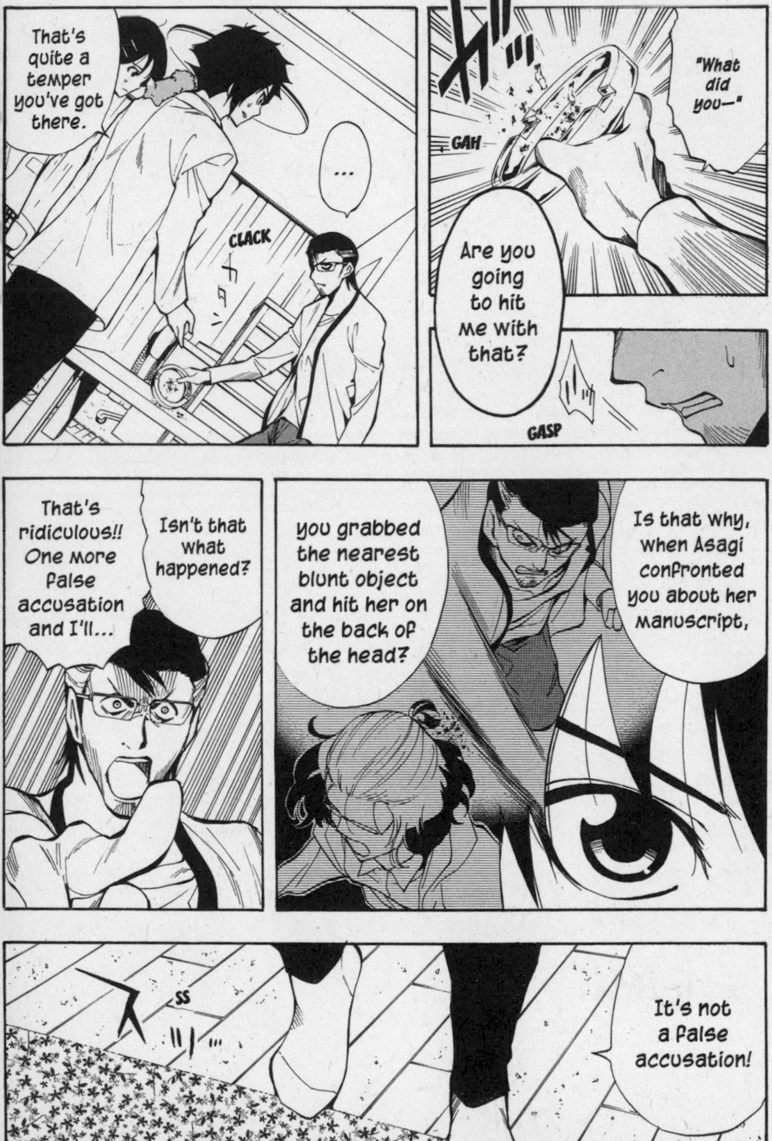

"What did you—"
GAH
Are you going to hit me with that?
GASP
That's quite a temper you've got there.
...
CLACK
Is that why, when Asagi confronted you about her manuscript,
you grabbed the nearest blunt object and hit her on the back of the head?
Isn't that what happened?
That's ridiculous!! One more false accusation and I'll...
It's not a false accusation!
SS

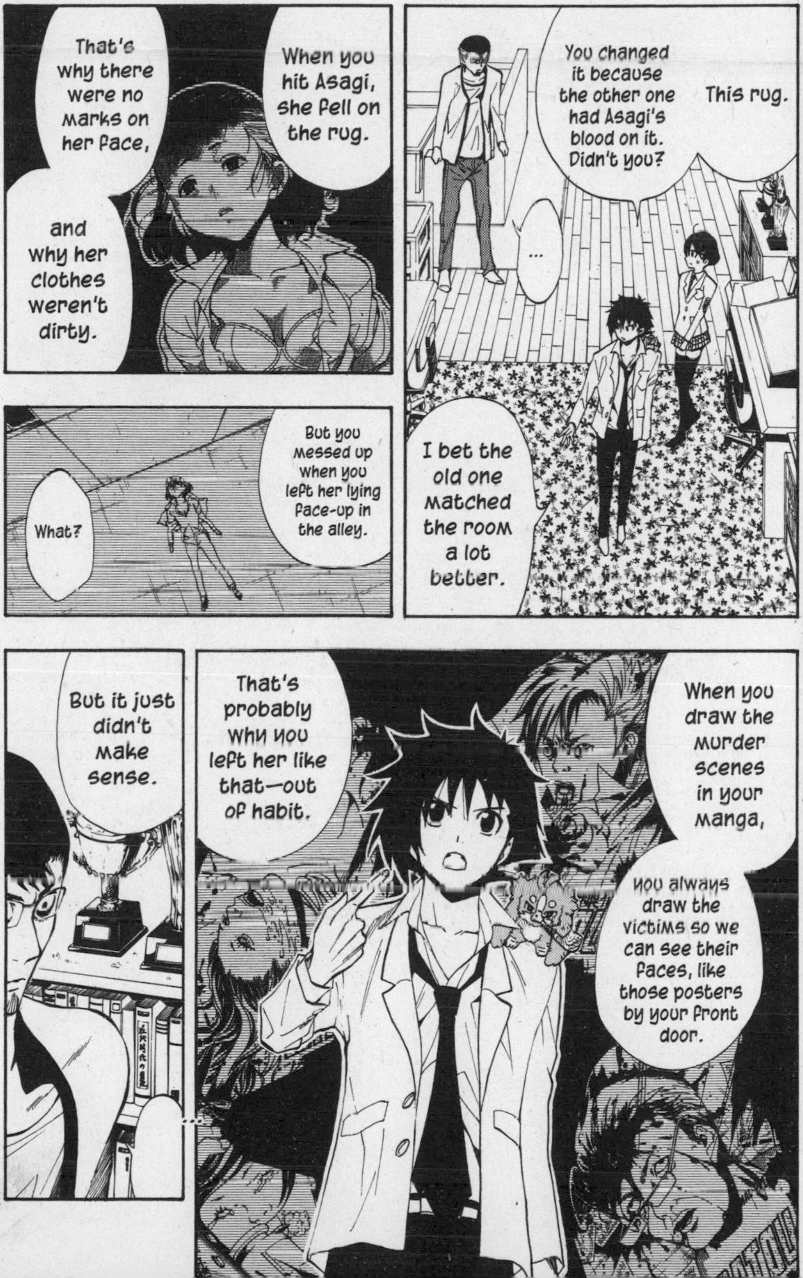
This rug.
You changed it because the other one had Asagi's blood on it. Didn't you?
...
I bet the old one matched the room a lot better.
When you hit Asagi, she fell on the rug.
That's why there were no marks on her face,
and why her clothes weren't dirty.
But you messed up when you left her lying face-up in the alley.
What?
When you draw the murder scenes in your manga,
you always draw the victims so we can see their faces, like those posters by your front door.
That's probably why you left her like that—out of habit.
But it just didn't make sense.
...

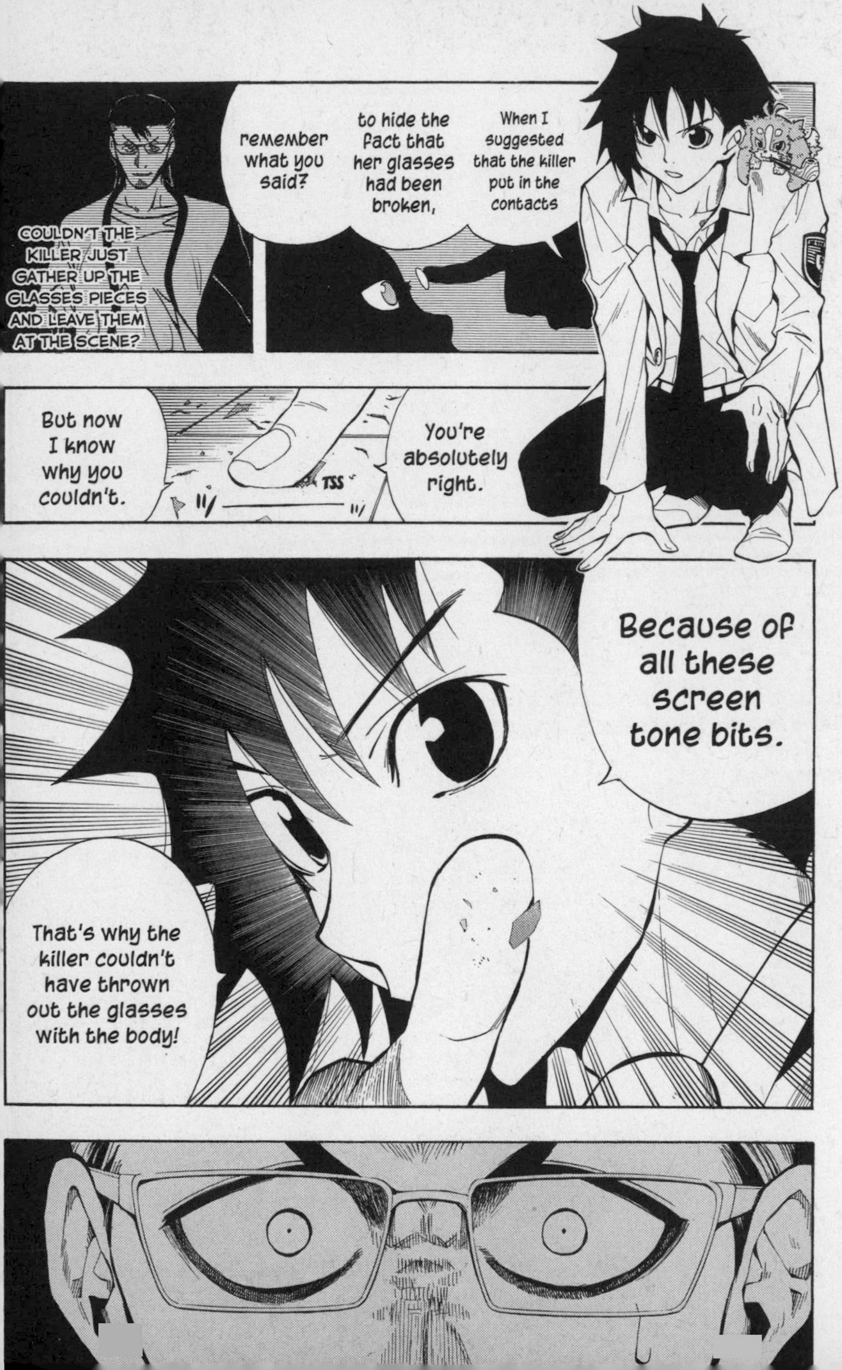
When I suggested that the killer put in the contacts
to hide the fact that her glasses had been broken,
remember what you said?
COULDN'T THE KILLER JUST GATHER UP THE GLASSES PIECES AND LEAVE THEM AT THE SCENE?
You're absolutely right.
TSS
But now I know why you couldn't.
Because of all these screen tone bits.
That's why the killer couldn't have thrown out the glasses with the body!

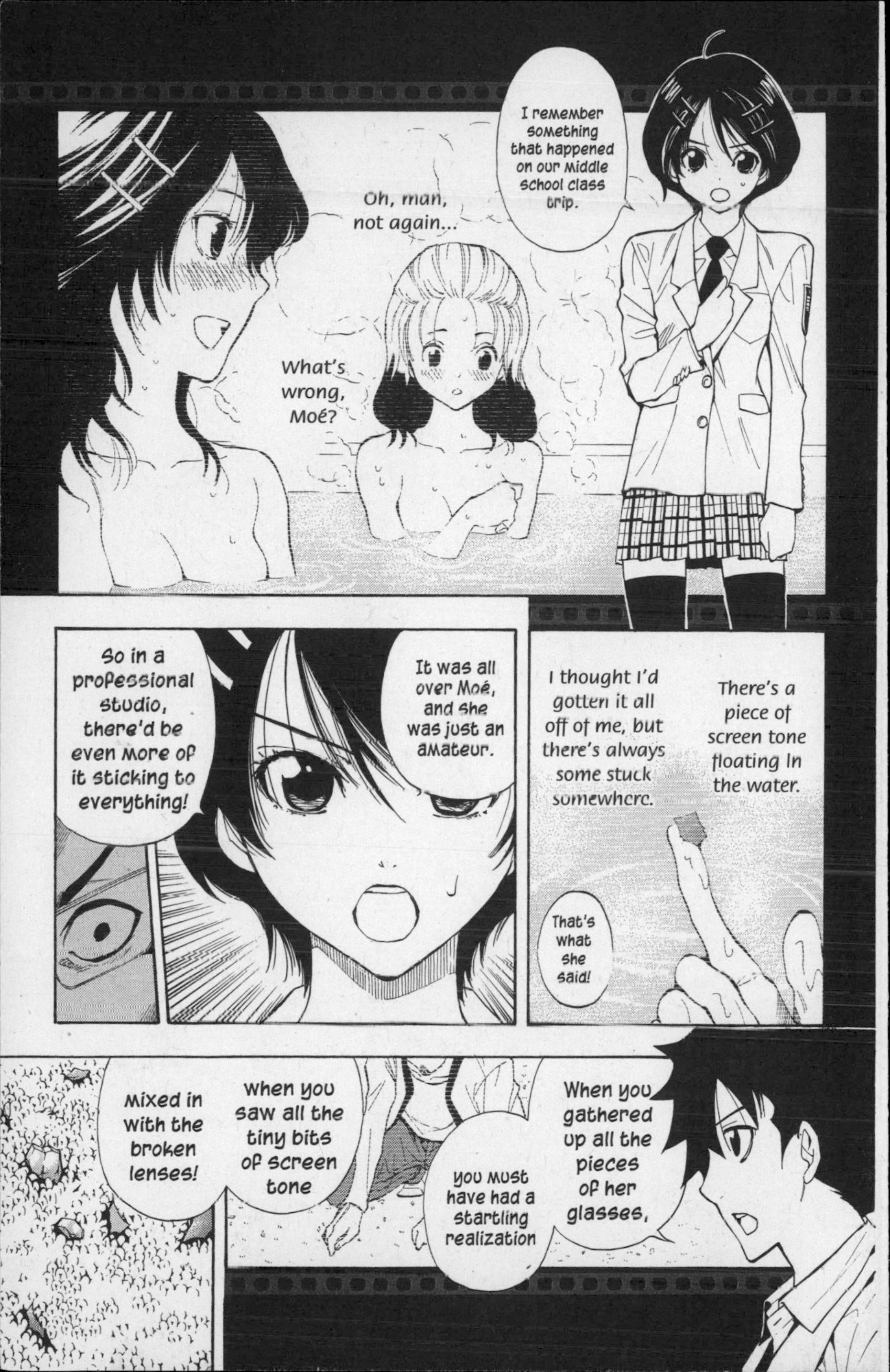
I remember something that happened on our middle school class trip.
Oh, man, not again...
What's wrong, Moé?
There's a piece of screen tone floating in the water.
I thought I'd gotten it all off of me, but there's always some stuck somewhere.
That's what she said!
It was all over Moé, and she was just an amateur.
So in a professional studio, there'd be even more of it sticking to everything!
When you gathered up all the pieces of her glasses,
you must have had a startling realization
when you saw all the tiny bits of screen tone
Mixed in with the broken lenses!

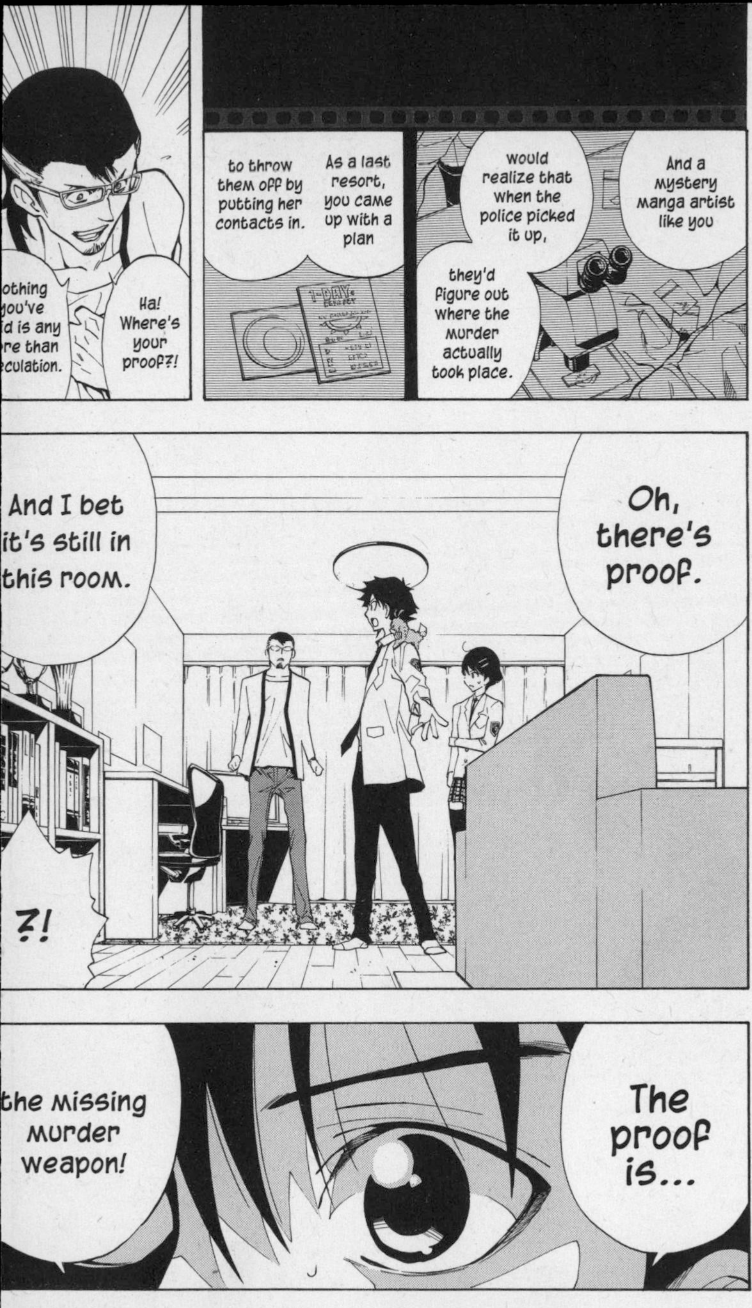
And a mystery manga artist like you
would realize that when the police picked it up,
they'd figure out where the murder actually took place.
As a last resort, you came up with a plan
to throw them off by putting her contacts in.
Ha! Where's your proof?!
othing you've d is any re than eculation.
Oh, there's proof.
And I bet it's still in this room.
?!
The proof is...
the missing murder weapon!

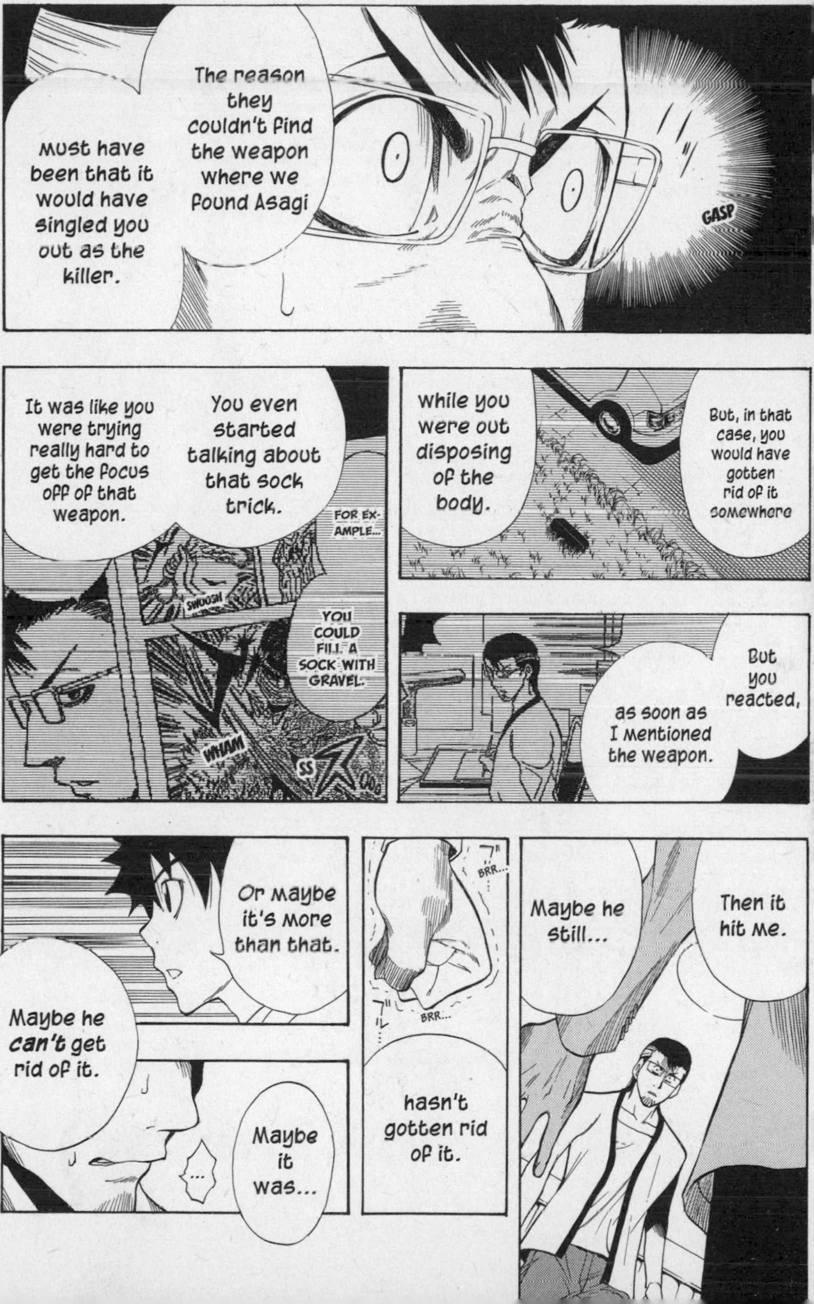
The reason they couldn't find the weapon where we found Asagi
Must have been that it would have singled you out as the killer.
GASP
But, in that case, you would have gotten rid of it somewhere
while you were out disposing of the body.
But you reacted,
as soon as I mentioned the weapon.
You even started talking about that sock trick.
It was like you were trying really hard to get the focus off of that weapon.
FOR EX-AMPLE...
YOU COULD FILL A SOCK WITH GRAVEL.
SWOOSH
WHAM
Then it hit me.
Maybe he still...
BRR...
BRR...
hasn't gotten rid of it.
Or maybe it's more than that.
Maybe he *can't* get rid of it.
Maybe it was...
...

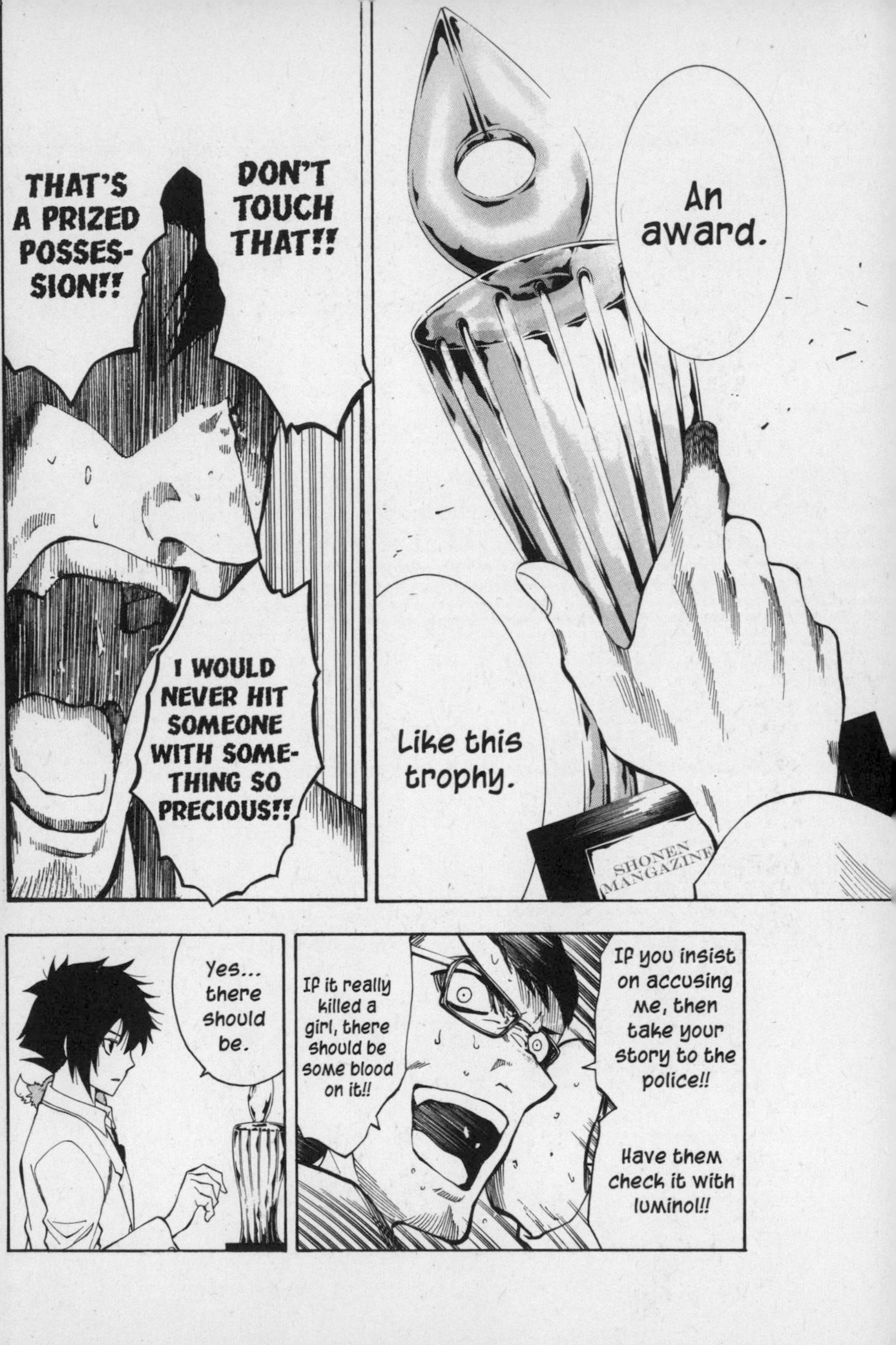
An award.
Like this trophy.
SHONEN MANGAZINE
DON'T TOUCH THAT!!
THAT'S A PRIZED POSSES-SION!!
I WOULD NEVER HIT SOMEONE WITH SOME-THING SO PRECIOUS!!
If you insist on accusing me, then take your story to the police!!
Have them check it with luminol!!
If it really killed a girl, there should be some blood on it!!
Yes... there should be.

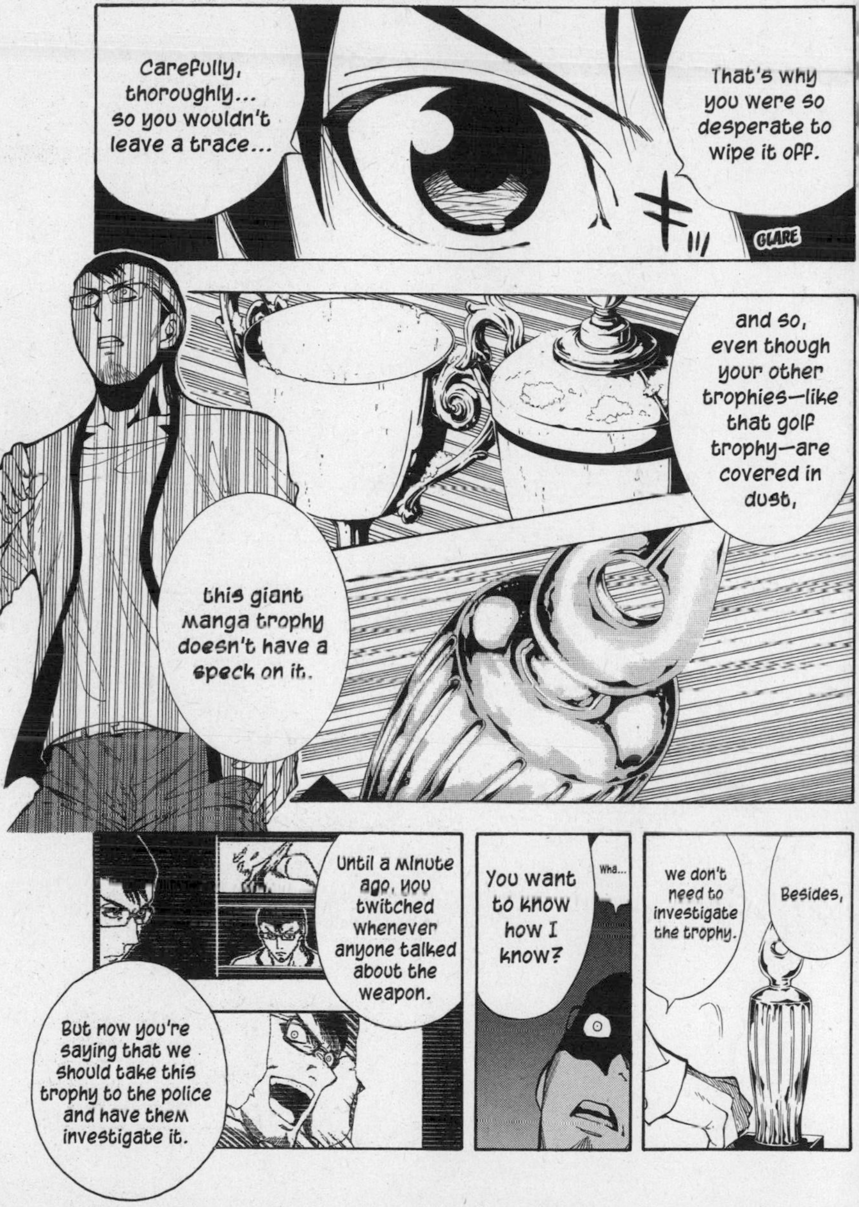
That's why you were so desperate to wipe it off.
Carefully, thoroughly... so you wouldn't leave a trace...
GLARE
and so, even though your other trophies—like that golf trophy—are covered in dust,
this giant manga trophy doesn't have a speck on it.
Besides,
we don't need to investigate the trophy.
Wha...
You want to know how I know?
Until a minute ago, you twitched whenever anyone talked about the weapon.
But now you're saying that we should take this trophy to the police and have them investigate it.

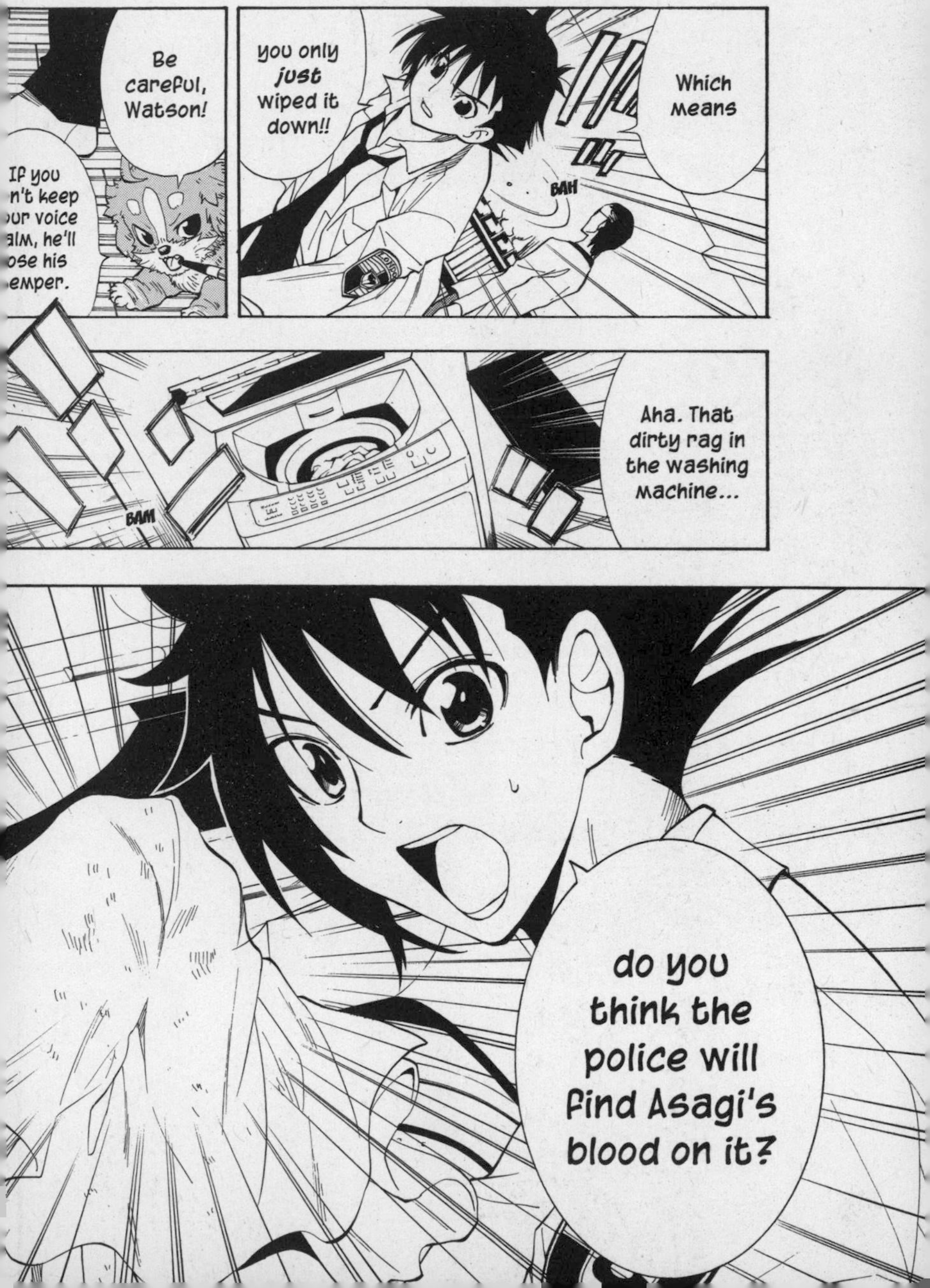
Which means
you only just wiped it down!!
BAH
Be careful, Watson!
If you n't keep our voice alm, he'll ose his emper.
Aha. That dirty rag in the washing machine...
BAM
do you think the police will find Asagi's blood on it?

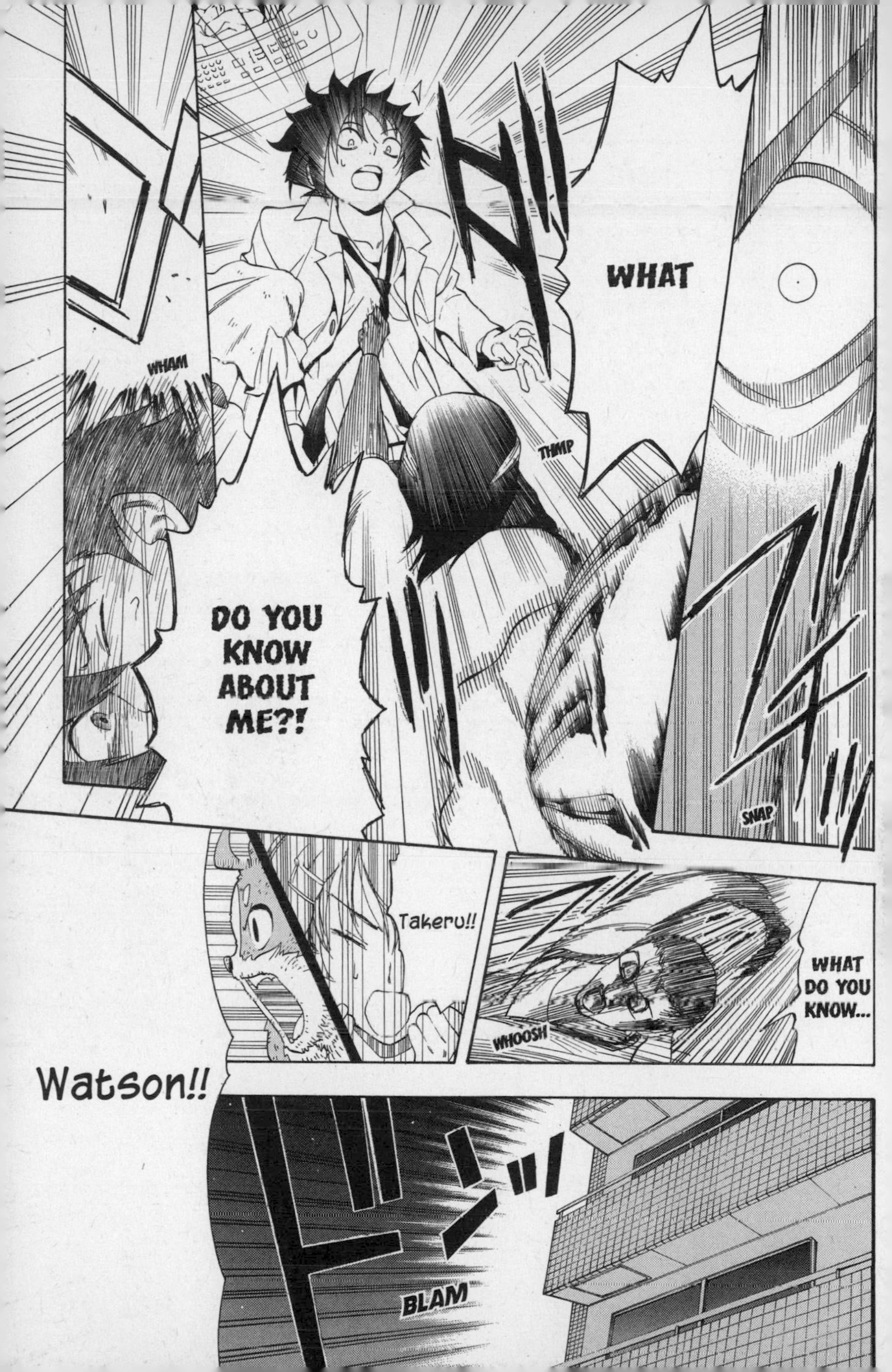
WHAT
THMP
SNAP
WHAM
DO YOU KNOW ABOUT ME?!
WHAT DO YOU KNOW...
WHOOSH
Takeru!!
Watson!!
BLAM

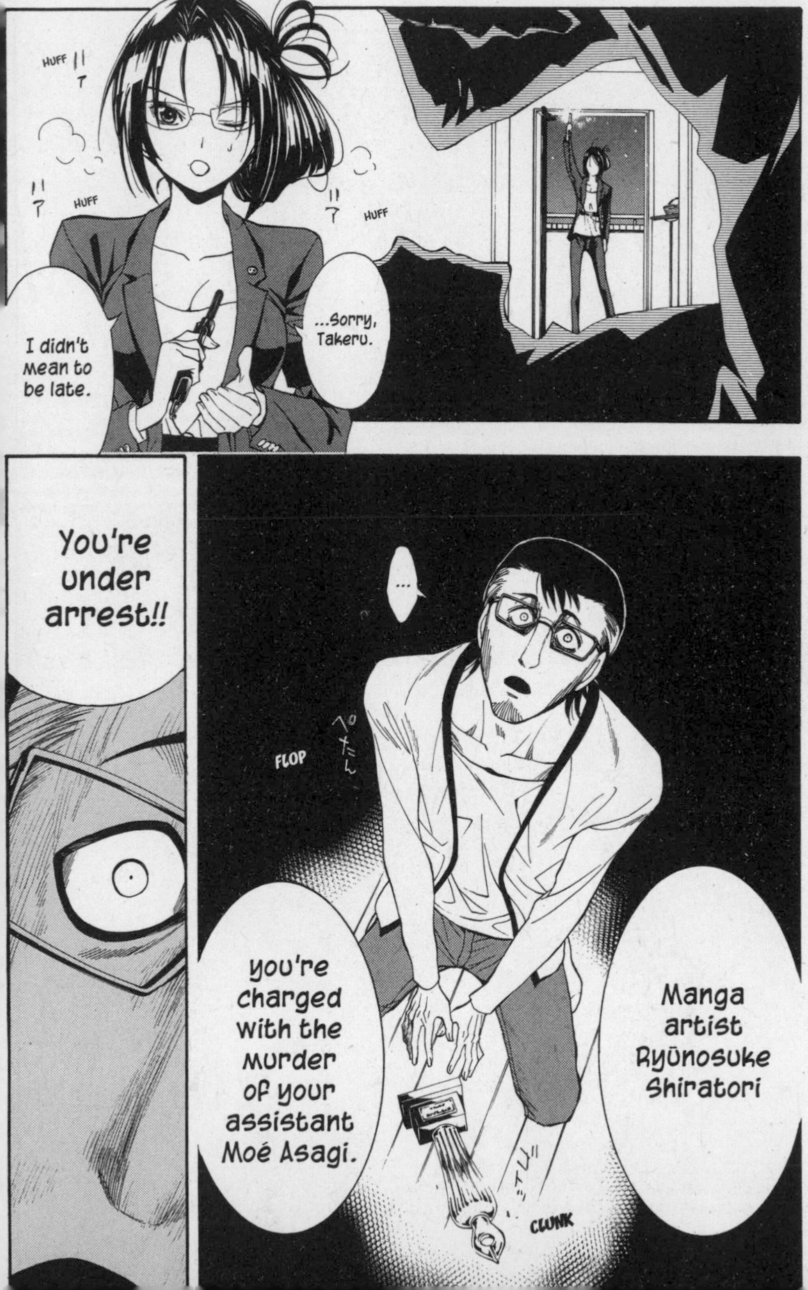
HUFF
HUFF
HUFF
...Sorry, Takeru.
I didn't mean to be late.
...
FLOP
Manga artist Ryūnosuke Shiratori
you're charged with the murder of your assistant Moé Asagi.
CLUNK
You're under arrest!!

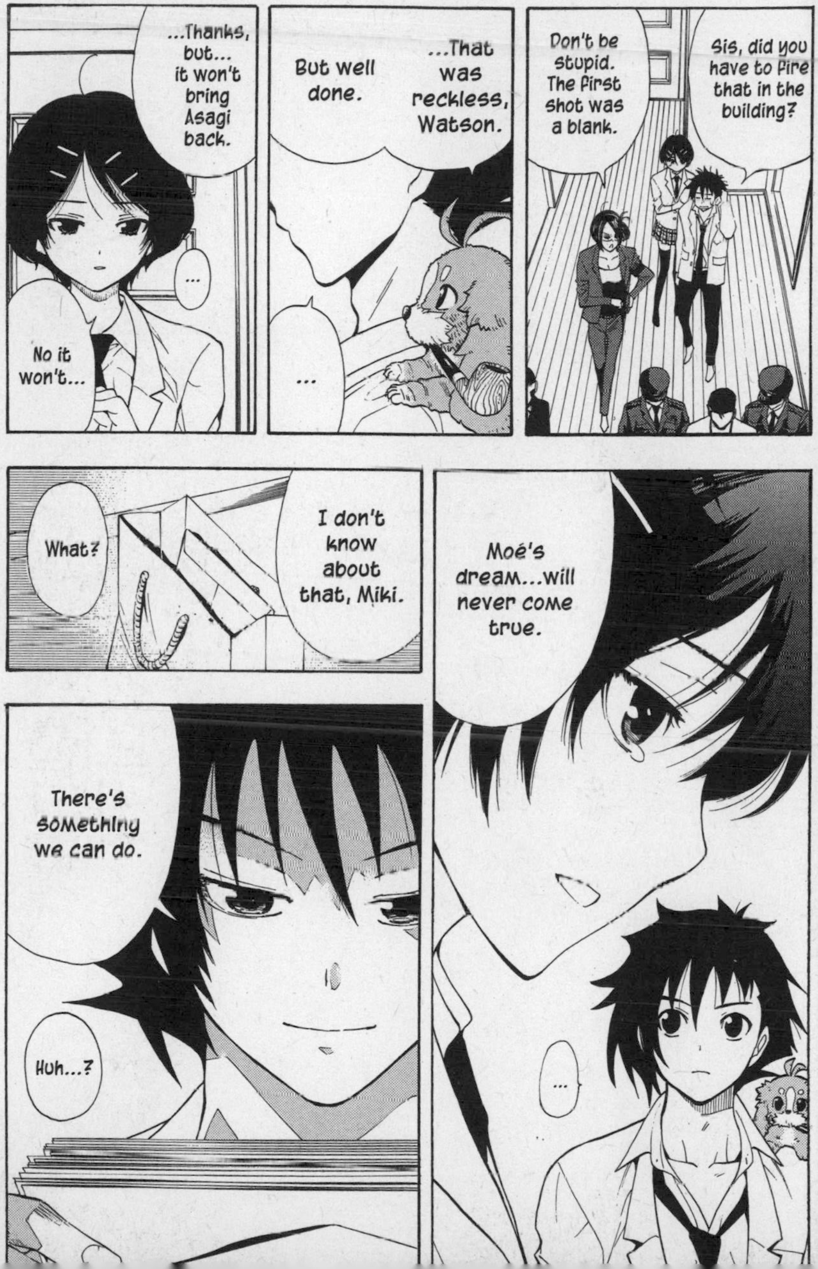
Sis, did you have to fire that in the building?
Don't be stupid. The first shot was a blank.
...That was reckless, Watson.
But well done.
...
...Thanks, but... it won't bring Asagi back.
...
No it won't...
Moé's dream...will never come true.
I don't know about that, Miki.
What?
...
There's something we can do.
Huh...?

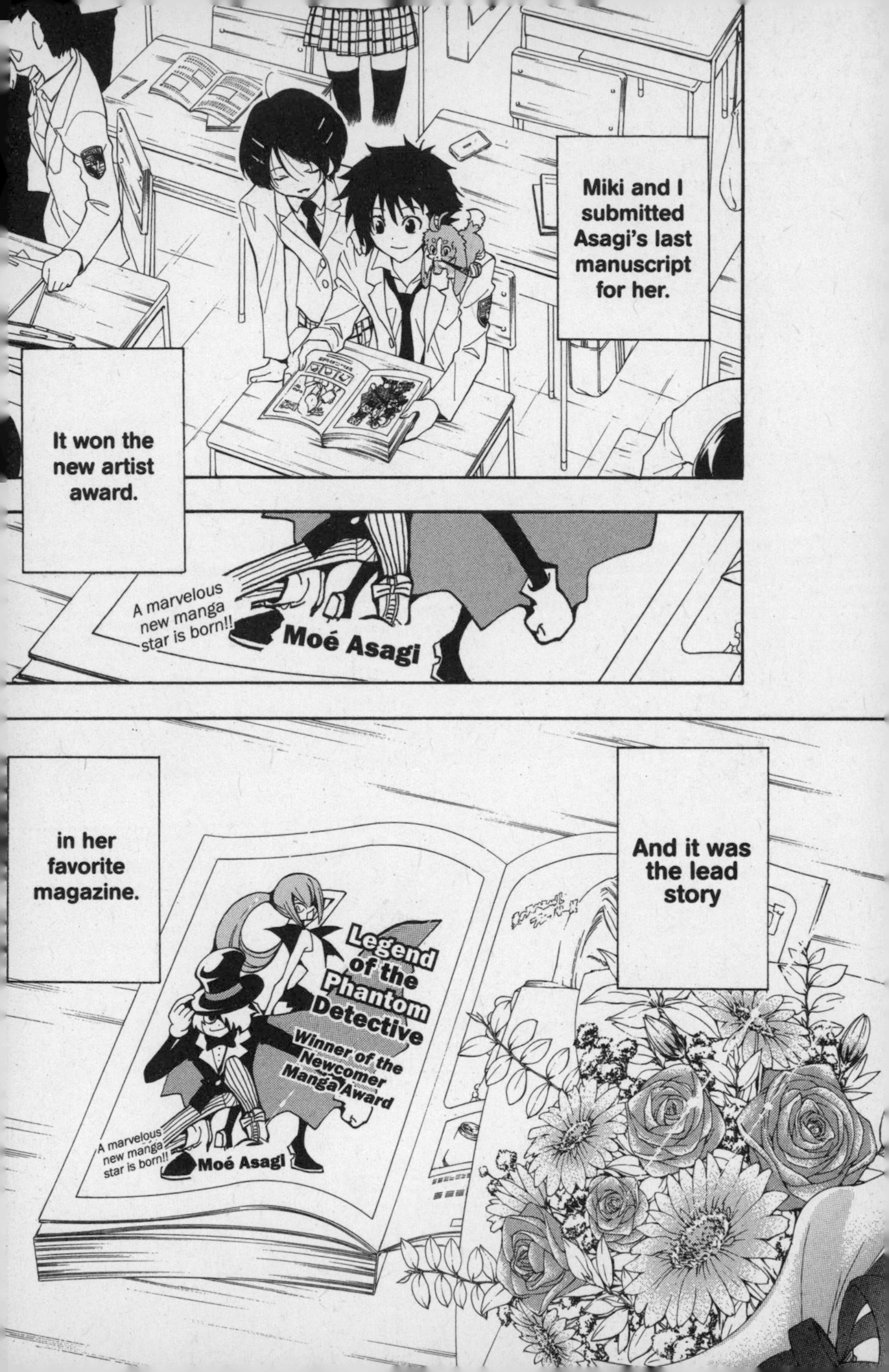
Miki and I submitted Asagi's last manuscript for her.
It won the new artist award.
A marvelous new manga star is born!!
Moé Asagi
And it was the lead story
in her favorite magazine.
Legend of the Phantom Detective
Winner of the Newcomer Manga Award
A marvelous new manga star is born!!
Moé Asagi

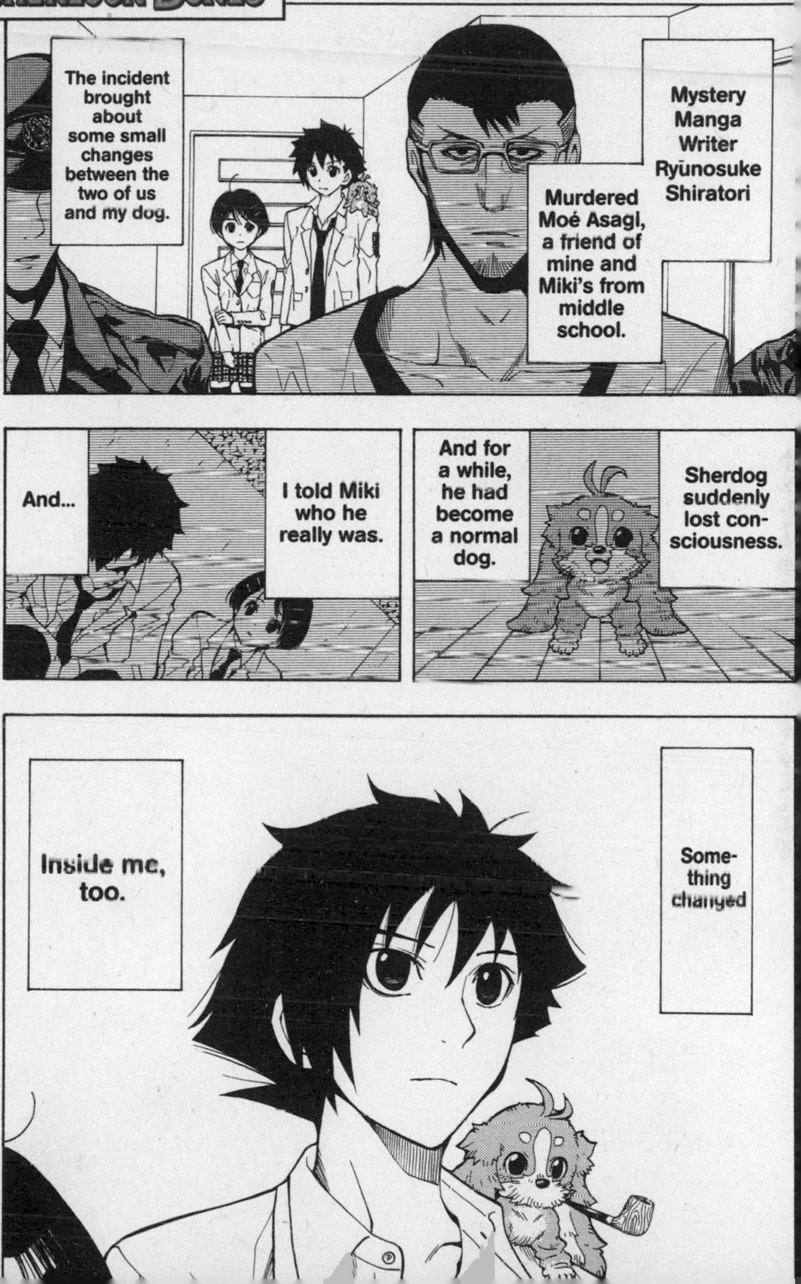
Mystery Manga Writer Ryūnosuke Shiratori
Murdered Moé Asagi, a friend of mine and Miki's from middle school.
The incident brought about some small changes between the two of us and my dog.
Sherdog suddenly lost consciousness.
And for a while, he had become a normal dog.
I told Miki who he really was.
And...
Something changed
Inside me, too.

Case 6: ⚜ The Lethal Left Hand, Part 1

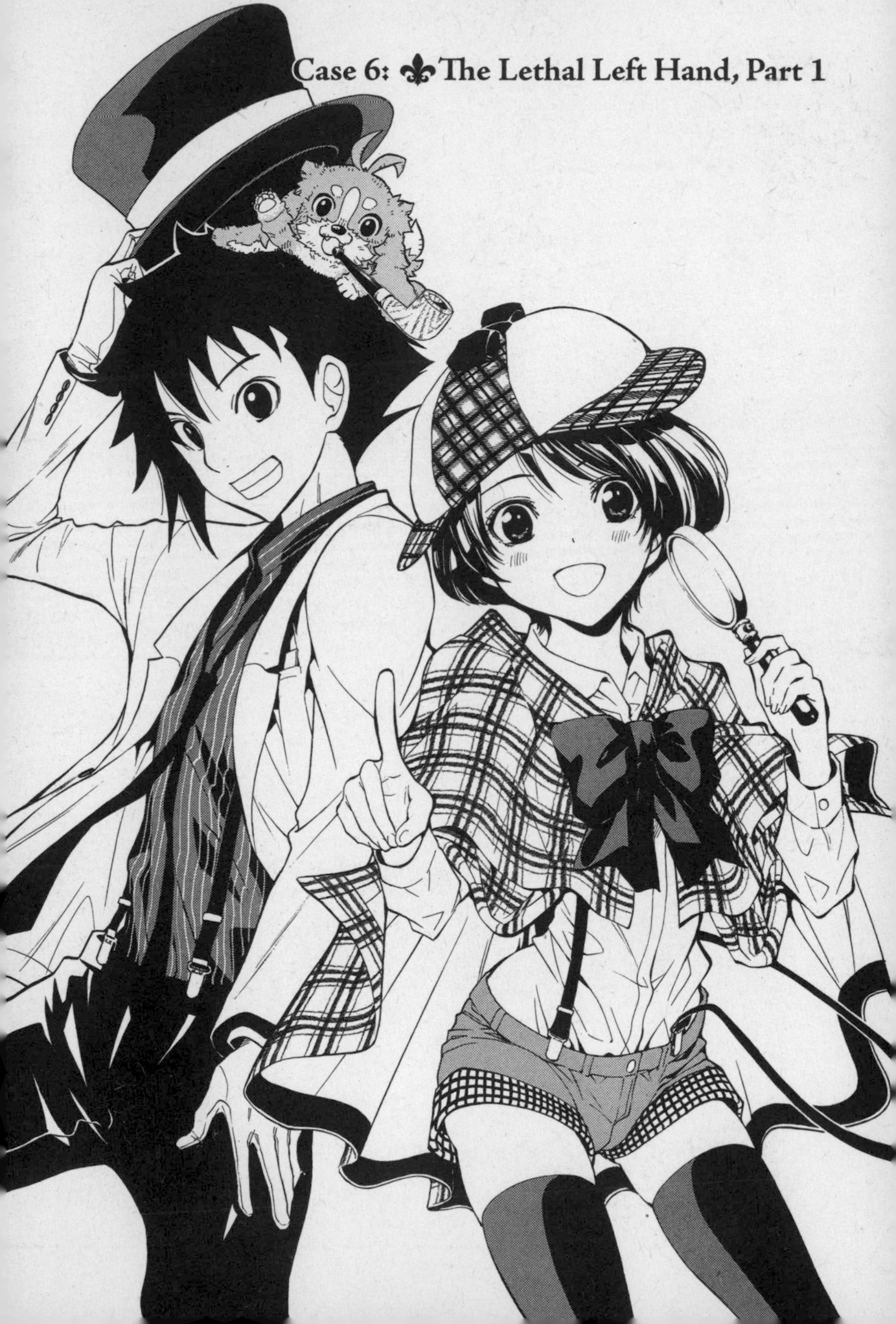

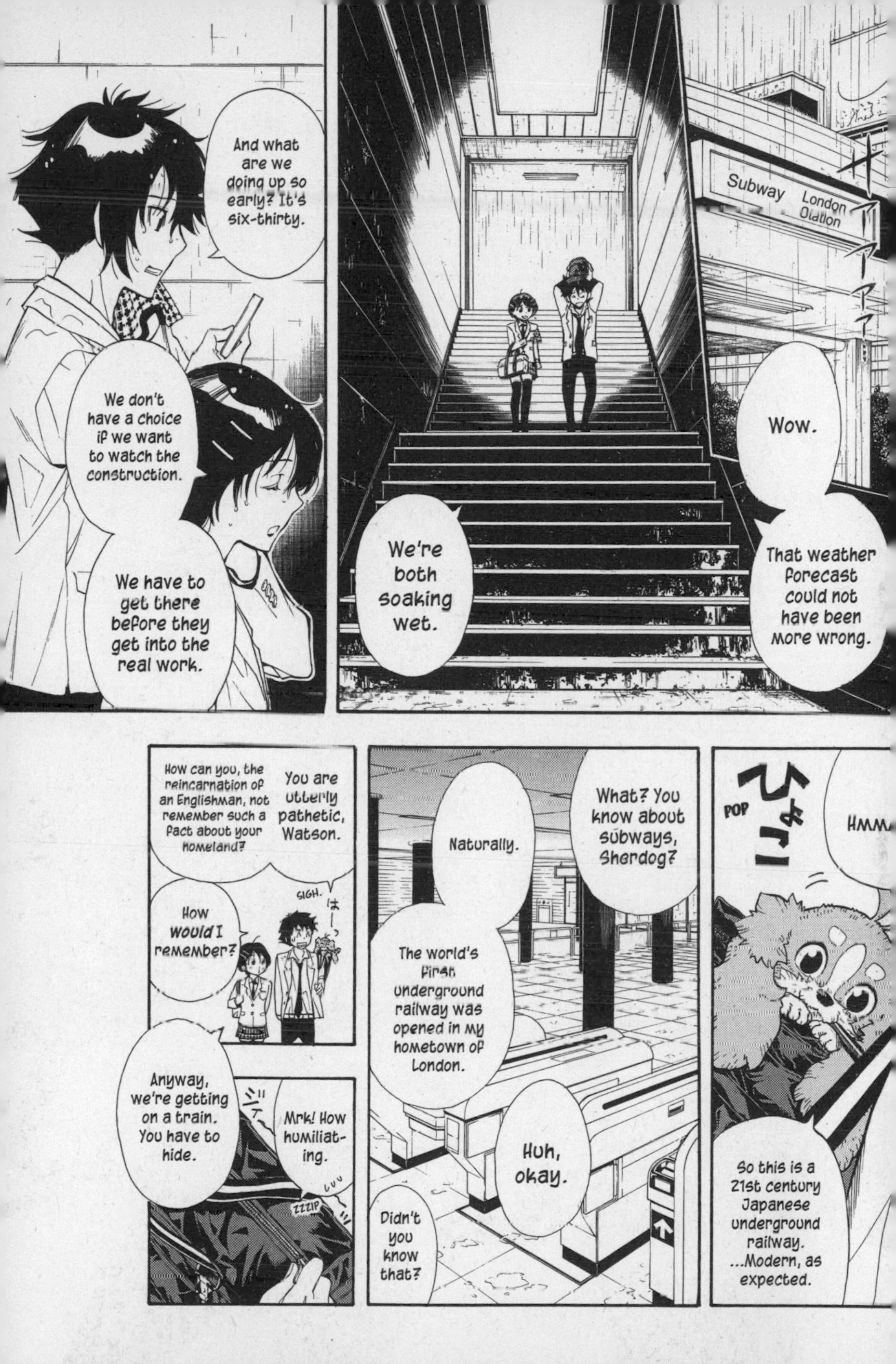
Subway
London Station
Wow.
That weather forecast could not have been more wrong.
We're both soaking wet.
And what are we doing up so early? It's six-thirty.
We don't have a choice if we want to watch the construction.
We have to get there before they get into the real work.
HMM
POP
So this is a 21st century Japanese underground railway. ...Modern, as expected.
What? You know about subways, Sherdog?
Naturally.
The world's first underground railway was opened in my hometown of London.
Huh, okay.
Didn't you know that?
You are utterly pathetic, Watson.
How can you, the reincarnation of an Englishman, not remember such a fact about your homeland?
SIGH.
How would I remember?
Mrk! How humiliating.
Anyway, we're getting on a train. You have to hide.
ZZZIP

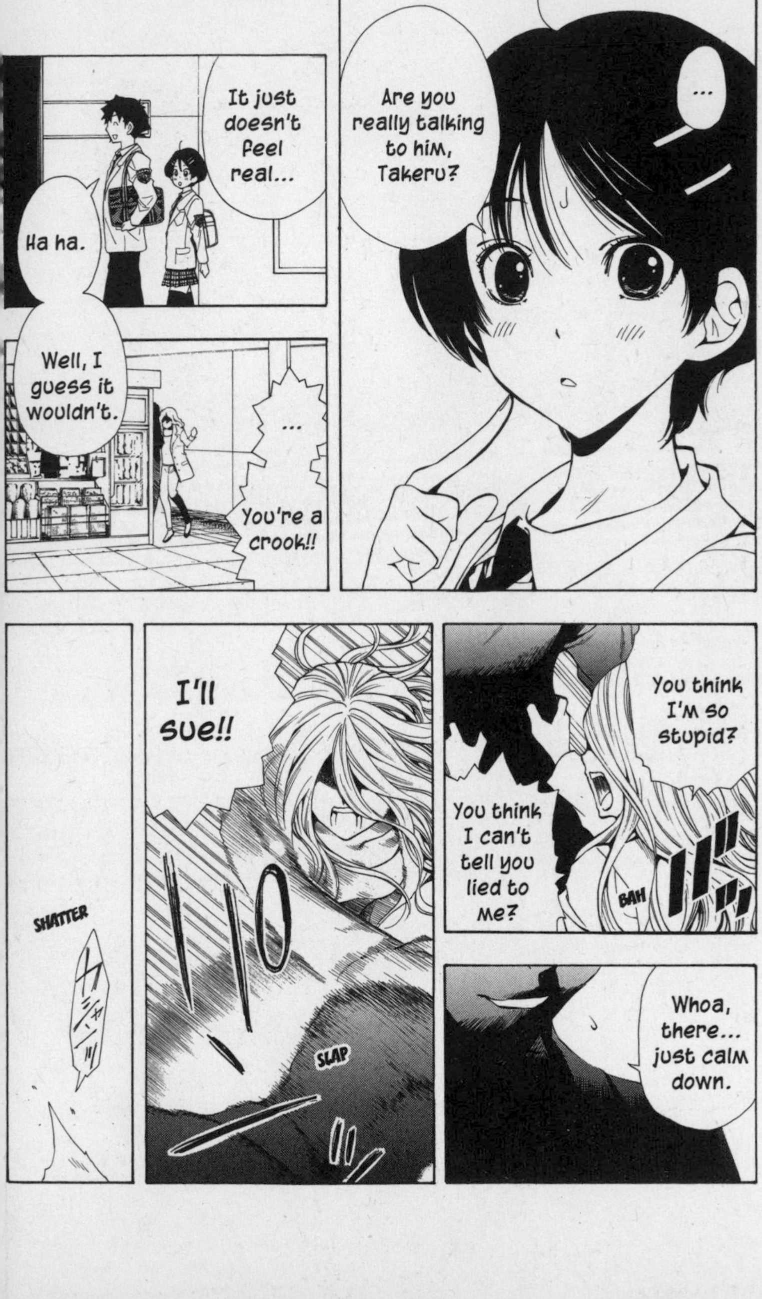
Are you really talking to him, Takeru?
...
It just doesn't feel real...
Ha ha.
Well, I guess it wouldn't.
...
You're a crook!!
You think I'm so stupid?
You think I can't tell you lied to me?
BAH
Whoa, there... just calm down.
I'll sue!!
SLAP
SHATTER

PERK
What were those voices just now?
And it sounded like someone hit something...
RIP
RIP
RIP
Train arriving on Line 2.
!
Dammit, let go...
No!
A man and a woman, fighting...
RRRING
HM...
WHUMP

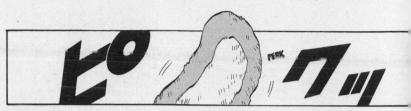

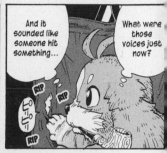

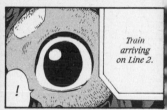

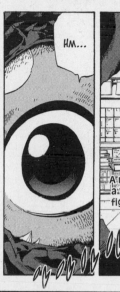

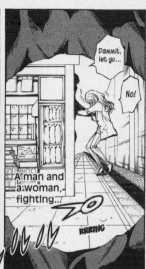

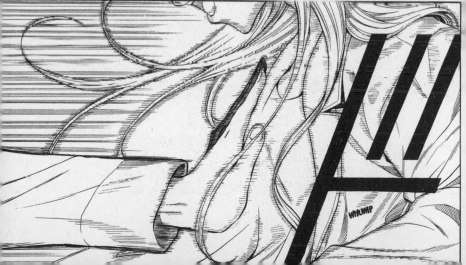

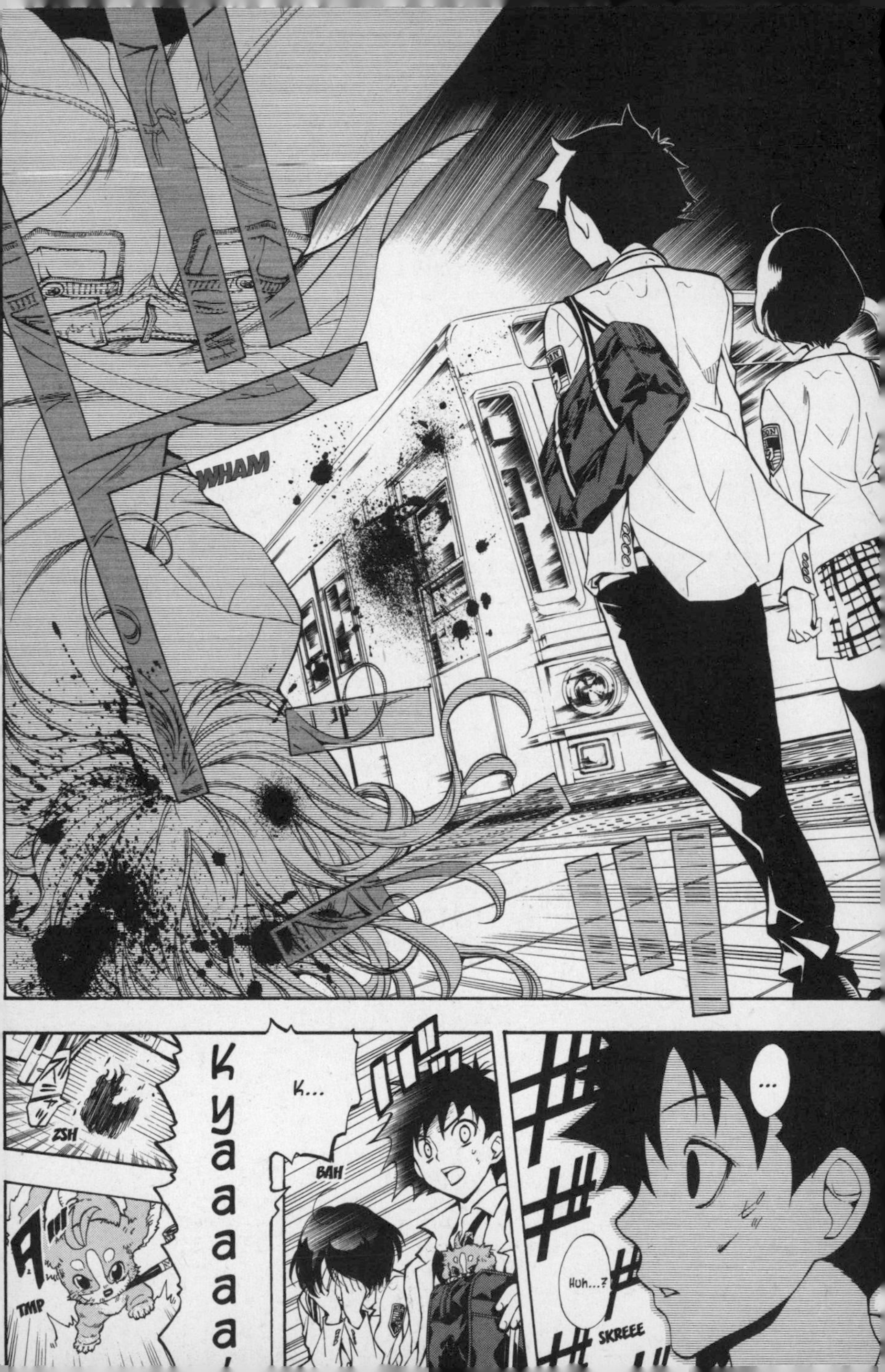
WHAM
...
Huh...?
SKREEE
K...
BAH
Kyaaaaa,
ZSH
TMP

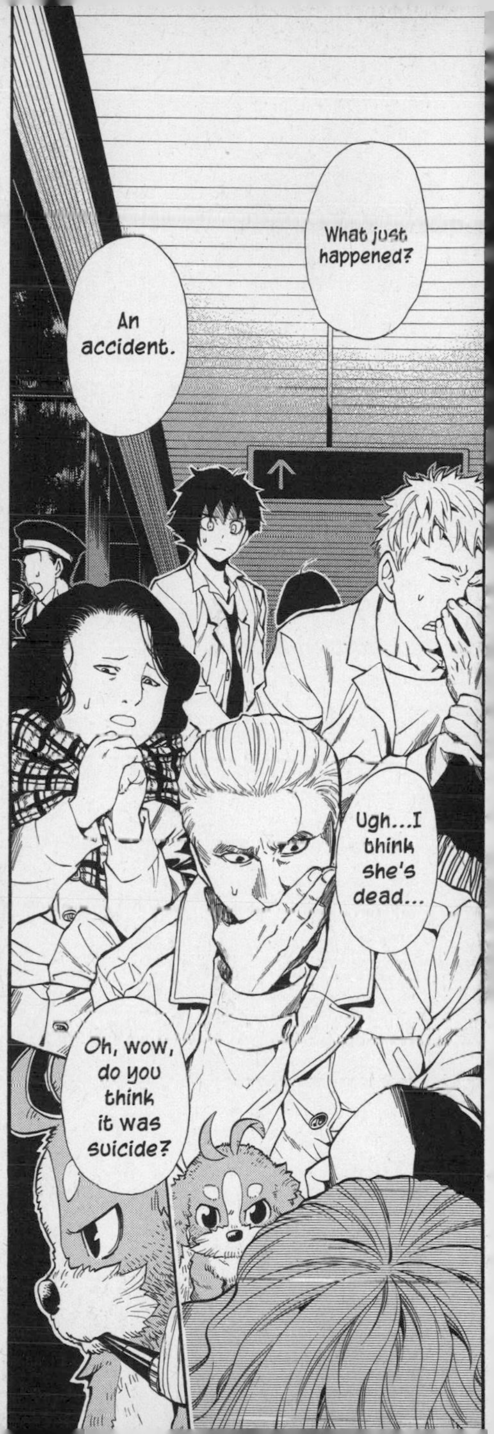
What just happened?
An accident.
Ugh...I think she's dead...
Oh, wow, do you think it was suicide?

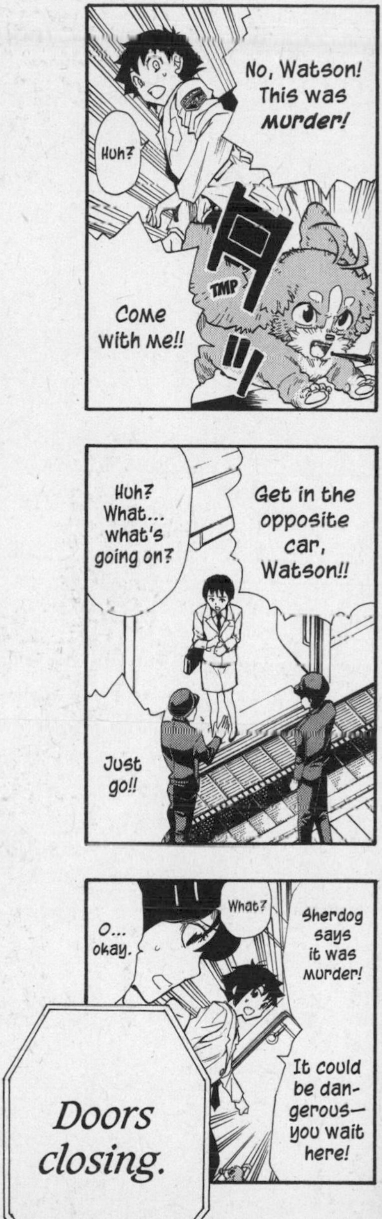
No, Watson! This was *murder!*
Huh?
TMP
Come with me!!
Get in the opposite car, Watson!!
Huh? What... what's going on?
Just go!!
Sherdog says it was murder!
What?
O... okay.
It could be dangerous—you wait here!
Doors closing.

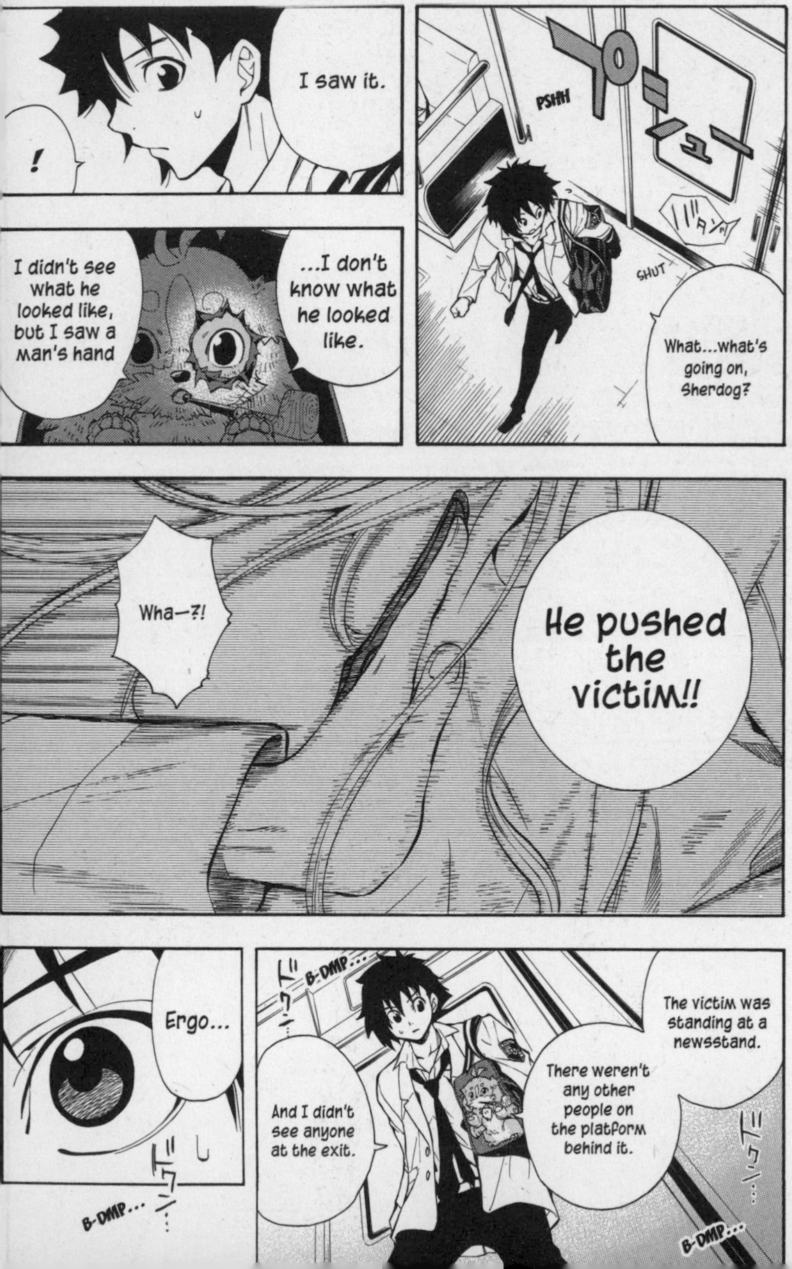

PSHH
SHUT
What...what's going on, Sherdog?
I saw it.
!
...I don't know what he looked like.
I didn't see what he looked like, but I saw a man's hand
He pushed the victim!!
Wha—?!
B-DMP...
The victim was standing at a newsstand.
There weren't any other people on the platform behind it.
And I didn't see anyone at the exit.
B-DMP...
Ergo...
B-DMP...

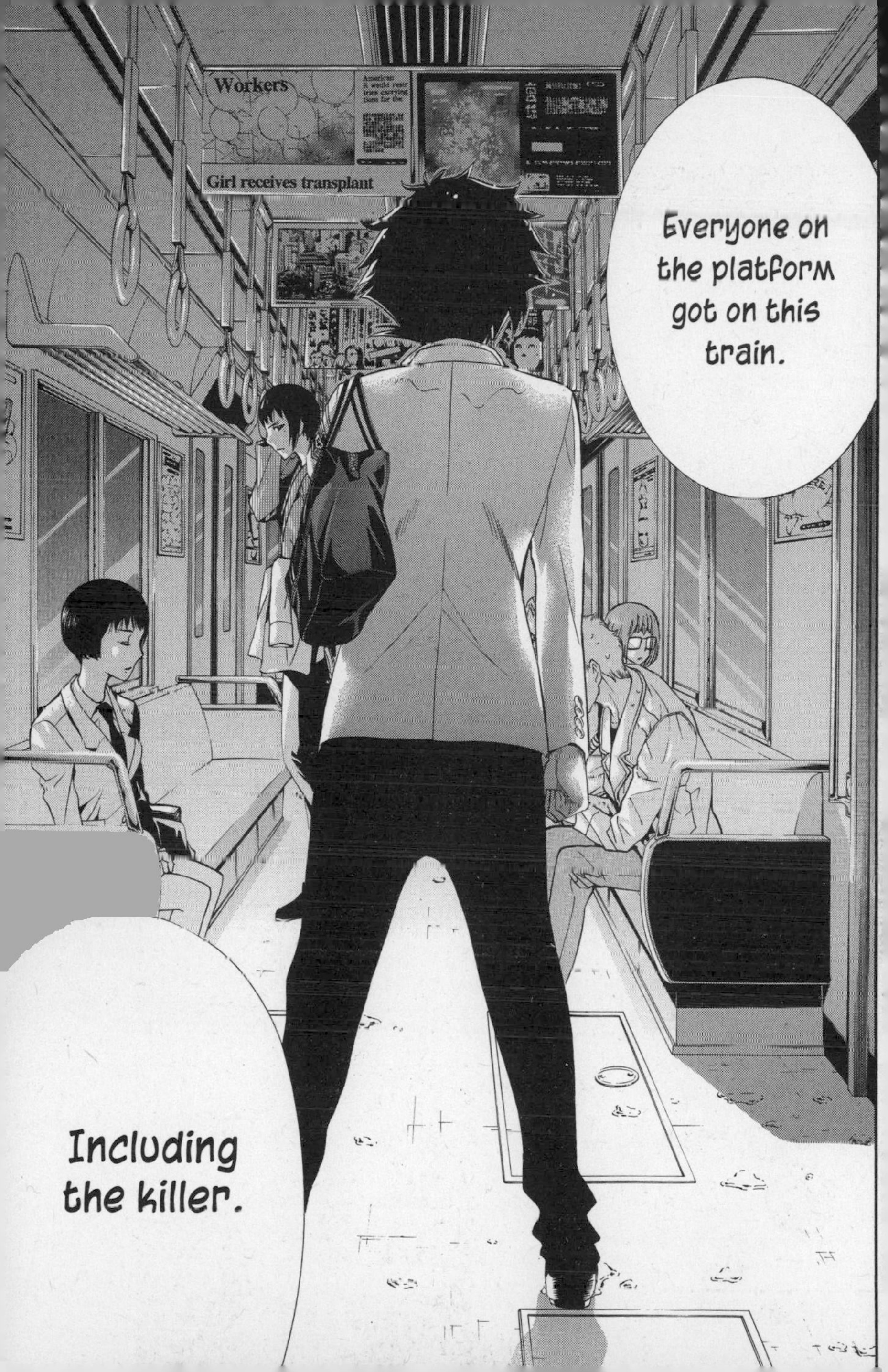
Everyone on the platform got on this train.
Workers
Girl receives transplant
Including the killer.

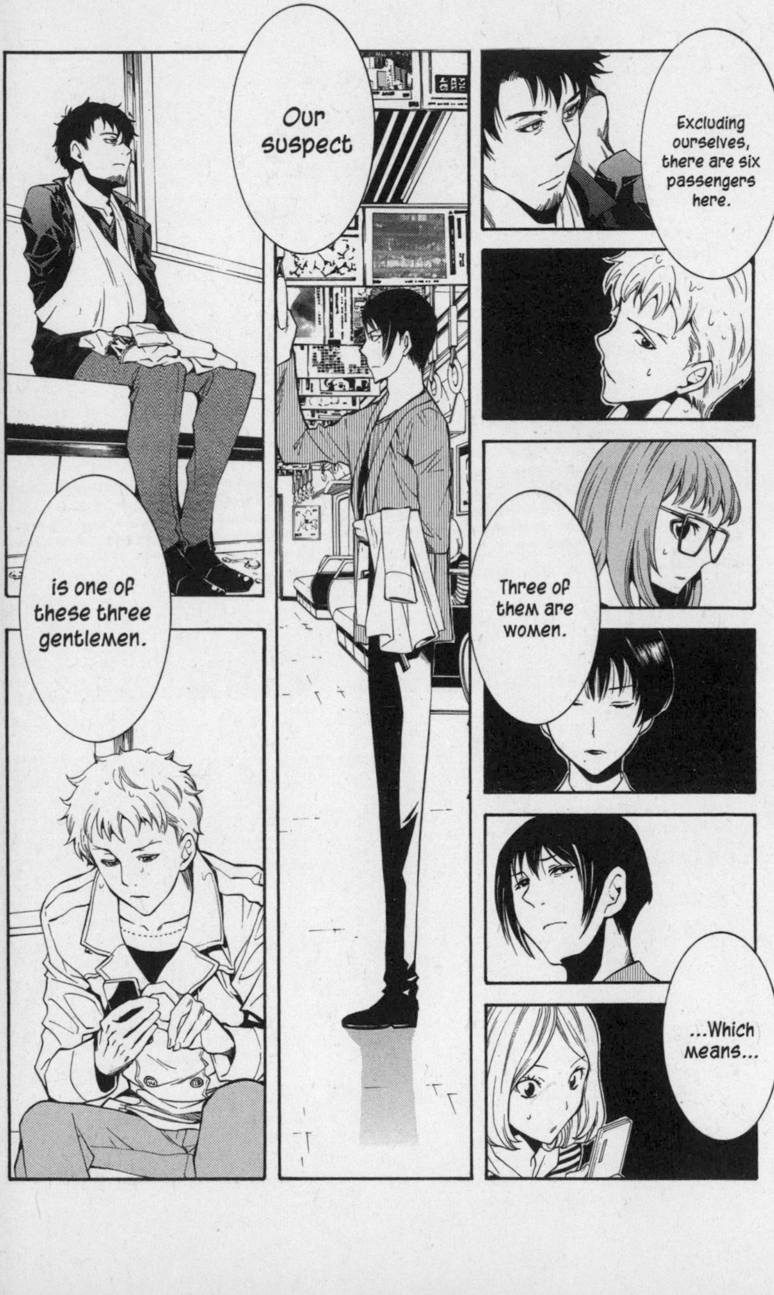
Excluding ourselves, there are six passengers here.
Three of them are women.
...Which means...
Our suspect
is one of these three gentlemen.

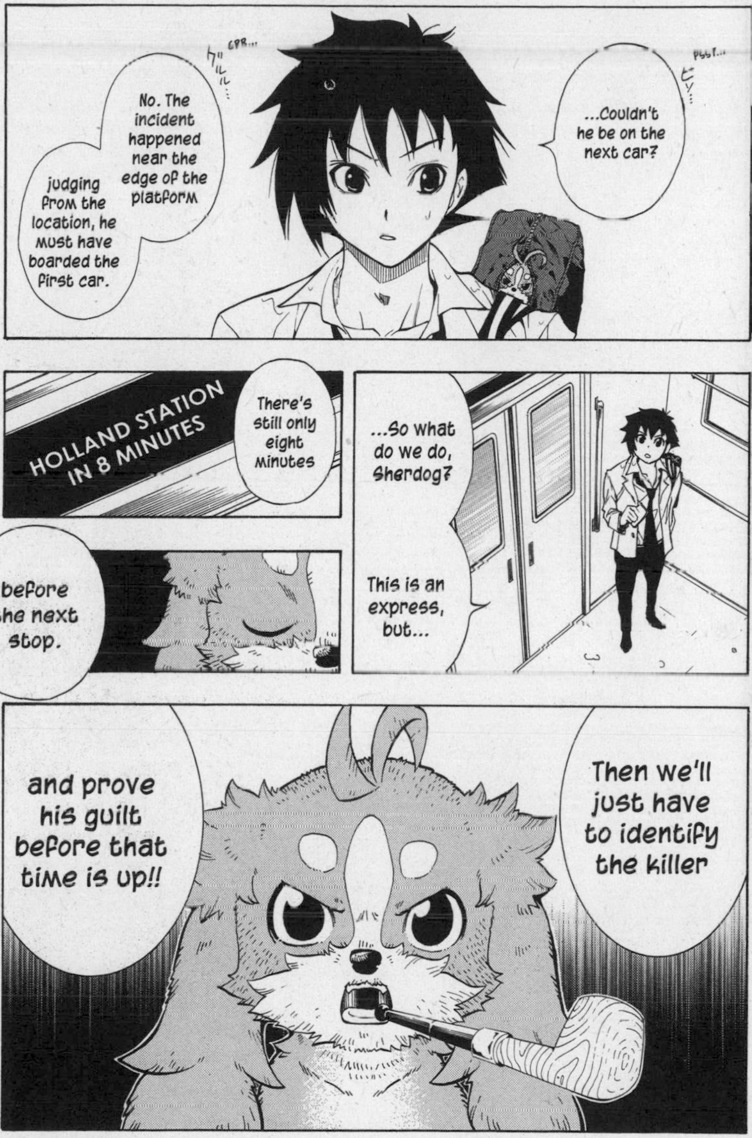
PSST...
...Couldn't he be on the next car?
GRR...
No. The incident happened near the edge of the platform
judging from the location, he must have boarded the first car.
...So what do we do, Sherdog?
This is an express, but...
HOLLAND STATION IN 8 MINUTES
There's still only eight minutes
before the next stop.
Then we'll just have to identify the killer
and prove his guilt before that time is up!!

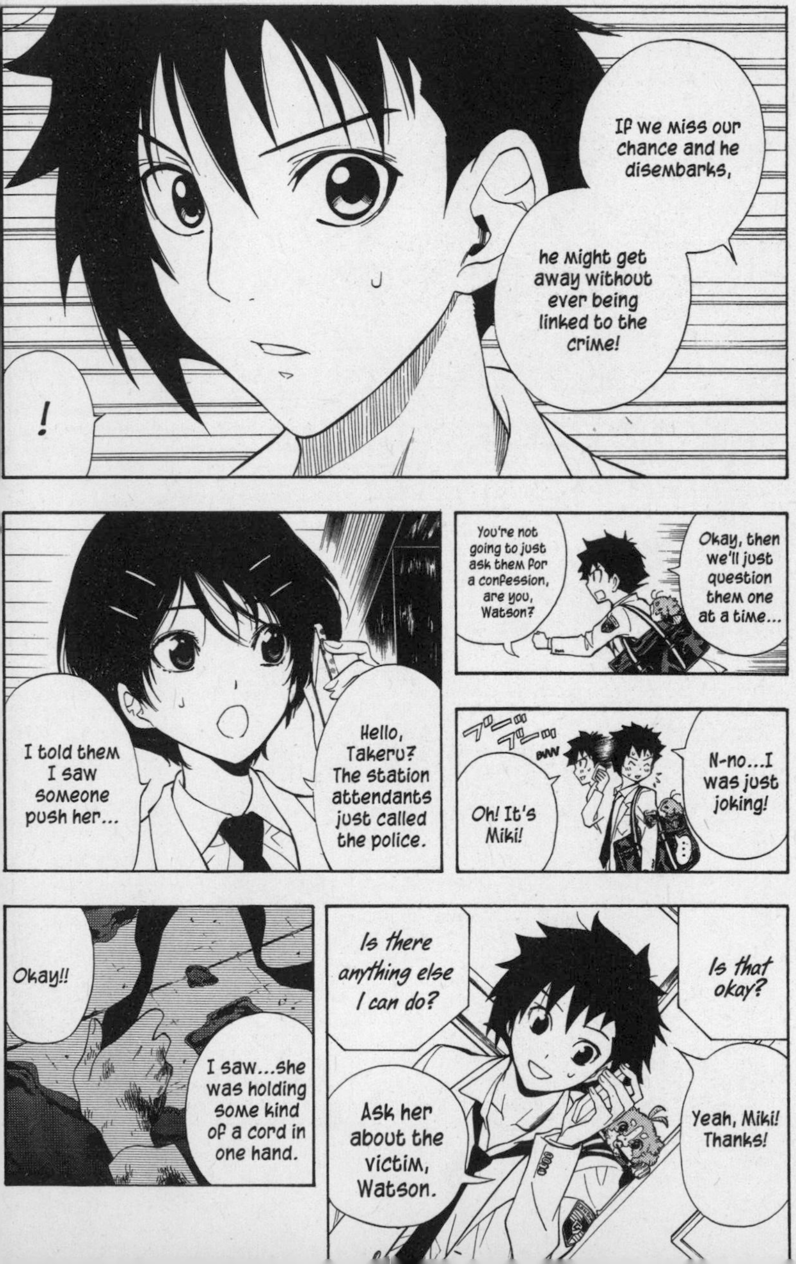
If we miss our chance and he disembarks,
he might get away without ever being linked to the crime!
!
Okay, then we'll just question them one at a time...
You're not going to just ask them for a confession, are you, Watson?
N-no...I was just joking!
Oh! It's Miki!
Hello, Takeru? The station attendants just called the police.
I told them I saw someone push her...
Is that okay?
Is there anything else I can do?
Yeah, Miki! Thanks!
Ask her about the victim, Watson.
Okay!!
I saw...she was holding some kind of a cord in one hand.

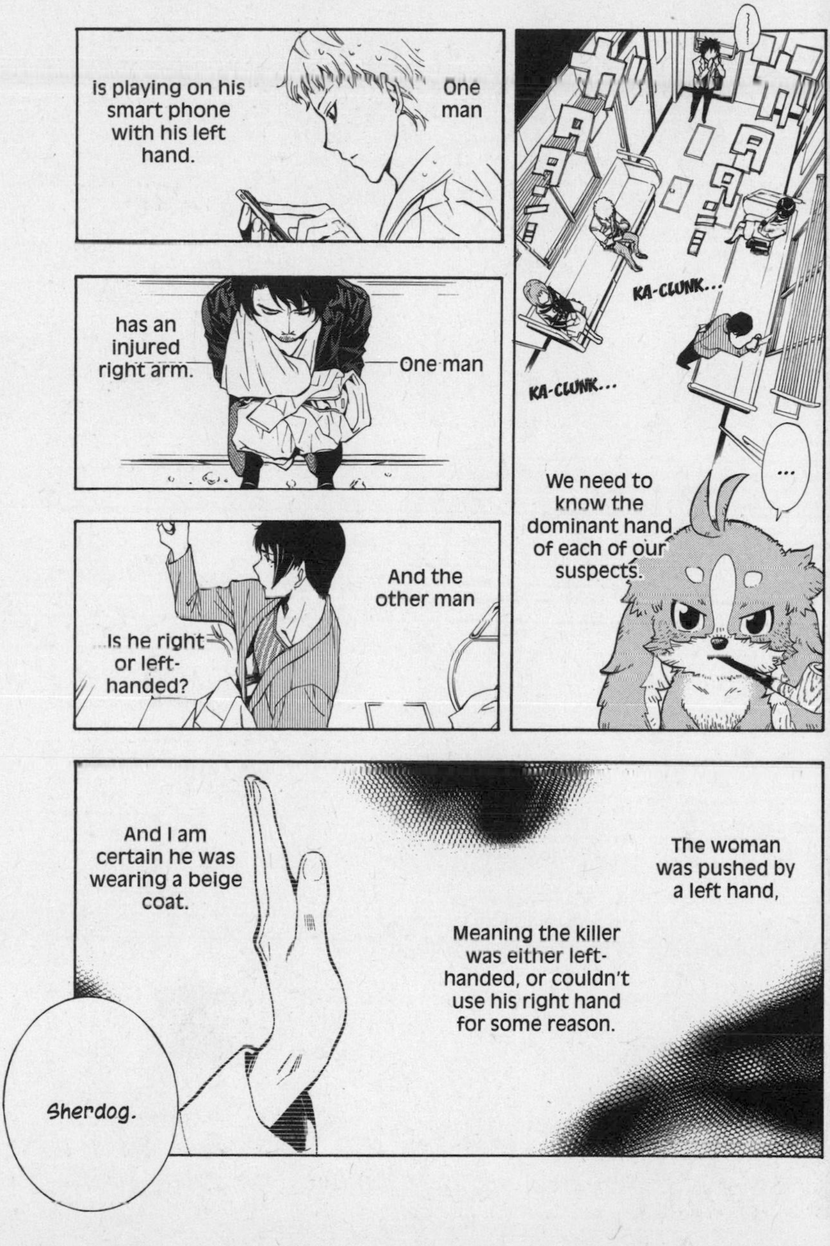

KA-CLUNK...
KA-CLUNK...
...
We need to know the dominant hand of each of our suspects.
One man
is playing on his smart phone with his left hand.
One man
has an injured right arm.
And the other man
...Is he right or left-handed?
The woman was pushed by a left hand,
Meaning the killer was either left-handed, or couldn't use his right hand for some reason.
And I am certain he was wearing a beige coat.
Sherdog.

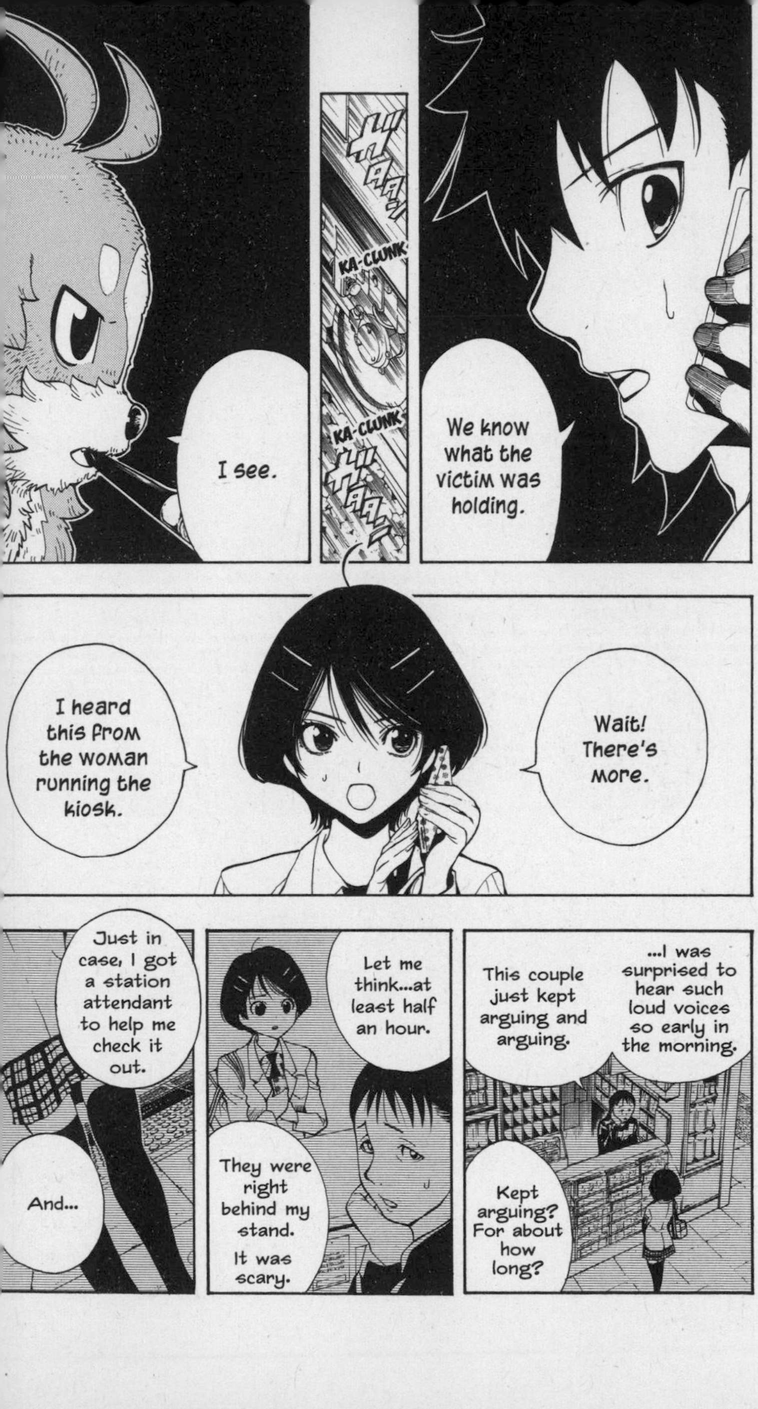
We know what the victim was holding.
KA-CLUNK
KA-CLUNK
I see.
Wait! There's more.
I heard this from the woman running the kiosk.
...I was surprised to hear such loud voices so early in the morning.
This couple just kept arguing and arguing.
Kept arguing? For about how long?
Let me think...at least half an hour.
They were right behind my stand.
It was scary.
Just in case, I got a station attendant to help me check it out.
And...

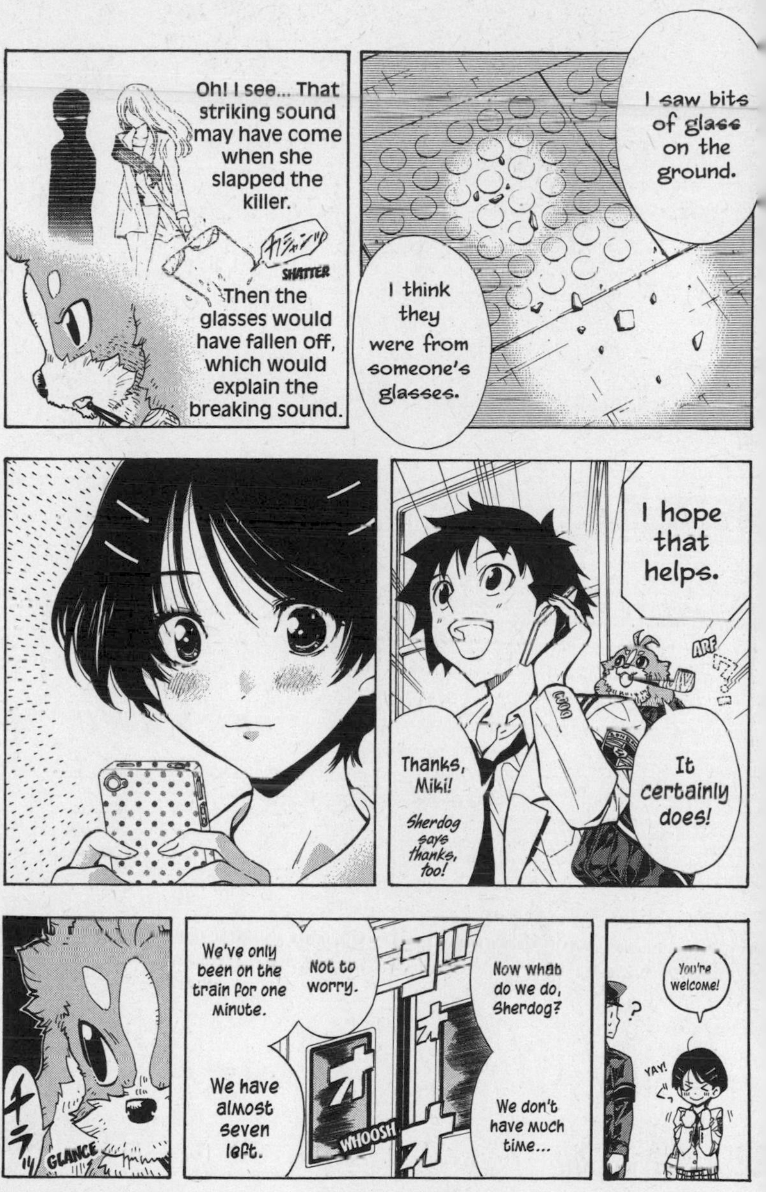
I saw bits of glass on the ground.
I think they were from someone's glasses.
Oh! I see... That striking sound may have come when she slapped the killer.
SHATTER
Then the glasses would have fallen off, which would explain the breaking sound.
I hope that helps.
ARF
It certainly does!
Thanks, Miki!
Sherdog says thanks, too!
You're welcome!
?
YAY!
Now what do we do, Sherdog?
We don't have much time...
Not to worry.
We've only been on the train for one minute.
We have almost seven left.
WHOOSH
GLANCE

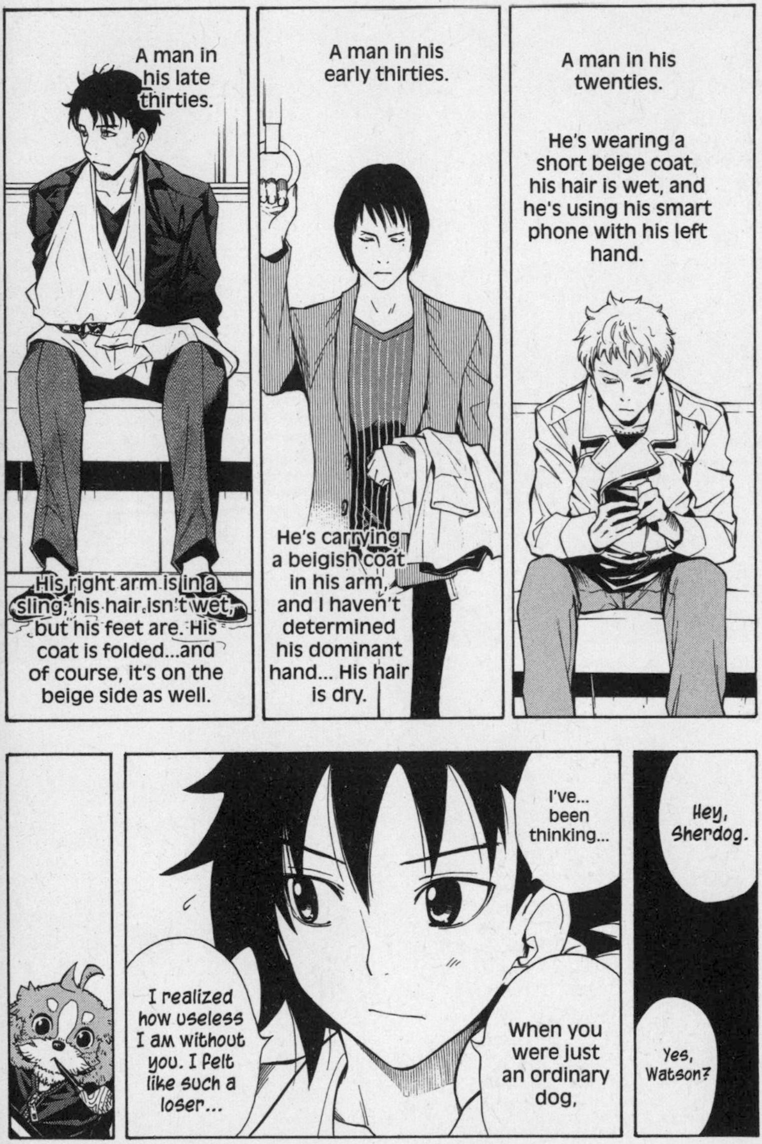
A man in his twenties.
He's wearing a short beige coat, his hair is wet, and he's using his smart phone with his left hand.
A man in his early thirties.
He's carrying a beigish coat in his arm, and I haven't determined his dominant hand... His hair is dry.
A man in his late thirties.
His right arm is in a sling, his hair isn't wet, but his feet are. His coat is folded...and of course, it's on the beige side as well.
Hey, Sherdog.
Yes, Watson?
I've... been thinking...
When you were just an ordinary dog,
I realized how useless I am without you. I felt like such a loser...

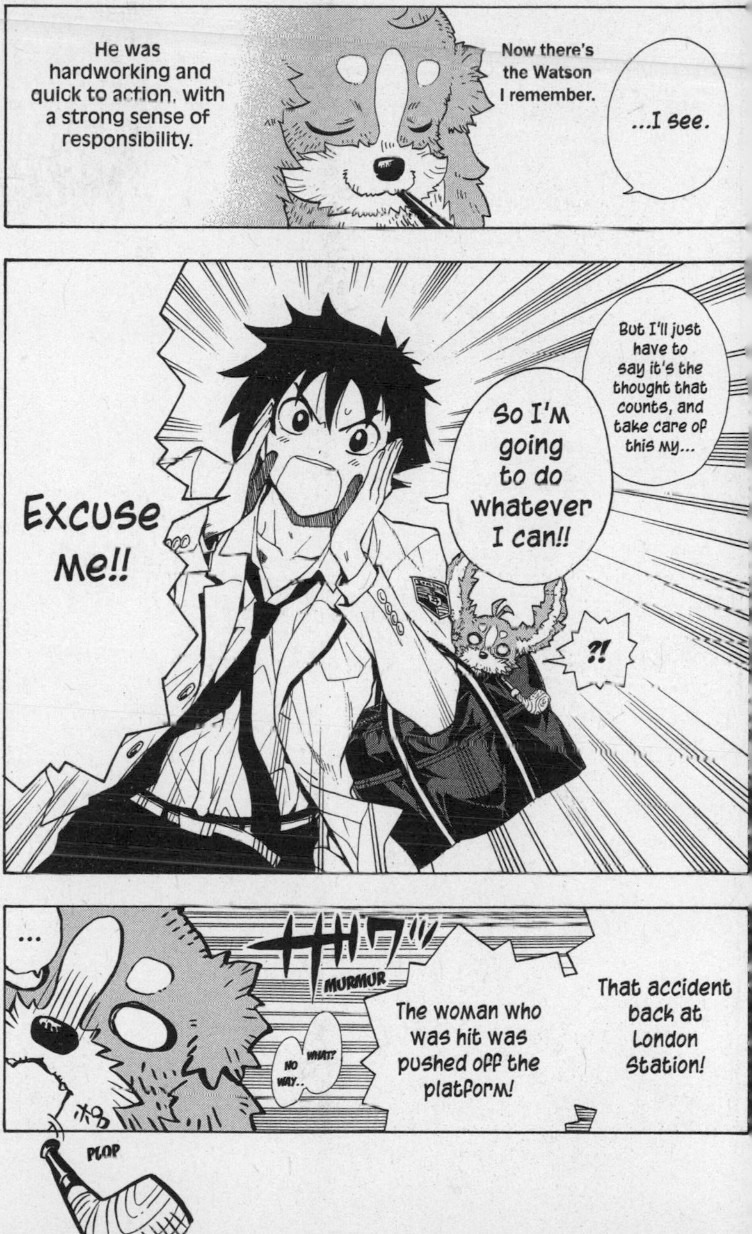

...I see.
Now there's the Watson I remember.
He was hardworking and quick to action, with a strong sense of responsibility.
But I'll just have to say it's the thought that counts, and take care of this my...
So I'M going to do whatever I can!!
?!
Excuse Me!!
That accident back at London Station!
The woman who was hit was pushed off the platform!
MURMUR
WHAT?
NO WAY..
...
PLOP

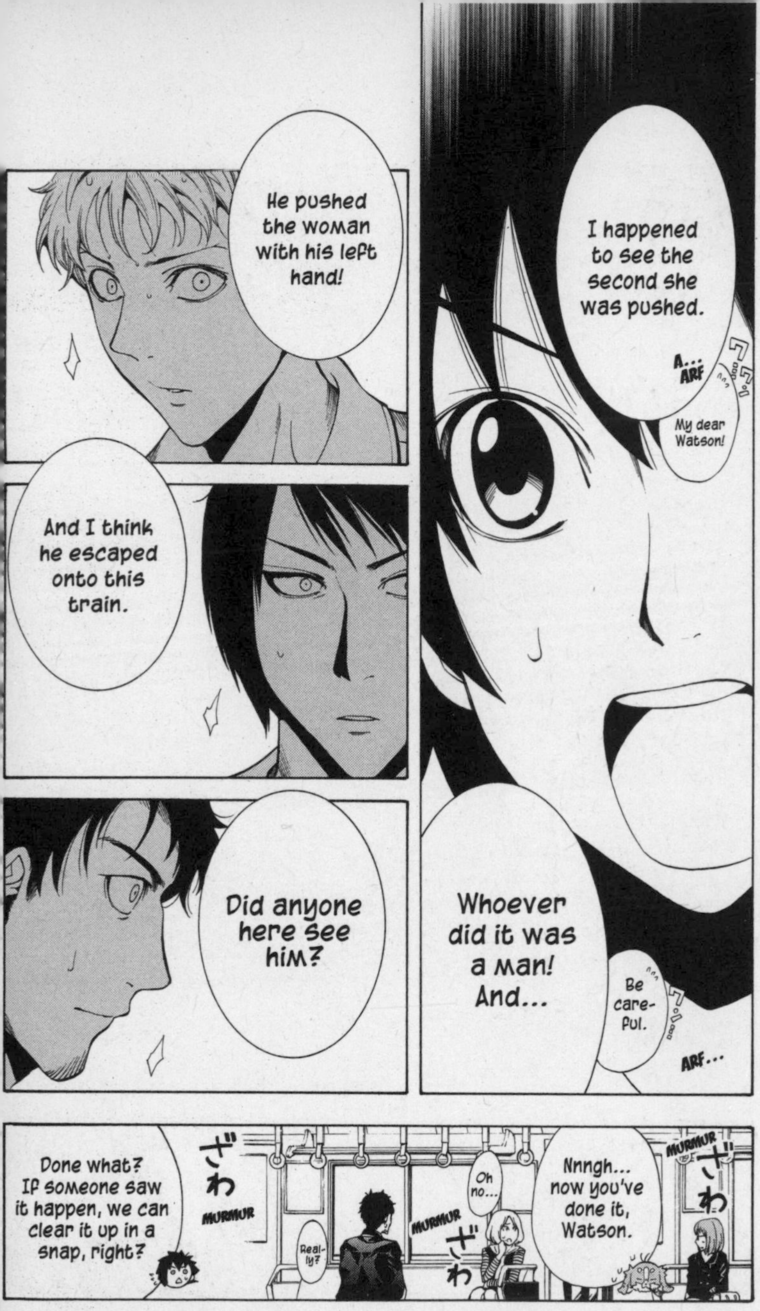
I happened to see the second she was pushed.
A... ARF
My dear Watson!
Whoever did it was a man! And...
Be care-ful.
ARF...
He pushed the woman with his left hand!
And I think he escaped onto this train.
Did anyone here see him?
MURMUR
ざわ
Nnngh... now you've done it, Watson.
Oh no...
MURMUR
ざわ
Real-ly?
Done what? If someone saw it happen, we can clear it up in a snap, right?
ざわ
MURMUR

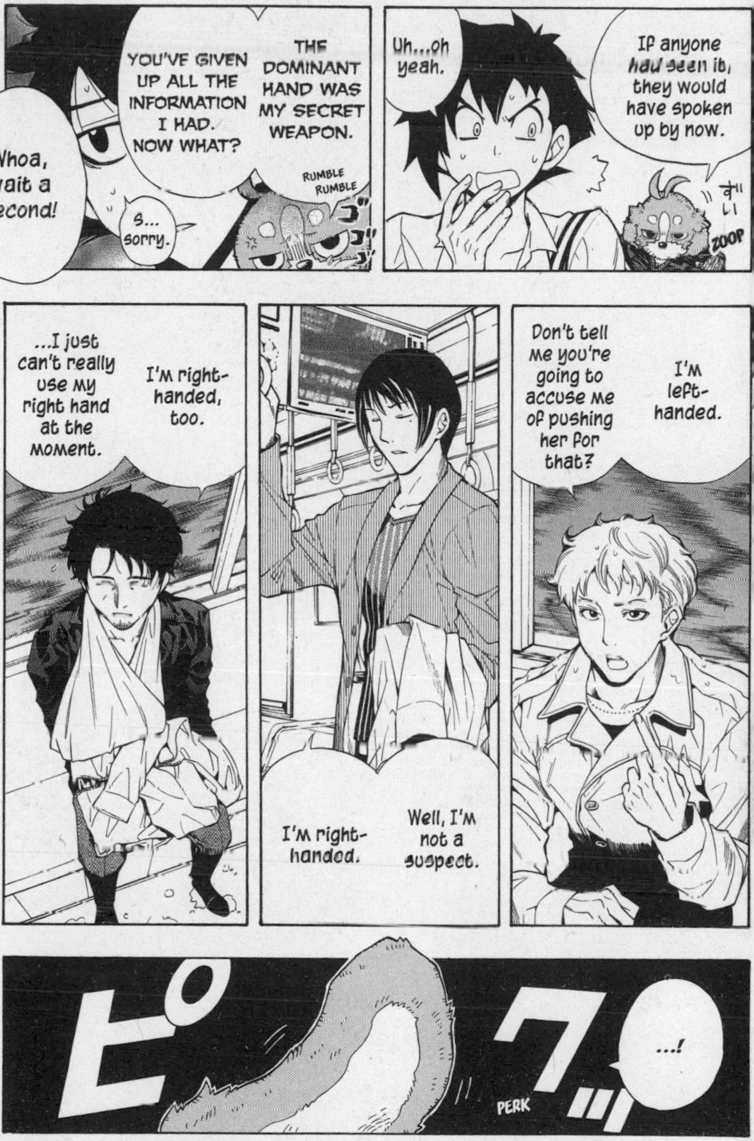
If anyone had seen it, they would have spoken up by now.
Uh...oh yeah.
ずい
ZOOP
THE DOMINANT HAND WAS MY SECRET WEAPON.
YOU'VE GIVEN UP ALL THE INFORMATION I HAD. NOW WHAT?
RUMBLE RUMBLE
ゴゴゴ
S... sorry.
Whoa, wait a second!
I'M left-handed.
Don't tell Me you're going to accuse Me of pushing her for that?
Well, I'M not a suspect.
I'M right-handed.
I'M right-handed, too.
...I just can't really use My right hand at the MoMent.
...!
PERK
ピクッ

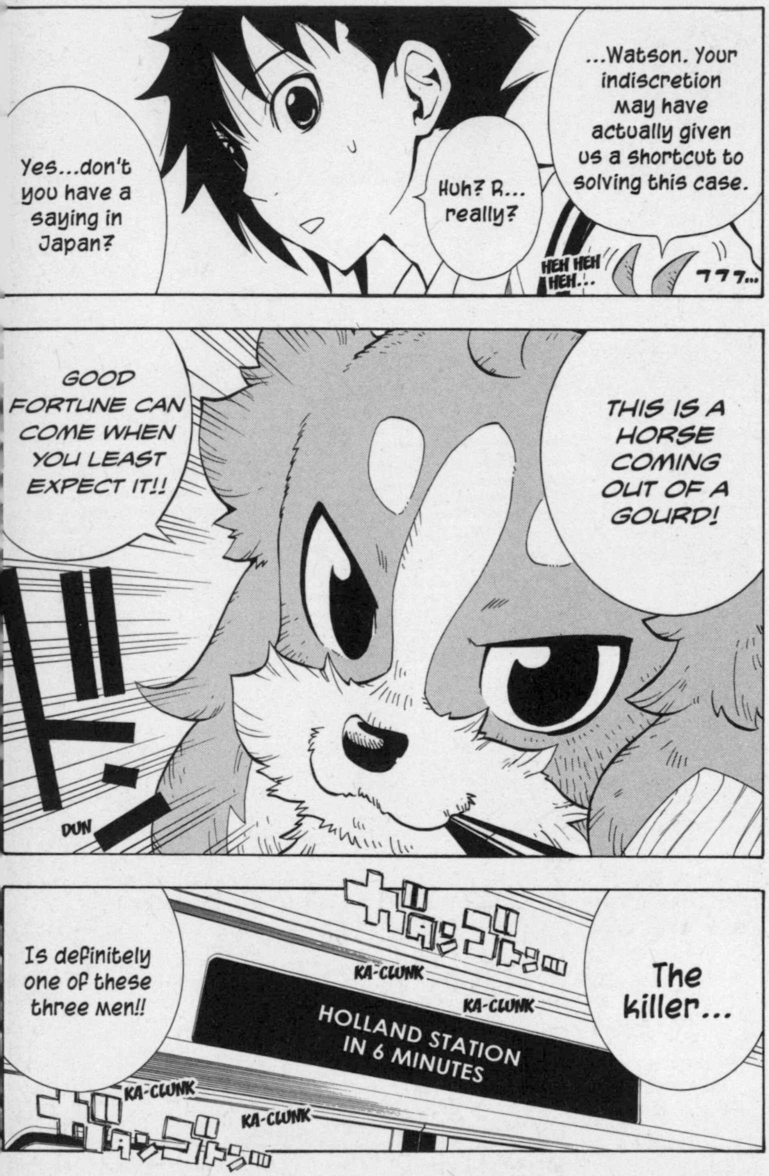
...Watson. Your indiscretion may have actually given us a shortcut to solving this case.
フフフ...
HEH HEH HEH...
Huh? R... really?
Yes...don't you have a saying in Japan?
THIS IS A HORSE COMING OUT OF A GOURD!
GOOD FORTUNE CAN COME WHEN YOU LEAST EXPECT IT!!
DUN
The killer...
KA-CLUNK
KA-CLUNK
HOLLAND STATION IN 6 MINUTES
Is definitely one of these three men!!
KA-CLUNK
KA-CLUNK

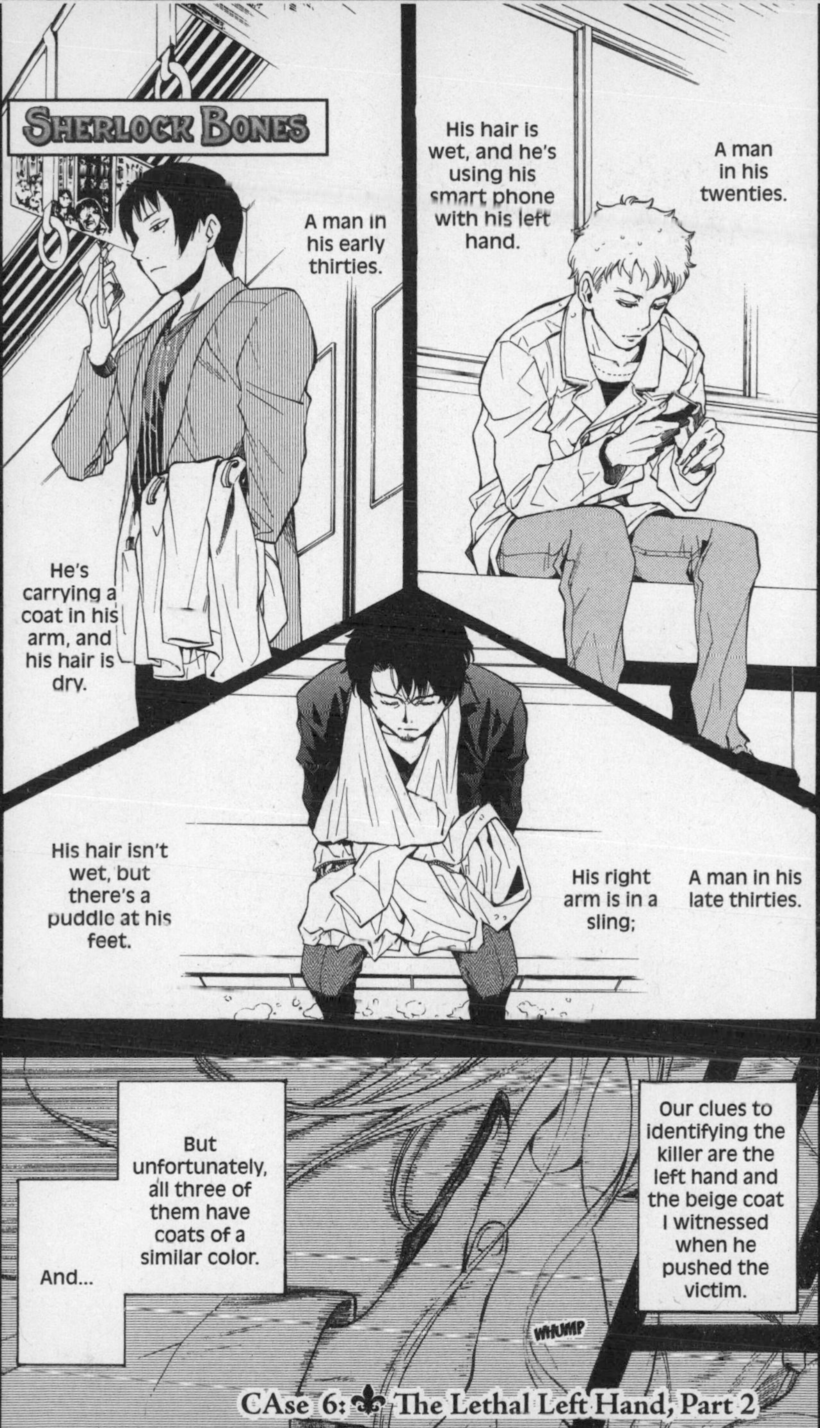
SHERLOCK BONES
A man in his twenties.
His hair is wet, and he's using his smart phone with his left hand.
A man in his early thirties.
He's carrying a coat in his arm, and his hair is dry.
A man in his late thirties.
His right arm is in a sling;
His hair isn't wet, but there's a puddle at his feet.
Our clues to identifying the killer are the left hand and the beige coat I witnessed when he pushed the victim.
But unfortunately, all three of them have coats of a similar color.
And...
WHUMP
CAse 6: ⚜ The Lethal Left Hand, Part 2

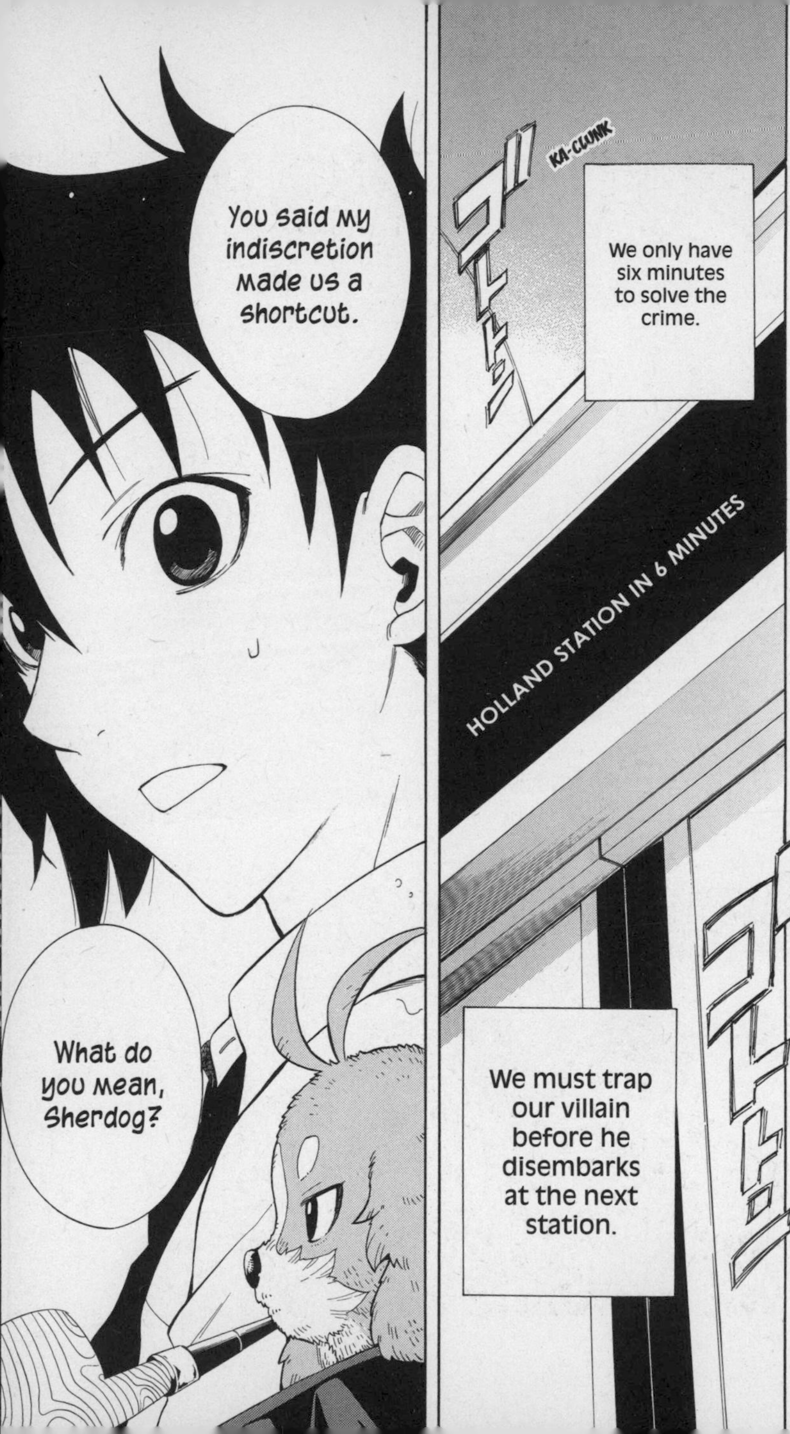
KA-CLUNK
We only have six minutes to solve the crime.
HOLLAND STATION IN 6 MINUTES
We must trap our villain before he disembarks at the next station.
KA-CLUNK
You said my indiscretion made us a shortcut.
What do you mean, Sherdog?

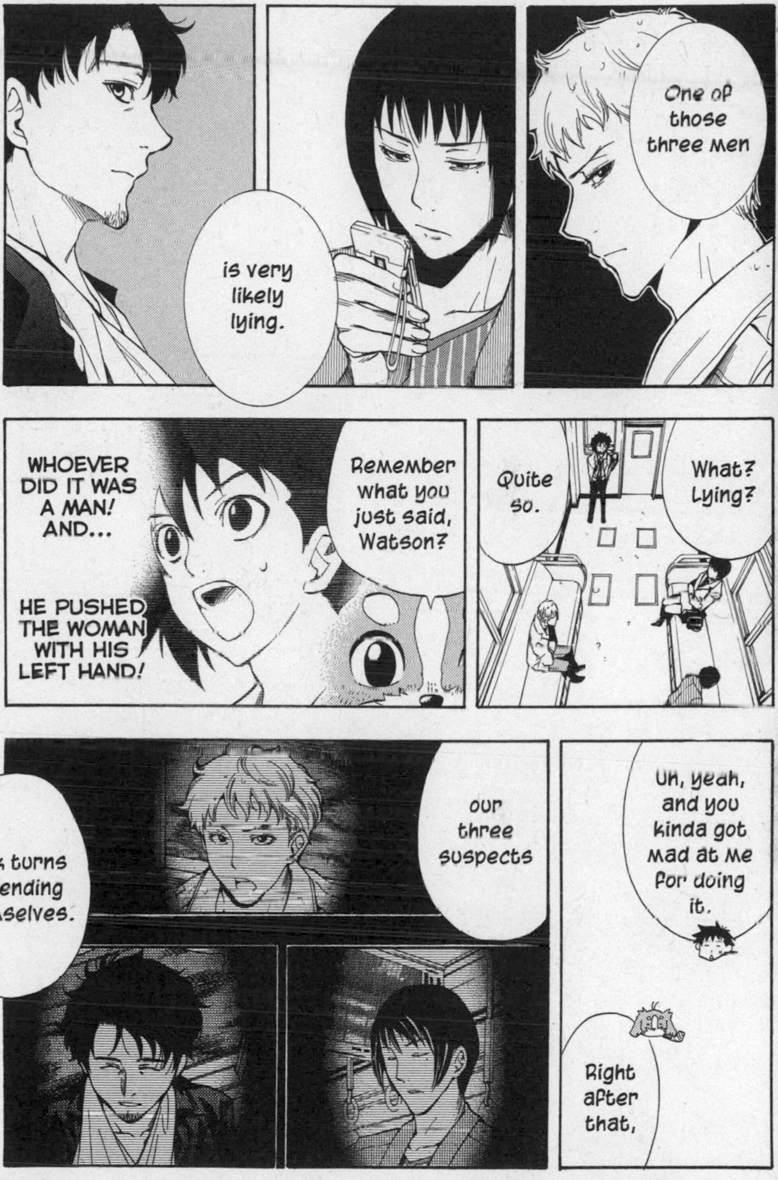
One of those three men
is very likely lying.
What? Lying?
Quite so.
Remember what you just said, Watson?
WHOEVER DID IT WAS A MAN! AND...
HE PUSHED THE WOMAN WITH HIS LEFT HAND!
Uh, yeah, and you kinda got mad at me for doing it.
Right after that,
our three suspects
took turns defending themselves.

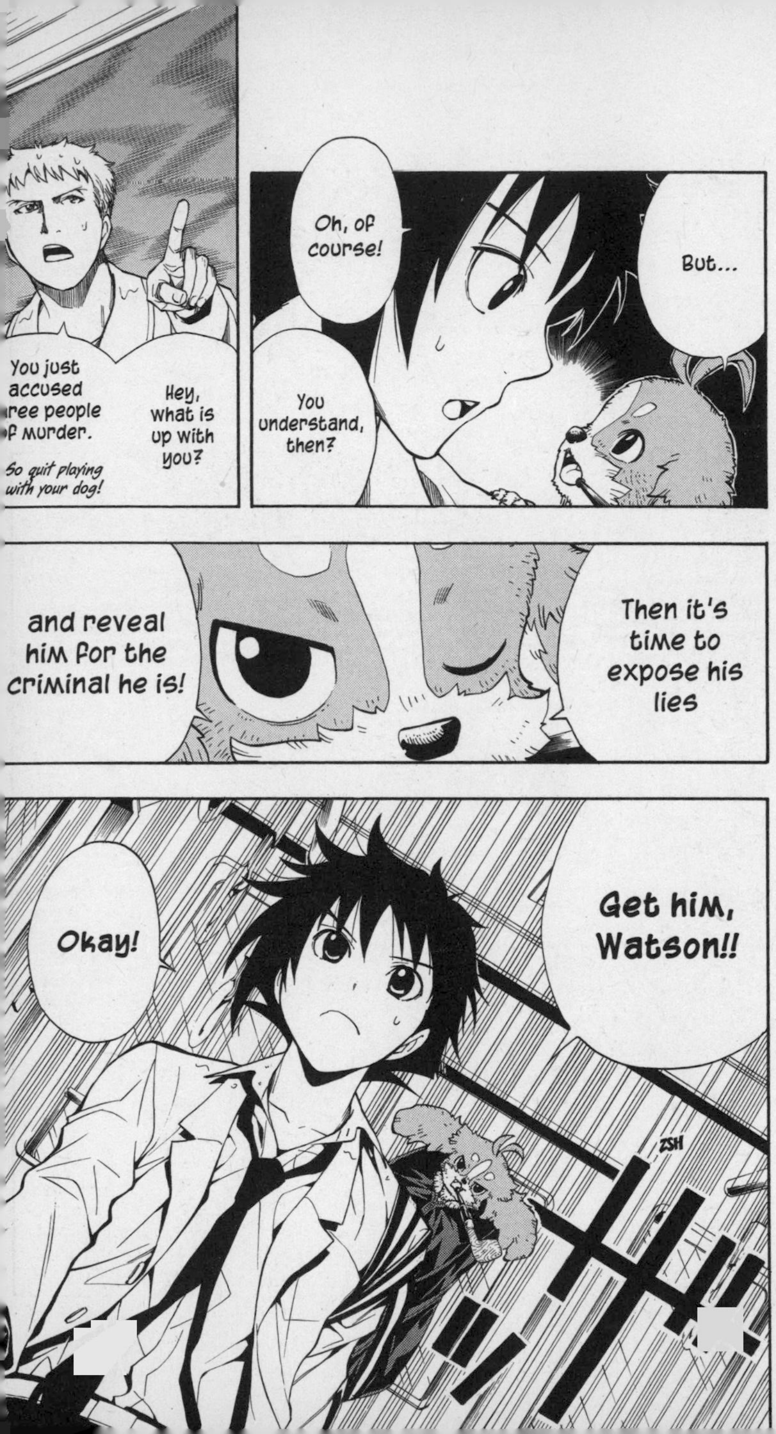
But...
Oh, of course!
You understand, then?
Hey, what is up with you?
You just accused ree people f murder.
So quit playing with your dog!
Then it's time to expose his lies
and reveal him for the criminal he is!
Get him, Watson!!
ZSH
Okay!

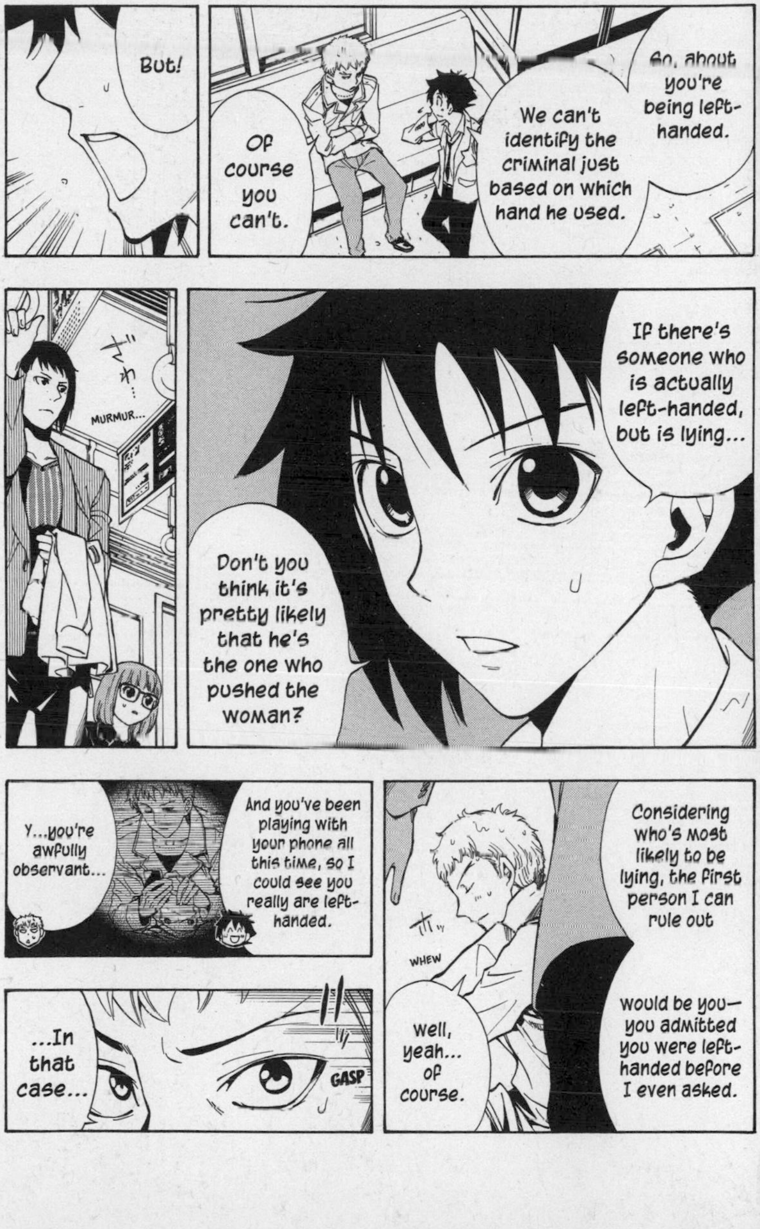
So, about you're being left-handed.
We can't identify the criminal just based on which hand he used.
Of course you can't.
But!
If there's someone who is actually left-handed, but is lying...
Don't you think it's pretty likely that he's the one who pushed the woman?
ざわ…
MURMUR...
Considering who's most likely to be lying, the first person I can rule out
would be you—you admitted you were left-handed before I even asked.
ホッ
WHEW
Well, yeah... of course.
And you've been playing with your phone all this time, so I could see you really are left-handed.
Y...you're awfully observant...
...In that case...
GASP

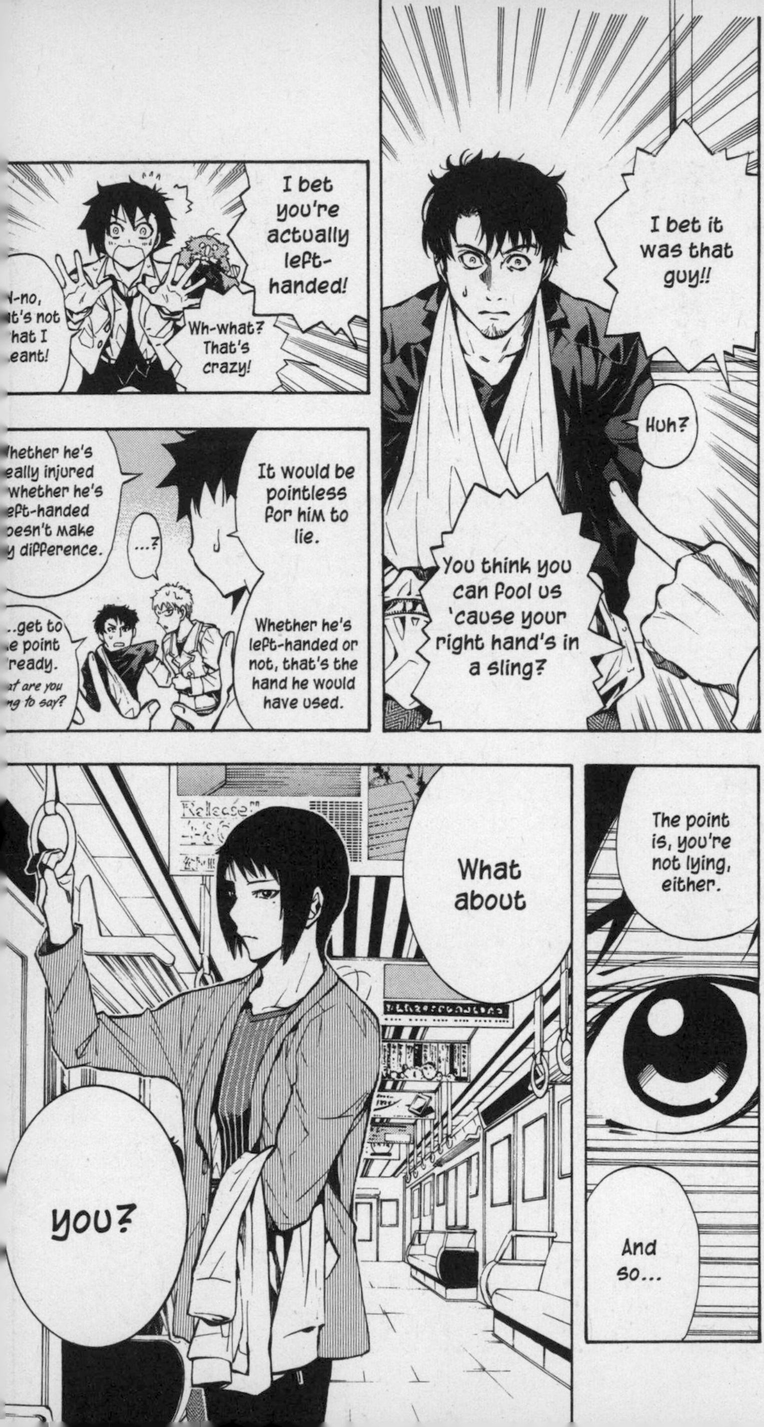

I bet it was that guy!!
Huh?
You think you can fool us 'cause your right hand's in a sling?
I bet you're actually left-handed!
Wh-what? That's crazy!
-no, t's not hat I eant!
It would be pointless for him to lie.
hether he's eally injured whether he's eft-handed oesn't make difference.
...?
Whether he's left-handed or not, that's the hand he would have used.
..get to e point ready. at are you ng to say?
The point is, you're not lying, either.
And so...
What about
you?

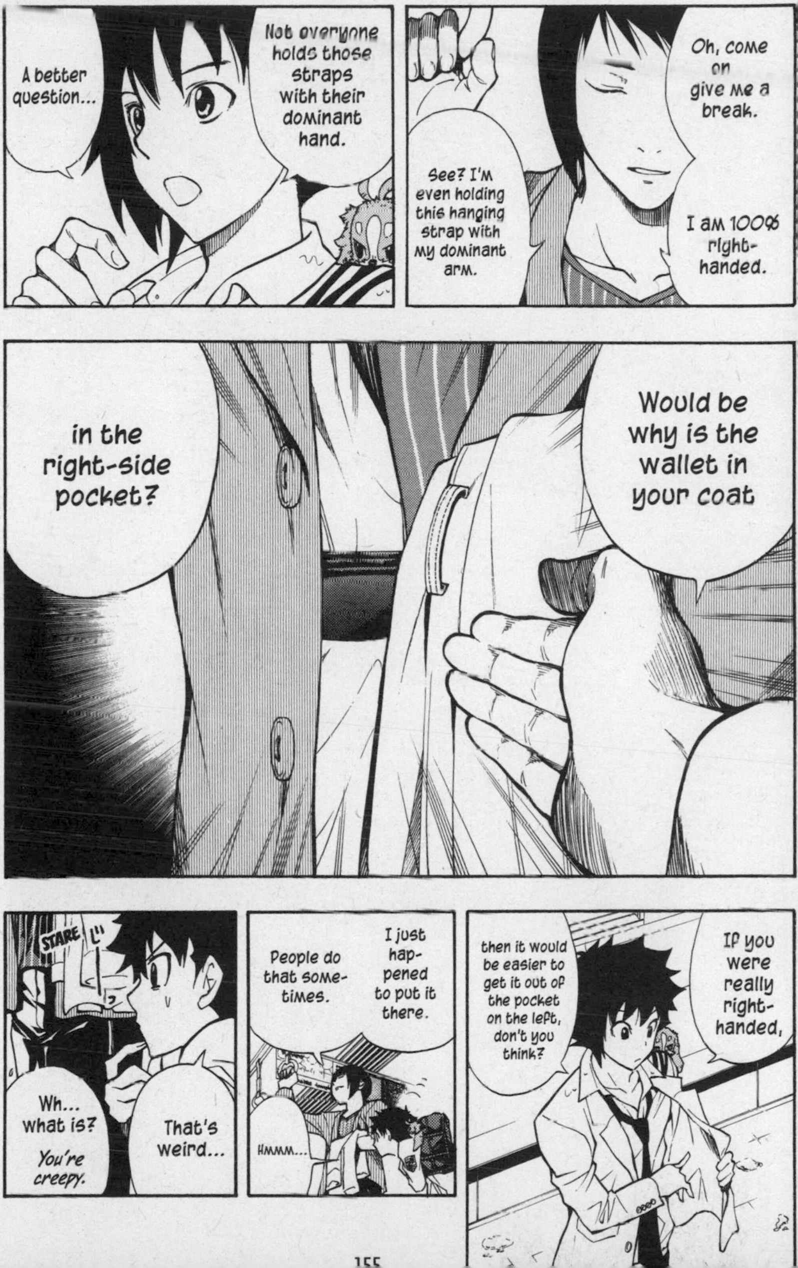
Oh, come on give me a break.
See? I'm even holding this hanging strap with my dominant arm.
I am 100% right-handed.
Not everyone holds those straps with their dominant hand.
A better question...
Would be why is the wallet in your coat
in the right-side pocket?
If you were really right-handed,
then it would be easier to get it out of the pocket on the left, don't you think?
I just hap-pened to put it there.
People do that some-times.
HMMM...
STARE
じ
That's weird...
Wh... what is?
You're creepy.

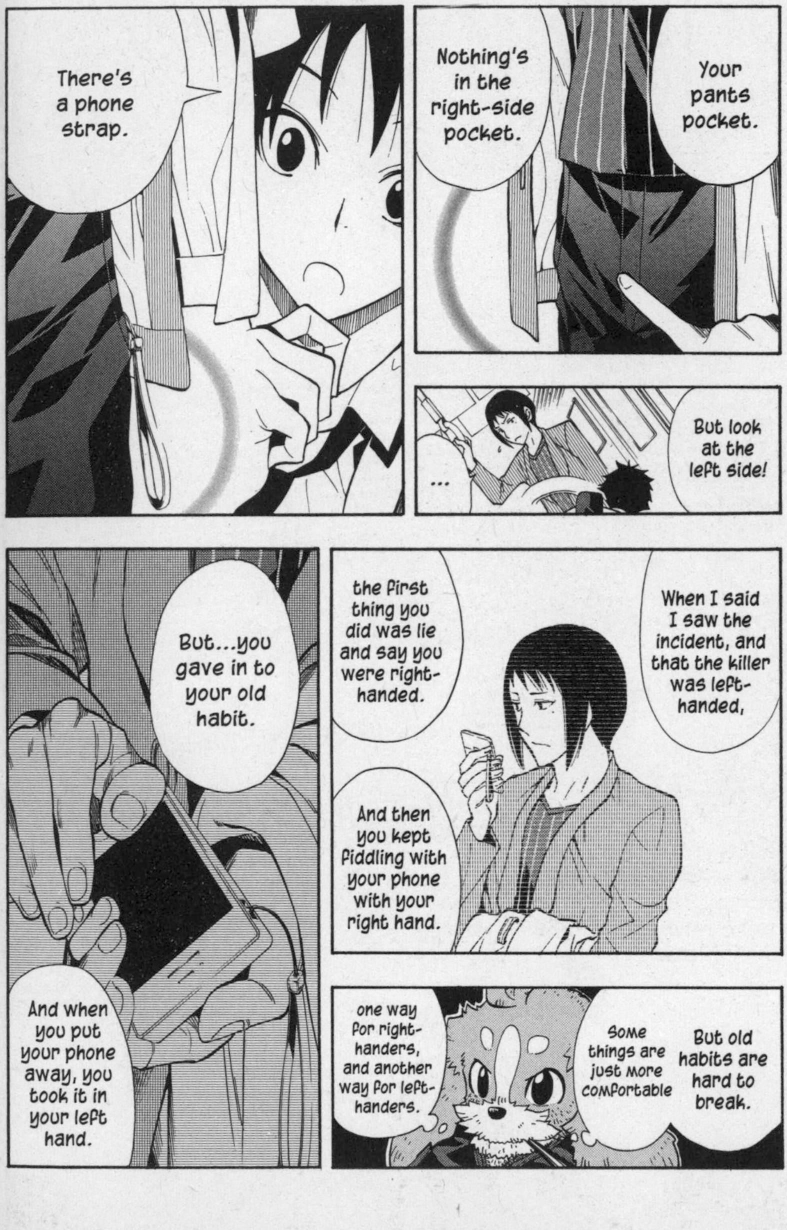
Your pants pocket.
Nothing's in the right-side pocket.
But look at the left side!
...
There's a phone strap.
When I said I saw the incident, and that the killer was left-handed,
the first thing you did was lie and say you were right-handed.
And then you kept fiddling with your phone with your right hand.
But old habits are hard to break.
Some things are just more comfortable
one way for right-handers, and another way for left-handers.
But...you gave in to your old habit.
And when you put your phone away, you took it in your left hand.

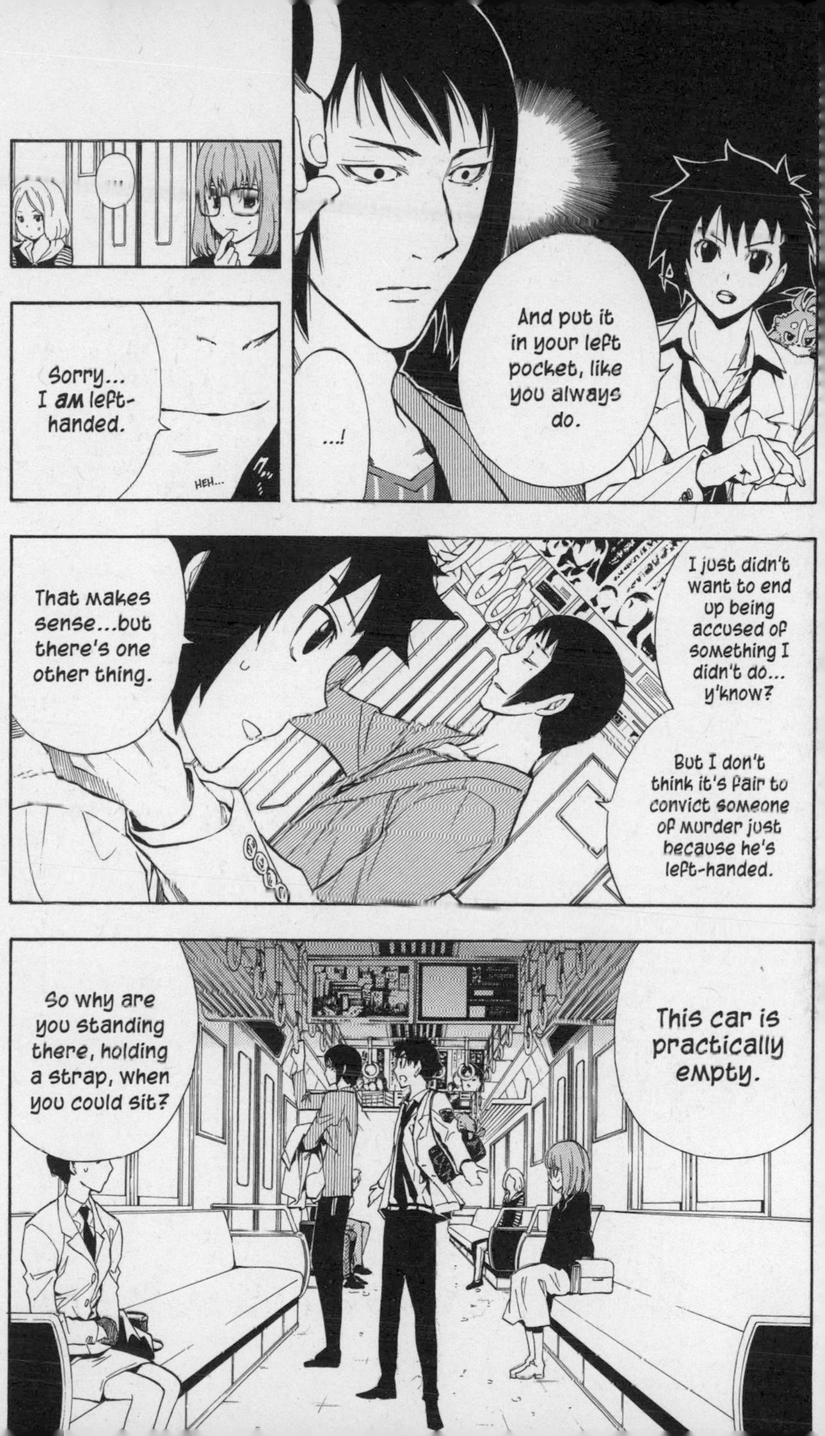
And put it in your left pocket, like you always do.
...!
...
Sorry... I am left-handed.
HEH...
I just didn't want to end up being accused of something I didn't do... y'know?
But I don't think it's fair to convict someone of murder just because he's left-handed.
That makes sense...but there's one other thing.
This car is practically empty.
So why are you standing there, holding a strap, when you could sit?

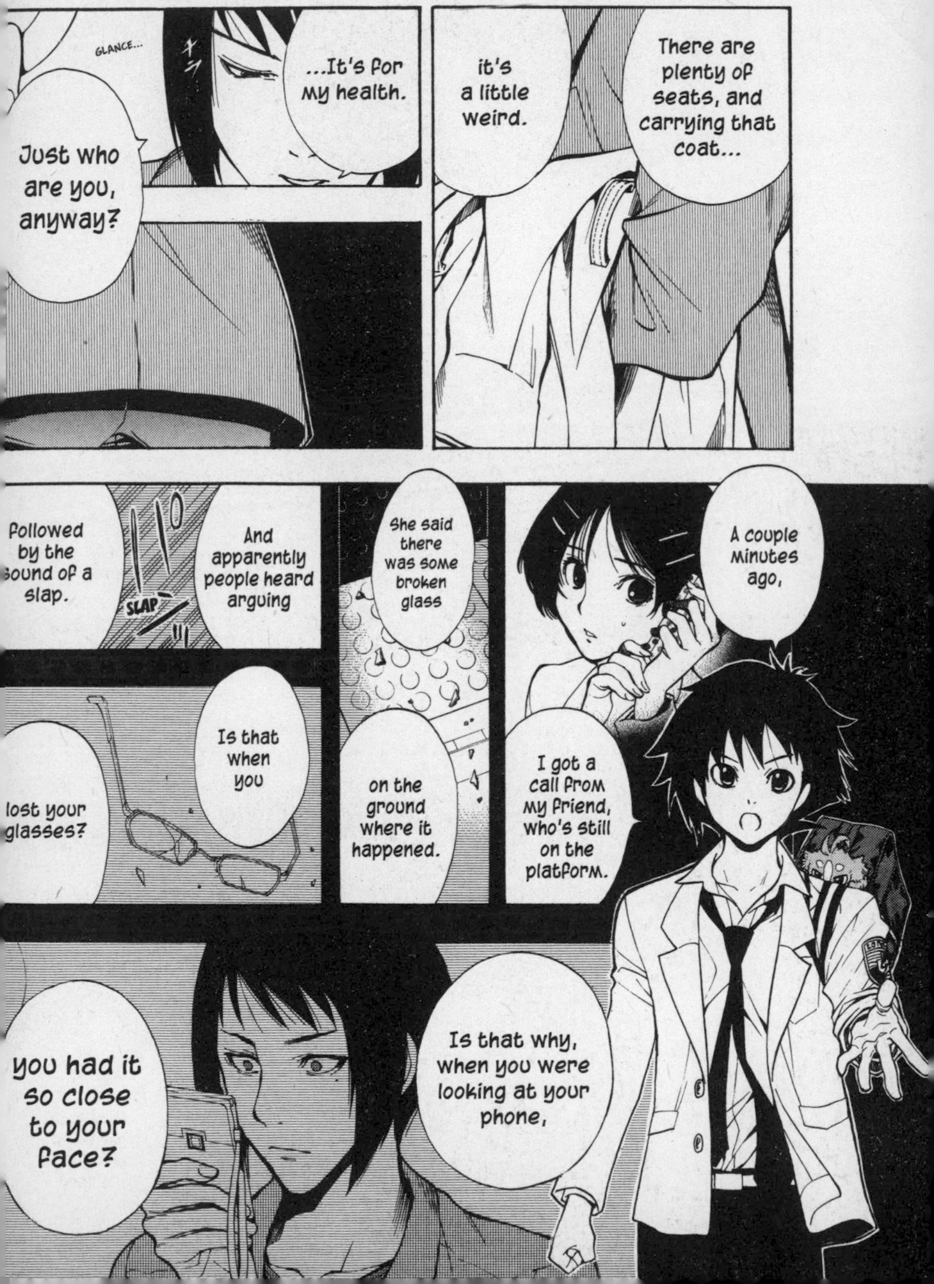
There are plenty of seats, and carrying that coat...
it's a little weird.
...It's for my health.
GLANCE...
Just who are you, anyway?
A couple minutes ago,
I got a call from my friend, who's still on the platform.
She said there was some broken glass
on the ground where it happened.
And apparently people heard arguing
SLAP
followed by the sound of a slap.
Is that when you
lost your glasses?
Is that why, when you were looking at your phone,
you had it so close to your face?

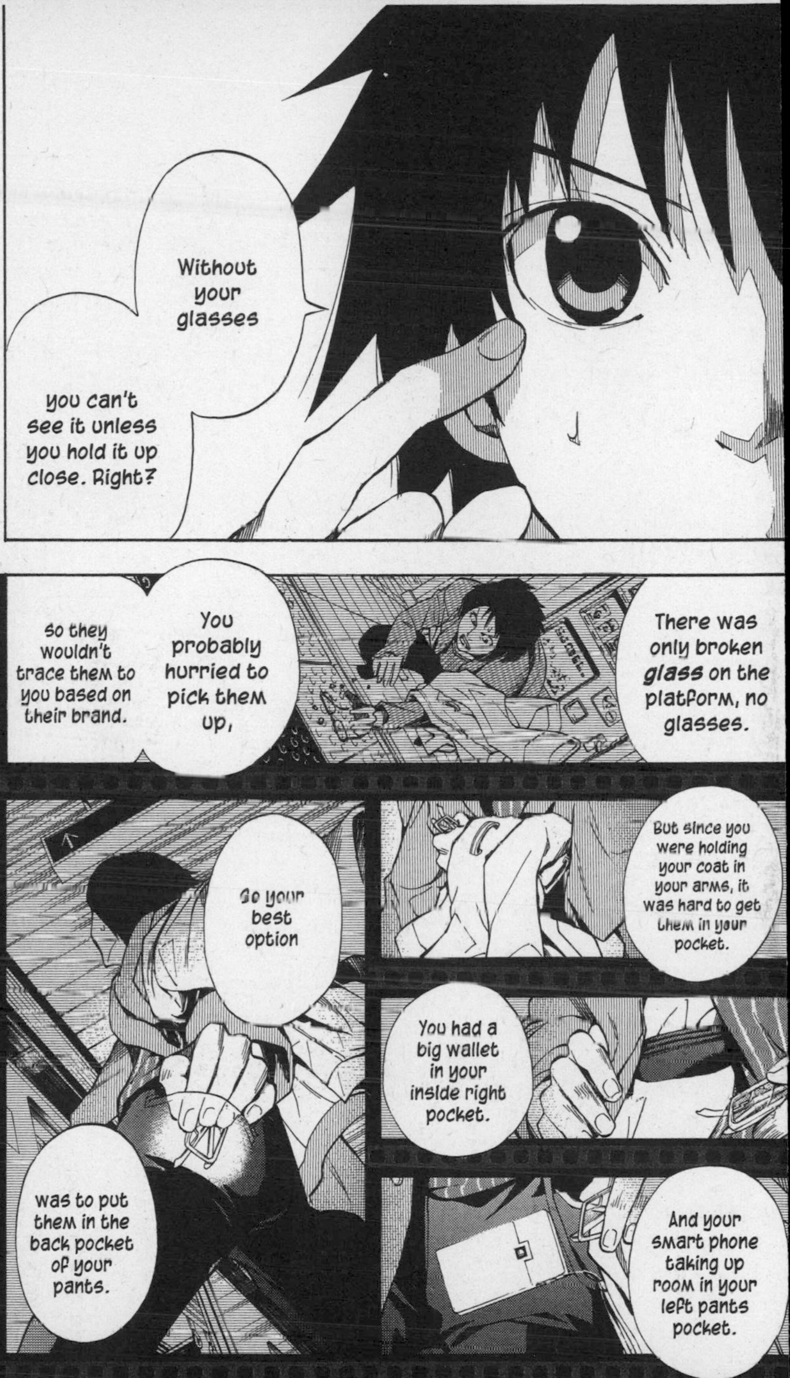
Without your glasses
you can't see it unless you hold it up close. Right?
There was only broken glass on the platform, no glasses.
You probably hurried to pick them up,
so they wouldn't trace them to you based on their brand.
But since you were holding your coat in your arms, it was hard to get them in your pocket.
You had a big wallet in your inside right pocket.
And your smart phone taking up room in your left pants pocket.
So your best option
was to put them in the back pocket of your pants.

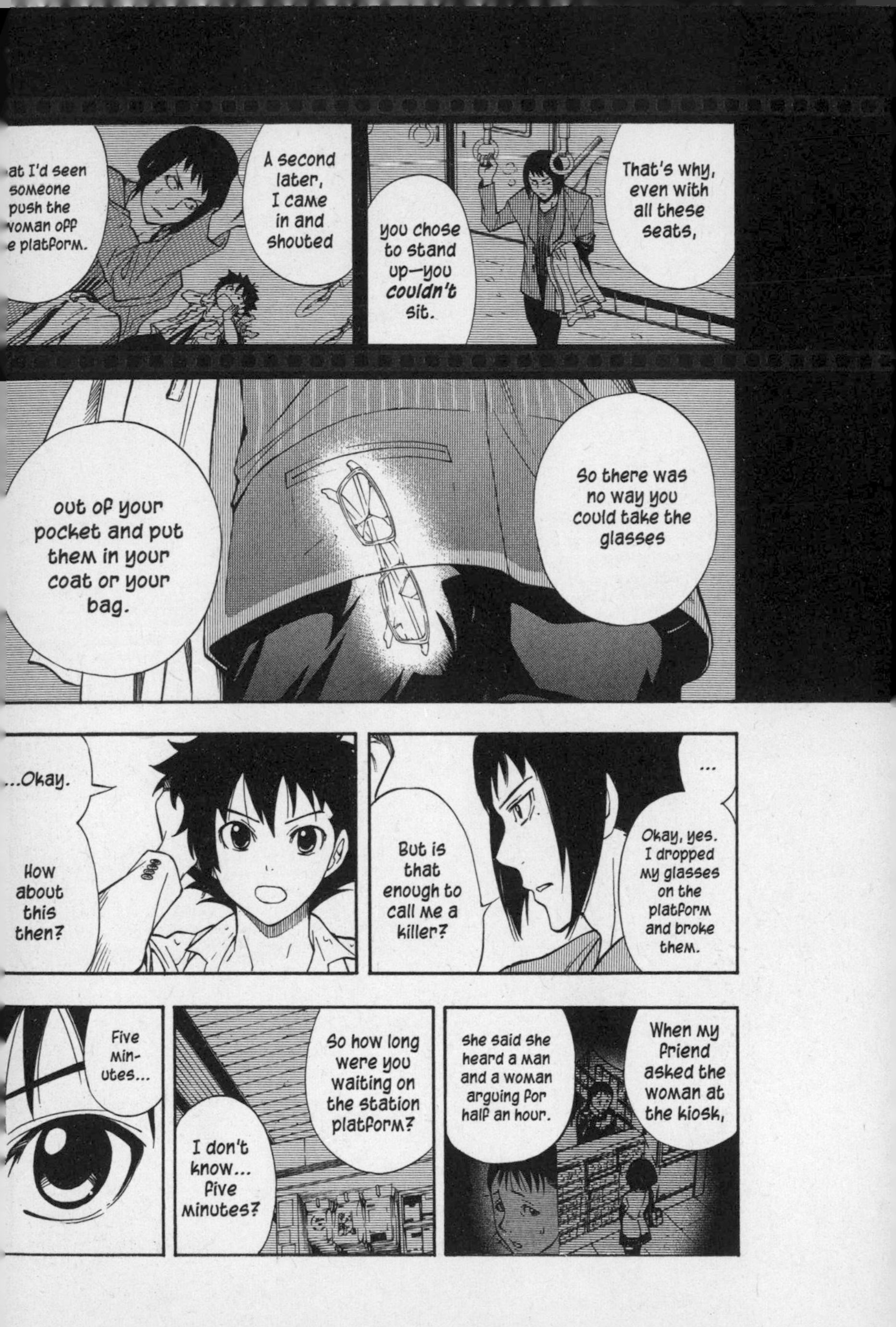
That's why, even with all these seats,
you chose to stand up—you *couldn't* sit.
A second later, I came in and shouted
at I'd seen someone push the woman off e platform.
So there was no way you could take the glasses
out of your pocket and put them in your coat or your bag.
...
Okay, yes. I dropped my glasses on the platform and broke them.
But is that enough to call me a killer?
...Okay.
How about this then?
When my friend asked the woman at the kiosk,
she said she heard a man and a woman arguing for half an hour.
So how long were you waiting on the station platform?
I don't know... five minutes?
Five minutes...

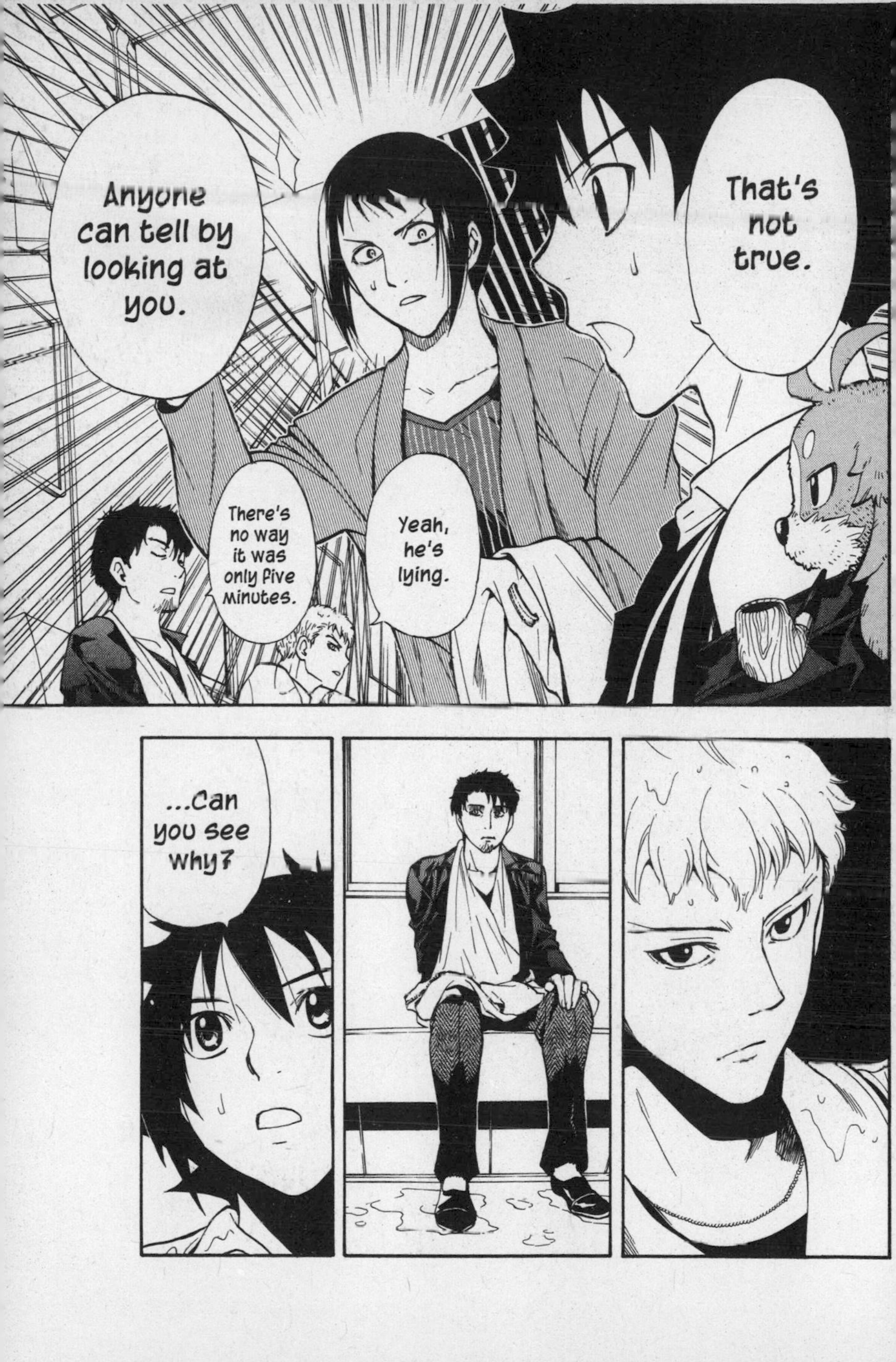
That's not true.
Anyone can tell by looking at you.
Yeah, he's lying.
There's no way it was only five minutes.
...Can you see why?

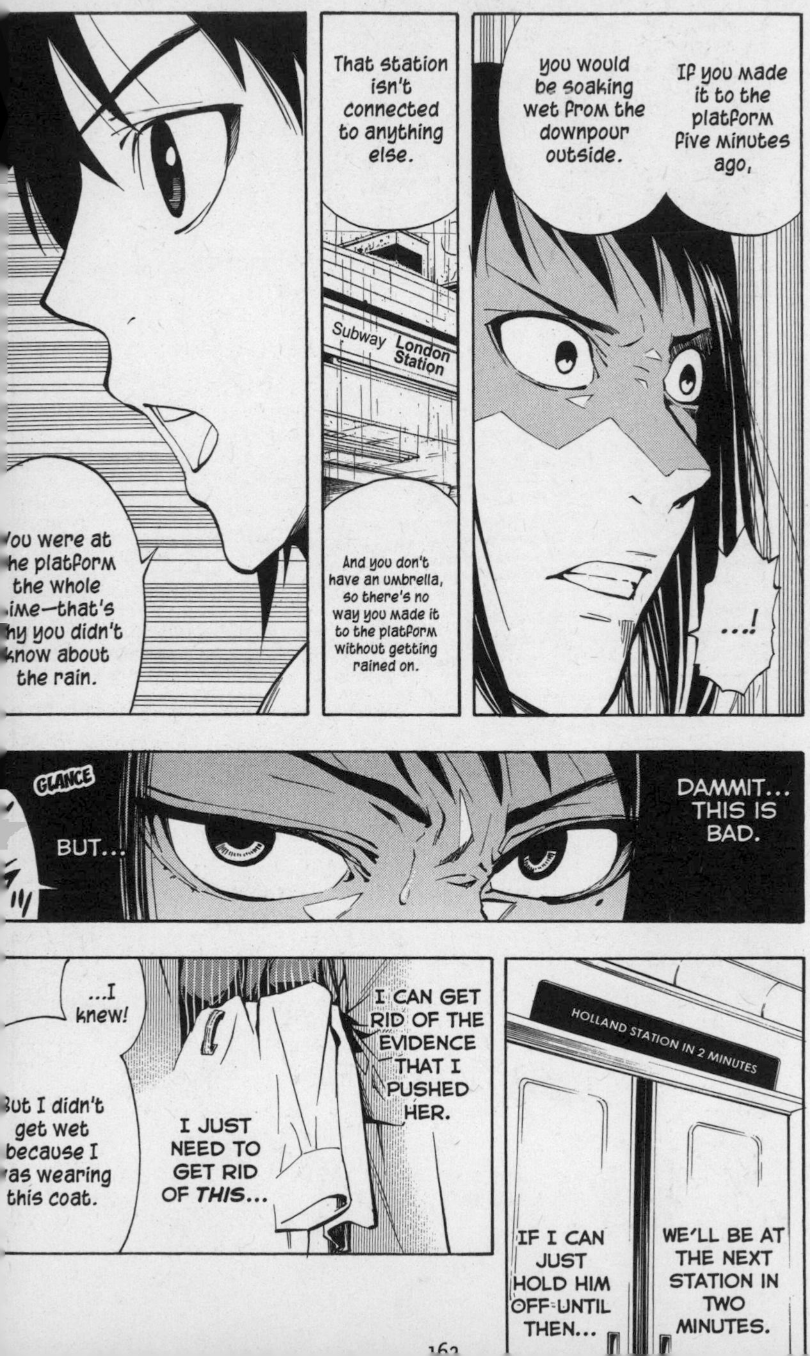
If you made it to the platform five minutes ago,
you would be soaking wet from the downpour outside.
...!
That station isn't connected to anything else.
Subway London Station
And you don't have an umbrella, so there's no way you made it to the platform without getting rained on.
ou were at he platform the whole ime—that's hy you didn't know about the rain.
DAMMIT... THIS IS BAD.
GLANCE
BUT...
HOLLAND STATION IN 2 MINUTES
WE'LL BE AT THE NEXT STATION IN TWO MINUTES.
IF I CAN JUST HOLD HIM OFF UNTIL THEN...
I CAN GET RID OF THE EVIDENCE THAT I PUSHED HER.
I JUST NEED TO GET RID OF THIS...
...I knew!
ut I didn't get wet because I as wearing this coat.

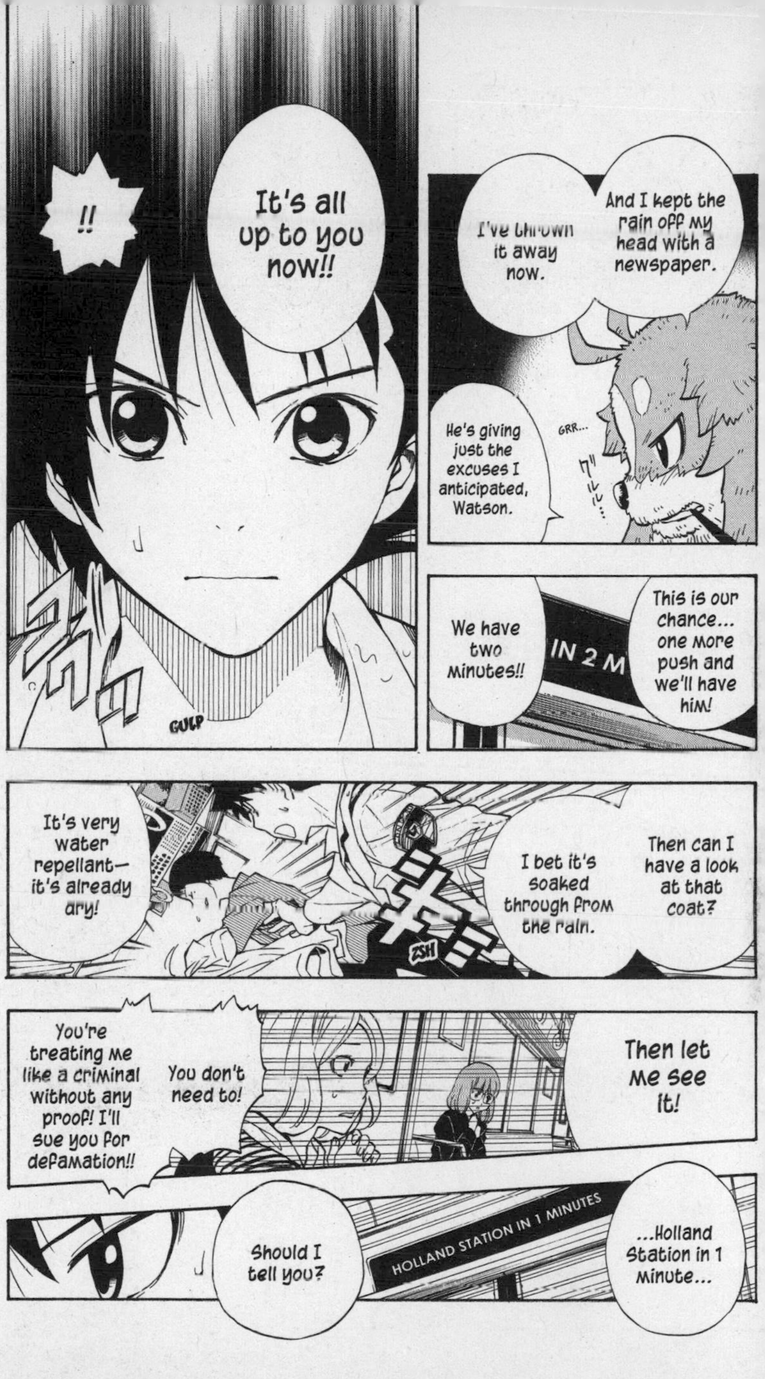
And I kept the rain off my head with a newspaper.
I've thrown it away now.
GRR...
He's giving just the excuses I anticipated, Watson.
This is our chance... one more push and we'll have him!
IN 2 M
We have two minutes!!
It's all up to you now!!
!!
GULP
Then can I have a look at that coat?
I bet it's soaked through from the rain.
ZSH
It's very water repellant—it's already dry!
Then let me see it!
You don't need to!
You're treating me like a criminal without any proof! I'll sue you for defamation!!
...Holland Station in 1 Minute...
HOLLAND STATION IN 1 MINUTES
Should I tell you?

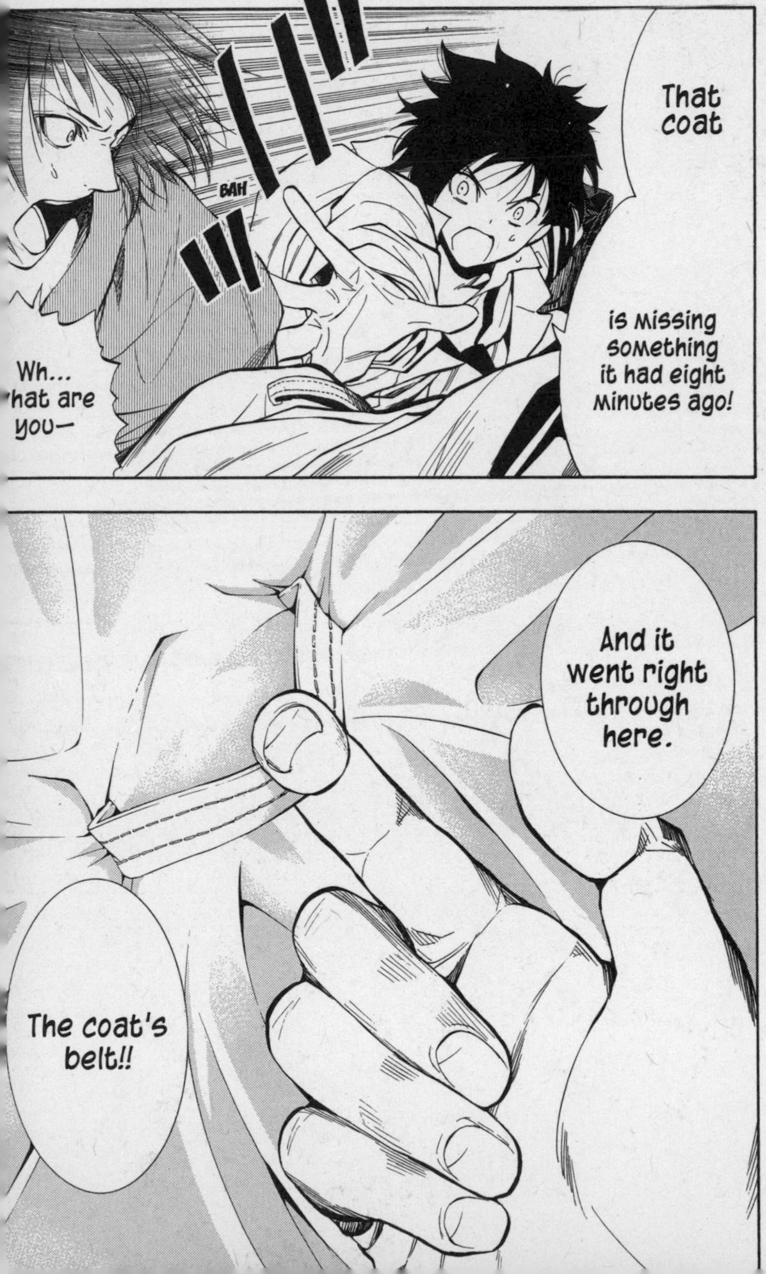
That coat
is missing something it had eight minutes ago!
BAH
Wh... hat are you—
And it went right through here.
The coat's belt!!

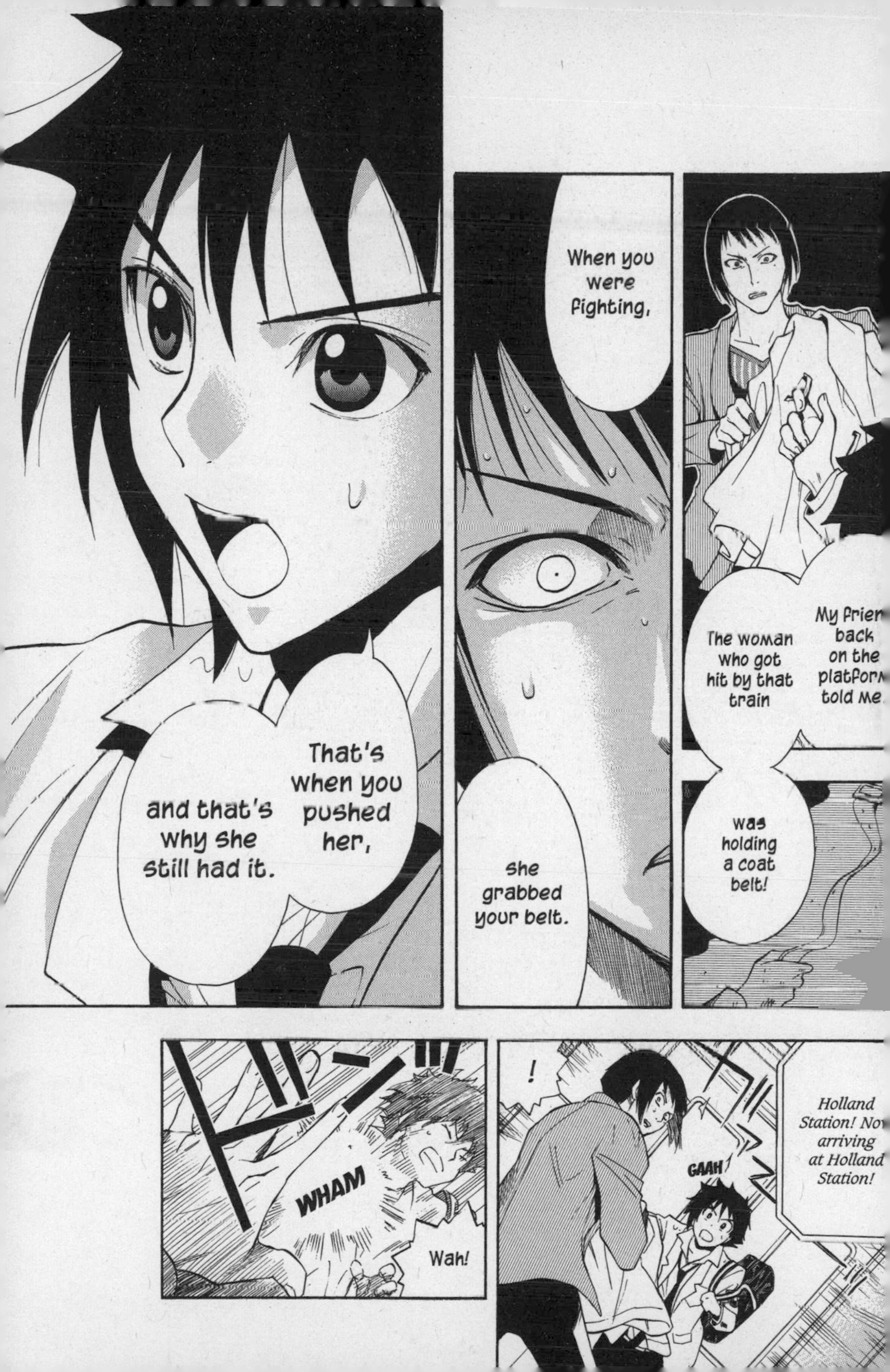
My frien back on the platfor told me.
The woman who got hit by that train
was holding a coat belt!
When you were fighting,
she grabbed your belt.
That's when you pushed her,
and that's why she still had it.
Holland Station! No arriving at Holland Station!
!
GAAH!
WHAM
Wah!

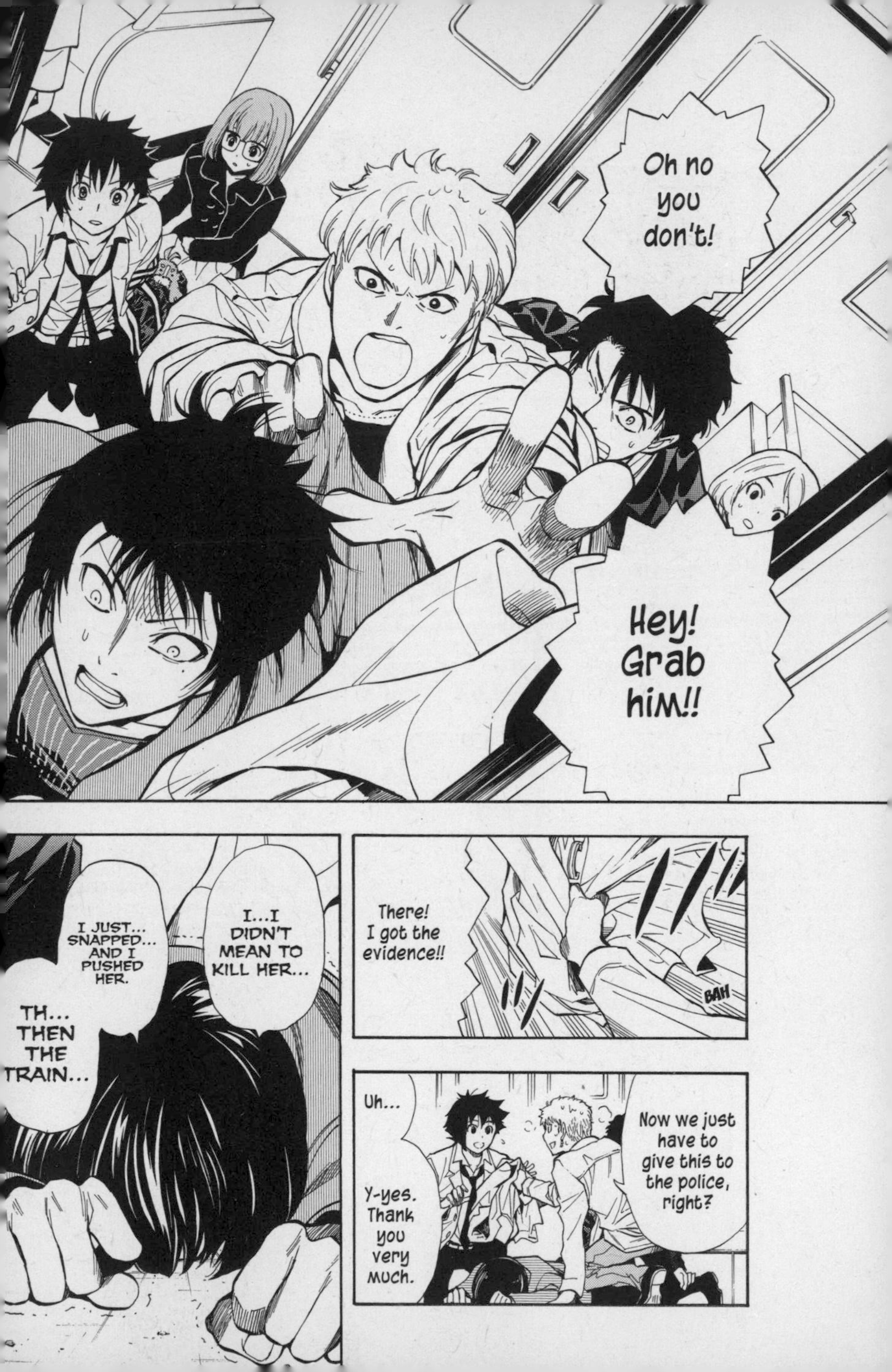
Oh no you don't!
Hey! Grab him!!
There! I got the evidence!!
BAH
Now we just have to give this to the police, right?
Uh...
Y-yes. Thank you very much.
I...I DIDN'T MEAN TO KILL HER...
I JUST... SNAPPED... AND I PUSHED HER.
TH... THEN THE TRAIN...

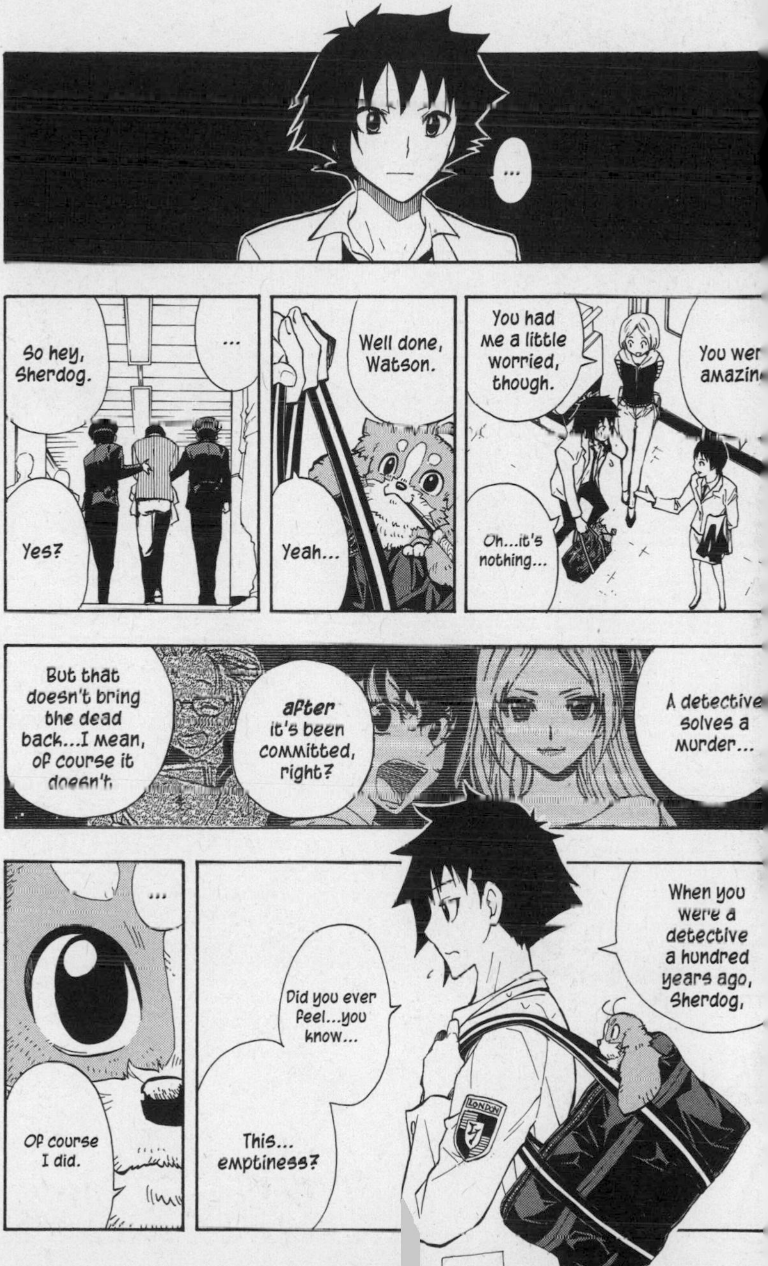
...
You wer
amazin
You had me a little worried, though.
Oh...it's nothing...
Well done, Watson.
Yeah...
...
So hey, Sherdog.
Yes?
A detective solves a murder...
after it's been committed, right?
But that doesn't bring the dead back...I mean, of course it doesn't.
When you were a detective a hundred years ago, Sherdog,
Did you ever feel...you know...
This... emptiness?
...
Of course I did.

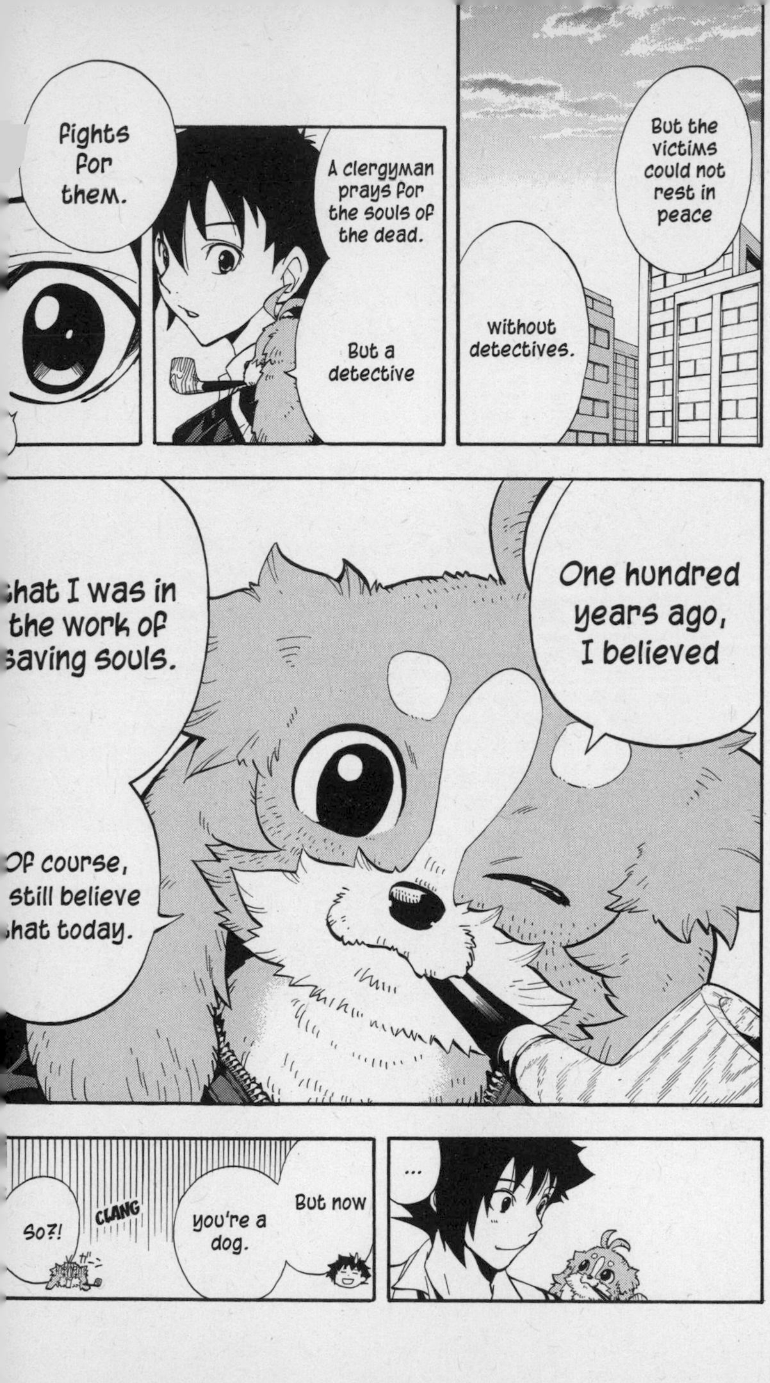

But the victims could not rest in peace
without detectives.
A clergyman prays for the souls of the dead.
But a detective
fights for them.
One hundred years ago, I believed
hat I was in the work of aving souls.
Of course, still believe hat today.
...
But now
you're a dog.
CLANG
So?!

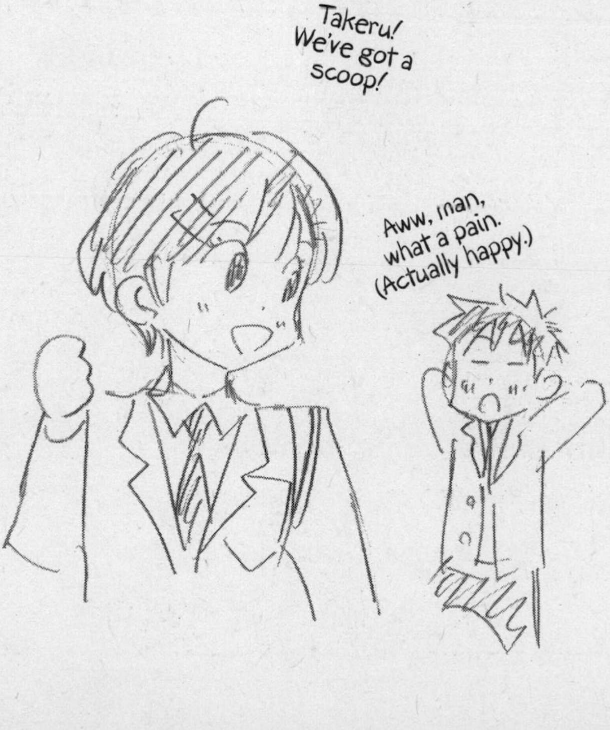
Takeru! We've got a scoop!
Aww, man, what a pain. (Actually happy.)

SHERLOCK BONES

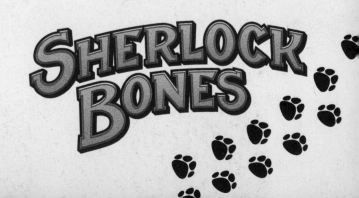

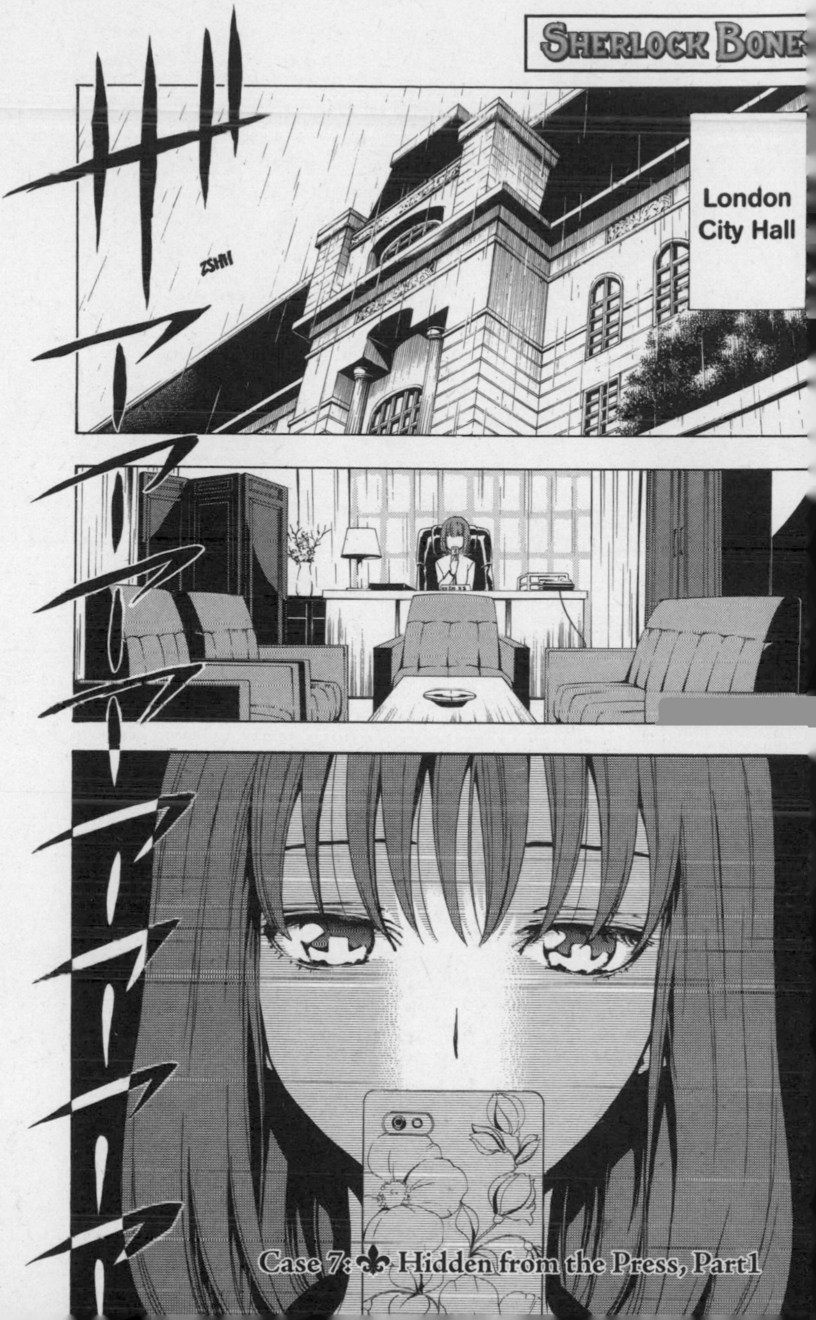
SHERLOCK BONES
London City Hall
ZSHH
Case 7: Hidden from the Press, Part1

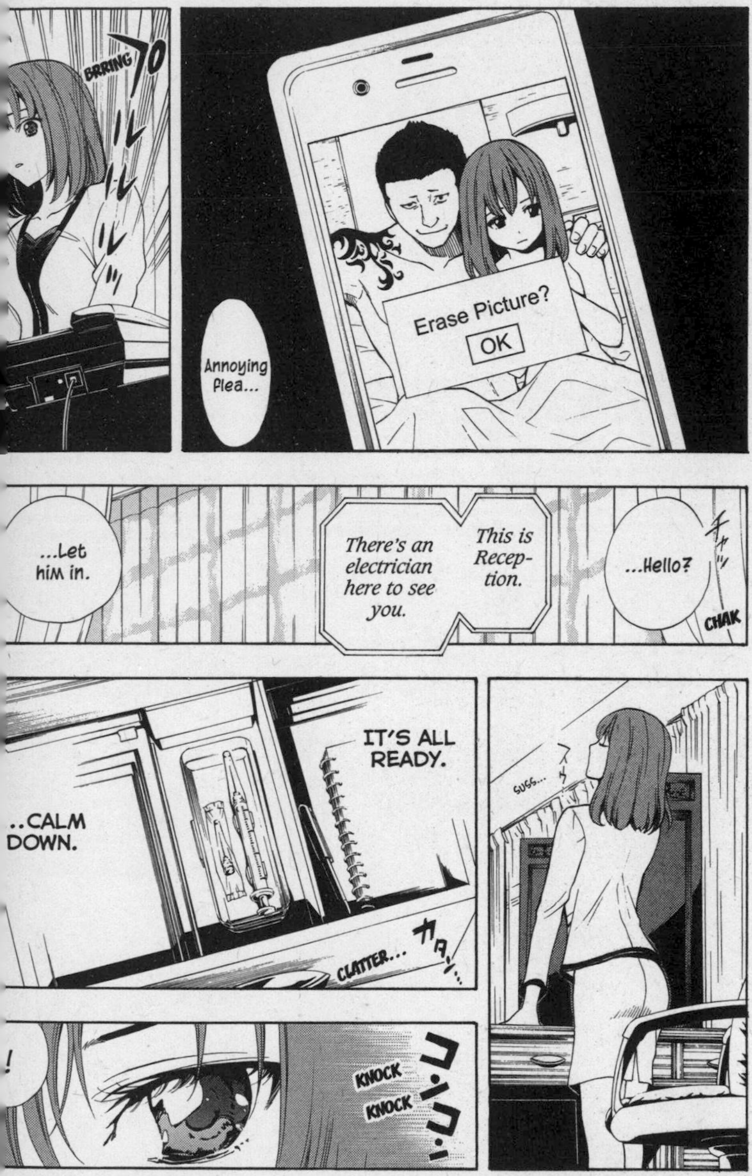
Erase Picture?
OK
Annoying flea...
BRRING
CHAK
...Hello?
This is Reception.
There's an electrician here to see you.
...Let him in.
SUGG...
IT'S ALL READY.
...CALM DOWN.
CLATTER...
KNOCK KNOCK
!

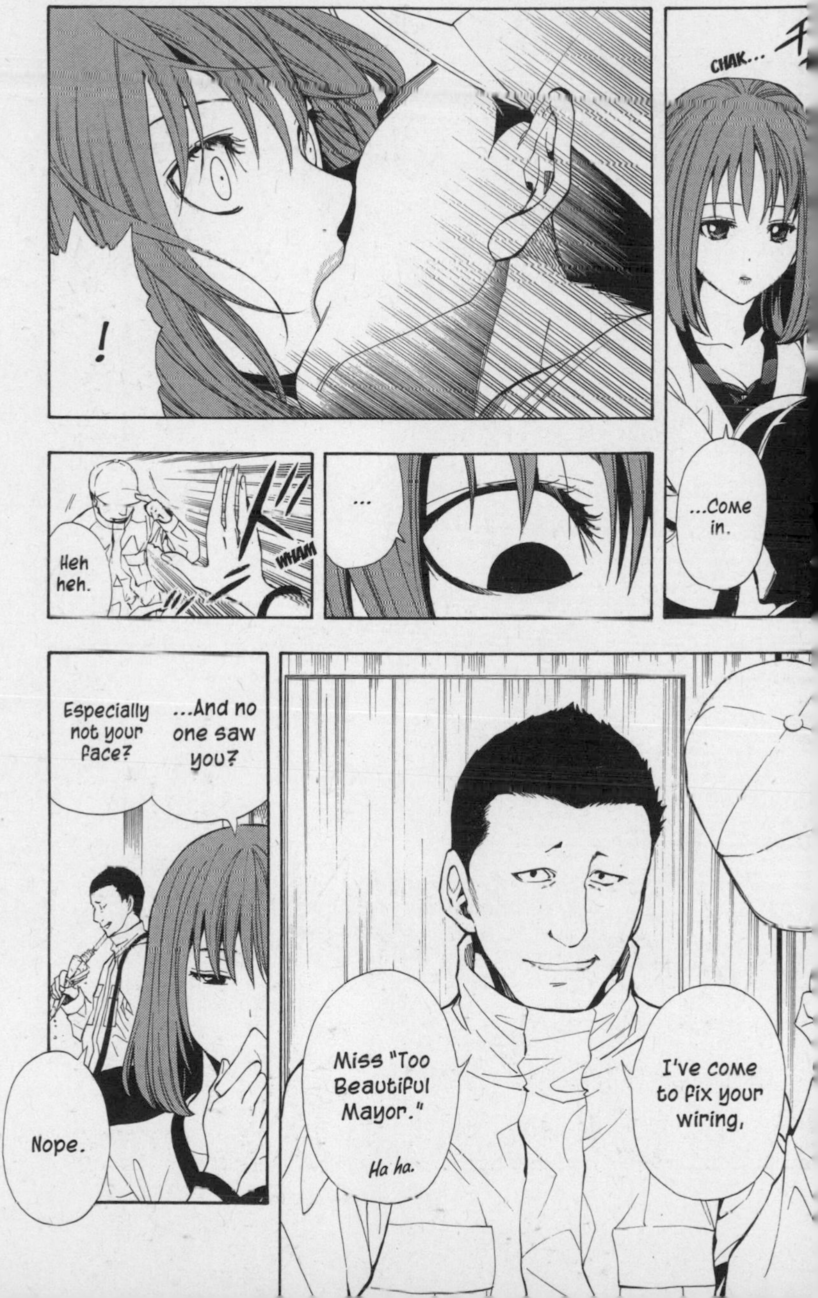
CHAK...
...Come in.
!
...
WHAM
Heh heh.
I've come to fix your wiring,
Miss "Too Beautiful Mayor."
Ha ha.
...And no one saw you?
Especially not your face?
Nope.

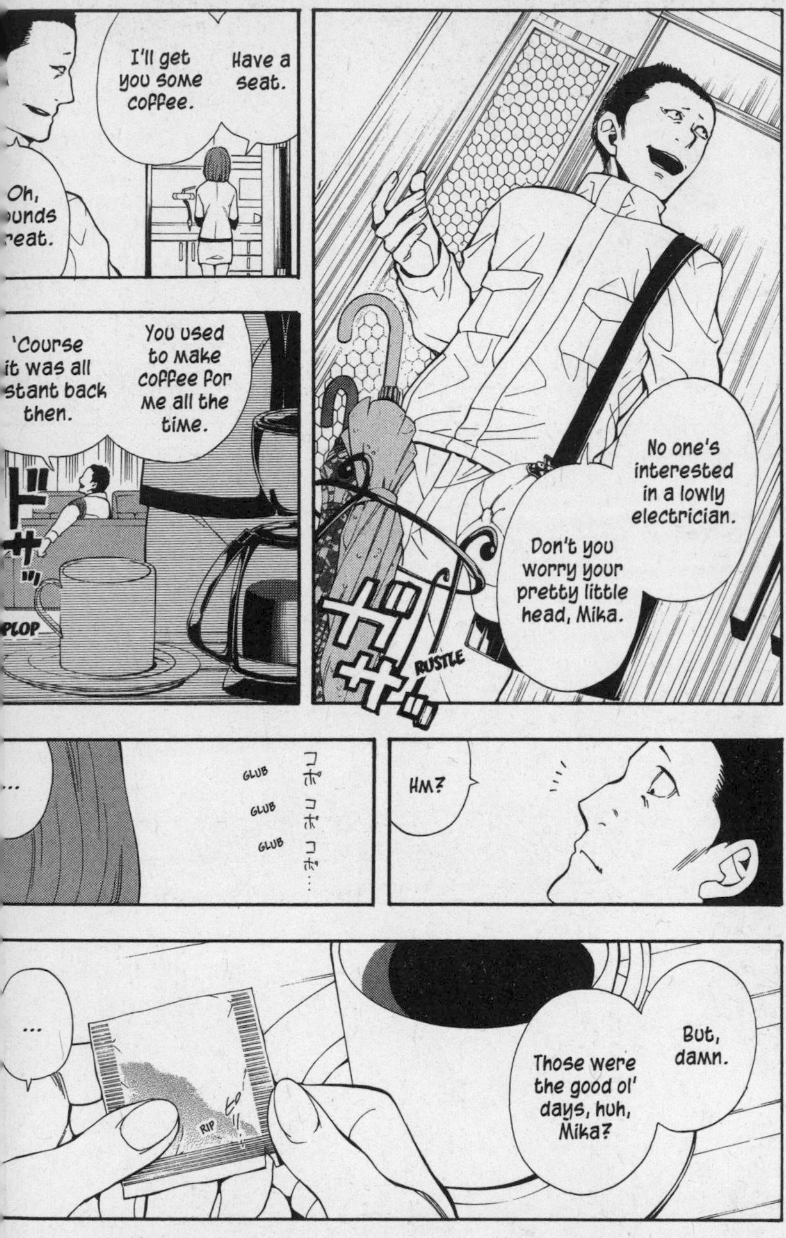
No one's interested in a lowly electrician.
Don't you worry your pretty little head, Mika.
RUSTLE
Have a seat.
I'll get you some coffee.
Oh, ounds reat.
You used to make coffee for me all the time.
'Course it was all stant back then.
PLOP
HM?
GLUB
GLUB
GLUB
コポコポコポ…
...
But, damn.
Those were the good ol' days, huh, Mika?
...
RIP

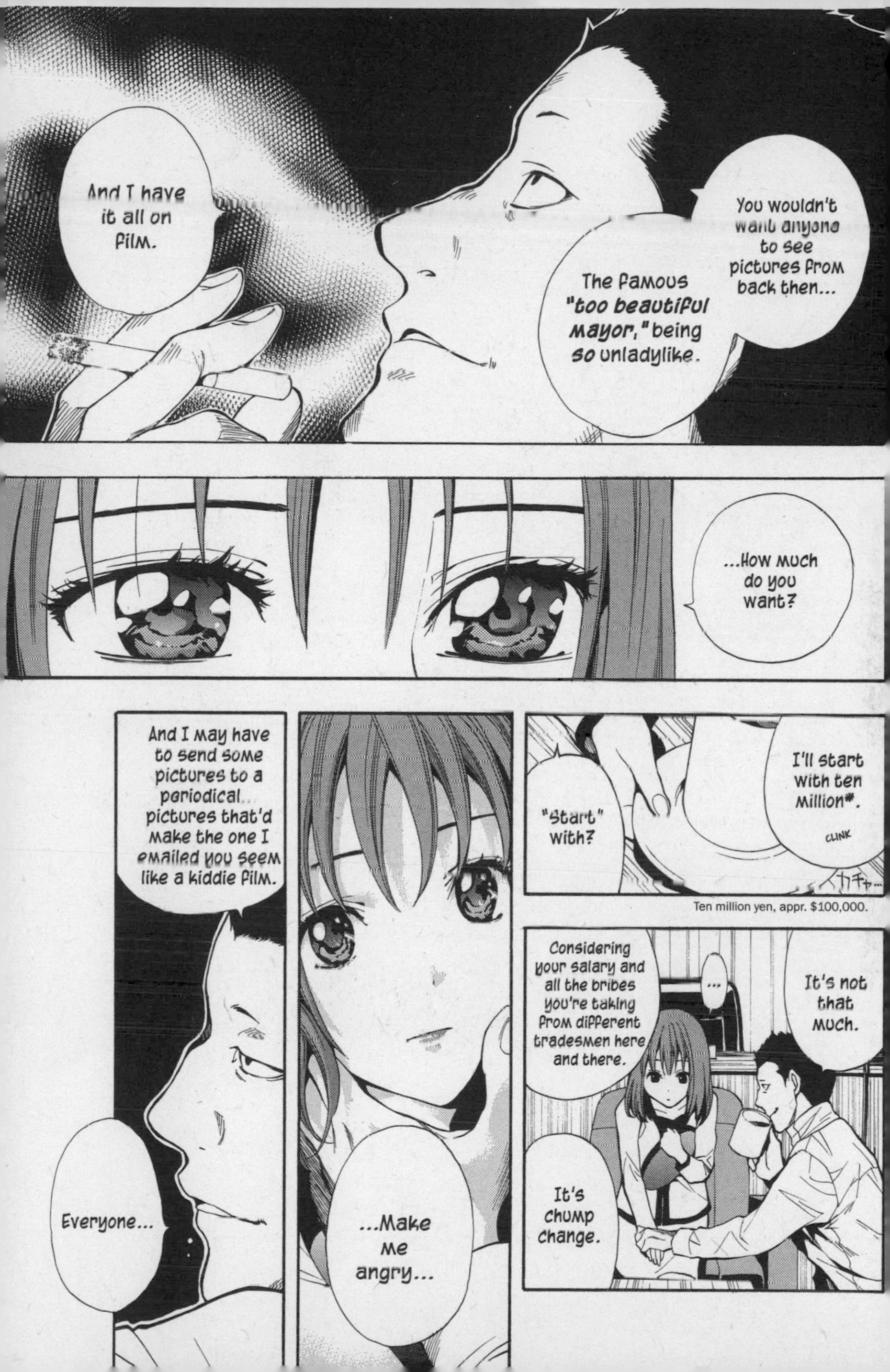
You wouldn't want anyone to see pictures from back then...
The famous "too beautiful mayor," being so unladylike.
And I have it all on film.
...How much do you want?
I'll start with ten Million*.
CLINK
カチャ...
"Start" with?
Ten million yen, appr. $100,000.
It's not that much.
Considering your salary and all the bribes you're taking from different tradesmen here and there.
...
It's chump change.
...Make me angry...
And I may have to send some pictures to a periodical... pictures that'd make the one I emailed you seem like a kiddie film.
Everyone...

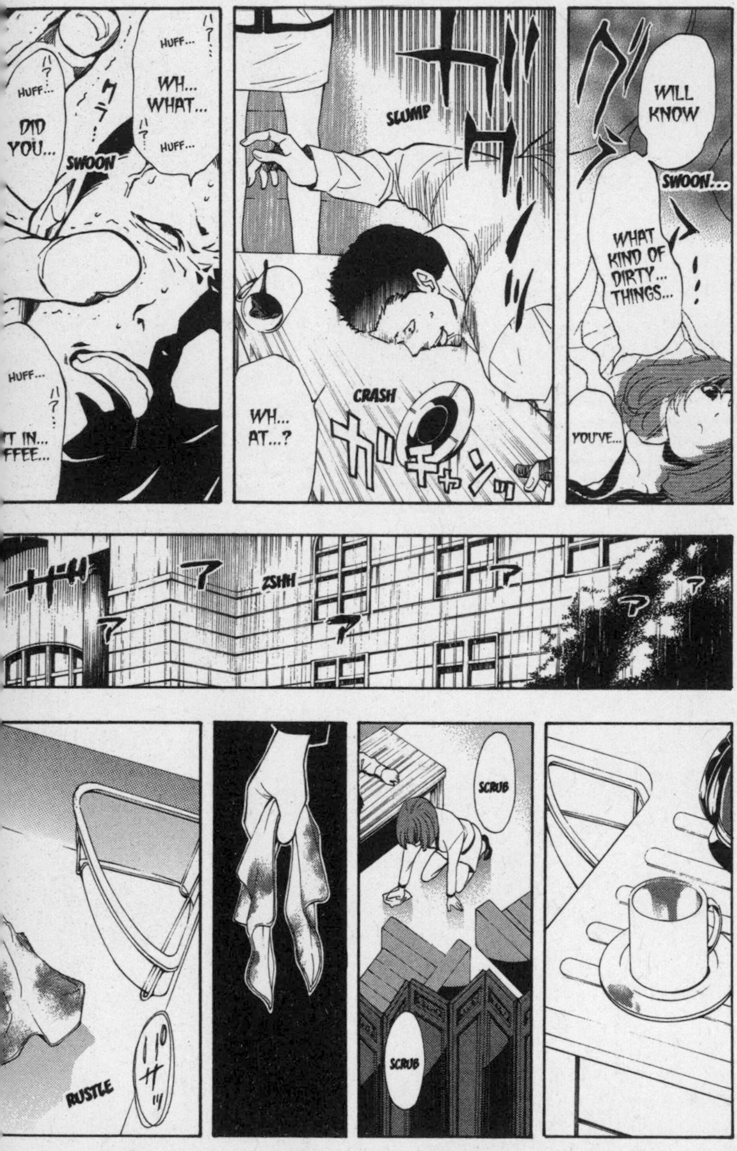
WILL KNOW
SWOON...
WHAT KIND OF DIRTY... THINGS...
YOU'VE...
SLUMP
CRASH
WH... AT...?
HUFF...
WH... WHAT...
HUFF...
HUFF...
DID YOU...
SWOON
HUFF...
T IN... FFEE...
ZSHH
SCRUB
SCRUB
RUSTLE

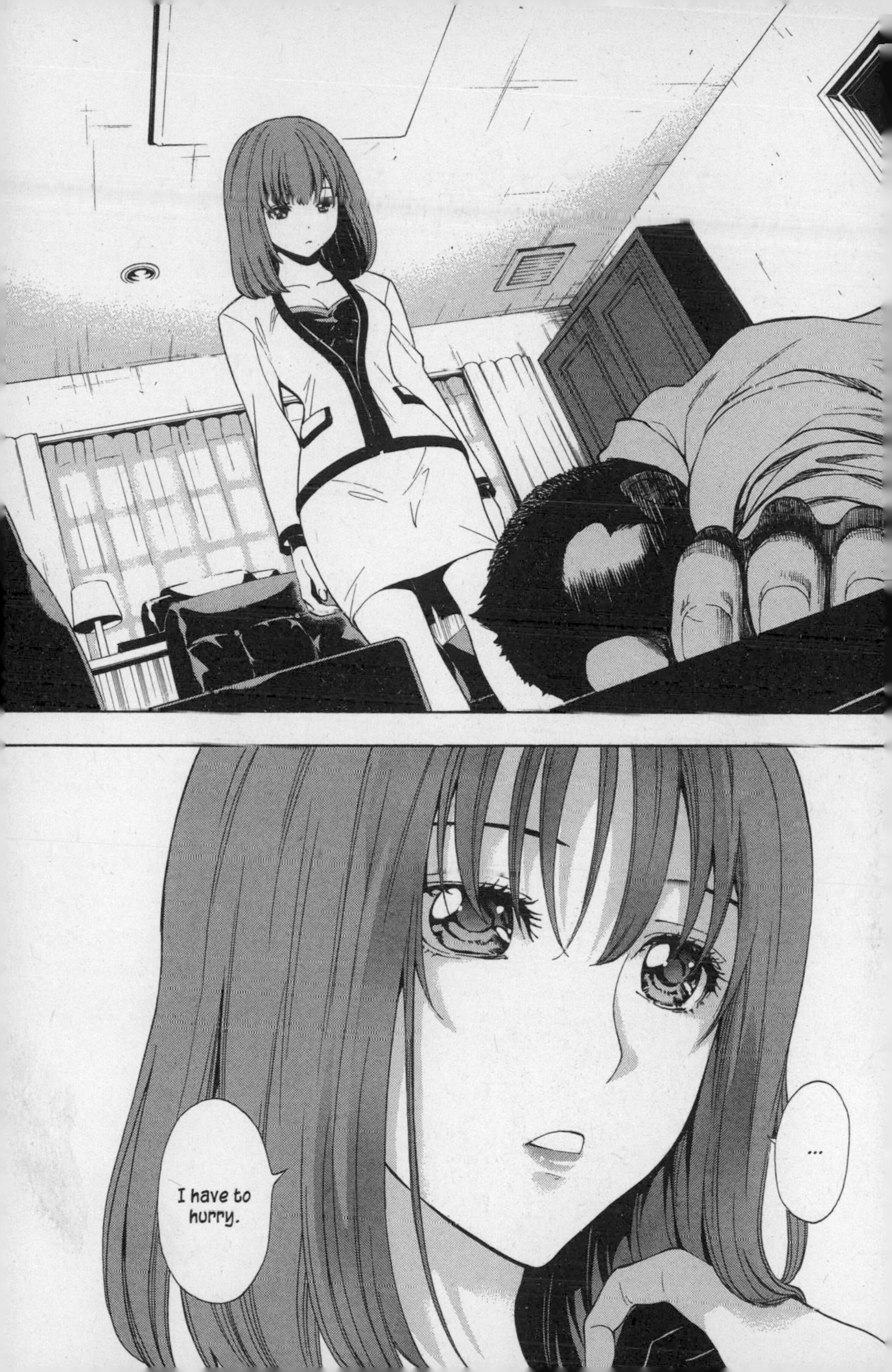
...
I have to hurry.

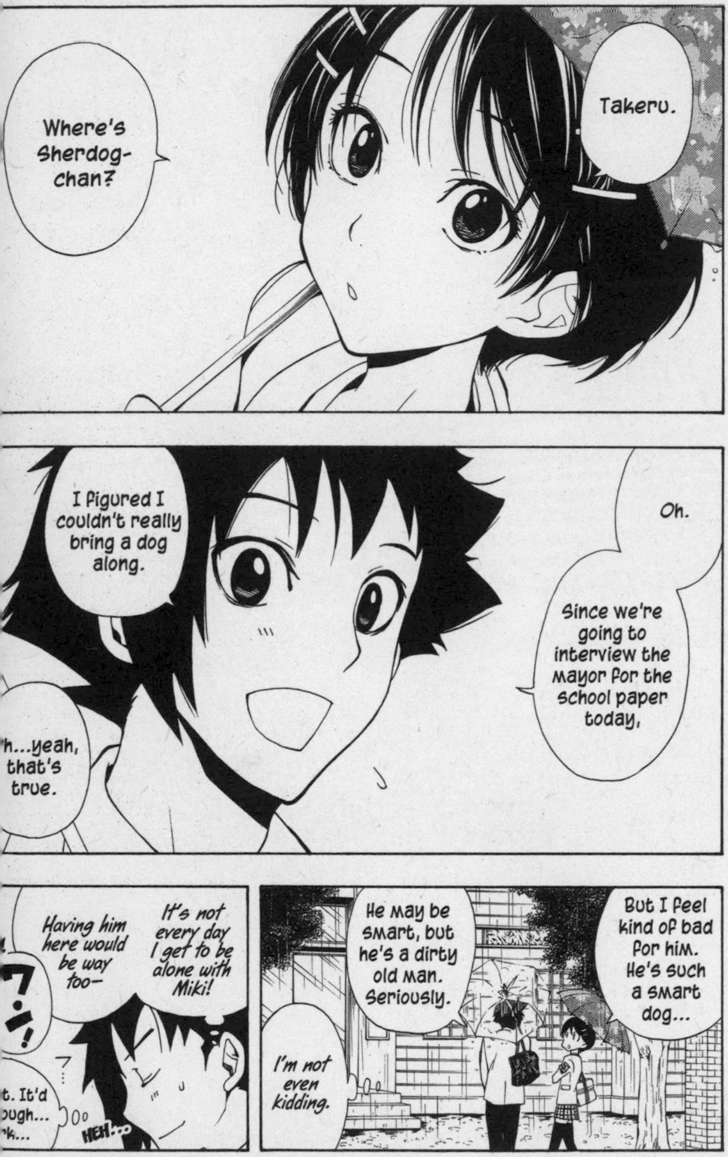
Takeru.
Where's Sherdog-chan?
Oh.
Since we're going to interview the mayor for the school paper today,
I figured I couldn't really bring a dog along.
h...yeah, that's true.
But I feel kind of bad for him. He's such a smart dog...
He may be smart, but he's a dirty old man. Seriously.
I'm not even kidding.
It's not every day I get to be alone with Miki!
Having him here would be way too—
t. It'd ough... rk...
HEH...

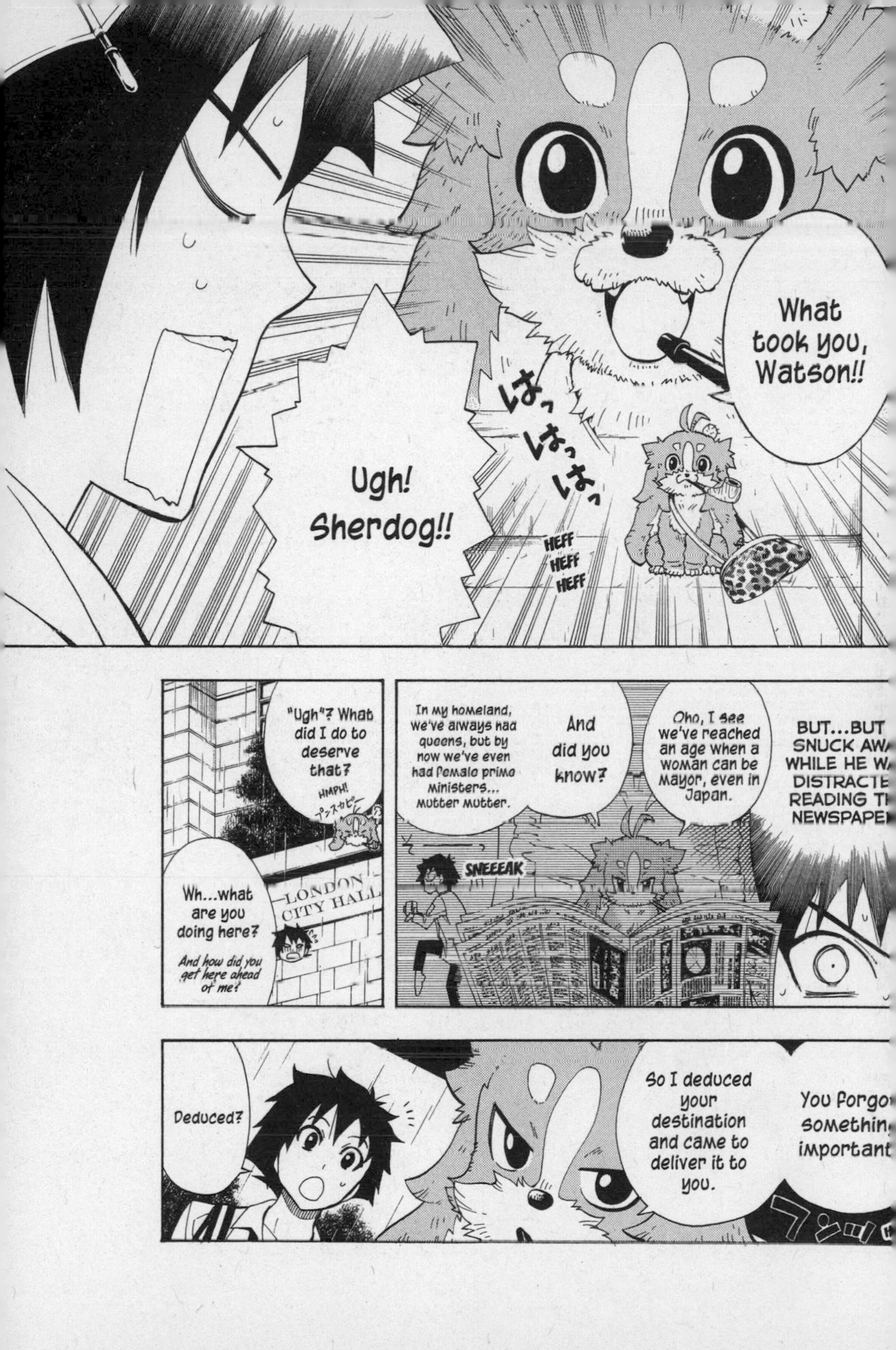
What took you, Watson!!
はっはっはっ
HEFF HEFF HEFF
Ugh! Sherdog!!
BUT...BUT SNUCK AWA WHILE HE WA DISTRACTE READING T NEWSPAPE
Oho, I see we've reached an age when a woman can be mayor, even in Japan.
And did you know?
In my homeland, we've always had queens, but by now we've even had female prime ministers... mutter mutter.
SNEEEAK
"Ugh"? What did I do to deserve that?
HMPH!
プンスカピー
LONDON CITY HALL
Wh...what are you doing here?
And how did you get here ahead of me?
You forgo something importan
So I deduced your destination and came to deliver it to you.
Deduced?

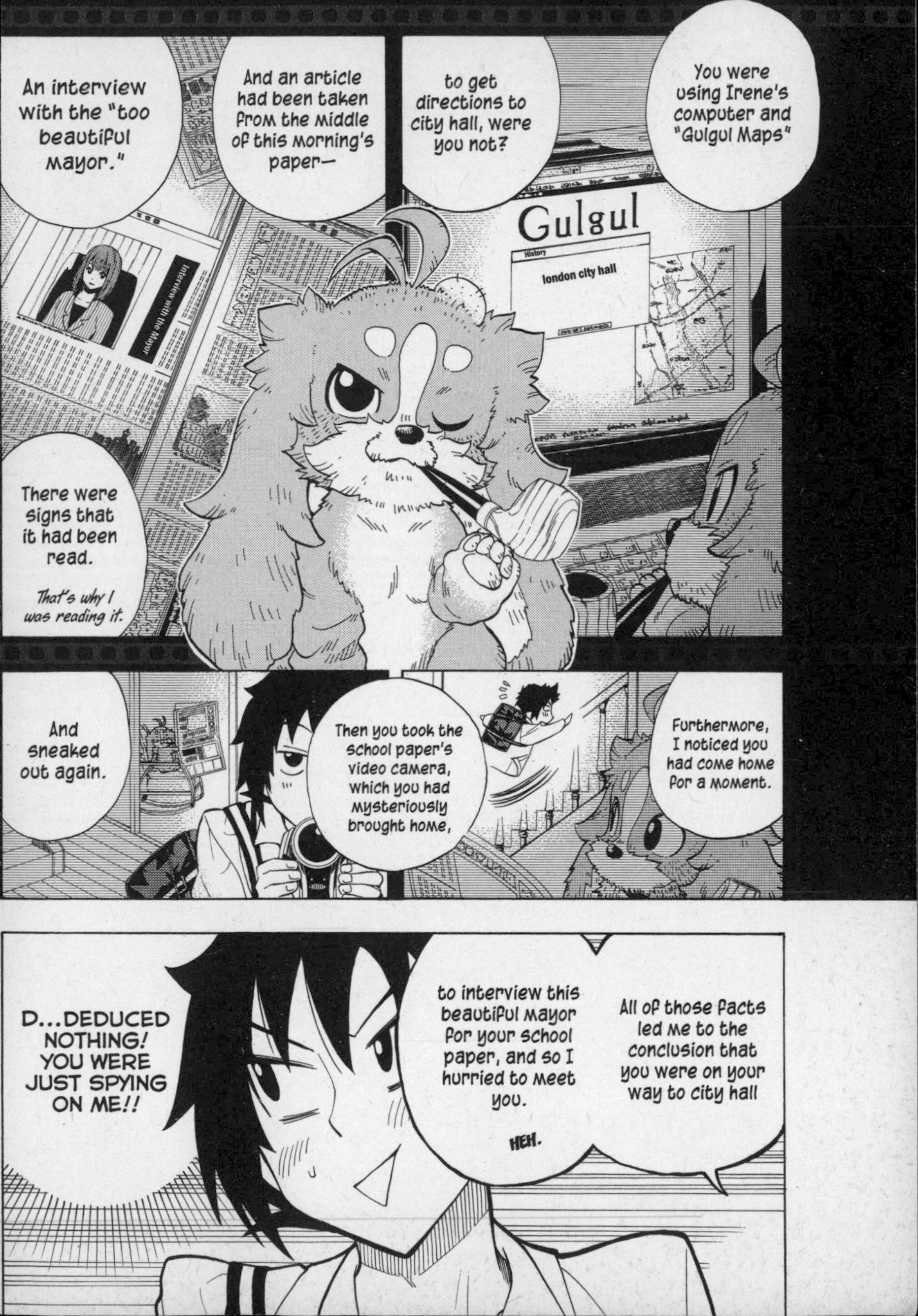
You were using Irene's computer and "Gulgul Maps"
Gulgul
History
london city hall
to get directions to city hall, were you not?
And an article had been taken from the middle of this morning's paper—
An interview with the "too beautiful mayor."
Interview with the Mayor
There were signs that it had been read.
That's why I was reading it.
Furthermore, I noticed you had come home for a moment.
Then you took the school paper's video camera, which you had mysteriously brought home,
And sneaked out again.
All of those facts led me to the conclusion that you were on your way to city hall
to interview this beautiful mayor for your school paper, and so I hurried to meet you.
HEH.
D...DEDUCED NOTHING! YOU WERE JUST SPYING ON ME!!

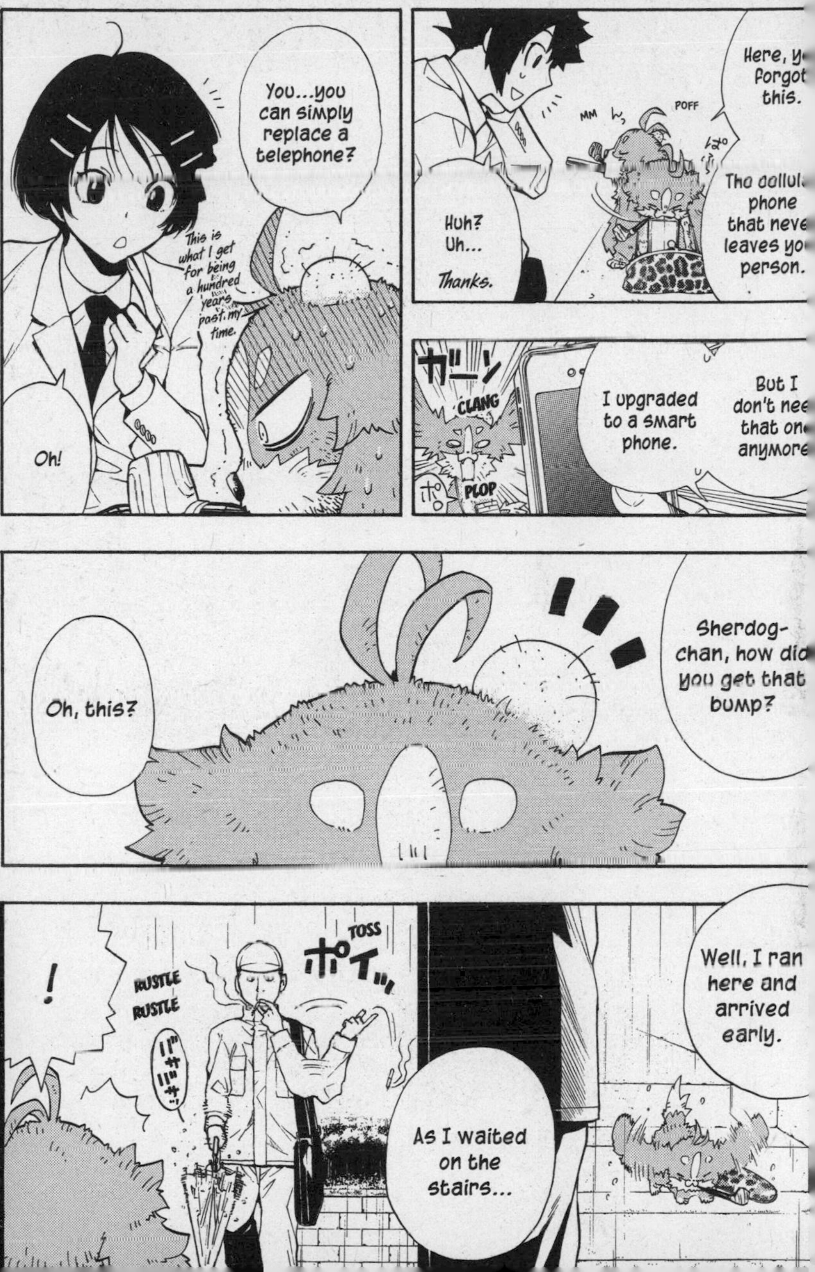
Here, y
forgot
this.
MM
POFF
The cellul
phone
that neve
leaves yo
person.
Huh? Uh...
Thanks.
But I don't nee that on anymore
I upgraded to a smart phone.
CLANG
PLOP
You...you can simply replace a telephone?
This is what I get for being a hundred years past my time.
Oh!
Sherdog-chan, how dic you get that bump?
Oh, this?
Well, I ran here and arrived early.
As I waited on the stairs...
TOSS
RUSTLE
RUSTLE
!

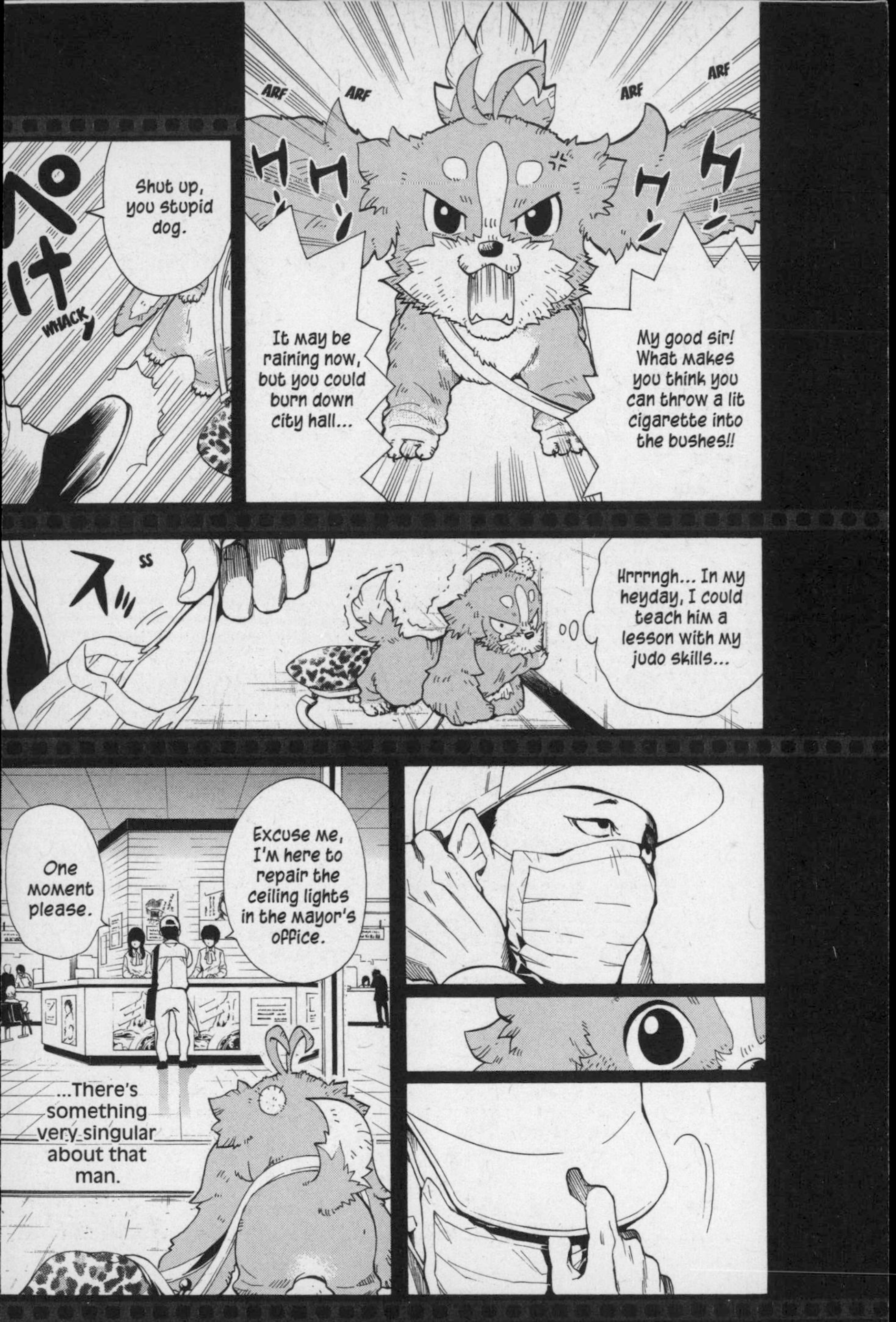

ARF
ARF
ARF
ARF
My good sir! What makes you think you can throw a lit cigarette into the bushes!!
It may be raining now, but you could burn down city hall...
Shut up, you stupid dog.
WHACK
Hrrrngh... In my heyday, I could teach him a lesson with my judo skills...
SS
Excuse me, I'm here to repair the ceiling lights in the mayor's office.
One moment please.
...There's something very singular about that man.

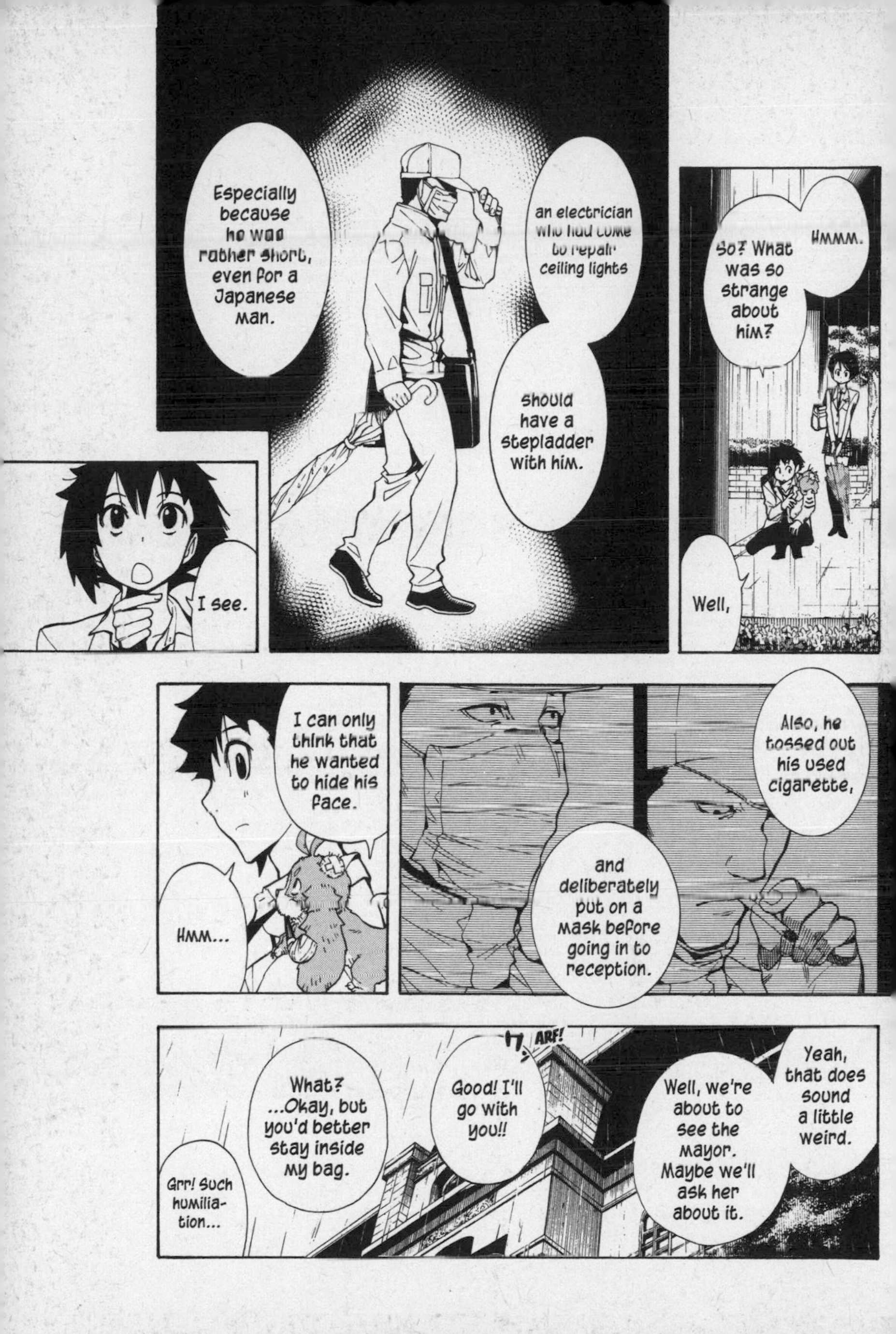
HMMM.
So? What was so strange about him?
Well,
an electrician who had come to repair ceiling lights
should have a stepladder with him.
Especially because he was rather short, even for a Japanese man.
I see.
Also, he tossed out his used cigarette,
and deliberately put on a mask before going in to reception.
I can only think that he wanted to hide his face.
HMM...
Yeah, that does sound a little weird.
Well, we're about to see the mayor. Maybe we'll ask her about it.
ARF!
Good! I'll go with you!!
What? ...Okay, but you'd better stay inside my bag.
Grr! Such humilia-tion...

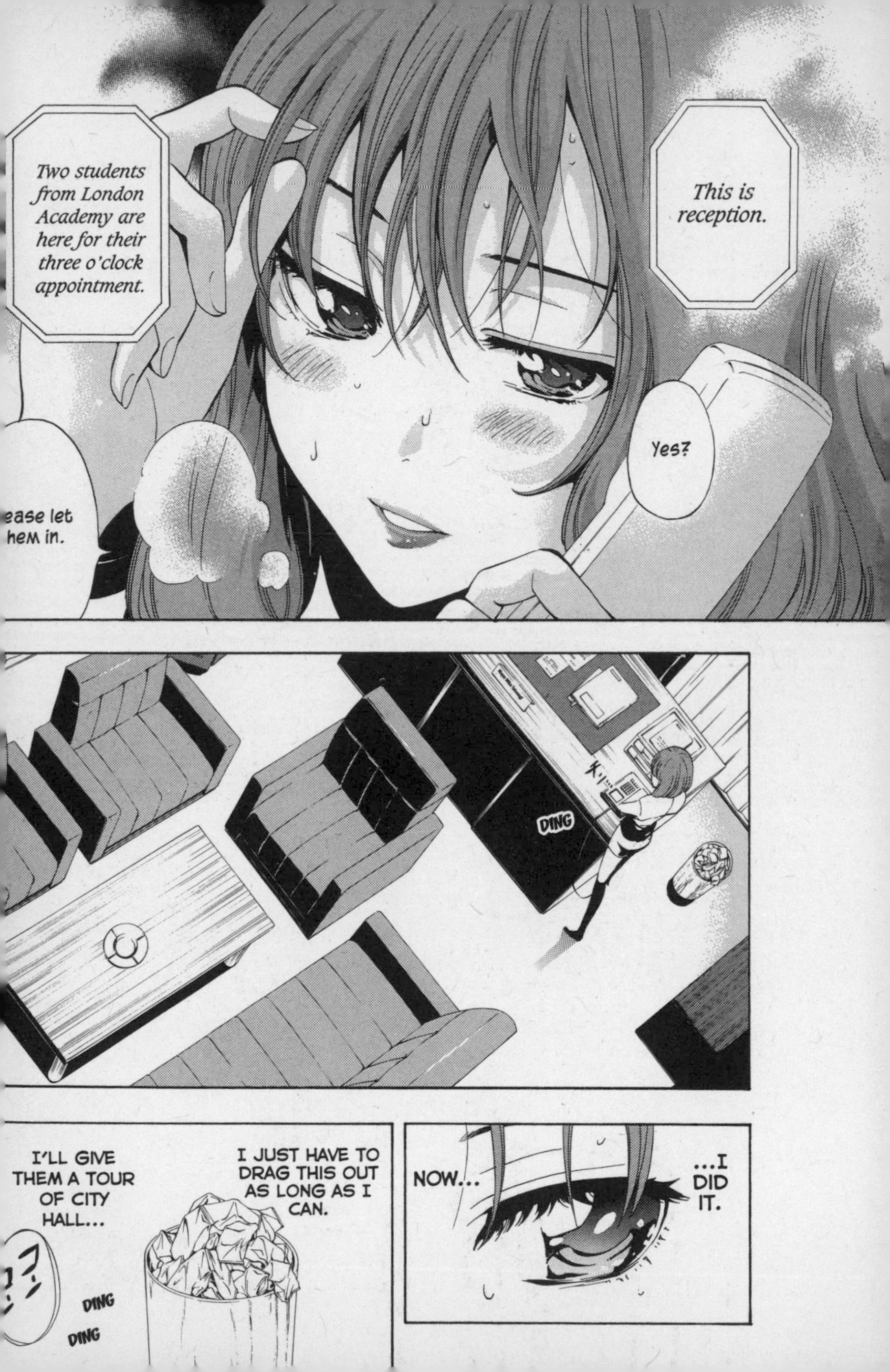
This is reception.
Yes?
Two students from London Academy are here for their three o'clock appointment.
ease let hem in.
DING
...I DID IT.
NOW...
I JUST HAVE TO DRAG THIS OUT AS LONG AS I CAN.
I'LL GIVE THEM A TOUR OF CITY HALL...
DING
DING

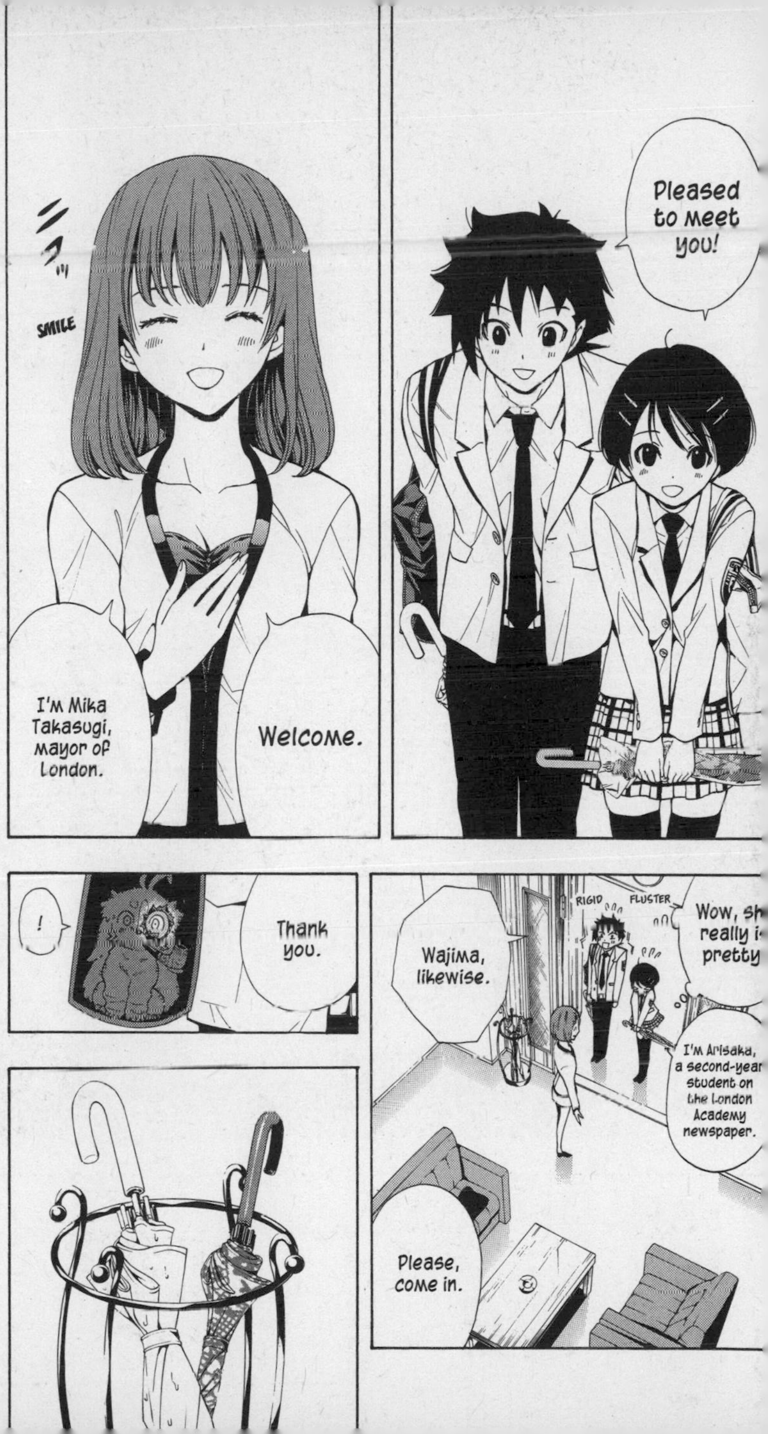
Pleased to meet you!
SMILE
Welcome.
I'm Mika Takasugi, mayor of London.
Wow, sh really i pretty
FLUSTER
RIGID
Wajima, likewise.
I'm Arisaka, a second-year student on the London Academy newspaper.
Please, come in.
Thank you.
!

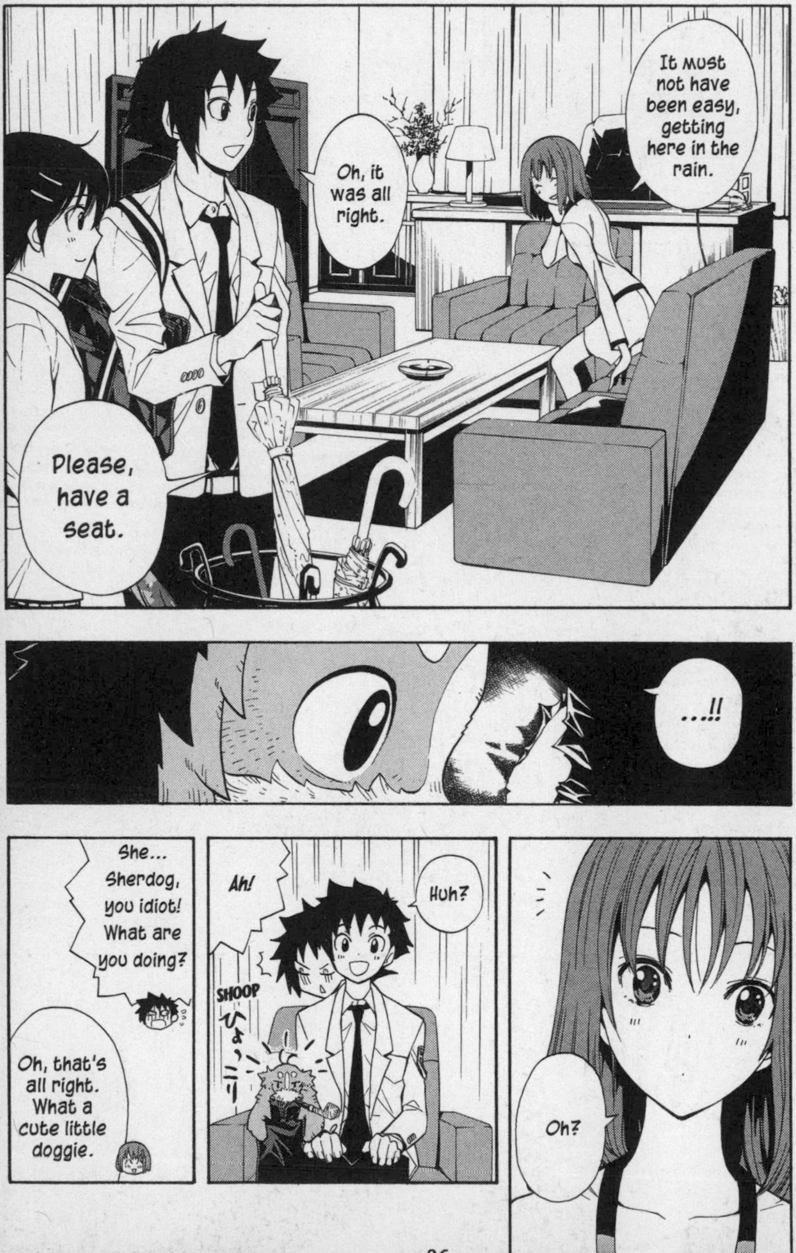
It must not have been easy, getting here in the rain.
Oh, it was all right.
Please, have a seat.
...!!
Oh?
Huh?
Ah!
SHOOP
She... Sherdog, you idiot! What are you doing?
Oh, that's all right. What a cute little doggie.

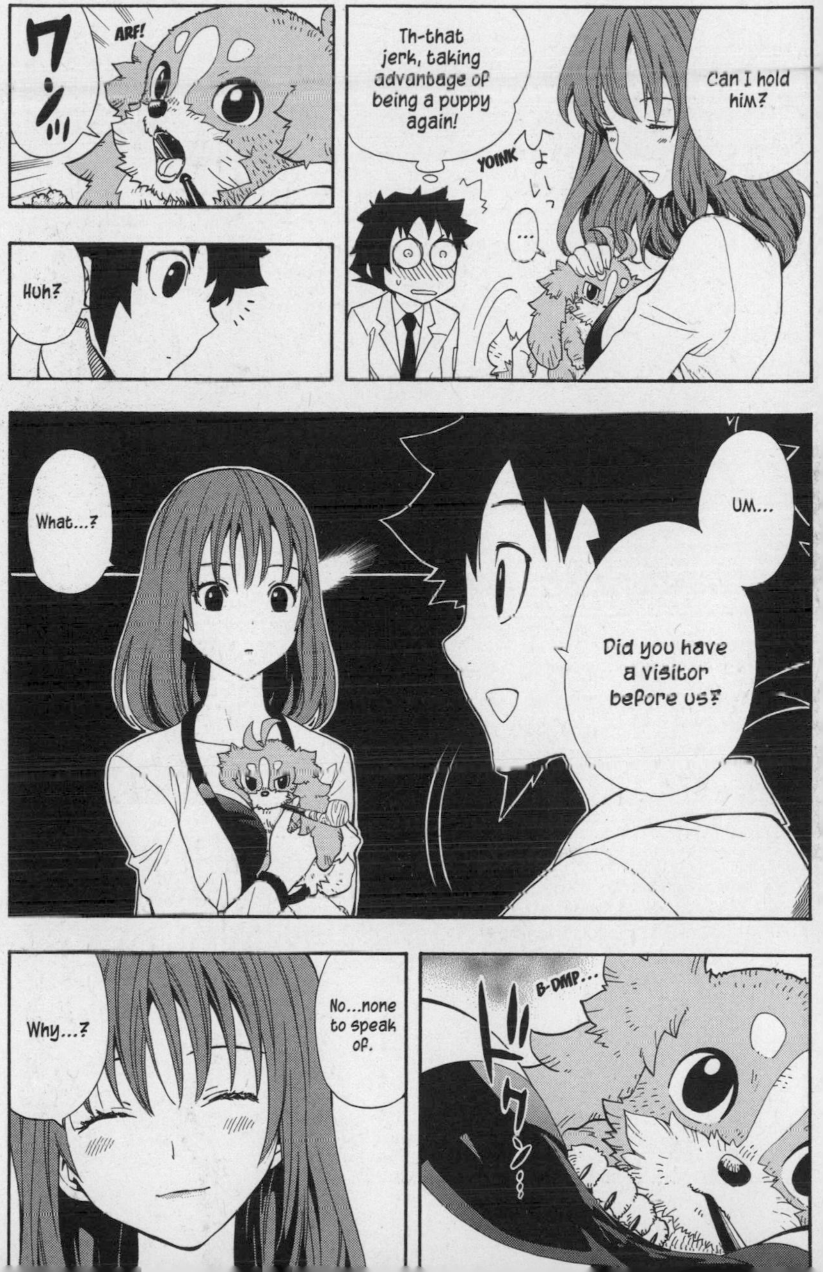
Can I hold him?
Th-that jerk, taking advanbage of being a puppy again!
YOINK
ひょいっ
...
ワンッ
ARF!
Huh?
Um...
Did you have a visitor before us?
What...?
B-DMP...
ドクン
No...none to speak of.
Why...?

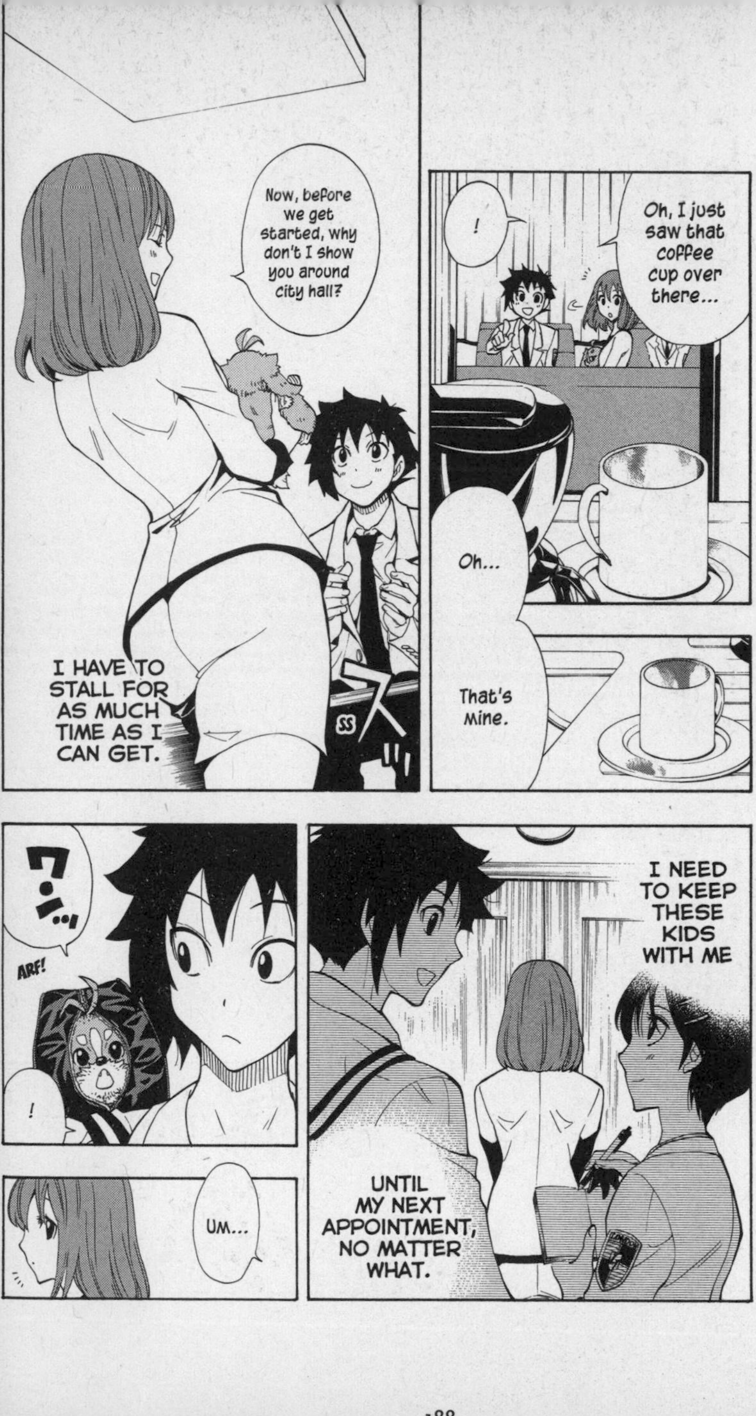

Oh, I just saw that coffee cup over there...
!
Oh...
That's mine.
Now, before we get started, why don't I show you around city hall?
SS
I HAVE TO STALL FOR AS MUCH TIME AS I CAN GET.
I NEED TO KEEP THESE KIDS WITH ME
UNTIL MY NEXT APPOINTMENT, NO MATTER WHAT.
?!
ARF!
!
Um...

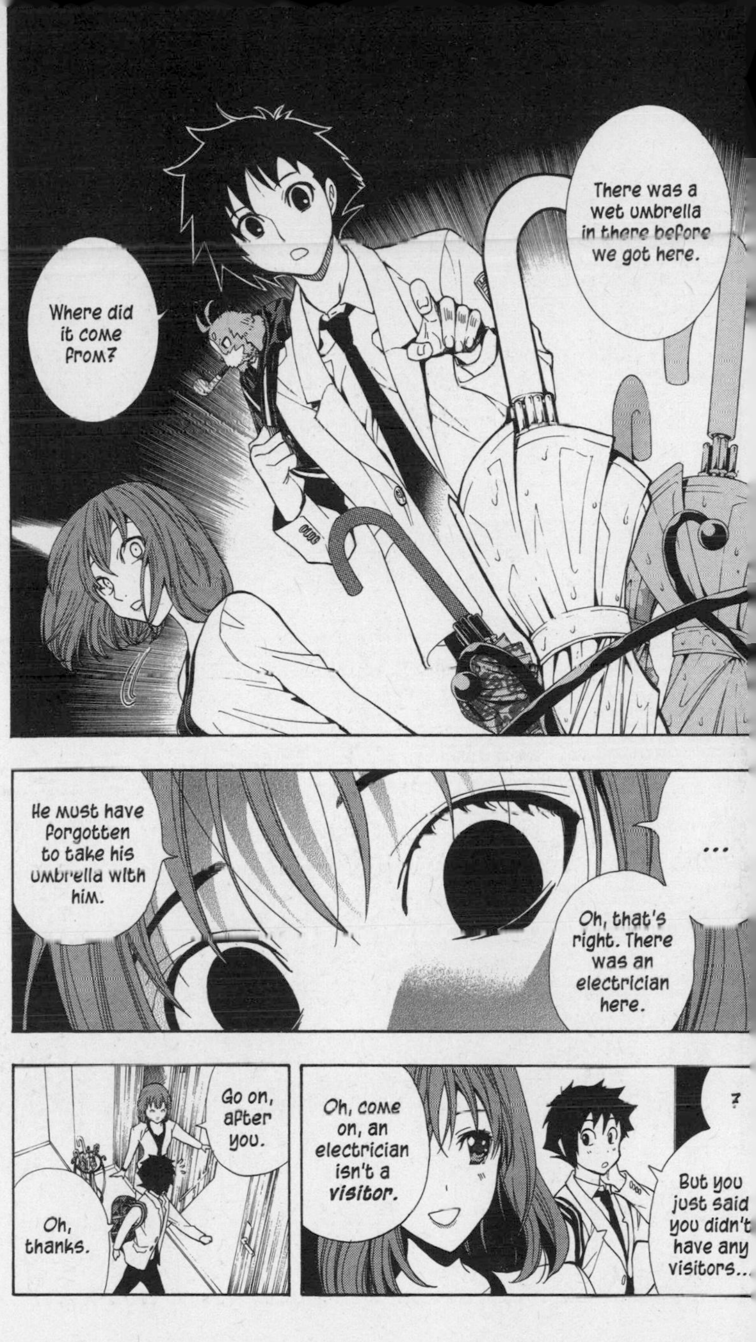
There was a wet umbrella in there before we got here.
Where did it come from?
...
Oh, that's right. There was an electrician here.
He must have forgotten to take his umbrella with him.
?
But you just said you didn't have any visitors...
Oh, come on, an electrician isn't a *visitor*.
Go on, after you.
Oh, thanks.

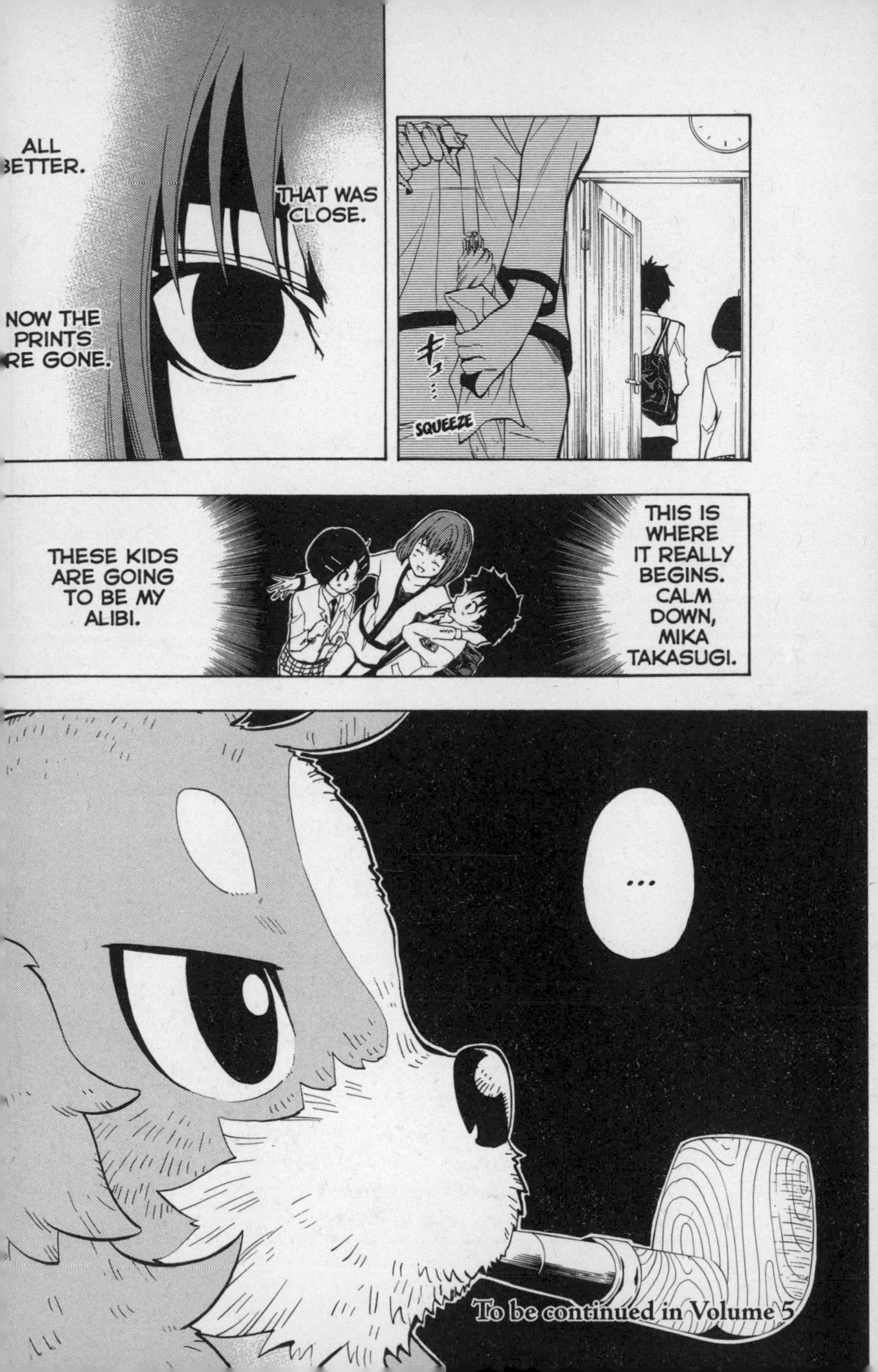
ギュ…
SQUEEZE
THAT WAS CLOSE.
ALL BETTER.
NOW THE PRINTS RE GONE.
THIS IS WHERE IT REALLY BEGINS. CALM DOWN, MIKA TAKASUGI.
THESE KIDS ARE GOING TO BE MY ALIBI.
...
To be continued in Volume 5

Bonus

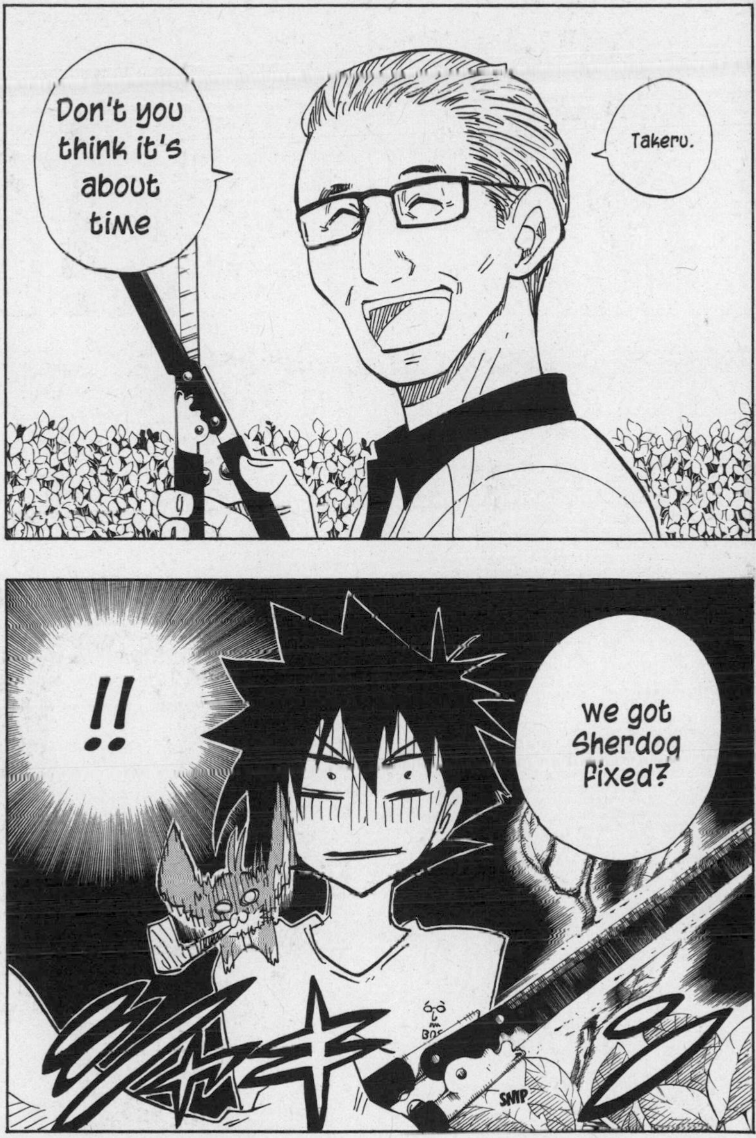
Takeru.
Don't you think it's about time
we got Sherdog fixed?
!!
SNIP

THAT WASN'T REALLY A GOOD STOPPING POINT, BUT IT'S TIME FOR A BONUS CHAPTER!!

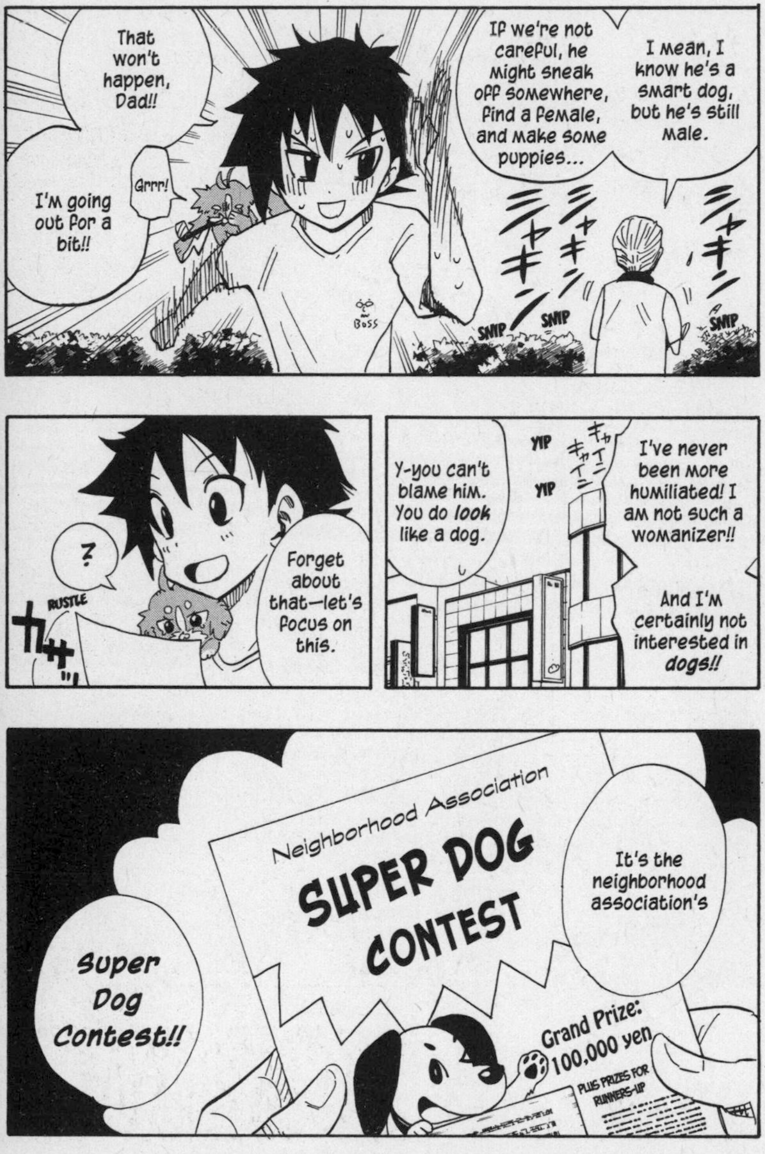
I mean, I know he's a smart dog, but he's still male.
If we're not careful, he might sneak off somewhere, find a female, and make some puppies...
SNIP
SNIP
SNIP
That won't happen, Dad!!
Grrr!
I'm going out for a bit!!
BOSS
I've never been more humiliated! I am not such a womanizer!!
And I'm certainly not interested in *dogs!!*
YIP
YIP
Y-you can't blame him. You do *look* like a dog.
Forget about that—let's focus on this.
?
RUSTLE
It's the neighborhood association's
Neighborhood Association
SUPER DOG CONTEST
Grand Prize: 100,000 yen
PLUS PRIZES FOR RUNNERS-UP
Super Dog Contest!!

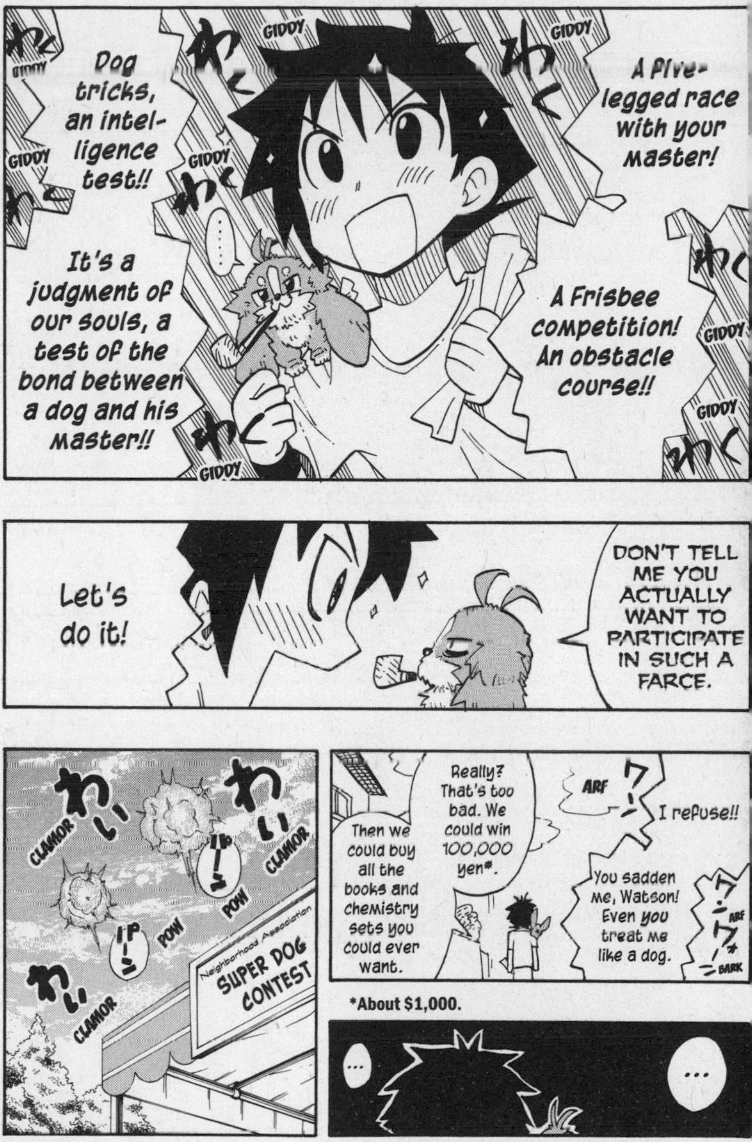

A five-legged race with your master!
GIDDY
Dog tricks, an intelligence test!!
A Frisbee competition! An obstacle course!!
It's a judgment of our souls, a test of the bond between a dog and his master!!
DON'T TELL ME YOU ACTUALLY WANT TO PARTICIPATE IN SUCH A FARCE.
Let's do it!
ARF
I refuse!!
Really? That's too bad. We could win 100,000 yen*.
Then we could buy all the books and chemistry sets you could ever want.
ARF
BARK
You sadden me, Watson! Even you treat me like a dog.
...
...
CLAMOR
POW
Neighborhood Association SUPER DOG CONTEST

*About $1,000.

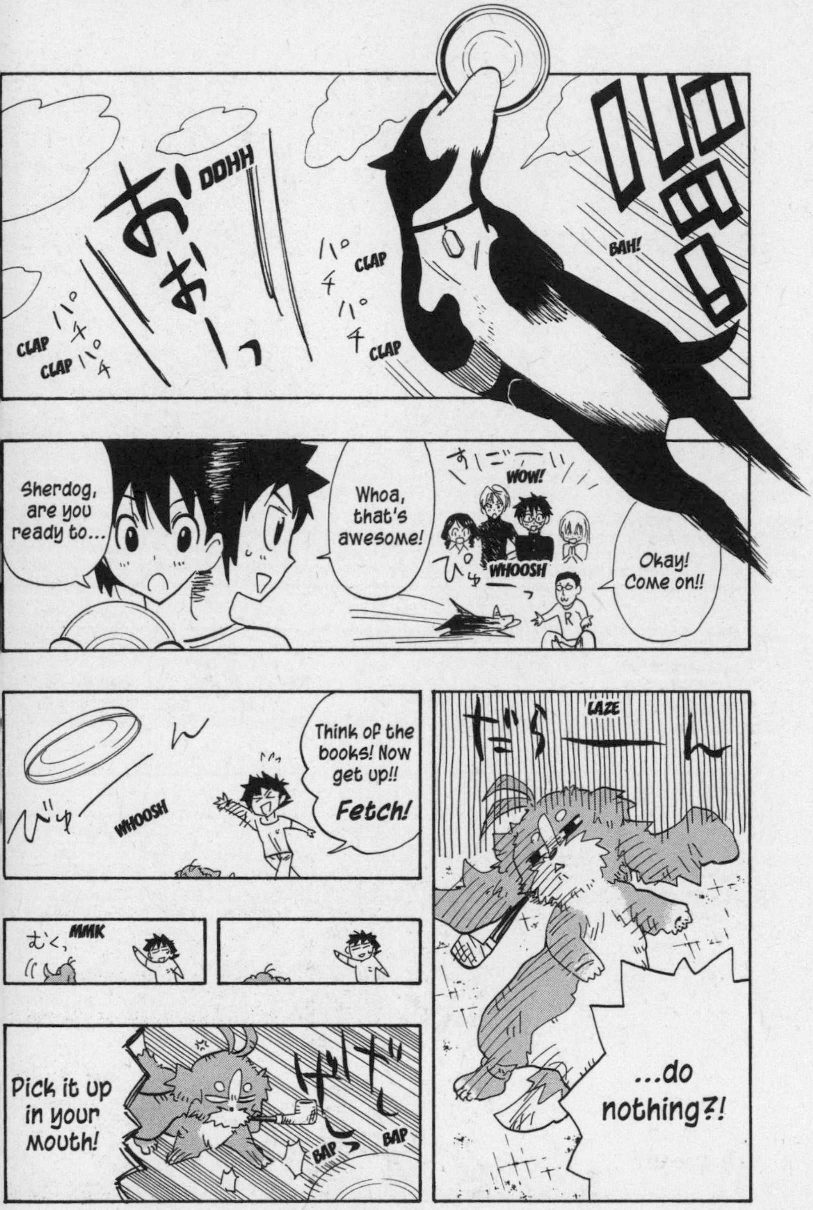
BAH!
CLAP
パチパチ
CLAP
おおーっ
DDHH
パチパチ
CLAP
CLAP
Okay! Come on!!
WHOOSH
ぴゅーっ
すごーい
WOW!
Whoa, that's awesome!
Sherdog, are you ready to...
だらーーん
LAZE
...do nothing?!
Think of the books! Now get up!!
Fetch!
びゅ
WHOOSH
むく
MMK
Pick it up in your mouth!
BAP
BAP

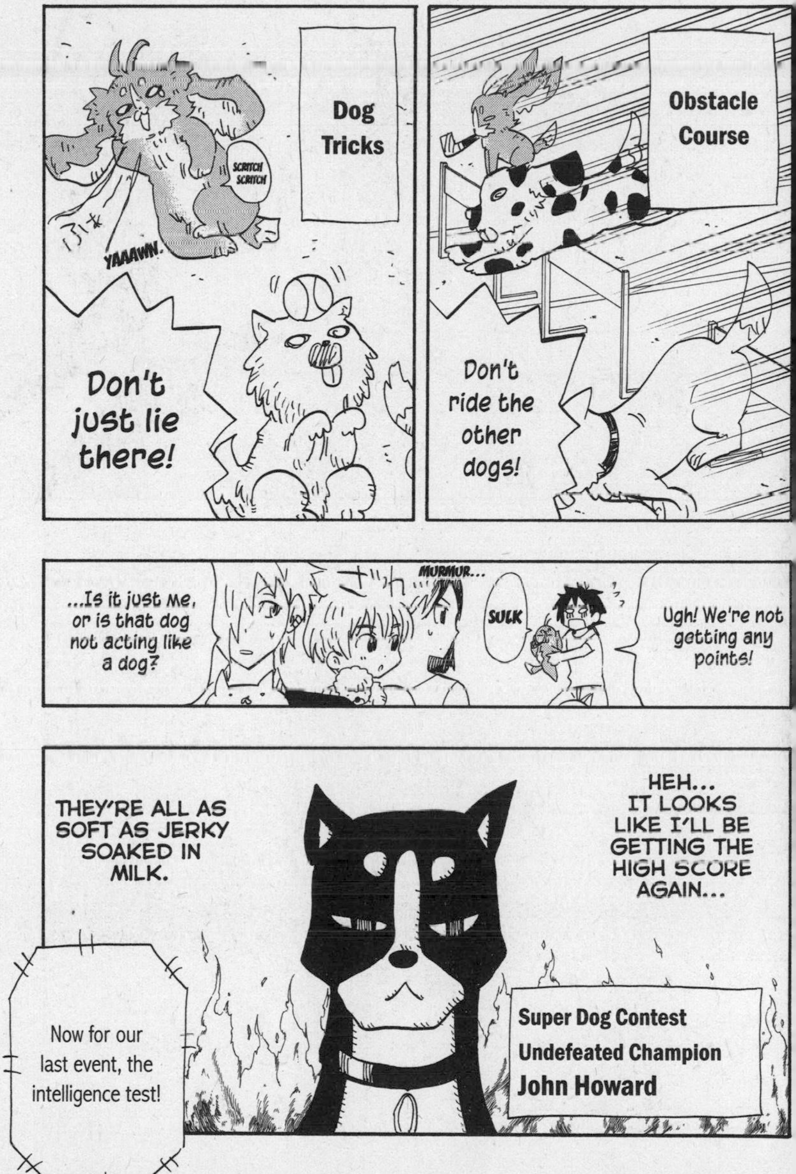
Obstacle Course
Don't ride the other dogs!
Dog Tricks
YAAAWN.
SCRATCH SCRATCH
Don't just lie there!
Ugh! We're not getting any points!
SULK
MURMUR...
...Is it just me, or is that dog not acting like a dog?
HEH... IT LOOKS LIKE I'LL BE GETTING THE HIGH SCORE AGAIN...
Super Dog Contest Undefeated Champion John Howard
THEY'RE ALL AS SOFT AS JERKY SOAKED IN MILK.
Now for our last event, the intelligence test!

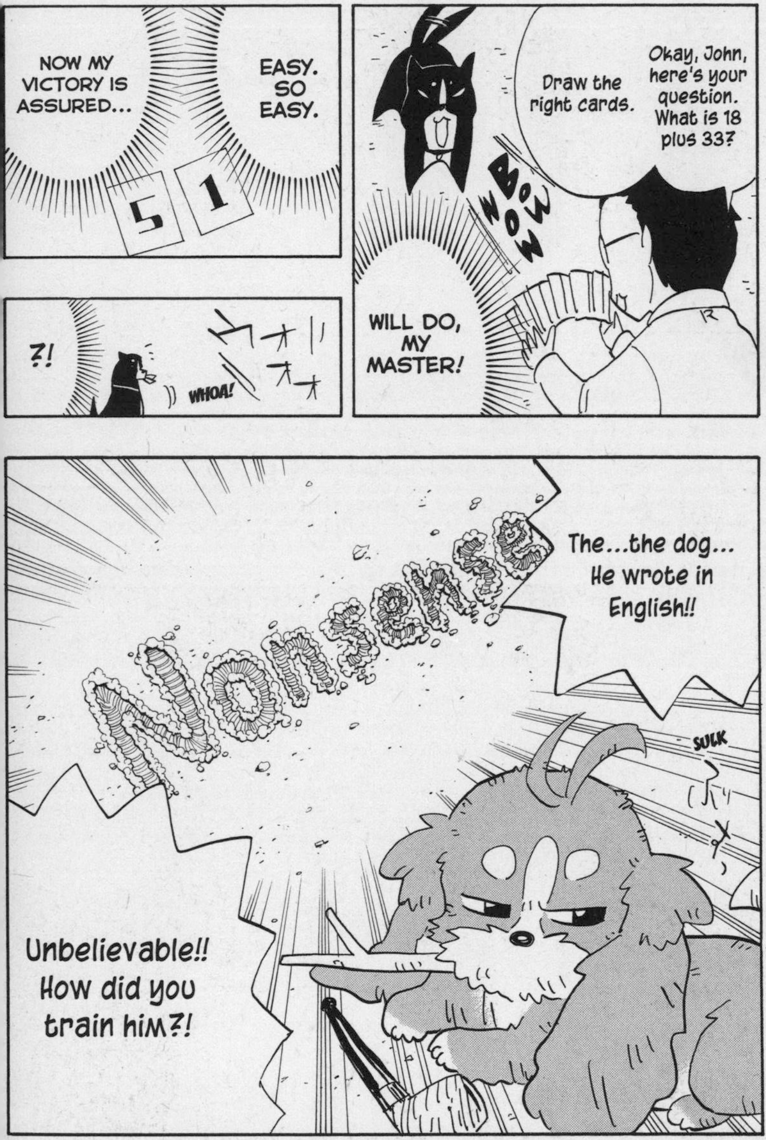
Okay, John, here's your question. What is 18 plus 33?
Draw the right cards.
BOW WOW
WILL DO, MY MASTER!
EASY. SO EASY.
NOW MY VICTORY IS ASSURED...
5 1
WHOA!
?!
The...the dog... He wrote in English!!
Nonsense
SULK
Unbelievable!! How did you train him?!

Ando-sensei, Editor I-san, Editor H-san, Graphic Novel Editor E-san, Designer Y-san, everyone at the publishing company,

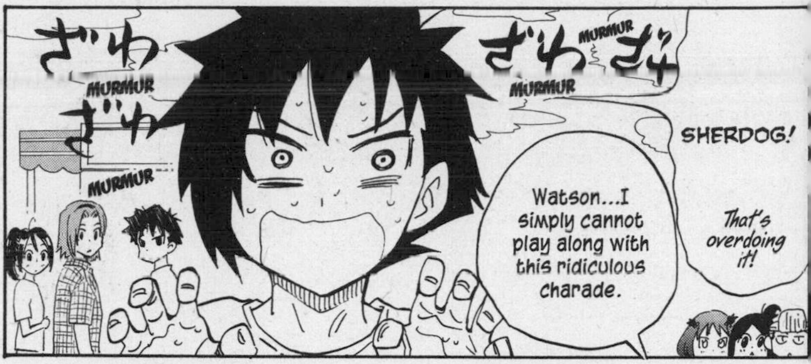
ざわざわ
MURMUR
MURMUR
SHERDOG!
That's overdoing it!
Watson...I simply cannot play along with this ridiculous charade.
ざわ
MURMUR
ざわ
MURMUR

Everyone in sales, my staff, my mentor, my friends, my family, and all my readers—thank you!

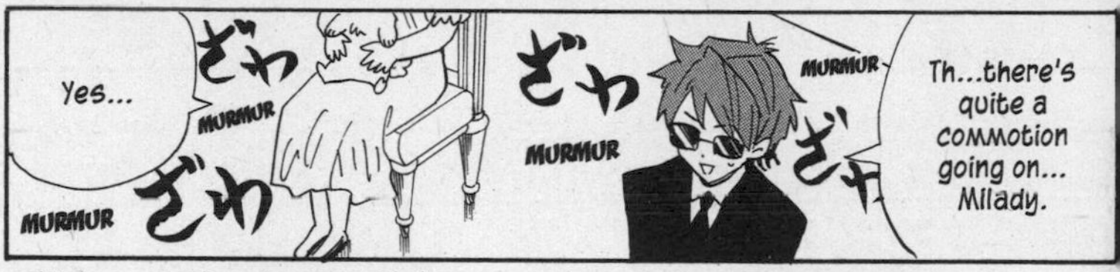
Th...there's quite a commotion going on... Milady.
MURMUR
ざわ
ざわ
MURMUR
ざわ
MURMUR
Yes...
ざわ
MURMUR

I'll keep working hard. ^^ Yuki

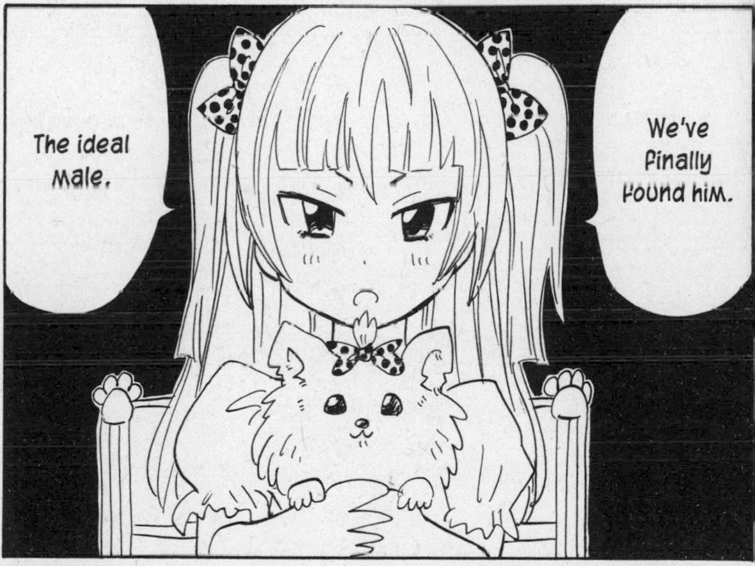
We've finally found him.
The ideal male.

Oops, we've ended on another cliffhanger... To be continued!!

Sherlock Bones 3 Translation Notes

Japanese is a tricky language for most Westerners, and translation is often more art than science. For your edification and reading pleasure, here are notes on some of the places where we could have gone in a different direction with our translation of the work, or where a Japanese cultural reference is used.

Idol collage, page 10

As you may have guessed from the context, an "idol collage" is a doctored photo of a celebrity, putting them in a situation they wouldn't normally be found in. The idol collage is such a common form of doctoring photos in Japan that the term "ai-kora," short for "aidoru koraaju" or "idol collage," has become synonymous with a photo of anyone doctored in that way, famous or not.

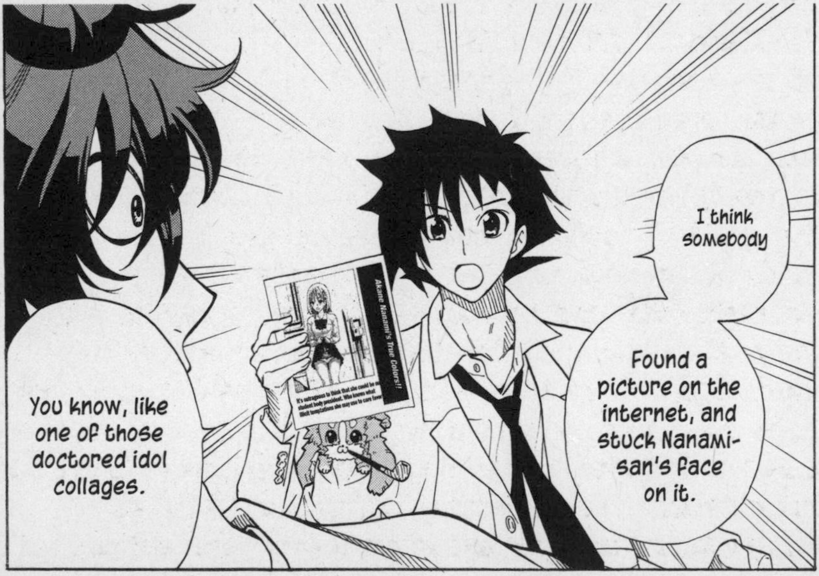
I think somebody
Found a picture on the internet, and stuck Nanami-san's face on it.
Akane Nanami's True Colors!!
You know, like one of those doctored idol collages.

Autocorrect, page 15

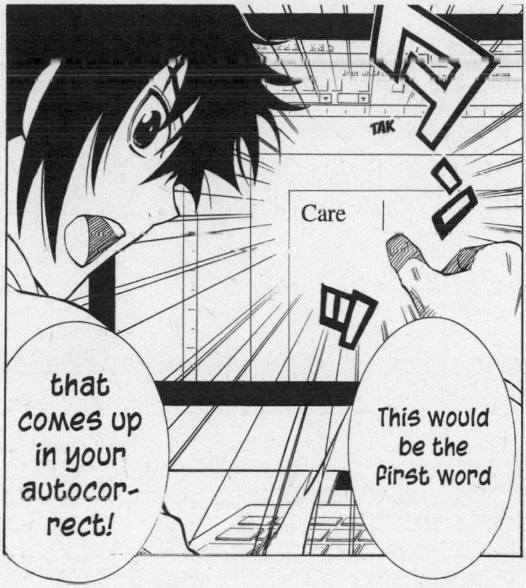

TAK
Care
This would be the first word
that comes up in your autocor-rect!

Japanese typing works a little bit differently than English typing, so "autocorrect" wasn't exactly the problem. The Japanese writing system uses a combination of two Japanese syllabaries, or kana (representing syllables), and adopted Chinese characters, or kanji (representing words or ideas). To avoid having to have thousands of different kanji available on a keyboard, in Japan, they use keyboards with the alphabet (in other words, their keyboards are just like ours). That means they use the alphabet to spell out Japanese words, then hit the space bar to select which kana or kanji to use in the text. Different kanji can be pronounced the same way, so if you type the same word, but choose the wrong kanji, your text could end up with a very different meaning the the one you intended. Like autocorrect's memory, the Japanese word input remembers which kanji is most like to be used by a device's user. In this case, the word in question is kanshin, meaning favor (歓心), as in "currying favor through illicit activities), or interest (関心), as in "I want students to take interest in the student council's activities."

***Coki Samejima*, page 16**

For the curious, the typo in question for the Japanese version turned the name Kōki, meaning "high and noble," into kōki, the first two kanji from kōkishin, meaning "curiosity."

***Screen tone*, page 118**

Screen tone is what manga artists use to "color" their manga. Any area that isn't black or white is made gray or given a texture or pattern with screen tone. It works like a sticker, and comes in sheets, or screens. The manga artist (or more likely, his assistants) will cut out a piece of screen tone roughly the size of the area that needs to be covered, then he'll lay it over the drawing and use a small blade to cut away the pieces that don't fit inside the lines. As a result, a bunch of little sticky bits get left all over the place.

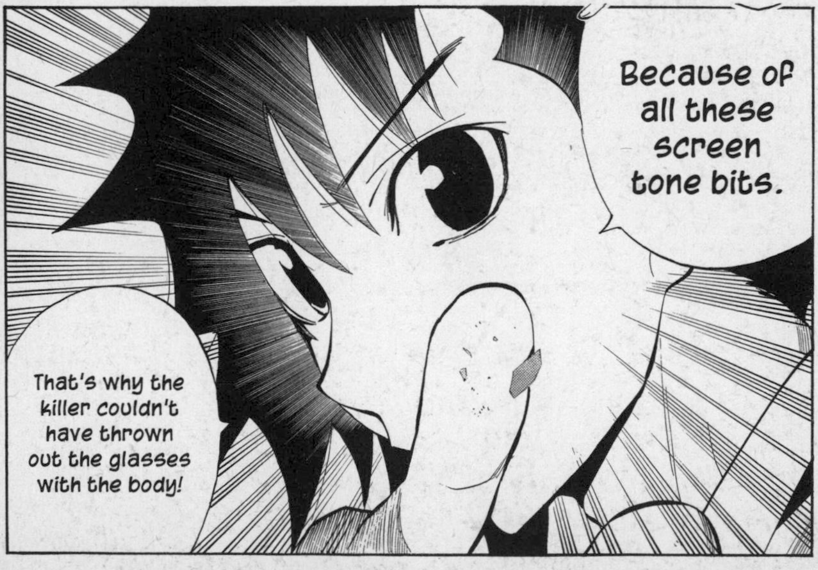
Because of all these screen tone bits.
That's why the killer couldn't have thrown out the glasses with the body!

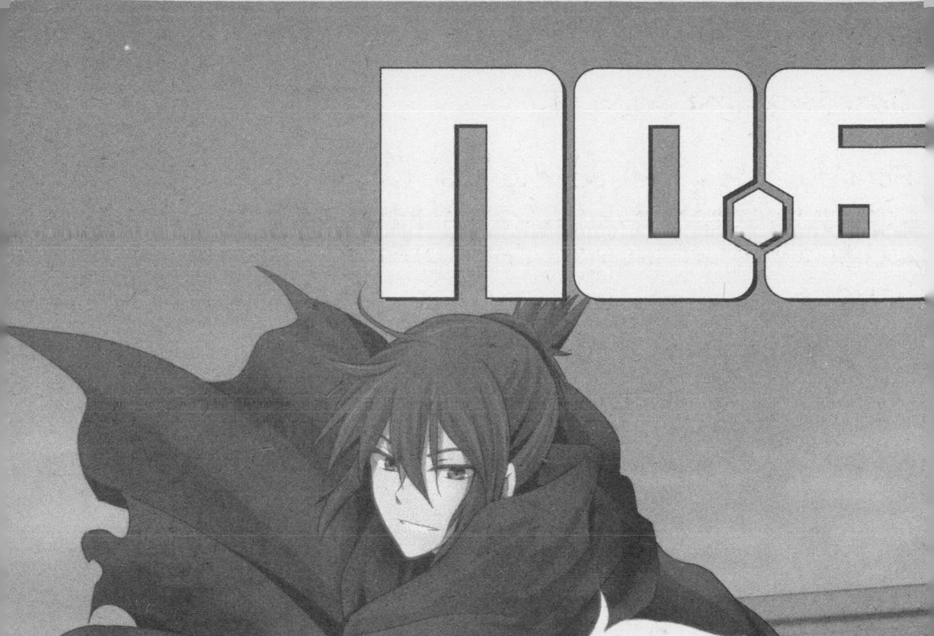
NO.6

A PERFECT LIFE IN A PERFECT CITY

For Shion, an elite student in the technologically sophisticated city No. 6, life is carefully choreographed. One fateful day, he takes a misstep, sheltering a fugitive his age from a typhoon. Helping this boy throws Shion's life down a path to discovering the appalling secrets behind the "perfection" of No. 6.

KC
KODANS

FROM HIRO MASHIMA,
CREATOR OF **RAVE MASTER**

Lucy has always dreamed of joining the Fairy Tail, a club for the most powerful sorcerers in the land. But once she becomes a member, the fun really starts!

Special extras in each volume! Read them all!

RATING T AGES 13+

VISIT WWW.KODANSHACOMICS.COM TO:
- View release date calendars for upcoming volumes
- Find out the latest about new Kodansha Comics series

Fairy Tail © Hiro Mashima / KODANSHA LTD. All rights reserved.

ANIMAL LAND

BY MAKOTO RAIKU

In a world of animals, where the strong eat the weak, Monoko the tanuki stumbles across a strange creature the likes of which has never been seen before—a human baby! While the newborn has no claws or teeth to protect itself, it does have the special ability to speak to and understand all different animals. Can the gift of speech between species change the balance of power in a land where the weak must always fear the strong?

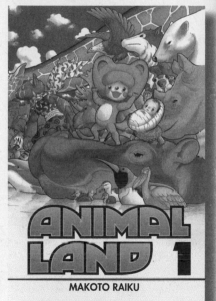

ANIMAL LAND 1

MAKOTO RAIKU

Ages 13+

VISIT KODANSHACOMICS.COM TO:

- View release date calendars for upcoming volumes
- Find out the latest about upcoming Kodansha Comics series

© Makoto Raiku / KODANSHA LTD. All rights reserved.

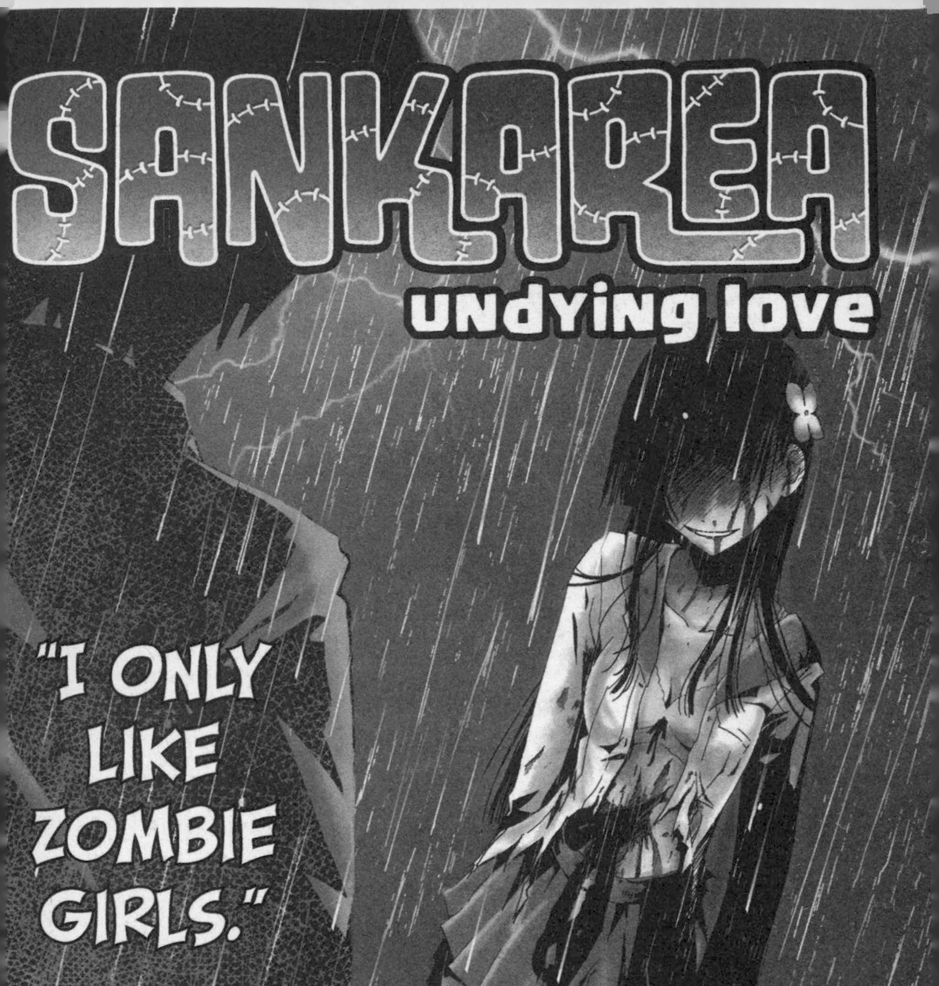

SANKAREA
undying love

"I ONLY LIKE ZOMBIE GIRLS."

Chihiro has an unusual connection to zombie movies. He doesn't feel bad for the survivors – he wants to comfort the undead girls they slaughter! When his pet passes away, he brews a resurrection potion. He's discovered by local heiress Sanka Rea, and she serves as his first test subject!

KC
KODANSHA
COMICS

NEGIMA!™
MAGISTER NEGI MAGI

BY KEN AKAMATSU

Negi Springfield is a ten-year-old wizard teaching English at an all-girls Japanese school. He dreams of becoming a master wizard like his legendary father, the Thousand Master. At first his biggest concern was concealing his magic powers, because if he's ever caught using them publicly, he thinks he'll be turned into an ermine! But in a world that gets stranger every day, it turns out that the strangest people of all are Negi's students! From a librarian with a magic book to a centuries-old vampire, from a robot to a ninja, Negi will risk his own life to protect the girls in his care!

1
FOR MATURE AUDIENCES AGES 16+
NEGIMA!
MAGISTER NEGI MAGI
by
KEN AKAMATSU
CREATOR OF LOVE HINA!

Ages: 16+

Special extras in each volume! Read them all!

KC KODANSHA COMICS

VISIT WWW.KODANSHACOMICS.COM TO:

- View release date calendars for upcoming volumes
- Find out the latest about new Kodansha Comics series

ATTACK ON TITAN

Winner of a 2011 Kodansha Manga Award

Humanity has been decimated!

A century ago, the bizarre creatures known as Titans devoured most of the world's population, driving the remainder into a walled stronghold. Now, the appearance of an immense new Titan threatens the few humans left, and one restless boy decides to seize the chance to fight for his freedom, and the survival of his species!

KC
KODANSHA COMICS